Imagining Difference

Leslie A. Robertson

Imagining Difference:
Legend, Curse, and Spectacle in a
Canadian Mining Town

UBC Press · Vancouver · Toronto

15   14   13   12   11   10   09   08   07   06   05   5   4   3   2   1

Printed in Canada on acid-free paper

Library and Archives Canada Cataloguing in Publication

Robertson, Leslie, 1962-
    Imagining difference : legend, curse and spectacle in a Canadian mining town / Leslie A. Robertson.

    Includes bibliographical references and index.
    ISBN 0-7748-1092-0 (bound); ISBN 0-7748-1093-9 (pbk.)

    1. Ethnology – British Columbia – Fernie. 2. Indians of North America – British Columbia – Fernie – Folklore. 3. Legends – British Columbia – Fernie. 4. Blessing and cursing. 5. Group identity. 6. Differentiation (Sociology) 7. Fernie (B.C.) – Social conditions. I. Title.

HN110.F47R62 2004   305´.09711´65   C2004-906031-7

Canadä

UBC Press gratefully acknowledges the financial support for our publishing program of the Government of Canada through the Book Publishing Industry Development Program (BPIDP), and of the Canada Council for the Arts, and the British Columbia Arts Council.

This book has been published with the help of a grant from the Canadian Federation for the Humanities and Social Sciences, through the Aid to Scholarly Publications Programme, using funds provided by the Social Sciences and Humanities Research Council of Canada, and with the help of the K.D. Srivastava Fund.

UBC Press
The University of British Columbia
2029 West Mall
Vancouver, BC V6T 1Z2
604-822-5959/Fax: 604-822-6083
www.ubcpress.ca

In memory of my grandmother,

Margaret Castle (1913-2003)

And our friends,

Victoria Kucera (1909-1998)

Maria Anebaldi (1900-1998)

Maria Gigliotti (1899-1999)

Tina Hesketh (1912-1998)

Wanda Slavens (1916-2004)

Contents

Illustrations

Acknowledgments

Perhaps the most important bestowal to a researcher is an openness to engage with her endeavour, and to contribute to a work that is not quite in focus. Ethnography is a social process and I have been greatly rewarded by those who participated in this project. It is somewhat of a travesty that the names of those whose stories have shaped the work are absent from this space of acknowledgment. Anonymity presents a dilemma for researchers in this regard. As this book attests, people in Fernie generously shared with me their histories, memories, and ideas, exploring sometimes-difficult issues. I am greatly appreciative of their warm acts of hospitality, the many hours of informative conversation they offered, and the ways in which they made me feel at home in Fernie. Research, writing, and publishing require all kinds and degrees of emotional, intellectual, and financial support. I am indebted to those people who generously provided these (sometimes intangible) gifts throughout the life of the project.

At the University of British Columbia, where this research began in 1995, Julie Cruikshank, Dara Culhane, and Martin Silverman challenged and inspired me as researchers, teachers, and writers. Their engagement with ideas fuelled my intellectual imagination and their contributions to this book are significant. Petra Rethmann, Bruce Miller, Richard Cavell, and Wendy Wickwire provided valuable comments on earlier versions of this work. Throughout the years of studying and research I was privileged to meet so many people on whose insights I have drawn. Many pointed me in locally or theoretically significant directions, offered me resources that I may not have stumbled upon, helped with translations, provided technical assistance, and read earlier drafts of chapters. I would like to thank Elizabeth Eley-Round, Liz Furniss, Darlene Luke, Mike Kew, Randall Macnair, Sybille Manneschmidt, Mary Menduk, Mike Pennock, Lexine Phillipps, Bev Sellars, Nevenka Stankovic, Femke van Delft, Ella Verkerk, and Nancy Wachowich. Noel Dyck drew my attention to the everyday sense of cursing as a social act during a conversation in 1994. Staff members at the Fernie and District Historical Society, the Fernie and District Hospital, and the Fernie Public Library were very helpful. I am grateful to members of the Ktunaxa-Kinbasket Tribal Administration and the Elders Traditional Use Study Team who spoke at length with me and read earlier drafts of chapters.

The weaving of text and voice that is at the heart of this ethnography owes much to many. Mary Giuliano translated interviews conducted for the Italian Oral History Project and Rose Anselmo typed the transcripts in her Calabrian dialect. The British Columbia Heritage Trust financially assisted the oral history project. The University of British Columbia funded my fieldwork through a fellowship. I am grateful for these forms of support.

The contributions of my family and friends are difficult to summarize. They have endured the best and the worst of this process and their wisdom and encouragement has greatly supported my efforts. My parents sustained me in many ways, always providing whatever support was needed. My mother's attachment to Fernie facilitated my social placement there and her stories originally sparked my sense of intrigue about that place. Femke van Delft helped me with some of the more tedious tasks of editing citations and preparing illustrations. Her humour and her meals nourished this process.

Jean Wilson and Darcy Cullen at UBC Press and copy editor Audrey McClellan provided insightful assistance throughout, improving the text and demystifying the publishing process. My appreciation extends to anonymous reviewers whose detailed readings and comments were also very helpful.

As this work takes on a public life, it is important to state that all interpretations and any errors appearing in it are my own.

Preface:
Knowing Who Your Neighbours Are

In my grandmother's house, the familiar yellow spines of *National Geographic* magazines fill two shelves. There is a picture book of Australia and another depicting the liberation of Holland by Canadian soldiers. Recipes torn from magazines fill one kitchen drawer. Yellowed, undated pages accidentally flip over to a description of "Mountain Men fighting Indians," an advertisement for a boy's first rifle, spice tips "from the British rule of India." Flyers appear in the milk box at the back door courtesy of the Jehovah's Witnesses. In them I read about genocide in Yugoslavia, the fiftieth anniversary of the United Nations Declaration of Human Rights, and relations between humans and angels. Such materials remind me of the busyness of information moving through people's lives and connecting them to larger relationships in the world.

I cannot ask my grandmother about the things in her house. She now lives a few blocks away in the extended care wing of the hospital. Alzheimer's has taken her memory; at least it has stolen her ability to communicate. Although I was virtually a stranger in Fernie, my family ties facilitated access to, and social placement within, the tight-knit community. I moved into my grandmother's house in May 1997. Like many anthropologists, I found my arrival in the field was marked by contradictory messages.

One day a worker came to replace the worn telephone line that sagged across the street into the side of the house. I was standing on the road, diverting traffic, while he dug his crampons into the pole, ascending it as if it were a palm tree. A group of elderly women were crossing the street. We exchanged greetings.

"Are you in this house?" one of them asked.

"Yes. It's my grandmother's house. I'm Leslie Robertson."

The most fragile of them lifted her arm from her walker and pointed to the house. "It was my understanding that no one would be living in Margaret's house!"

Twice. She said it twice, and in between I enthusiastically told her how great it was to be able to stay here a year or so to do research.

Another woman was consoling. "Have you come from the city, dear?"

"Yes."

"You'll like living in a small town. You know who your neighbours are here!"

Fernie is, officially at least, a city, with a population of just over five thousand people. It is located in the southeast corner of British Columbia, within the larger region of the East Kootenays. Here the Elk Valley intersects with the Crowsnest Pass, the lowest and southernmost corridor across the Canadian Rocky Mountains. Throughout the 1900s, Fernie was the destination of immigrants who sought prosperity in the coal mines, re-unification with relatives, and lives free from political upheaval and economic depression. I spent eighteen months living in Fernie conducting ethnographic research that, though grounded in one locale, taps into ideas and images from elsewhere. I was interested in ideas of human difference, intrigued by the possibility of working with people whose diverse histories converge and collide in this community. My contacts with people began with my grandmother's friends. Belonging to an "old family" in Fernie carried a significance that I had initially underestimated. Eventually, I did come to know who my neighbours were.

Homes separated by gardens and low fences look deceptively similar in Fernie. Their insides, however, are lined with languages, aromas, and objects bearing the symbols of complex journeys. Regional dialects from southern Italy or Czechoslovakia enliven kitchens steeped in the aroma of espresso, poppy-seed pastry, or pig-fat cookies. Some people lament the passing of these word-worlds, commenting on national programs of language "purification" or the difficulties of keeping language alive in exile. Medallions of saints, dream catchers, shields, crucifixes, fine cutwork, samovars, landscape paintings, war medals, carvings of wildlife, calendars from Germany, Scotland, Czechoslovakia – all belong to the stuff of selves. The figure of Buddha appears surprisingly here and there, on a mantel below the glass eyes of an elk or in St. Anthony's peripheral vision. For some, the objects symbolize friendships with – or marriages of sons and daughters to – people from different backgrounds. They are the manifestation of social relationships extending beyond cultural traditions and, in many cases, across boundaries of class and privilege in a place where many acknowledge the idea of ethnic hierarchy.

There is an uneasy blend of old and new in Fernie. I am told there is a room still dusted with coal above the cappuccino place on the main street. It makes me realize the layers of time separating what is seen from what is vanishing and what is now invisible. Brick buildings uptown bear the engraved names of Anglo-European men. Advertisements for businesses long gone are barely discernible on the weathered bricks of the Elks' Lodge and the hardware store. The newest shops display mirrored sunglasses, Gore-Tex suits, backpacks, skis, and snowboards. In the window of an art gallery is an image of a Masai man leaning on his staff. Next to this is a photo-realistic print of wolves, while inside the store is a watercolour of an "Indian Princess." The dynamic figure of a Plains "warrior" atop his horse is stencilled large on the outside of Fernie's ice arena (see Figure 1). I am intrigued by these public representations that seem so conspicuous in the present highly charged context of treaty negotiations in British Columbia.

I lived in Fernie doing research for this book between 1997 and 2000. At the time of writing – January 2004 – the Ktunaxa-Kinbasket First Nation had signed a Treaty Framework Agreement and was negotiating an Agreement-in-Principle that will provide the terms of the treaty. The Akun'kunik, or People of the Place of the Flying Head, are members of the Tobacco Plains Band in Grasmere, the closest reserve community, about a thirty-minute drive southwest of Fernie. It is one of seven bands located across two states and one province, which make up the Ktunaxa-Kinbasket First Nation. The others are the A'qam, or Woodland People, of the St. Mary's Band in Cranbrook, the Yaqan Nukiy, or the People of the Place Where the Rock Is Standing, in Creston. The Klitqatwumlat, or the Not

Figure 1 In 1997, the Fernie Junior "A" Ghostrider hockey team painted its logo on a side wall of the ice arena. The image was patterned after a shadow on Hosmer Mountain. *Photograph by L. Robertson, 1997.*

Shirt People of the Shuswap Band live in Invermere, and the Columbia Lake Band, or the Akisq'nuk, live at Windermere. In the United States, the Akaqlahalxu, or the Meadow People, live in Bonners Ferry, Idaho, and the Ksanka Band, or the Akicqa (Fish Trap People), live in Elmo, Montana (Kootenai Cultural Committee 1997:xiii-xiv).

Maps of traditional Ktunaxa territory include the region around Fernie and extend into the United States. The treaty-making process in British Columbia is unsettling established colonial relationships and ushering in new representational conventions. It is a reminder that changing political structures shape ideas of proximity and acts of exclusion between people.

When I hear old people in Fernie speak about neighbourhoods, there is a sense of the ground beneath them continuously shifting, rearranging in response to war, immigration policy, and the strategies of industry. The South End, which to many is where the "moneybags" live, was in times past the (Anglo) district of mining and railway "bosses," bankers, and businessmen. English-speaking Europeans tell me that the North End is the Italian district. Most Italians I spoke with commented on the mixture of ethnic groups here, especially before the male residents of Chinatown "just died out." Across the highway, which was once the Great Northern Railway track, is the district called the Annex. Homes here were built upon piles of slack (small pieces of coal) dumped near the Elk River. I have heard about the now-vanished French grocers and lumbermen from Italian, "Slav," and "Scotch" residents. "Workers" lived in West Fernie. Like my great-grandfather, many of them travelled several miles to work in the mines at Coal Creek. Before the sawmill shut down in West Fernie there was an area there known as the "mill shacks," where "Hindus" lived. West Fernie is enigmatic; its citizens have strongly resisted incorporation into the city for over a hundred years. Moving up the sides of the valley are post-1970s suburbs built in the wake of Kaiser Steel's takeover from Crowsnest Industries. Currently, the Elk Valley rings with the sound of construction as new houses for skiing vacationers fill the cracks in scenic valleys.

A more detailed social history of class, gender, age, and religion is inscribed in the hillside cemetery above the city. Names, dates, and epitaphs appear in Italian, English, Russian, Polish, and, less frequently, Chinese. Mining explosions, railway accidents, and epidemics are among the causes of death etched into the headstones of Welsh, Irish, and Hungarian residents. The symbol of the United Mine Workers of America appears on some gravestones. Many more are impressed with insignia of the Loyal Order of Moose, the Masons, Oddfellows, and sister signs of Rebekahs and Eastern Star. White stone altars stand as memorials to those who lost their lives in the First and Second World Wars. Children's graves are marked by the statue of a lamb. Visually, the boundary between Catholics and

Protestants is easily discerned. Ornate iron fences surround Greek Orthodox crucifixes; other crosses, carved from stone, bear Christ near statues of the Virgin Mary. My great-grandparents are buried in the Protestant area beneath a flat, plain stone inscribed only with their names and dates.

Below the cemetery, Fernie spreads to fill the gaps between the winding Elk River and the thickly forested base of mountains. The city's ever-extending boundaries are held tight by Hosmer Mountain to the north-east, close by Proctor and Trinity mountains, each draped with stories based on "Indian legend." Old-time residents have been socialized into these narratives, now offered as important symbols of local identity. To the west is the Lizard Range, where a thousand-hectare ski area attracts enthusiasts from around the world. Here an ironic, modern cornucopia of myth and ritual circulates around the figure of "The Griz," a stout, whiskered man dressed in skins, holding a powder musket. As drivers arrive in Fernie from the east or the west, The Griz appears on highway signs inviting them to "Discover Us."

When I first arrived in Fernie, long-time residents expressed a sense of isolation, of no longer being known outside of the region. During my research, the community began the uneasy transformation from a predominantly working-class, coal-mining town to an internationally recognized destination ski resort. I wanted to know where, in a socially diverse setting, people draw lines of human difference, what criteria they use, and how they speak about it.

I have structured this book around a popular local legend about a curse cast on Fernie by indigenous people. I use the story to introduce the multiple locations from which residents spoke to me about particular issues, tracing changes in the details of a legend that is narrated across generations within shifting ideological contexts. Cursing is an important theme throughout this work. It is both a verbal act wielding the force of intentional social action and a potent symbolic gesture implicating ideas of justice. I explore several forms of what I call cursing – contexts in which words constitute a powerful social force: gossip and rumour, representation, political correctness, and beliefs around word magic. As a metaphor, cursing implies the power that stories have to carry and construct meanings about who people are.

Stories wield social and political power; they are vessels for ideas of human difference transmitted across generations and geographies through mass media and official and social networks. I work with the narratives of people from different age, ethnic, gender, class, and religious locations in order to bring into relief the imaginative resources they draw upon to reckon human difference. I examine forms of social knowledge circulating within local and distant settings that constitute shared understandings, commonsense views of the world and social relationships within it.

People summon imagery from folklore; they draw upon official and contested histories using concepts popularized from scholarly theories or the edicts of political discourses. Poetics of human difference are woven into complex webs of representation used to justify, explain, or negotiate conflicts and affinities. As Beth Roy writes:

> Group actions are formulated from the experience of identity ... the complex construction of an individual's location in the community and her ties with others. Similarly, the will to action is born of detailed ideologies that often are experienced as commonsense or unexamined assumptions about rights and powers. Both identity and ideology-making draw deeply at the well of ... shared histories constructed through story-telling that serve to define memberships within groups and relations among them. (Roy 1994:3)

My intention in this book is to identify repertoires of difference and to highlight the processes through which these ideas enter our social imaginations. I trace images, legends, and theories that people use to negotiate various relationships within contexts of colonialism, immigration, labour strife, wars, treaty making, and development for tourism. Each context activates particular narratives where social categories are revived or newly constructed and difference is negotiated. There is an alarming consistency in the ways that essentialized categories of race, class, religion, gender, age, and sexuality persist across time. Different eras, characterized by shifts in social consciousness, generate new criteria; however, the list remains salient. Our repertoires of difference constitute a kind of commonsense social knowledge. This book is about the interplay of imageries of difference manifest in social practice.

Introduction:
Ideas Make Acts Possible

> Ideas make acts possible ... and then they make it possible for acts to be accepted.
>
> – Etienne Balibar, "Is There a Neo-Racism?"
> in *Race, Nation, Class*

An elderly woman in a wheelchair moved closer to another woman who was beginning to wail. She spoke softly, reaching out to touch her arm. "Try to think of something happy," she said in a thick accent. It was to no avail. The woman in the chair moved towards me as she began to sing a song. I asked her what language she was using. "Russian," she said. "Russian, Ukrainian, we all know each other's songs." When I asked where she was from she said, "The farm." Leaning over, she asked the crying woman if she had an education. The woman shook her head. They spoke together about hauling sacks of grain, milking cows, raising their children, and attending church. Then the crying resumed. "I don't know why she cries all the time. There's a few of them here [in the seniors' home] that cry all the time." Silence.

Then "Row, row, row your boat gently down the stream. Merrily, merrily, merrily, merrily, life is but a dream. That's it," she said. "You're in school, then you work, then you get old and die and you have to leave it all behind." Looking up, the other woman smiled and nodded. The singing woman continued: "There were many people before us. And nobody knows where they came from. The blacks were here first. They're the oldest, the first. Then the whites came from somewhere. Then they got together and danced. Nobody knows." She laughed. (Fieldnotes, 9 December 1997)

Memory begins in the present, hauling the past through time and place, through what we know, what we have lived, and what we imagine. It is a solitary process made social through selectively chosen utterances crafted to fill a particular moment. These women share time leading to the end of their lives. They speak in a language that neither regards as her own. Beyond their divergent religions and national histories, they arrive at a place they both inhabit. I am made aware of the inadequacy of words, the distance between what is said and what it means.

This book is structured by what people told me during fieldwork. All of the narratives that appear here are edited excerpts from conversations between individuals and me, an ethnographer. They reflect differing degrees of acquaintance and rapport; implicitly, they map out lines of friendship that I was privileged to experience. Most of my work was conducted with self-identified "old-timers," local residents who range in age between sixty and one hundred years.

Settings for our conversations were living rooms and kitchens in participants' homes; rooms in hospitals or in the seniors' facilities; mountainsides, dry creek beds, fast-food outlets, gardens, fairs, cemeteries, and long drives. Husbands and wives often sat down with me together. Three teenagers sat with me for a group interview, and I spoke more informally with younger children as they bustled in and out of conversations with their parents. I established contact with participants largely by word of mouth. During conversations about my research, people directed me to others who were regarded as knowledgeable historians or authentic representatives of a particular cultural or occupational group. Sometimes I was intentionally introduced to people with controversial views. I argued with some people about ideas we did not agree on, but these ongoing dialogues did not create irresolvable tensions. They were treated with humour and an "agreement to disagree" over ideas that everyone recognized as controversial. I transcribed interviews as soon as possible and returned them to participants who clarified misheard words, provided correct spellings, and made any edits they wished to make. I make no claims that these people are representative of the ethnic, age, or gender groups to which they affiliate. My analysis looks at how people express their ideas, the discursive resources they draw upon to configure human difference. My presentation is based on patterns in content and form that emerged from these conversations.

Like all researchers, I am faced with inevitable dilemmas that accompany the inscription of others. Beginning in the 1980s, the "crisis of representation" steered anthropology's gaze inward towards a critical evaluation of ethnographic works: "Fieldwork produces a kind of authority that is anchored to a large extent in subjective, sensuous experience ... But the professional text to result from such an encounter is supposed to conform to the norms of a scientific discourse whose authority resides in the absolute effacement of the speaking and experiencing subject" (Pratt 1986:32).

In any ethnography, the writer is faced with several decisions that reflect uneasy power relations between those who represent and those who are represented (Fabian 1990). Undeniably, participants' words are the viscera of ethnography; without them we are left to the often elegant, but disembodied, machinations of theory. Having said this, I recognize that the words of participants appear throughout this book in text, severed from the rich particulars of their relationships and histories. Editing personal narratives is the first active move towards classification, and I have marked voices with categories of nationality, gender, age, and sometimes neighbourhood and region. The descriptors follow from categories of identity relevant to each chapter. At present, this seems an inevitable reduction, given my attempts to preserve the anonymity of participants and the detail of their locations. My intention is not to reduce the complexity of individual narrators, but to highlight their perspectives and the imaginative resources they use to speak about human difference.

Most ethnographies are written from a distance. They are a complicated collage of "on the spot" observations, evolving understandings, and finally a sort of re-entry into the realm of theoretical and methodological questions. Among those questions is how to translate the research experience into text (see Boon 1982 and Bruner 1986). Fieldwork is an idiosyncratic process of reflection and documentation that generates several forms of information or "data." I have adopted a visual style to represent these forms in an attempt to remain self-conscious about ethnographic rhetoric and the layers of information acquired through experience, analysis, and, finally, through scholarly interpretation. Lengthy excerpts from participants' audiotaped interviews are inset from the main text block, in order to reinforce the primary materials upon which I have built this book. Unedited fieldnote entries appear in a sans serif font along with their date of entry. I flag distinctions between taped interviews and participants' comments or my observations of events that I later wrote from memory in my fieldnotes.[1] Other passages include quotes "from" my fieldnote entries or from notes written on whatever was available (these are not in sans serif). The remainder of the book represents my analytical interpretations and the words of others borrowed for their insights.

The rationale for this strategy is, in part, based on the fact that there are several audiences for this book. In the past I have used this form of presentation and received feedback from community members who appreciated the option to read the work variously through elicited narratives or through my inscription of events and theoretical observations (Robertson 1994). Anthropological fieldwork involves crossings between systems of knowledge, subjective realities, and social orders. My methods of information gathering focused on mass media, personal narrative, public social performances, and ideas of place and space.

During fieldwork I met many people simply through day-to-day encounters in Fernie. My routine included a visit to my grandmother in the hospital each evening. Here I spoke with staff and other residents, met religious leaders, and witnessed the passing of a generation of collective memories. I attended funerals and flea markets, went berry picking and fossil hunting, was guided to sites where the towns of Morrissey and Coal Creek once bustled. I went to ceremonial events: at the Legion Hall on

Remembrance Day, to Roman Catholic masses and Ktunaxa powwows in Fernie and Creston. The Mogul Smoker and Griz Days events opened a view to the social world of skiers and tourists. I spoke often with friends' children and attended events surrounding the closure of the historic Fernie High School and a performance of Mesmer the Hypnotist. I joined a committee to commemorate Italian heritage in the Elk Valley and coordinated an oral history project for the Fernie and District Historical Society.[2] Whether public performances are scripted as entertainment, as formal ritual, or as community spectacle, they are infused with historical references and symbols of local identity that provide researchers with a sense of what is valued.

I spent some time at the local museum looking through historical records and speaking with historians and archivists there. The public library provided me with microfiche copies of the local *Fernie Free Press* newspaper dating from 1898. Transcripts from an oral history project carried out in 1971 were also a rich resource. People invited me to peruse their personal archives: eloquent write-ups of family histories, collections of old newspaper articles and school textbooks, pay stubs and immigration forms, photographs and home movies. Many showed me documents from the "old country"; religious images that commemorate communions, weddings, or saints' days; items of propaganda from the Second World War; frail books, newspapers, and magazines in many languages. All of these materials provided me with access to descriptions of events and people through the imagery of distant times and places.

Articles and advertisements from the *Fernie Free Press* newspaper, postcards, and photographs appear throughout this book. My approach to these materials of popular culture is informed by Arjun Appadurai's concept of "mediascape," in which mass media is inextricably tied to the local, national, and global contexts within which it circulates. The many forms of media "provide repertoires of images, narratives and ethnoscapes to viewers in which politics, news and commodities are profoundly mixed" (1991:7; see also Ginsburg 1994:5).[3] These materials serve to highlight "hegemonic forms ... the creation of national and other social imaginaries; and the development of new arenas for political expression and the production of identity" (Ginsburg 1994:8). Forms of mass media provide a sense of official and popular discourses circulating locally and internationally during particular moments in time.

Situating Myself

I am the fourth generation in my mother's line to live in Fernie. Introductions always included this vital piece of information. I was, at times, taken aback by the spontaneous and vivid accounts of my relatives that were offered. It was a little eerie to see my great-grandfather in home movies, tipping his hat to the camera, or a book of poetry inscribed in his handwriting. I met people who spoke to me about the care my grandmother had provided as a nurse during the birth of their children. In the extended care wing of the hospital, I passed time with a woman who used to cook supper for my mother and other children in West Fernie. Several people recounted meetings they had with me as a child. Sometimes during interviews people told me that we were related through marriage. Clearly, old-time residents in Fernie are able to place me socially through their acquaintance with my ancestors. Many, in fact, knew more about my family than I do. My research included a foray into my own family history. I eventually interviewed my mother.

Could you tell me about our family history in Fernie?
Our family history as I know it. Phyllis Nattrass and Alec Henderson married in Nine Banks church in Northumberland, travelled over to Canada, and, as I know it, they were on the train station just outside of Allendale in a town that no longer exists. They, with a group of other immigrants, go on the train, travelled to a port in southwest England. Got on a boat, travelled across – probably to Montreal. Disembarked and travelled by train all across Canada to Fort Macleod, Alberta. Where, as I understand it, they had homestead property. I don't know too much of what happened at that time except that my grandmother became very, very ill. That was around 1905-06, because, historically, 1907 or 1908 have gone down in the history books as being one of the coldest winters of all time. And as my grandfather told me, my grandmother became very ill with one of the infectious diseases of the time – it could have been diphtheria. I was led to understand that his homestead property wasn't the best, and because of the illness and possibly other reasons, they picked up and moved to Fernie. Where he went back to the mines. Of course, when he left England he'd hoped to have had his own farm, to be a farmer or a rancher. So his plan didn't work out, and of course the mines were booming at this stage. So they got on the train again and went further west into the Crowsnest Pass and stopped off in Fernie. It was probably around 1909 or '10. Because my mother was born in 1913.

My grandfather was down in the mines. As he told me, there was a terrible mine accident – he wasn't in the accident. There was fairly severe loss of life. He told me that he decided at that stage he would never go down again. It was in Coal Creek I think. So he decided he was going to stay up on top, and as far as I know, that's when he became, he was in charge of the horses. As I grew up, I knew him to be the blacksmith at Coal Creek. (Interview, 12 May 1998. English-Canadian woman, born 1937.)

Stories of arrival are narrative links to distant places, cornerstones of identity that hint at the complex journeys of ideas. My ignorance of my own family history reflects the tenuous connection I have to this place as part of an expatriate family. I spent my childhood in Australia. While my research was conducted in a small, rural town in British Columbia, many of those with whom I worked are also connected personally, or through their parents, to transnational contexts. Most of the participants in this research originally arrived in Fernie as members of labouring classes in large-scale migrations. Appadurai (1991:198) uses the term "deterritorialization" in reference to movements of "persons, images and ideas" in "local" places. Ulf Hannertz (1990:239) asserts the need to examine networks of people who carry "collective structures of meaning" across the globe.[4] Ideas are carried with people as they embark on great journeys; upon arrival they are revived and applied in new settings.

Personal Narratives

As my familiarity with people in Fernie deepened, I recognized several forms of narrative circulating in this town. People's stories draw from different social realities and inter/national events. During fieldwork I heard life stories, family histories, place histories, national histories, and accounts of war, arrival, and work. As Julie Cruikshank (1994:408) notes, personal narratives are striking for "what they reveal about social history ... the complexities of daily life and contradictions in relations of power." Perhaps the greatest challenge for those working with oral materials is to "demonstrat[e] how all social constructions, including our own, factor into social processes we are trying to understand, and how they connect generations, times, and places" (418).

Throughout this book I analyze flows and ruptures in social knowledge, and how narratives reveal strategies of political regimes and propagate social theories. People's stories reveal places where categories of human difference become visible, the criteria these categories are based on, and how they are spoken about. Through personal narratives I gained a sense of the ideas that are passed on, reconfigured, and sometimes lost.

Details of arrival are perhaps the most authenticating aspect of Anglo-European and non-Anglo-European[5] narratives. Old-timers are able to recite to me the bare bones of other people's arrival stories. Itineraries of ports and stations, problems with officials, seasickness, and exhaustion fold into descriptions of a new and seemingly endless landscape. Food and language are the most immediate terrors encountered by newcomers in the stories of non-Anglo Europeans. Others, forced to leave behind children and extended family, spoke of the intense grief they experienced on their journeys. There is something else in these narratives. It is the collision of images about the new country – not paved in gold, but rough and rural and without a kind of cosmopolitanism that people were accustomed to.

Romantic ideas forged by the stories of returning compatriots, or by literature and song, dropped into the black ocean during trans-Atlantic crossings, or they snapped off in the lonely and barren days of a first winter in Canada. Fantasies of cross-cultural interaction were also counted in the cargo lost through immigration. Some people spoke of the Wild West, of anticipating cowboys and Indians, expectations seeded by motion pictures and embodied in childhood games. Early Welsh immigrants who interacted with Ktunaxa people believed that they had met the mythical "Welsh-speaking Red Indians" of their own nationalistic lore. Others held on to the terror sown through stories of savagery and rebellion in the New World. Clearly, expectations about the new country were set in elaborate and somewhat fantastic imagery.

For many immigrants, the strangeness offered new horizons detached from grim postwar realities of Europe, political oppression, or desperate unemployment. Some people describe stepping onto the rail platform in Fernie and feeling dread because of the closeness of the mountains. Many women, reunited with husbands and relatives, felt only relief that they had arrived. The accounts are most vividly narrated by those with first-hand experience, although the subsequent generation was also able to provide details. Children of immigrants spoke often about the melancholy of their parents, especially mothers. Narratives of arrival provide important clues about how "foreigners" are received and imagined by the host nation. I examine shifting perceptions of European otherness through personal narratives, policies, and theories affecting immigration during different eras.

Unravelling the past involves paying attention to ideas, images, and objects passed on through time by people in their complex journeys from other places. Details of ancestry were often cited when I was introduced to people in Fernie. They are a powerful symbolic form by which people reckon their origins and a way of locating someone within a dense social network – a network *known* by people in a small community.

Over and over I was told about the vital links to some other place through stories of immigration, language markers, and national histories.[6] Particular cultural conventions are used to reckon connectedness to distant places and peoples. Some do this through objects. Religious artifacts signify saints' identification with home villages, and figurines depict regional dress. I was shown coats of arms and genealogical charts, tartans and clan histories. Many families have compiled texts of their families and nations. One woman showed me her history of Bohemians traced back through three centuries of Austrian reign, then through the tenth- and thirteenth-century dynasties of "native princes," and finally to a Celtic tribe called "Boii" in the fifth century BC. A northern Italian family showed me a written description of their "forefathers' lives" that commenced in the fourteenth century when the popes took up permanent residence in Avignon. Their history emphasized self-governing regions in Italy manifest in "dialect, custom and cooking."

Calabrians from southern Italy use oral forms of remembering origins. One man born in Fernie had been taught by his father to memorize the sequence of villages on the roads leading to his home in Italy. The convention of the "supra nome" or "over-name" was frequently brought up. These are descriptive nicknames that follow family lines through at least four generations. Often the supra nome refers to a special talent or occupation of a male or female ancestor. I was told that when travelling in Italy or overseas, people "would not be seen" (socially recognized) until an over-name was mentioned. Some Calabrian women changed their names after marriage; however, many continued to be addressed by their supra nomes and maiden names in Canada.

Everyone knew stories about their respective old country. These narratives of elsewhere are important carriers of ideas about people, nations, and events. Participants recalled turbulent experiences of wartime in different nations, as well as labour unrest, revolutions, and poverty. Some invoked pastoral beauty, the sense of closeness to extended family, and ways of living that fulfilled their social needs. People often spoke about the ruptures in their religious lives – the sudden loss of daily spiritual involvement or the absence of their particular faith – in the new country. First-generation Canadians pull in and out of their parents' stories. As one woman told me: "My thoughts are my mother's memories. My real memories are here in Canada." Ideas passed on and kept alive from the old country include impressions about people from different nations. I learned that ideas are transmitted from one setting to another and, in some cases, passed on through generations. These ideas carry taxonomies of difference that have become "traditionalized" in the repertoires of people from different nations (Bendix and Klein 1993:6; see also Dundes 1971b:187; Görög-Karady 1992:114). Ideas from distant times and places continue to inform contemporary interpretations of human difference.

Old country ways include oral performances at the hearth of distant homes, sculpted by religions, beliefs, histories, and landscapes now part of collective memory in exile. Oral traditions defy the ordinary. I was told Czech fairy tales in which animals and insects interacted in a tight network of kinship, and stories that described mountains as animated social actors. Calabrian women told me about villages threatened by burning logs in the sky, or earthquakes caused by slips in faith. Their stories are filled with faith-promoting miracles of saints whose statues are inextricably bound to the destiny of each small village. For Eastern Europeans, revolutionary traditions revive identities scourged by political oppression. The poetry of Taras Shevchenko lives on in Ukrainian liberation songs. In kitchens in Fernie, freedom songs were sung proudly in Slovakian dialects finally released from the bonds of Magyar. I heard about Bonnie Prince Charlie, "that madman." A Scottish woman sang a song describing the deception that culminated in the historical slaughter of the House of MacDonald. Closer to home there is a locally inspired phantasmagoria that includes testimony about flying saucers, speculation that "degraded" persons reincarnate as crows, and ghost stories about a nun who haunts the museum and a murdered miner at the abandoned site of the town of Coal Creek.

I was surprised by the complex work histories in Fernie. For men, the flexibility of occupations corresponded with wars, fluctuations in the coal market, and strikes or injuries. Everyone spoke about periods of unemployment and poverty, of times when they went "into the bush" to hunt rather than leave the area in search of work. Other informal economic strategies included labour in exchange for rent, food, and sometimes language lessons. Changes in technology and workers' rights are embedded in these accounts. Old-timers were particularly nostalgic for an era when people worked together, a kind of mutual dependence, knowing that you and your neighbour were in the same boat. Often these reminiscences revolved around ideas of community shaped by shared experiences of class or relationships to a dominant ethnic group. Work is deeply implicated in expressions of identity.

Women's narratives included the work histories of their male relatives. For the wives and children of early miners, anticipation of the dreaded emergency siren was a daily burden. Non-Anglo-European women offered detailed work histories; many cleaned the homes of wealthier residents, worked as chambermaids in the hotels, or scrubbed pots in the kitchen of the Chinese restaurant. Others took in boarders, usually coal miners, tending to their laundry and meals. The eldest generations of women told me about prostitution, once prolific in this region where, demographically, working men are still in the majority. In their narratives, these women also mentioned strategies of berry and mushroom picking, fishing, and sometimes working a trapline. For the eldest generations, tending to livestock was a daily routine and all women mentioned their vegetable gardens, still a vital topic of conversation in Fernie. Gendered difference was ever-present in the narratives of the eldest generations of women. Usually this took the form of a moral discourse directed at particular ethnic groups and their perceived treatment of women in spousal relations. In Fernie, people of all ages speak about the curse legend in terms of gender transgression.

Founding Legends: The Curse as a Key to History

> Folkloric expression itself can be a political act, even without a
> necessarily political interpretation ... [It] raises issues of unequal
> power and social exploitation ... When and where these forms
> are expressed – and where they are not, either forbidden or
> hidden – carries enormous weight in both their symbolic and
> their practical value.
>
> – William Westerman, "The Politics of Folklore"

There are many forms of collective lore circulating in Fernie that meld
fantasy to history. Local legends are embedded in the surrounding mountains; they are alive with contested meanings brought into service during periods of local conflict. Some stories describe interactions between
Aboriginal characters or between indigenous people and Euro-Canadians.
Others tap into folklore traditions from other places, now transposed onto
new landscapes. Norse mythology surrounds the Lizard Range, where the
ski hill is located. Hosmer Mountain and Trinity Mountain are draped in
narratives detailing gender transgression and unrequited love. Written
history, on the other hand, is contentious in Fernie. A litany of disasters
and conflicts resurfaces in each new publication about the area's past. These
accounts describe uneasy relations between Anglo and non-Anglo Europeans. In town, some old-timers talk about people identified as "foreigners," who seem destined to remain forever frozen in these accounts. Like
these non-Anglo Europeans, indigenous people are also reified through
folklore, a kind of popular history that reinforces taken-for-granted
notions of who people are. I draw from the work of scholars who analyze
forms of folklore as symbolic resources through which power is negotiated, contested, and controlled (Brunvand 1971; Dundes 1971a; Shai 1978;
Gaudet 1988). Throughout this book I approach folklore as "ideological
narratives" whose "purpose is to come to terms with a social and historical reality" (Görög-Karady 1992:114; see also Taussig 1984; Linke
1990:118; Klein 1992:465; Westerman 1996:571-574).

"Indian legends" circulating in Fernie initially appeared to me as narratives carrying cross-cultural information. The main actors in these stories
include all of the characters of colonialism: chiefs, braves, princesses,
explorers, and businessmen. There are scenes of exploitation and mystical revenge, and skirmishes of power embedded in the contours of mountains. The most ubiquitous legend now surrounds Hosmer Mountain. It is
the story of the curse through which people implicitly and explicitly
address gender, class, ethnicity, and age.

Old legends tell of Captain William Fernie courting an Indian Princess
of the Kootenay Indian band to learn the source of her necklace's "sacred

black stones." Upon learning the location of the Morrissey coal seams, Fernie jilted his Indian bride. Her angry mother then placed a curse on the Elk Valley ... a curse officially lifted by the Kootenay Indian Band in 1964. (Postcard inscription. Purchased in Fernie 1996)

The story appears on a postcard depicting the Ghostrider of Hosmer Mountain, a horse-and-rider-shaped shadow visible in the early evening light on a rock face above the city of Fernie. According to the writer, the image is that of the ghost of William Fernie, destined eternally to "flee the angry Indian Chief and his daughter." The postcard evokes a narrative landscape of sorts, where the story is visible to those who reside there. During my research, the curse narrative was repeatedly offered to me as *the* story of Fernie. It is offered to "strangers" as a narrative hinge upon which local identity swings. Some present the tale as belonging to a widespread rural genre almost expected in casual encounters between people from different places. The message here is that the story travels well. Others acknowledge market value, the managing and packaging of the story, and its power to lure tourists into the mystique of an unknown place. Newcomers are very aware of the latest incarnation in popular media, especially advertising for tourism. I asked everyone who participated in my research about the curse. It became a kind of barometer to trace the way that a story flows through a community. Where does it stop? How is it used? The legend of the curse and the image of the Ghostrider are dynamic imaginative resources. I track their transformations and link them to shifting historical contexts of representation.

When I first began interviewing people in Fernie, I was drawn into the quest for origins of the curse narrative. There is little consensus about the story's origin, its truth-value, or its function. I abandoned investigations into the genesis of the narrative when I became aware of how malleable it is, and how individuals use it to address issues and events that are relevant to them. To some, the curse is an innocuous tale, an heirloom passed between generations, vitally connecting them to their birthplace. Interpretations swing between different ideologies, beliefs, and explanations rooted in personal identity. What is clear is that the legend is firmly lodged in a repertoire of social knowledge that is local but not uniform in its expression. There is always the possibility of new situations that will breathe life into the old story.

The curse is well documented in published accounts of Fernie's history, and residents freely offer their versions, some of which include real people and witnessed events. William Fernie arrived in the Elk Valley in the mid-1800s. Ktunaxa traditionalists officially lifted the curse in a public ceremony in 1964. According to some people who attended the curse-lifting, the curse was subsequently reinstated. Like Richard Bauman (1986:2),

I am interested in an ethnographic and contextual view of narratives "in order to discover the individual, social, and cultural factors that give [them] shape and meaning in the conduct of social life." It became clear to me that long-time residents have been socialized into the story that is deeply embedded in landscape and history. Participants' narratives anchor my analyses in this book. My approach to history, therefore, reflects what social historian David Cohen (1994:4) calls a "popular processing of the past" that highlights "multiple locations of historical knowledge."

I discussed my intention to use the curse as a main thread in this work with an active community member in Fernie. She was, at first, hesitant, concerned about community morale and the consequences of dredging the story up – feeding a pessimism she felt was not useful. She told me about an editorial in the local newspaper in 1999 that revived the curse, and how angry she was that this writer was casting the story again, making people feel helpless. This is the essence of the story to her – the feeling that the people here can't control what will happen. I told her that I was interested in the legend for what it says about cross-cultural relations. This interpretation both surprised and intrigued her. Like many people in Fernie, she did not interpret the narrative through ethnic relations, a significant point, I will argue, in the colonial process of inscribing indigenous people.

The curse legend has remarkable plasticity; it is brought into service within the historical contexts of discovery and colonization, local industrial strife, and current tourism development. I am interested in the curse story as a popular narrative that takes on different meanings in particular circumstances. In the context of the colonial encounter, I look at the historical grounding of the curse legend and what it reveals about relationships between European and indigenous people leading up to the twentieth century. I examine popular narratives as successful forms of colonial propaganda, reinforcing a story that marginalizes indigenous people. I also analyze the legend through different cosmologies and changing regimes of belief, through ways that the story makes sense as something to "think with" (Darnton 1984:4). The curse was, perhaps, initially an origin story for the Crowsnest Pass Coal Company. In the context of development for tourism and skiing, the curse story is fading behind new industrial legends and the commodified image of the Ghostrider shadow.

While everyone I spoke with had a sense of the story, it is important to note that not everyone could narrate the details of the curse legend. Some non-Anglo-European immigrants were hesitant. Younger people sometimes blended elements of it with details of other local legends and more than a hint of Western fairy tales. Uneven knowledge of the legend highlights the notion of story-sharing communities within which people become socialized. Different versions from different age groups also provide insight into how such narratives transform over time, which elements remain significant, and which are dropped. During fieldwork, the story of the curse led to discussions about curse beliefs, while my questions around human difference prompted many to comment on what they perceived to be constraints on free speech. I came to understand that silences and hesitations are bound up with perceptions of traditional, political, and social power.

Politics of Information: Controlling the Flow

I was constantly reminded of the politics surrounding whom one speaks with, and what one speaks about.

> I brought some berries in today [to the seniors' home] for my
> grandmother and Mrs. _____. Two of the nurses asked me where
> I was picking. I hesitated and smiled. One of them burst out laughing
> and pointed at me, saying: "You're becoming a Fernie-ite! She's not
> saying where her patch is!" We laughed. She said: "When someone asks,
> just say 'up the mountains.'" (Fieldnotes, 1 September 1997)

While berry picking has its political dimensions, other topics around which information is guarded evoke more serious tensions between locals and outsiders, and between members of different generations, classes, genders, and language or ethnic groups. Stories carry ideas and images of people; they are a form of social action used to contest or maintain hegemonic views. With this in mind, it is important to examine both how people express themselves and how they feel constrained in their expression. While conducting research I became acutely aware of contexts in which speech acts and particular representations were seen to be breaches of appropriate behaviour. Conceptually, cursing is a potent idea through which to explore connections between thought, speech, and action.

I explore cursing through traditional knowledge (*mal'uocchiu* and other European examples), informal networks of talk (gossip and rumour), and scholarly ideas about representation and political correctness. Although they draw from different contexts of meaning (traditional, social, and political), each of these forms of what I call cursing is driven by recognition of the repercussions of speech acts. Not surprisingly, anthropologists interested in the social power of words explore connections between witchcraft or sorcery and gossip (Paine 1968:278; Gluckman 1968). Regarding gossip, Karen Brison (1992:4) concentrates on the salience of "dangerous words" and their power to "constitute social worlds." Cursing is, at base, a speech act with serious ramifications.

Many people with whom I worked expressed belief in cursing. I obtained the clearest views on the subject from Calabrian women who told me about mal'uocchiu, translated to me as "the crooked eye." Like rumour, beliefs that fall within this complex may be viewed narrowly as a mechanism of social control. Unlike gossip, mal'uocchiu requires only thought (conscious or unconscious) to affect the physical being of others. As Sam Migliore (1997:x, 13-15) notes, both representations of the crooked eye and the actual complex of beliefs surrounding it are "inherently ambiguous, vague, and variable." Most writers agree, however, that the evil eye phenomenon should be approached through the contexts of its use in a particular social setting. According to participants, to be watchful of mal'uocchiu is to deter any sentiments of envy *(invidia)* that may arise from careless boasting or displays of prosperity, beauty, and health. Class-consciousness is acute for residents of this traditionally working-class community. Many of the anxieties expressed revolve around displays of "being better than" one's neighbours. In much the same way, people were also apprehensive about participating in certain informal networks of talk. Without providing examples, they spoke about the harsh power of gossip in this small community.

Power is implicated in most scholarly works on rumour and gossip. What is most potent about this form of talk is the power of such stories to affect "social processes extending beyond the immediate social encounter" (Goodwin 1982:799). Gossip functions as a form of sanction to powerful economic corporations (P. Turner 1992) or a way of indirectly challenging leaders and public personalities (Brison 1992). Rumour is particularly effective in "dense social networks where people share many acquaintances" (10). As strategic interpretations of events and persons, these narratives transmit moral evaluations affecting "how people perceive and react to events" (18-19). They provide, in effect, an immediate critique of hegemonic assumptions through the circulation of alternative interpretations.

Rumour is also, at times, generated by dominant discourse-makers. During periods of conquest, warfare, and political or economic strife there is a kind of "talk" in circulation that demonizes particular people, naturalizing enmity and essentializing difference. To Veena Das (1998:111), the "perfomativity of rumour" is based in the "perlocutionary force of words; their capacity to do something by saying something." In Fernie, people's explanations reflected atrocity myths, official forms of propaganda, and scholarly theories cast into circulation during particular times of conflict. They are powerful narratives imbued with authority that propagate particular taxonomies of difference. Old stories are revived in new settings. New ideas are brought into circulation, bolstering commonsense understandings about who other people are in relation to oneself.

In scholarly, political, and social arenas during the late 1990s there was an intense awareness of the use of words, particularly those through which difference is ascribed. Political correctness rests on the assumption that language propagates ideas and images that could harm certain groups of

people or justify acts of exclusion, inequality, or violence. Although folk-
lorists categorize cursing as a verbal genre, others suggest that writing,
too, may be viewed as "constitutive of social action" (Danet and Bogoch
1992:133). This is the power of representation.[7] In academia, and particularly in anthropology, representation has come to occupy a central and
somewhat scratchy place in cultural politics. I hope to show that concepts
and beliefs that underlie cursing resonate in social *and* academic realms.
Legacies of representation are tangled up in particular fields of power and
deeply affect the lives of people belonging to inscribed groups. They also
influence perceptions of relationship with others.

There is, however, a more expansive level of social consciousness at play,
affecting how people, myself included, express ourselves. In his extensive
work on "racist and nationalist ideas in Europe," Leon Poliakov (1974:5)
describes the present in which a kind of "anti-racist dogmatic orthodoxy"
reigns. Many of us live in a current context where sanctions against or for
what we say or write are popularly named political correctness. Meaning
is negotiated within particular social contexts extending from local face-
to-face situations to larger societal arenas where particular ideas are agreed
upon and challenged. Management of information takes place within particular contexts where expression is shaped by collective sanctions and
protocols guiding social behaviour. Moira Smith and Rachelle Saltzman
(1995:86-87) view interventions on speech as "traditional acts" by audiences of "expressive culture" that serve to reinforce a moral universe.[8]

This theory of word power deeply implicates notions of justice. Political correctness operates as an "ideological code ... in the field of public
discourse to structure text or talk" (D. Smith 1995:26).[9] Concepts of racism
and civil and human rights are relatively recent additions to popular consciousness. During other times and in other places, political suppression
also followed the "party line" of ideology makers. Clearly, successive eras
of social thought are characterized by particular guidelines for acts of
speech and behaviour:

> As oral historians we have frail but precious tools: attention to language
> and form, to how things are remembered, or forgotten; and not only to
> the contents of memory, but also to what is not remembered, to silences.
> (Passerini 1992:15)

People in Fernie spoke often about silence. It is an enigma both between
generations and within. Silence hovers around the subjects of imperial occupation, war, immigration, and politics. Men who experienced the two world
wars as soldiers do not speak about their experiences. First-generation
Canadians noted their parents' silence about harsh conditions in their
home countries or about circumstances of persecution after they arrived.

Silence is audible in the whispers about oppressive political regimes and in the pronounced hesitations to speak about beliefs not sanctioned by religious, medical, and/or educational authorities. Several people with whom I worked have experienced life under Nazi and Fascist regimes. Some have experienced the abrupt closure of communication with their families in Soviet territories. A few participants openly critiqued the social taxonomies imposed by national regimes, others chose to speak "off the record," and some presented these categories as natural and unquestioned. Theoretically, these responses may be approached through Luisa Passerini's (1992:7) idea of "totalitarian mentalities": that is, social systems requiring consensus and authority and involving "a system of propaganda as well as control of expression and communication." Totalitarian states use "the technology of amnesia" (Watson 1994:6), which includes official censorship, propaganda, and a system of enforcement that imposes a kind of personal silencing (see also Passerini 1992; Khubova, Ivankiev, and Sharova 1992; Cruikshank 1994). Throughout this book I identify methods used by different political regimes, including British imperialism, to manage the appearance of particular social problems and peoples. I look to the places where these impressions and images intersect with personal narratives.

Invoking Difference

> Implicit social knowledge is not simply a passive, reflecting, absorbing faculty of social being; it should also be thought of as an experimental activity, essaying this or that possibility, imagining this or that situation, this or that motivation, postulating another dimension to a personality – in short, trying out in verbal and visual image the range of possibilities and near-possibilities of social intercourse, self and other.
> – Michael Taussig, *Shamanism, Colonialism, and the Wild Man*

I draw from many fields contributing to studies about difference: folklore, inter-ethnic relations, the history of anthropology, and oral history. I am interested in hegemony, in processes that generate and maintain a "commonsense" view of the world and social relationships within it. Recognition of different kinds of knowledge circulating within particular contexts is key to these investigations. Knowledge refers "to what people employ to interpret and act in the world: feelings as well as thoughts, embodied skills as well as taxonomies and other verbal models" (Barth 1995:66). What I present in this book is a body of ideas circulating in theoretical and popular contexts that signals shifts in the ways human difference is spoken about.

I wanted to know what information is conveyed between parents and children, between members of the same social group, and between members of different social collectivities. I was told stories and anecdotes, legends, political doctrines, and scientific theories that reveal taxonomies of difference. Some people made reference to mass media and products of popular culture. In most cases there were overlapping ideas from members of the same cultural group. "Culture" was not, however, the salient shaper of perceptions about difference. Instead, I heard people speaking from their experiences as men and women; as members of a certain generation; as "foreigners," "enemy aliens," "DPs," and those who are racialized; as people with spiritual convictions; as members of particular economic classes; and as residents of a region. These distinctions serve to dissipate monolithic categories constructed at particular historical junctions.

Looking Sideways

A kind of web of alliances that cuts across normalized boundaries of ethnic identity became apparent to me. I borrow the term "looking sideways" (Palsson 1993:12) to describe lines of affiliation cast laterally between people who, superficially, do not share group membership. Non-Anglo Europeans of different nationalities look sideways at each other, based on their treatment as "foreigners" in Canada. Italians expressed an understanding and affinity for indigenous people through their shared sense of ritual and deep commitment to faith. A Ktunaxa woman who was raised in Fernie spoke about her sense of closeness to Italians through their common experience of racialization by dominant "white" society. Others met on equal ground, interacting eye to eye in the context of shared poverty or compatible ideology.

Ideas of affiliation and estrangement shift within particular contexts of interaction between people. For each act of looking sideways there are implicit acts of looking down on, or being looked down upon by, a culture or class group, an age grade with radically different perspectives, nonbelievers or faith promoters, regional outsiders or locals. Each scenario pivots around some arrangement of unequal power through structural relationships or representational control. What I hope to make clear is a changing constellation of relationships where concepts such as race, class, age, gender, nationality, religion, sexuality, and culture intersect. They are markers in the malleable discourses of human difference.

Working with members of more than one ethnic group turns attention away from the idea of isolated units to relationships grounded in ordinary social activity. I approach ideas of difference within larger ideational contexts that are influenced by changing scholarly theories, political realities, and localized social formations (Balibar 1991:17; see also Stolcke 1995). I investigate how these resources are used by people (or not) to make sense of their social environment.

Scholarly Theories

> Philosophies and theories, like political opinions, should be
> regarded as part and parcel of the world in which we live rather
> than transcendent views that somehow escape the impress of
> our social interests, cultural habits, and personal persuasions.
> – Michael Jackson, *Things As They Are*

I brought to this project certain dissatisfaction with ethnographic inquiry and the writing that inscribes it. I struggle with the philosophical and political underpinnings of the master concepts of culture, tradition, and history. These constitute the disciplinary language at our disposal. Our analytical idiom seeks out distinctions marked by these heavy concepts of group membership and, perhaps unwittingly, creates images of mono-lithically discrete and bounded "cultures" framed by academic categories that have been sculpted by their own dynamic histories. Not surprisingly, scholarly theories that serve to naturalize distinctions between people and normalize their relations also have a part to play in the popular imagina-tion. In this work, I have tried to portray the slipperiness in our reckon-ings of affiliation and strangeness, concentrating instead on the complex experiential contexts in which we formulate our impressions of human difference. Fantasy has an often startling role to play in the ways that our imageries interweave and diverge.

Dialogues about social theory inform the ways that people express their ideas about human difference. These theories have long intellectual his-tories and have been used at various points in time to delineate European and indigenous peoples. Social evolution, race theory, Nordic superiority, and eugenics each provide a way of imagining human difference. Explor-ers, government officials, medical authorities, politicians, and scientists have wielded them to classify people. These theories and the taxonomies they dictate have been applied to indigenous people in an alarmingly con-sistent manner across time. By contrast, the official application of these ideas to Europeans in Canada has been erratic.

Although rephrased throughout the history of anthropology, portrayals of cultural difference lie at the philosophical heart of the discipline. The most influential concepts are race, culture, and ethnicity. Nineteenth-century notions of the "primitive" and the "civilized," and scientific the-ories of race, social evolution, and other influential mythologies have been well noted in the intellectual histories of disciplinary thought. I trace the way that "race" is used in both official and popular arenas. Scholars have long debated the usefulness of "culture" as a grand concept reifying dif-ference; as many have argued, it maintains notions of uniqueness and self-containment of "systems of shared meaning" (Rosaldo 1989:27-28;

see also Clifford 1988:234; Abu-Lughod 1991; Wikan 1992:472). Ethnicity emerged in the 1960s as a concept recognizing power relations and processes of identity construction within and between groups previously conceived as cultures. Perceived racial and cultural differences remain central to studies of ethnicity:

> The term "ethnic identity" can ... refer to origin, uniqueness, passing on of life, "blood," solidarity, unity, security, personal integrity, independence, recognition, equality, cultural uniqueness, respect, equal economic rights, territorial integrity, and so on, and these in all possible combinations, degrees of emotional content, and forms of social organization. (Roosens 1989:19)

Historically, broad sociological survey methods have been used to measure ethnic phenomena including racial/ethnic classifications, sentiments, and types of social organization (R. Cohen 1978). Traditional studies focused on an ethnic group and its contact across boundaries with other groups. Important theoretical perspectives include the recognition of subjective, contextual processes of group identification (Barth 1969), scholarly and local traditions of conceptualizing such processes (Boon 1982), and the entanglement of the latter in larger political fields (Memmi 1968; Said 1978; Wolf 1982). Current approaches focus on power relations and the problems of conceptualizing identities, cultures, and peoples. Ideological contexts, including nationalism, colonialism, and scholarly debates of ethnicity, explode previous strategies of inquiry. Critics of the literature on ethnicity agree that standard works (however eclectic) tend to normalize concepts that are extremely problematic (Roosens 1989; Thompson 1989; Balibar and Wallerstein 1991; Barth 1995). Notions of static boundaries, homogeneous groups, and the taken-for-granted fact of conflict interest me. As narratives in this book show, these assumed notions break down in everyday evaluations of human difference.

There is a rich legacy in anthropology exploring the spaces between interacting cultural groups. Initially, research dealt with the ambiguity in constructions of cultural boundedness between non-European peoples (Leach 1954; Barth 1969). More recently, studies include self-conscious discussion of the role of theorizing difference and its place in the western European imagination (Thomas 1994; Wolf 1994). Ethnographers dealing with ethnic relations in Canada focus on the indigenous-European social divide and structural realities of inequality (Braroe 1975; Stymeist 1975; Lithman 1984). In recent works there is a central and necessary reference to history and the ways that nations narrate a story of colonial interaction (Culhane 1987, 1998; Furniss 1999).[10] A prolific literature details the history of misrepresentation of indigenous people in official and popular mediums (Pearce 1953; Berkhofer 1979; Bieder 1986; Clifton 1990; Francis 1992). Throughout this book I highlight continuities in the visual and ideational representations of indigenous people across different historical contexts. Within the body of works detailing indigenous views of Europeans (Lips 1937; Basso 1979; Hill 1988; Holden 1976; Wickwire 1994), many are relegated to the academic margins of ethnohistory, folklore, or linguistics. These contrast with the politically charged demands for interrogations of "whiteness" by non-European scholars. Through consultations with members of the Ktunaxa-Kinbasket Nation, I was informed of current protocols of self-representation that have shaped the focus of this work.[11]

What appears in this book is documentation of popular and official discourses now "traditionalized" in European repertoires of human difference (Görög-Karady 1992:114). Rather than viewing these discourses as some pathological divergence from a natural state, what I am suggesting is that they are well instilled within conventional European traditions of speech and thought. While many people do not adhere to such essentialized visions or to the power that I have awarded these discourses, they remain central in popular configurations of the social world. I hope to contribute to the project of analyzing the European production of social knowledge about human difference.

In Europe, theorists are currently identifying new discourses of exclusion and examining the role these play in conflicts between "foreigners" and "natives." These discourses suggest "a resurgence of essentialist ideologies" in a world where race theory is now "discredited politically" (Stolcke 1995:2; see also Bendix and Klein 1993). According to Verona Stolcke, "cultural fundamentalism" has replaced older ideas of race through which biological inferiority was naturalized (1995:2). In contrast, new expressions of xenophobia essentialize conflict itself, making it seem natural and inevitable.[12] In Fernie, xenophobia is apparent in a typology generated through regionalism that distinguishes between rural and urban people, locals and newcomers. Essentialized difference also appears in discussions about sexuality as the latest frontier of otherness. Queer theorists negotiate similar discursive terrains bounded by binary oppositions of gay and straight (Ingraham 1994; Seidman 1994; Epstein 1994). I explore how essentialized ideas of difference are expressed through discourses of regionalism, nationalism, class, sexuality, and ethnicity.

My consideration of difference also includes age, an angle that is often underdiscussed in ethnographic works. Many classificatory schemes assume continuity across time and space, fixed through ethnicity, nationality, class position, sexuality, or gender. In Fernie, old-timers look sideways at each other, based on their shared experiences of poverty and marginalization as a working class. However, class-consciousness, in particular, has lost the vibrancy an idea requires to move between age grades. Several scholars examine the spaces where images and practices are not successfully translated across generational lines, thus creating conflict (Ackelsberg 1992; Muratorio 1998). Intergenerational differences point to ruptures in "memory and meaning; politicization, de-politicization and politics" (Ackelsberg 1992:126). What has been identified as the "Problem of Generations" (Mannheim 1952) pivots on the "historically situated redefinition of meanings" (Mahon 2000:291; see also Ginsburg 1989:62-64). I hope to portray the ways that age cuts across normalized boundaries, highlighting categories and discourses shared by people whose ideas have been shaped within different historical contexts.

Scholarly theories of human difference carry political ramifications; they do not belong strictly to the world of academe, but are used in multiple ways by those with power to control populations. "Race," culture, and ethnicity are part of the apparatus of public representations used in popular and political arenas.

Political Realities

> [The] partitioning of the human species ... makes possible a
> variety of political and ethnographic projects: particular
> populations may be visible as objects of government; they may
> serve as ethnological illustrations or subversive counter-examples
> in comparative social argument; and these reified characters
> may be available for appropriation in anti-colonialist, nationalist
> narratives.
>
> – Nicholas Thomas, *Colonialism's Culture*

My research is complicated by the diversity of political regimes within which participants have experienced their lives. I suggest similarities in the ways that National Socialism, Italian Fascism, British imperialism, and Soviet Communism have made use of conventional symbolic codes and created particular taxonomies of human difference. Major political discourses include what John Borneman (1992:46) calls national narratives: "Different state strategies for defining nation, manifested in ... how it narrates ... political history ... and official codes for group membership." Official histories are saturated with popular understandings of difference.

In British Columbia at present, the question of how to narrate the violent history of colonial incursion is at the centre of public and legal debates. "History provides societies with categories of thinking or mythologies through which they might represent and relive their past" (Wachtel 1990:11-12). My work weaves in and out of popular mythologies narrated through the Canadian state. Dara Culhane (1998:37-57) names perhaps the two most powerful colonial narratives that are central to understandings about the imagined identity of indigenous people: Terra Nullius (unoccupied, empty land) and Terra Incognita (unknown land). Marina Roseman (1998:108) calls the political erasure of indigenous peoples "the aboriginal absent presence," while to Elizabeth Furniss (1999:60) it is a case of the historically "invisible Indian." Several scholars identify "frontier mythology" as another such powerful story of indigenous-European interaction (Slotkin 1973; Klein 1992; Furniss 1999). Central to this narrative is the "mythic icon" of the pioneer as first settler, whose "heroic characteristics and actions" become the focus of history rather than the "complex economic and political forces" of colonial power (Furniss 1999:90).

In Canada, non-Anglo-European immigrants are encompassed within what D.H. Stymeist (1975:10-11) calls "mythologies of capitalism," in which suffering and discrimination are coupled with rising above levels of perceived inferiority through hard work and perseverance. While I encountered these narratives in my research, I found more nuance in the ways that people reckoned their relationships with others. Immigrants' perceptions of indigenous people are expressed through comparison with their own experiences of exclusion and their particular national histories and forms of religious knowledge.

Many Anglo Europeans, however, had conspicuously little to say in terms of perceiving historical injustice. John Mackenzie's (1984) work on imperial propaganda serves to highlight the intersection between political and popular narratives. He is a social historian who looks to the places where everyday materials and expressions are infused with imagery that propagates values of British imperialism. These projections of empire play a role in the negotiations of difference between Anglo and non-Anglo Europeans and between indigenous and settler peoples. My book contributes to a view of British imperialism from many perspectives, examining narratives that both maintain dominant political discourses and contest them. I discuss particular historical contexts in which ideas and images are part of the political apparatus used to manage appearances during colonial conquest, European settlement, and different periods of immigration.

The Canadian state recognizes three primary categorizations of people: Aboriginal, immigrant, and charter (English and French) populations. I explore the narrative construction of difference from each of these perspectives while looking to the places where people obscure the categories. A nation's sovereignty is based on the "definition and enforcement of social and territorial boundaries" (Borneman 1992:45). I am concerned with social boundaries, although it is important to note that physical barriers are also part of the administrative apparatus of colonialism and immigration.

In Canadian history, state control over people's movement is most significant. Under the early colonial regime, indigenous people were legislated to reserves. In the 1870s the Indian Act came into force. It is state legislation that delimits diverse indigenous populations. It does so by defining and categorizing linguistically, politically, and socially diverse people as "Indians," while instituting sanctions that effectively partition them from Euro-Canadian society. (The privilege to classify through naming is one manifestation of state power. Throughout this book I use the terms "indigenous" and "Aboriginal" in reference to people known variously as "Indian," "Native," and, increasingly in British Columbia, "First Nation." Given the complexity of issues raised through colonial classifications, I have chosen terms that evoke a more international discourse of human rights that highlights unequal power. I use the names of particular communities when I am discussing specific situations or events.)[13]

Superficially, the criteria of classification in the Indian Act have changed from racial and cultural difference to legal status. Originally the definition was based on blood; the legal definition was instituted in 1951. Given the enforcement of patrilineal descent in Canadian Indian policy, the insignificance of blood is debatable. The current act reads: "'Indian' means a person who pursuant to this Act is registered as an Indian or is entitled to be registered as an Indian" (Canada, RSC 1985, c. 1-6, s. 1:2). The state differentiates between people of First Nation, Inuit,[14] and Métis heritage. Indigenous people are divided into categories of "status" under the Indian Act and "non-status" or nonregistered. Inuit and Métis people, as well as those with status, fall under the term "Aboriginal" within the Canadian Constitution.[15] Officially and unofficially, there is a complex array of classifications applied to and by these people:

> There are status Indians, non-status Indians, Métis, Inuit Dene, Treaty Indians, urban Indians, on reserve Indians, off reserve Indians; there are Indians who are Band members and Indians who are not Band members. There are First Nations peoples, descendants of First Nations, Natives, Indigenous peoples, Aboriginal peoples, mixed bloods, half-breeds, enfranchised Indians, Bill C-31 Indians ... And these are just some of the labels we must consider in identifying ourselves. There are also definitions based on Tribal/First Nations affiliations, on language, on blood quantum. (Damm 1993:11)

To Ktunaxa people with whom I spoke, the constellation of meanings around the term "Indian" has remained consistent throughout colonial history.

Within larger Canadian society, the Indian Act enforces separateness in governmental, educational, medical, residential, and social spheres. In 1951 a series of revisions to the Indian Act erased prohibitions against religious and political expression. State policy at this time turned towards more legalistic definitions of "Indians" and a project of assimilation. As it applies to indigenous populations, assimilation is a strategy to displace the history of domination based on the construction of racial and cultural differences. I discuss a kind of "psychological apartheid, an apartness that ... is institutionally reinforced" (Crapanzano 1986:xxii), and I look at the ways that separateness is bolstered through representational strategies and physical distances. My purpose is to identify significant political discourses that maintain a stubborn hold in popular social consciousness.

The "Canadian mosaic" is a vivid image of nationalist identity that evokes multiculturalism and propagates a "public ideology of harmony and balance" (Stymeist 1975:1). To John Porter (1965), this is a "vertical mosaic" where indigenous people are undeniably the lowest class. D.H. Stymeist (1975:10) suggests that assimilationism provides a metanarrative of sorts, which remains central to immigrants' ideas of cultural difference. Early immigration was linked inextricably to nation building in North America. Shifts in immigration policy reflect relationships between different nations and the demands of industry. Canada's immigration policy has meandered between periods of demand for inexpensive and often dangerous labour, during which international borders were dissolved, and periods when the state has imposed exclusionary policies and restrictive penalties on particular populations of people. Policy makers tapped into theories of human difference that held sway at the time and constituted taken-for-granted ideas about the character and productivity of certain populations.

Officially, multiculturalism was instituted in Canada in 1971 in response to demands for equality from "ethnic immigrant collectivities" (Kallen 1982:165; see also T. Turner 1993:413). Ideologically, the policy challenges assimilationism in favour of pluralism. The rationale is: "In a culturally pluralist society, ethnic groups are believed to share some aspects of a common *culture* and participate collectively in its economic and political life while retaining their *unique ethnic culture* in their social networks, residential enclaves, churches and languages" (Li 1988:8, my italics).

Critiques of multiculturalism revolve around the abyss separating the ideal from the structural realities. Put differently, it is the "illusion of multiethnic harmony and equality without seriously undermining the dominant ethnic group's hold on state power" (Thompson 1989:132). My research examines intersections between what people told me and official political narratives. What came across clearly was a map of differently situated perspectives that implicate national histories and political categories but also individual realms of experience.

Non-Anglo Europeans I spoke with were articulate about changing ethnic hierarchies embedded in mythologies of this nation. The terms "alien," "foreigner," "displaced person," "peasant," and "Slav" were mentioned frequently. They are official labels used by the Canadian government that are now firmly entrenched in social repertoires. Some people, personally or through the stories of their parents, remember the trauma of internment as "enemy aliens" during the First World War. Many recall the humiliation of compulsory registration, surveillance, and curtailed mobility during the Second World War. Most recall stories of exclusion: name-calling, harsh enforcement of English-only on school grounds, postwar tensions. As Europeans who do not fall within the category of a charter population, these people offered articulate impressions of British imperialism.

Local Histories

I conducted my research within a general climate of political awareness. In British Columbia, the treaty process fuelled public debates grounded in ideas of difference that evoked national narratives and the recital of collective histories. Reconciliation of the colonial past has generated flows of information from the academy and from the state. In Fernie, state narratives of difference are apparent in official renditions of the past that collide with unwritten versions of events from marginalized perspectives. Local written histories celebrate the "many nationalities" of the region (see Fernie and District Historical Society 1977; Crowsnest Pass Historical Society 1979, 1990; Scott and Hanic 1979; Turnbull 1983; B. Dawson 1995; Norton and Miller 1998; Norton and Langford 2002). Most people with whom I spoke had much to say about the ways that "foreigners" continue to be represented in many publications. The history of Fernie has been scripted as violent both in terms of clashes between Europeans and in terms of labour exploitation, crime, and physical disasters. Fernie's turbulent past coincides with huge-scale movements of migrant labourers, wars, revolutions, and shifting immigration policy. Corporate power has always been a force to contend with.

The Crow's Nest Coal and Mineral Company (est. 1889)[16] first hired immigrants from across the world to work in the mines. Passage from Europe and the price of accommodation, food, and equipment were deducted from wages. Miners worked on a contract basis and were fired if they were injured or if they did not meet set quotas of coal production. Child labour was used in the mines until 1920. In 1902, 128 miners were killed in an explosion in the Coal Creek mine, six miles from Fernie. Two years later a fire wiped out the commercial district of town. In 1908, three miners were killed in a "bump" in the Coal Creek mine; two days later, six thousand residents were left homeless by another fire that killed ten people. Before its closure in 1958, the Coal Creek mine was the site of a further forty-four deaths: six in 1912 from a rock and snow slide, thirty-five in 1917, and another three in 1938 in mine explosions. During the First World War, 306 "enemy aliens" were arrested and interned in Fernie and nearby Morrissey. The early 1920s were marked by labour unrest in the form of a series of strikes. Periods of international conflict and labour strife ushered in new regimes of difference dictated by the state that resonated in face-to-face interactions among people in Fernie.

Colonialism also shapes ideas and images associated with Aboriginal peoples. Ethnographically, Ktunaxa-Kinbasket people have been inscribed as a tribe inhabiting the Plateau culture area between the coastal mountains and the Rocky Mountains; linguistically they are mapped as a language isolate. Here and there in the early ethnographic representations of Ktunaxa people, writers mention resentment and hostilities between "Indians" and "the whiteman" (Boas 1918; Turney-High 1941; Baker 1955; Schaeffer papers). Disputes over the establishment of the US boundary, and thus the severing of Ktunaxa-Kinbasket communities, are especially noted. According to H.H. Turney-High, Chief Michel "laid a stricture of silence on the Kutenai" in response to relocations enforced by the US government (Turney-High 1941:17-19). Further "resentments" have been inscribed by Paul Baker (1955:54-55) as the inevitable results of colonial oppression. Most of these works are concerned with the stuff of culture: religious and economic systems, forms of warfare and subsistence technology, language classifications, and toponyms. One ethnography is titled *The Forgotten Kutenai* (Baker 1955). My book does not focus on these people, their customs, or their beliefs. I am instead interested in the ways that non-Aboriginal peoples have come to imagine indigenous societies and how these imaginings constitute a lingering curse in Canadian society.

Within anthropology there is a certain unease about the conceptualization of a field setting (see Clifford 1997; Okely 1996). Scholarly renderings of other societies often reflect taken-for-granted notions of geographical distance and isolation of place. In the past, anthropologists have overlooked regions like the Elk Valley as "zones of cultural invisibility" where processes of assimilation are complete (Rosaldo 1989). Perhaps perceived to be familiar, contemporary, and non-isolated, Euro-Canadians have been largely precluded from ethnographic attention, and studies of western societies tend to be institutionally marginalized within the discipline of anthropology.[17] Several scholars are now complicating the criteria used to think about groups. Many identify the tendency to essentialize and homogenize "The West" in the project of understanding others. Occidentalism is manifest most profoundly in assumptions of history and privilege. As readers will see, Fernie is anything but a homogeneous social community. It is alive with dialogues and memories that are fuelled by the many realities people have experienced and imagined.

Fieldwork is always conducted within a particular temporal context that frames the way people express themselves. Events in the larger world lead to discussions about current events. At the time I was in Fernie, media attention was held by the deaths of Princess Diana and Mother Teresa; the crisis of immigration for Czech Roma; media reports on the green-house effect and El Niño; the appeal decision of *Delgamuukw;* the speech of "reconciliation" by the Canadian Department of Indian Affairs and Northern Development (DIAND); anxiety about Y2K; and debates around same-sex benefits. Many of these topics inspired dialogues about "race," class, age, and sexuality. They also unlocked and revised histories held tight in memory, bringing them into service in new contexts.

In what follows, the curse legend is my doorway to different historical contexts. Each chapter begins with a different rendition of that legend through which I introduce early methods of colonial inscription (Chapter 1); discourses surrounding immigration (Chapter 2), belief (Chapter 3), and war (Chapter 4); new colonial narratives (Chapter 5); current tourism development (Chapter 6); and ultimately the disappearance of the curse story as it folds into the image of the Ghostrider (Chapter 7), an alluring artifact of globalization. In Part One, titled "Politics of Cursing," I present three distinct but overlapping historical contexts in which important dis-courses of human difference were established. I argue that images and ideas generated at these points in time have come to constitute a kind of curse for many indigenous and non-Anglo-European peoples. Part Two, titled "Imagining Difference," analyzes social contexts where ideas and images are revived, recontextualized, or sometimes lost. Through observations on local performances, narratives about space and place, and the transmis-sion of ideas, I portray an intergenerational landscape of contemporary social imagination in Fernie.

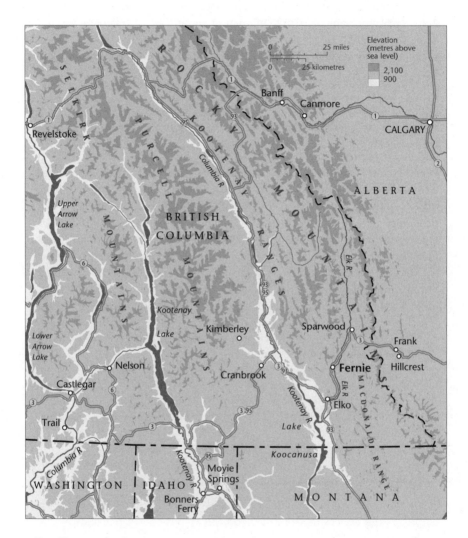

East Kootenay region

Part One
Politics of Cursing

The recognition of the political nature of all forms of
construction is what allows a logic of democracy to emerge.

– Aletta Norval, *Thinking Identities*

I had dinner one night with four elderly women. Throughout the night
we ate food and laughed a great deal. I was astounded by the topics
that came up in our conversations. At one point the eldest woman said
to another: "Look! There's another one of you over there!" We all looked
to see her reflection in the front window. She ran with it: "It's your
clone! I wonder if it can cook? It would be exactly the same – that's
how they make clones." They spoke about pensions, health care, and
snow removal. One of them mentioned a new subdivision at the base of
Fernie Mountain. "One day," she said, "that mountain will just step right
across the river and destroy those new condominiums that the moneybags have bought!" Another woman pulled out an old journal and told
us about a day in 1983 when a "gush of water" erupted from one of
the peaks on Trinity Mountain.

We spoke about geology and prehistory in the Elk Valley. Someone
said that people think Fernie Mountain is a volcano. Two women talked
about the fish fossils they have found – how the valley was once part of
a great inland sea, and then it was a lake closed off at the present railway tunnel. The woman with the journal began a discussion around
"Indian paintings," which, she said, "couldn't be genuine because they
were below the waterline" at some point in time. Then she talked about
the "so-called paintings" that are on rock walls recently blasted away for
road construction and said a geologist had told her that markings on
rocks are made by escaping gases and minerals.

The eldest woman asked me if I met "the Indian who was selling soap
at the fair." Someone else said she had bought some. They told me the
soap seller was a great storyteller from Cranbrook. The woman with
the journal said that she "never saw one Indian growing up." Then she
told us about being on the Tobacco Plains reserve a long time ago and
hearing that the Elk Valley is haunted and people won't come here.
"Then," she almost shrieked, "[a man] told me there's a site where an

Indian maiden died. Which is true?" The eldest woman began
reminiscing about her childhood, walking with her father and greeting
and speaking with many "Indians" on many occasions.

We talked about history. The eldest woman said: "History is never the
same. How's somebody supposed to know what's true?" The youngest
woman began to imagine, out loud, kayaking up the valley when it was
full of water. Her friend said to her: "It's easy to romanticize the past.
It must have been a really hard life." The woman with the journal
mentioned the idea of "savagery," said she was reading about
"barbarous tortures" where they staked people to the ground to be
eaten by ants. I asked her who it was that did this. She said it was "an
Indian group" she "didn't remember." The kayaking woman interjected,
told us she had read about the "old country" in Europe where people
were strung upside down over ant hills and their eyes were eaten first.
The woman with the journal mentioned "burning arrows." The other
began talking about the Druids. The woman with the journal said that
she thought Stonehenge was technologically impossible and that
perhaps the stones were left there after erosion. She rationalized this
through demographics. "There just weren't enough people to manage
that!" Again the demand: "What's true?!" A discussion of independent
invention ensued around fire signals, how so many different peoples
used them but they did so without a universal signal system. The oldest
woman spoke about the pyramids and how ingenious they are. Then she
said: "Atlantis." (Fieldnotes, 23 November 1997)

Our social imaginations provide the symbolic resources we use to configure the past and other people. These women summoned the worlds of
genetics, folklore and mythology, geology, demography, archeology, and
popular history. They debated ideas about "savagery" and the presence of
indigenous peoples in the valley, comparing "Indians" with peoples of the
"old country." There is a kind of ethno-anthropology at work here where
people draw upon personal reservoirs of social knowledge to discuss ideas
of human difference that are contested.

Not long after our visit, I was again drawn into conversation with two
of these women. We had been speaking about multiple interpretations of
the same event. One of the women said: "It's like seeing a burning house.
One person is on the side that sees a man jumping out the window – but
if you were on the other side you wouldn't see it!" The other woman said:
"Cats jumping into a fire!" We prompted her to continue. She told a story,
pointing south, about a house on the edge of town, burning wildly out
of control: "Cats came from everywhere leaping into the flames."

This story is enigmatic, inaccessible from where I sit. In my search for
a methodology to approach a sense of the everyday in another time, I

turned to works in history. Here, ironically, I was referred back to anthropology and folklore. "We constantly need to be shaken out of a false sense of familiarity with the past, to be administered doses of culture shock" (Darnton 1984:4). People act and express themselves through an invisible sheath of ideas and images, through repertoires of rituals and symbols that inform their everyday lives. Sam Migliore (1997:4) is succinct when he writes: "Meaning is context-dependent. To understand something it is necessary to examine how people interpret and make use of it in specific circumstances." My analysis is complicated by diverse traditions, beliefs, and forms of expression used by residents in Fernie.

In "Politics of Cursing," I attempt to get at an understanding of the kinds of social knowledge useful for thinking about the curse on Fernie. Chapters in Part One depict overlapping historical contexts of colonialism (until 1900), early immigration (until the 1920s), and Fernie's local history (until 1945). These histories are entwined with representational processes that continue to assert powerful assumptions in popular ideas about human difference. Tensions between popular interpretations, scholarly theories, and official categories reveal the resilience of particular ideas.

1

Conversations among Europeans and Other Acts of Possession

> A prospector, William Ferney [sic], who worked at times with Michael Phillips who was the Hudson's Bay trader on the Tobacco Plains south of Elko, was informed by the trader that huge seams of coal existed in a valley near them that was taboo as far as the Indians were concerned and nothing could be learned from the Indians as they refused to discuss anything about the valley.
>
> – Sydney Hutcheson, *The Curse and Other Stories from the Wella Board*[1]

So begins this Fernie old-timer's published rendition of the story. It is prefaced by a question: "How many have heard of the 'Curse' that the Kootenai Indians placed on the coal fields and the whiteman in the Crow's Nest Pass?" (Hutcheson 1973:35). Hutcheson begins with a hypothetical conversation between trader and entrepreneur, one instance of interaction in a seemingly endless dialogue between Europeans about others. The categories of "Indian" and "whiteman" are monuments to "race,"[2] still salient in the relatively modern context of this version. There is a kind of self-evident tone in the mention of "taboo," an understanding that presupposes belief as an explanation for the "Indians'" silence. But there is something else – it is the recognition that in order to access the land, Europeans were dependent on indigenous peoples' knowledge. In the 1992 video *Ktunaxa Land Claims Presentation,* narrator Lexine Phillipps states emphatically that knowledge of the land is the basis of Ktunaxa culture. Popularized accounts of European settlement effectively erase the relationship between indigenous knowledge and land.

I am interested in ideas deeply embedded in the colonial imagination that are kept alive by forms of storytelling. In this chapter I follow the story of the curse as a colonial narrative, a politically managed form of information that enforces particular categories of human difference. Such stories constitute a kind of "social knowledge ... transformed into an agent of power" (Linke 1990:118). As John Mackenzie (1984:2) notes, officially managed "propaganda of Empire" served to propagate a cluster of popular ideas in Great Britain: militarism, adoration of royalty, a "contemporary cult of personality," and racial typologies that were based in the premises of social Darwinism.[3] Colonial narratives suggest absence and presence: the absence of socially placed and named others exercising intentional agency, and the presence of a "produced reality" operating through popular and official channels of information spread (Thomas 1994:41). Hegemony is useful here as a concept whereby the "means of mental production" (Mackenzie 1984:8) are controlled by a dominant class in order to enforce a "commonsense" view of the world and social relationships (R. Williams 1976:145). I am not concerned with a linear presentation of historical fact; however, my writing follows a loose chronology sketching an outline of different forms of information and how they serve to bolster a very old story of indigenous-European relations.

The story of the curse begins at a critical moment in relations between Aboriginal peoples of British Columbia and the British colonial project, a moment reflected in the meeting of two men who represent the economic and social changes then occurring. Michael Phillipps[4] was the son of a clergyman, born in Hertfordshire, England, and employed by the Hudson's Bay Company at the age of nineteen. He purchased land and established a trading post at Tobacco Plains around 1865. Like many men who worked for the company, his work history was diverse. He was a postmaster, rancher, trapper, orchard farmer, magistrate, interpreter, Indian Agent, prospector, and trail builder (Miller 1998:29; see also I. Turner 1977b:17). William Fernie left his birthplace in Huntingdonshire, England, at age fourteen. He set sail for the Australian gold fields at Bendigo and was later a quartermaster on a mail boat between North and South America. Before his journey to southeastern British Columbia, he worked as a miner and gold commissioner in the north (*Free Press* 20 May 1921). These were the years following the fur trade, a time of surveying lands and boundaries and imposing a system of institutions to control populations and ready the region for the mass incursion of European peoples that was to follow.

For those who knew and inhabited the land, the mid-1800s were the beginning of confinement on reserves, thus impairing access to traditional territories and resources. It was also a moment in European history when the age of discovery shifted to the project of settlement, when absolute dependence on indigenous knowledge shifted to exploitation of that knowledge in order to enforce systems of state control. Silence figures greatly in the popular story of the curse. Although frequent social inter-actions between Aboriginal people and Europeans occurred during the fur trade period, a clearly defined social distance developed in the years following. Effectively, colonial writing attempted to marginalize indigenous economic structures, inscribe irreconcilable difference, and thus rationalize procedures and techniques of imperial control. I will be tracing such acts of erasure through the curse legend and other dominating narratives that feed into and reinforce colonialism.

More official forms of history also depict early years of European colonization. On the highway between Fernie and Sparwood stands a plaque dedicated to George Mercer Dawson, emblazoned with the coat of arms of British Columbia. A bursting sun shoots rays through wavy lines of water below a crown embedded in the Union Jack. The suggestion of empire above nature symbolically suits this tribute to a nineteenth-century scientist. It reads, in part: "In 1883 Dr. Dawson explored the Crowsnest Pass for the Geological Survey of Canada. His report demonstrates his extra-ordinary ability to provide not only geological and geographical evaluation of the area but also practical inventories of the natural environment, all of which were used by capitalist and settler alike. Motivated by Dawson's findings Colonel James Baker organized the Crow's Nest Coal and Mineral Company in 1889."

All of the European characters of colonialism are inscribed: scientist, military man, capitalist, and settler. I am interested in this plaque for two reasons. First, it represents a strange necessity to mark difference, for below Dawson's photograph, authorless text notes his "physical disability" while stating that it did not impede his work in any way. Second, the plaque is an official, physical marker in a specific place, commemorating a particular moment in time – a moment when discovery and capitalist expansion relied upon the collection and dissemination of information, now separate from indigenous peoples.

This plaque and the curse narrative converge as a kind of origin story of the Crow's Nest Coal and Mineral Company established by Fernie and Baker. Both are markers of history with their own social trajectories – one aimed towards popularizing official history, the other a popular form in itself, orally passed on, here and there inscribed in written form. I intend to show the interplay of different forms of information that feed popular understandings of colonial history. "The telling of the story is a sort of necessary mediation between concept and practice that ensures the re-production of the everyday world" (Taussig 1987:107). The story of the curse conveys powerful concepts necessary to the resilience of colonial narratives.

There are two well-defined periods in early relations between European men and Ktunaxa peoples. The first involved men of commerce in their mission of trade. The second called for explorers – map-makers, who would secure possession and "rights of discovery." In Ktunaxa territories, the objectives of discovery were initially to open fur trade relations with indigenous groups, and later to find passable routes, preferably for a railway, through the southern Rocky Mountains. Information about the land was intended as reconnaissance for settler possibilities and industries of resource extraction. The project sought to displace indigenous peoples from their land, economic networks, and independent forms of government. I am concerned here with the ways in which the colonial experience was managed and mapped in correspondence between European men. Courting and cursing played an unofficial but significant role in these European processes of discovery and settlement.

Colonial Discovery: Managing Appearances

During the middle years of the nineteenth century, Great Britain held uncontested reign over the seas. A system of "informal empire" existed through the "imperialism of free trade" (Stocking 1987:240). George Stocking describes the political structure in white settler nations at this time as a kind of self-government, a "trusteeship" involving assumptions of "dominance over 'dark-skinned' populations" (240). For the strategy of indirect rule to work, what was needed most was knowledge of indigenous values. In Britain the establishment of professional and middle classes coincided with university reform and the celebration of "practical men" who were mobile and whose entrepreneurial adventures were crucial to British colonialism. What John Mackenzie (1984:3, 18) calls the "Imperial adventure tradition" included the literature of exploration, missionizing, and biographies of famous travellers. At this time the general public had gained a new level of literacy, and scientific publications were accessible to many at affordable prices. Writers at home and away had a "mobile symbolic realm in which they could represent and justify their violent interventions ... as rational humanistic responses to social disorder" (Povinelli 1994:126). This is the assertion of colonial power through "moral suasion and display" (128). The colonial imagination depended on the idea that "particular races constitute definite entities that can be known" (Thomas 1994:81). Idealized versions of Indians and whites were prolific. What they had in common were descriptions, presented as fact, that these groups shared no social features in common, especially not moral and economic features.

Among Britain and Australia, India, the West Indies, Canada, and the African Cape flowed a steady stream of products, people, and information. The products "opened up new tastes" for tea, chocolate, soaps, oils, tobacco, and meat extracts celebrated through the seed of mass media in the form of advertising. Advertisers were interested in promoting not only a product, "but also the world system which produced it" (Mackenzie 1984:16). The people travelling within the new world system came from all classes of British society. Many of the so-called middlemen were Scottish, Welsh, or Irish. British class structure was mirrored abroad. Colonial and trade company administrators, explorers, military men, and men of- science came from emerging middle classes. Many were from gentry. Towards the end of the nineteenth century these "colonial heroes" appeared on posters, pamphlets, and postcards. Magic lantern slide shows and lectures were increasingly popular and accessible to all classes of British society. Overseas, intense projects of information gathering focused on the location and quality of resources as well as detailed descriptions of peoples. Conversations among Europeans took the form of written correspondences between officials in the new lands and those who managed the information in Britain.

In western Canada the exchange took several forms. Irene Spry (1963:6) outlines an oral communication network among "Indians" and local traders, many of whom were Métis or had significant kinship alliances within indigenous communities. In turn, these communications were rendered into the official reports of traders, explorers, and scientists.[5] In corporate dispatches, "List(s) of Queries" were sent from England to inscribe "Charts of the Country" and histories of exploration (Simpson 1828 in Rich 1947:167). Secret military reports were procured from the British war office in 1845. Accounts of expeditions of discovery were presented before the Royal Geographical Society by John Palliser in 1859[6] and the colonial office by Thomas Blackiston in 1858.[7] George Dawson testified before the Immigration and Colonization Committee of the House of Commons in 1883.[8] Missionaries published their journals (DeSmet 1905).[9] From these traders, explorers, scientists, and missionaries surged a stream of information gradually working to flood the gaps in existing knowledge about the Dominion of Canada.

Men employed by the Hudson's Bay Company were involved in a prolific transmission of information on the East Kootenay region, then called New Caledonia. Fur traders' records and maps were not publicly accessible. These were the secret properties of corporations worried about competition and not wanting to encourage settlement. During the fur trade period, "public and politicians alike had only rumour, conjecture, and controversy as a basis for decisions as to policy" (Spry 1963:6). All of that changed in the face of competing claims by the Americans and a race to establish possession of territory before the international boundary was surveyed in 1860. In the Hudson's Bay Company dispatches at this time, genealogies of exploration, travel, and trade (read rights of possession) were being inscribed. As Elizabeth Povinelli (1994:127) notes, writers across the British Empire were "making, changing, and accounting for history, not simply describing it."[10] To Michael Taussig (1987:107) these were "histories not *of* but *for*" colonial powers.

Empty and Unknown Lands
Addressing the explorations of Lewis and Clark undertaken in 1806, Sir George Simpson of the Hudson's Bay Company wrote:

> In order to give the Expedition as much as possible the air of a *Voyage of Discovery*, and to make it *appear* as if they were exploring and taking possession of an *unknown Country* (though in fact the Country in the Interior

was well known to the traders from Canada) the Americans as they went
along bestowed new Names on Rivers, Mountains &c ... forgetting or *affecting to forget* ... previous surveyed routes and possessed territories. (Simpson
1822 in Rich 1947:183, my italics)

The passage is telling. Simpson made reference to an obviously popular genre of discovery, thus acknowledging its symbolic power. He also
recognized the management of appearances: of making lands *appear* to
be unknown. Colonial representatives used written information to feed
the "management of public opinion within colonizing nations" (Thomas
1994:57). The question was, how to manage two very different representations: that of an empty land free for the taking and the other of dangerous and war-like indigenous people.

In 1824, Simpson was sent by John Pelly, then the Hudson's Bay Company governor, to "acquire more correct information respecting the Country on the west of the Rocky Mountains" (Pelly 1825 in Rich 1947:164).
Pelly's 1825 dispatch (in Rich 1947:161-164) is worth considering in some
detail; the rhetoric of managing the appearance of an empty land *and* uncivilized people is evident, as are the legal and representational strategies
that powered the acquisition of lands. Thus, Governor Pelly wrote that
title to territories included justifications "on the grounds of first discovery, priority ... continued occupation and actual possession." International
law at this time recognized sovereignty on three commonsense criteria:
cession, conquest, and occupation of territory. Importantly, land could be
peopled but not possessed (Povinelli 1994:126).

Pelly strongly urged the establishment of the international boundary
in light of a map published by the Americans and already brought to "the
attention of Congress." On this map "the Line of Lat. 49 is continued
from the Rocky Mountains to the Seacoast ... This line would deprive Great
Britain of a valuable country" (165). He argued against American assertions of rights to the Columbia River region, citing a voyage of 1792.
In his history, the British Lieutenant Broughton had performed an act of
"formal possession ... in His Britannic Majesty's name, having every reason to believe that the subjects of no other civilized Nation or State had
ever entered this River before."[11] The idea of possession based on civil
presence deserves attention. The terms of an empty land were those not
owned, added to, transformed (read cultivated) and not peopled by "fully
human" (read civil) subjects and nations (Povinelli 1995:507; see also
Wolfe 1991:210). The imagery was to remain an important fixture in representations of nineteenth-century Canada. In his "Sketches of the ... Indians
of Canada," Dawson (1879:16) uses the rhetoric of a "Great Lone Land"
and refers often to the "Indian problem."

Implicit in all of this is the justification of conquest through moral and political-economic arguments. "Civilization" was inextricably bound up in the cultural values of middle-class Britain.[12] Morality here meant taming and controlling "instinctive passions" that left people at the irrational mercy of nature (Stocking 1987:35). Indigenous technologies were viewed as mere strategies of survival. Forms of family, and customs surrounding marriage and belief systems, were especially scrutinized through comparison with Protestant moral ethics. The result was a standard description of what was absent. "Civility" was, in general opposition to "savagery," measured primarily through comparisons of "social order and ordered knowledge" (R. Williams 1976:58). Order was tied to notions of human productivity in terms of agriculture and technology. Evaluations of knowledge drew from the increasingly influential rational and scientific approach to the world.

In a list of queries sent to Sir George Simpson in 1825, M.U. Addington of the British Foreign Office enquired about climate, soils, game, profits, American activities, navigation routes, and British rights to trade. Regarding "Character of the Natives," Addington asked: "Are ... [they] warlike or pacific, inclined or averse to intercourse with the whites? Is the Country between the Rocky Mountains and the Columbia densely or thinly inhabited?" (in Rich 1947:167). Simpson replied that the "Tribes" were "generally bold and warlike" towards each other, but that they were "well disposed towards the whites ... The best understanding exists between us and them" (168). However, Simpson ended the dispatch with concerns for safety and recommended that trading posts be fully manned as the "population is very great" (174). The ever-present possibility of rebellion was reinforced as a kind of social knowledge producing "effects on consciousness of an atmosphere of uncertainty" that depended largely upon "terrifying narrations" (Taussig 1987:103). In *Elementary Geography of the British Colonies,* George Dawson (1892:35) described indigenous peoples as "a source of great and constant danger to the scattered early European settlements." The greatest trope available to European writers was, perhaps, the charge of cannibalism. As Henrika Kuklick (1991:103) notes, cannibalism was equated with "the basest savagery in the popular mind." In a summary of "customs and modes of thought," Dawson (1879:3-4) noted the practice as a form of survival. Atrocity myths circulating about indigenous peoples constituted an important social force on the frontier.

The 1800s were also notorious for romantic accounts of great war chiefs and a literary focus on the "warpath" (Bieder 1986:201). Travelling up the Missouri River in 1862, Henry Morgan made note in his journals of the bragging of traders and the "humbug" of stories depicting Indian princesses or bloody tales of intertribal violence (in White 1993:222). In Anglo-European literature, a tradition that induced "Indian-hating" through the figure of the "frontier hero" was firmly established by the late eighteenth century. The idea of savagery was already well instilled in the colonial imagination. Questions about territorial possession, however, required formal inscription through imperial presence and performance. The matter became crucial in light of the competition from Americans to secure rights to land. Clearly what was needed were British explorers and mapmakers who would perform the necessary acts of discovery and inscribe, through journals and charts, procedures of conquest.

Mapping

> Ferney [sic] checked out the areas where the Indians were camped and spent the winter with a band of Indians on St. Mary's Prairie, which is northeast of Cranbrook. The Indian chief's oldest daughter wore a necklace of beads made of coal, and [Fernie] put the pressure on the band to try and find out where the beads came from.
> – Sydney Hutcheson, *The Curse and Other Stories from the Wella Board*

In this excerpt there is a sense of the freedom of movement enjoyed by European men at this time. A prerogative to join the Ktunaxa winter camp also portrays the social nature of interactions. Most significantly, there is an admission of "pressuring" these people for information, recognition of dependence upon indigenous knowledge. Fernie arrived in Ktunaxa territories at least a decade after British explorers had secured rights of discovery. In explorers' journals there is an intense anxiety around collecting information. Over and over, these men recorded the process of interviewing, eliciting, and listening for information that would allow them to "discover" what was on the other side of the European frontier. Discovery relied upon the inscription and publication of accurate information.

Exactly how these men communicated deserves some attention. The people who guided Europeans into Ktunaxa territories were often members of enemy tribes, identified by explorers in their journals as half-breeds, Cree, Blackfoot, Stoney, or simply Indian; sometimes they have a single European name. Later, Ktunaxa guides included parties of women and children. In his 1858 memoir, John Palliser described his first meeting with a Ktunaxa man who spoke "an extraordinary, chuckling language" (Spry 1963:137). His guides and interpreters included a "half Blackfoot" man named Paul and "a Stoney Hunter," both of whom had difficulties, according to Palliser, with Ktunaxa sign language. Thomas Blackiston's party first met with a Ktunaxa man who spoke some Blackfoot. James Hector, a botanist and map-maker on the expedition, travelled with Alick, a Ktunaxa guide who spoke fluent Cree. It is significant that at this time Blackfoot and Ktunaxa communities were mutually antagonistic. Histories of interaction between indigenous societies must surely have influenced the quality of rapport between explorers and the people with whom they met.

There are striking differences in the ways that Palliser, Blackiston, and Hector described Ktunaxa people. Due partly to personality conflicts and to the objectives of the expedition, the explorers split off and conducted their own forays into Ktunaxa lands. Blackiston was guided by a Ktunaxa party of four men and two women whom he described as "honest," "civil and hospitable" (in Spry 1963:173-175) people who shared their valuable knowledge of passes and rivers. On this expedition he learned of the Crowsnest Pass through a "report of the Natives that it was a very bad road and seldom used" (174). Hector's descriptions were also positive: "These Kootenais are very fine Indians, being remarkably free from all the usual bad qualities of the race" (256). Hector in particular provided details of incident after incident where local knowledge was of the utmost importance to the survival of his party and to his botanical explorations of the region (255-257, 297-302). The farther these explorers travelled from the European frontier, the more dependent they became on Ktunaxa people for the preparation of their food and clothing, fresh horses, and information of routes. Personality also affected the nature of exchanges between these Europeans and the people who aided them.

In contrast to those of his colleagues, Palliser's descriptions were largely negative. In late August 1859 he reinforced his European point of comparison through negative descriptions based on economic grounds noting that Ktunaxa people he met "were starving," "all living on berries," "destitute of clothes and ammunition" (in Spry 1963:291). Palliser's details may have had more to do with the impending loss of financial support from the Royal Geographical Society. His description of Ktunaxa people was included in a letter justifying the need for more funds: "I first obtained the best information I could collect, which proved so vague as to be utterly valueless ... The fact is that the knowledge the Indians possess of the mountains is very small ... their knowledge is very limited indeed" (295).

His letter included the warning that, if it did not fund another expedition, the Society might as well put "the possibility of the easy construction of a railway across the Rocky Mountains for ever at rest." This was no idle threat. These men were invested with the power of claiming territory through mapping and naming.

Naming

Explorers' memoirs became crucial tools in securing British rights of discovery. This was a symbolic exercise recognized politically among European colonial powers. New names were laid down, signifying conquest and celebrating values of imperialism. Palliser thus eagerly reported the naming of the "British Kutanie Pass" to the Royal Geographical Society in 1859. In keeping with the cult of personality popular at the time, Blackiston dropped prominent British names upon the landmarks of the country. In 1858 Blackiston named a mountain "Gould's Dome" and another region "Waterton," both after prominent British naturalists. The range of mountains at the eastern slope of the Rockies he named after Livingston, by now a famous African explorer, and later he named "Railway River" in anticipation of the imagined pass through the mountains.

In their journals, explorers described landscapes already riddled with trails and with named and storied places and people. As early as 1807, according to Claude Schaeffer (1965:212), Ktunaxa people had drawn a map for David Thompson that included the people and territories all the way to the west coast. The European act of naming sometimes followed from "local Indian legends" associated with sites and used by people who knew the areas (Palliser 1858 in Spry 1963:133). Despite the publication of European maps, colloquial or "Indian place names" were still in common use by 1892 (Dawson 1892:35).[13] Europeans relied upon established camping and village sites. Travel, or "internal communication" as it was known, also occurred along "Indian routes" (56). Clearly Europeans found themselves in a relationship of dependence upon indigenous knowledge and practice.

Explorers wrote detailed descriptions of vegetation, rocks, rivers, animals, humans, and soils, punctuated by the continuous measurements of distance and altitude. These were men of military and scientific precision, whose reliance upon aneroids, barometers, compasses, sympiesometers, and chronometers created a good deal of anxiety (see especially the journals of Hector 1858 and Blackiston 1858 in Spry 1963). The explorers were also meticulously classifying – through description and naming – the people who greeted them along the way. The predominant mode of human classification followed from natural history in the form of "biocultural" descriptions (Stocking 1987:106). Body types and physical appearance, geographical distribution, and languages of peoples were charted and mapped in much the same way as the flora and fauna. This information was then turned over to armchair scholars in Britain who were working on theories that were to set the stage for ideas still popularly held. During this period, "naturalized typifications" of others drew on the model of differentiation of species and problematic connections between animals and humans (Thomas 1994:84). The line between "savagery and civilization" had obsessed French and British scientists for close to a century.

Social Rituals: Performing Difference

Journeys of exploration gave rise to new forms of social ritual performed by traders, explorers, and the indigenous people with whom they interacted. Such performances served to secure symbolic understandings. Protocols of greeting and methods of exchange between European and indigenous people are clearly noted in the journals of fur traders and explorers. The Welsh trader Peter Fidler is cited as the first European to make "contact" with Ktunaxa people in 1792. Anthropologist Claude Schaeffer worked with Fidler's journals. In his archived papers he noted the intimate nature of this first meeting, writing that the Ktunaxa chief "greeted each person and saluted him with a kiss" (Schaeffer M1100/37).[14] In 1807, David Thompson noted in his journals that trade did not commence until pipes were shared and conversation began (Schaeffer 1965:205, 212). What Blackiston later called "the language of presents" (1858 in Spry 1963:171) also included "the necessity of shaking hands" and "evening(s) spent in talk." He described being "inundated with presents" from women and children (171-173). Hector noted offerings of meat and berries from women in exchange for "trinkets" (256). These were interactions of an entirely social nature that included physical contact between men, women, and children.

While Europeans participated in culturally appropriate protocols in order to secure information and goods, they were also performing their own symbolic acts that reified conquest and hierarchies built on the concept of race. One such ritual was inscribed by Blackiston on his journey through Ktunaxa territory: "as usual, when with or near any Indians, my flag, a St. George's Jack, was hoisted on a pole in front of the tent" (165). It is not without significance that St. George is the patron saint of England and of the Order of the Garter, a society whose membership includes knights and professional soldiers. Blackiston later shouted from a mountain ridge, celebrating, on "public record" as the first "Whiteman over the Kootenai Pass" (168). He also presented himself as a conduit between colonial subjects and monarchy, thus imbuing these interactions with the air of formal negotiation: "I told them plainly for what reason we had been sent to the country: that Her Majesty was always glad to hear of their welfare, and that any message which they might have for Her, I would take down in writing" (August 1858 in Spry 1963:166). It is important to note that on this occasion, Ktunaxa people with whom he spoke had much to say about the depletion of wild animals they were witnessing and the poor treatment they had received from "traders and Plains Indians" (166). In another journal entry a month later, Blackiston wrote: "I made a rule never to hide from Indians ... and to go to them as soon as I knew of their proximity. I also told them for what reason the British Government had sent the expedition to the country; and I never failed to receive manifestations of goodwill" (175). The inscription of such details suggested that Europeans and indigenous people shared common understandings about the colonial acquisition of lands through dialogue. These symbolic acts of greeting and oratory were recorded and published. They served to reinforce the legal grounds for colonial acquisition" (see Povinelli 1994:127; and Thomas 1994:57).

In nineteenth-century Britain, literature describing colonial others streamed in from all corners of the empire. Explorers' published memoirs were a very popular genre that became the vehicle through which public policy and moral progress were argued (Strong 1986:175-183).[15] Popular accounts of the American frontier revealed an anxiety around the meeting of "races" in the form of miscegenation (Hallowell 1963). There was a particular fascination with Métis communities that followed from a current theory of the "heritability of acquired characteristics" (Stocking 1968:240). At this time, blood was seen as the determinant for advancement towards civilization. In America, theorists were rigorously debating human origin(s) through monogenism – a single, shared line of descent – and polygenism – different lines of ancestry corresponding to distinct categories of humanity. It is important to consider the meeting of cultural systems involved in this relationship, the proximity of European and indigenous people before settlement.

Courting: Frontier Intimacy

> The valley was taboo and the beads were sacred and the girl
> was the only one who was allowed to wear them. Ferney [sic]
> was out of luck for information so he checked the country over
> the summer with no success and at that time he figured out he
> would have to marry into the tribe and be an Indian to get the
> information so that winter he asked the Chief for the girl's hand
> and they were married. He was told the secret of the coal and
> the valley and he could hardly wait for the spring ... after one
> look at the exposed seams of coal ... in the Morrissey Valley he
> knew he had found his "El Dorado" ... When the bridegroom
> did not come back to his wife, the Indians figured he was dead
> and after a time they forgot about him.
> – Sydney Hutcheson, *The Curse and Other Stories from the
>   Wella Board*

What understandings of reception and incorporation existed between indigenous and European people that led Fernie to believe he would become an Indian through marriage? How were such unions used to gain access and rights to knowledge? How was belief, here evoked through "taboo" and sacredness, used to promote colonial ideology? The questions implicate cultural practices and theories of human difference that mediated relationships between people.

Conceptually, "transculturation" looks to the place where members of categorically different social groups meet. Irving Hallowell (1963:523) defines it as a "process" whereby "individuals enter the web of social relations of another society and come under the influence of its customs, ideas, and values to a greater or lesser degree."[16] Social distance is mediated by ideas of inclusion or exclusion circulated and practised by members of a group. "The degree of receptivity depends on social values, attitudes, and institutions to mediate the induction of alien individuals" (528). In the context of the American frontier, this process was largely one way. The institution of adoption practised by some Native American groups ensured social placement of "others" within their own kinship structures. In contrast, within European social systems, indigenous persons were limited to specific roles. Incorporation into "civilization" was limited, by a moral imperative, to occupational positions, most especially those of missionary and translator. Hallowell emphasizes the importance of viewing transculturation "in the context of the expanding frontier" (525), and within the ideas and values of both European and indigenous groups. In Europe, images of the frontier sparked ideals of progress and the promise of freedom from binding class structures. On the other hand, the frontier evoked a dangerous intimacy with "savagery."

The ambiguity of the frontier situation is best highlighted through two popular motifs in nineteenth-century literature: the "Indian princess" and the "white renegade." Hallowell (1963:520) notes that "it was the ... novelist rather than the scholar, whose interest has been caught by the phenomenon" of transculturation.[17] The "Wild West" conjured an imagery built upon distanced impressions about trade relationships, warfare, religious conversions, intermarriage, and captivity (520). As a genre, the captivity narrative had been well entrenched since the story of Pocahontas was inscribed by Captain John Smith and published in 1624 (Strong 1992). In the context of the frontier, the image of the "princess" evokes a "chief" and is heavy with assumptions of mediation between cultures, as women are turned over from one influential man to another. Traders sometimes gave their indigenous partners nickname titles like "Princess," "Duchess," and "Lady" (Van Kirk 1980:30, 141). At different times and places, changing representations, practical models, and theoretical discourses compete (Thomas 1994:50). The nineteenth century was such a time. Alongside the romanticized image of these women was the appearance of the white renegade who "symbolized the rejection of progress, civilization and Christianity, and was easily cast as a villain" (Hallowell 1963:521).

During the fur trade period, trading companies oscillated in their policies, alternately discouraging and then promoting intermarriage.[18] Indigenous women came to be "icon(s) of the commingling of blood" and "mediators between men with power" (Strong 1999:23; see also Van Kirk 1980:75). In the early 1820s, Hudson's Bay Company governor Simpson "recommend[ed] that the officers should form connections with the principal families immediately upon their arrival as the best security we can have of the goodwill of the Natives" (in Rich 1947:392).[19] The recommendation was overturned five years later in a Hudson's Bay Company resolution that forbade employees stationed on the western side of the Rockies from intermarrying. This apparent ambiguity reflected changes in the social and political landscape.

There was an element of practicality in all of this. The unions served an important function in the conscious strategies of obtaining access to information, resources, and labour. Indigenous women were guides, interpreters, and teachers of languages and traditions; they prepared food, clothing, and campsites for Europeans who were ill-prepared for the rigours of the unfamiliar terrain (Van Kirk 1980:53-64). This meeting of men and women across what was then a "racial" boundary created a distinctive society unparalleled in other colonial contexts. Families of these people formed a new social category whose identity, vis-à-vis Britain, was malleable. Necessities of travel and communication called for people able to negotiate two cultural worlds, and Métis peoples were undeniably useful to the Hudson's Bay Company.

In his appeal for funding of a trapping expedition into the territory west of the Rockies, Governor Simpson recommended enlisting the services of "Red River half breeds," contending: "This party if well formed ... the leaders are men of great activity, are thoroughly acquainted with the Indian Character, are all Hunters by Trade and accustomed to Indian Warfare and if brought into contact with either Savage or civilized will not I think allow themselves to be insulted with impunity" (Simpson 1826 to the governor of the York Factory, in Rich 152-153). His reference to "the Indian Character" suggests an identity already fixed, monolithic, and knowable. This he contrasts with the social knowledge and industry of the men from Red River. Regarding their expenses, Simpson wrote: "The men are on the spot, they will have no wages ... pay will be the price we shall give for their Skins" (153). He was careful to add that this payment should exceed the price that the Americans would pay.

By the nineteenth century the categories "full blood" and "mixed blood" were socially fixed. "Mixed blood" became the acceptable class for marriage prospects as fur trade society developed. Until the early nineteenth century, indigenous wives were also forbidden to settle in Rupert's Land. The corporations justified their positions against intermarriage through an economic discourse translated today into fiscal concerns for family benefits.

Marriages between company employees and local women are entirely absent in the official records of the Hudson's Bay Company. They were, however, apparent in the wills left by traders (Van Kirk 1980:48). As European women began to arrive in the mid-nineteenth century, yet another act of erasure took place. It became important to manage the (in)visibility of intimate connections. Indigenous wives were forbidden to accompany their European partners to Britain.

A relatively stable pattern of intermarriage and alliance between European men and indigenous groups became overshadowed by the looming reality of settlement. During the latter half of the century, fur traders were seen by Victorian society to be "tainted with barbarism" (181). What may be called a moral cult of "the lady" was also gaining symbolic hold. Victorian morality held that "promiscuous tendencies were supposedly inherent in ... blood" (146). By the 1850s, "mixed blood" people were already guarding the secrets of their ancestry.[20]

Blood and "Race"

In western Europe at this time, international expositions and learned societies were displaying peoples of non-European ancestry billed as "cannibals, savages and barbarians" (Bogda 1988:176; see also Corbey 1995). The popularity of such cross-cultural spectacles corresponded with the rise of ethnology and the opening of popular museums. Importantly, the form of presentation mimicked the scientific lecture. Raymond Corbey (1995:72) views the "narrative plots" of museums, expositions, and imperialist and scientific institutions at this time as a way to instill in the citizens a story that made sense of radical differences and maintained the "orderliness of empire."[21] These popular forms of media reinforced the inevitability of war and conquest, presenting them as "endemic to civilization" and "evidence of superiority" in a time when different cultures constituted "races," hierarchically categorized (Mackenzie 1984:6-7). With the popularity of science, "race" began to refer to a biological type of human being. A hierarchy emerged in which people were ranked and ascribed social and psychological traits.

Some sense of the criteria of human difference may be gleaned from the work of British writers in the middle and late nineteenth century. Fur traders, explorers, and scholars were embedded in successive eras of ideas, each era with its own language within a shared climate of understandings. In his 1859 report to the Royal Geographical Society in London, Palliser described leading his "half breed" men in prayers conducted in Cree "through the medium of an interpreter" (in Spry 1963:284). He wrote: "I mention this circumstance to show the respectful tendency and the absence of bigotry of these men" (284). The brief entry conveys a sense of Christian brotherhood, and it identifies "bigotry" as a social dynamic on the frontier. In the correspondences of European men, indigenous persons were labelled in generalized terms as "Indian," "Native," or "Red Man." Tribal affiliation was noted and the use of "Nations" was common. People were categorized as "half-breed," "pure blood," and "Métis." The labels evoke a social context in which knowledge of one's ancestry or blood quantum was both relevant and public.

Within an empirical and scientific worldview, "blood" was a measurable and quantifiable "thing" that constituted a commonsense way to distinguish between colonizer and colonized (Strong and Van Winkle 1996:554). In his reference to the project of "civilizing the Indians," George Dawson (1879:25) clearly saw Métis people as "exerting a moral influence over their race" through the "recognition of their position among the whites." Notably, Dawson advocated full citizenship and independence. His position must be approached within a political context where the "Indian problem" was a public issue of vital social importance.[22] Bureaucratic structures mirrored the social theories in circulation at this time.

The political context codified a discourse on blood through the legal structures of policy. In 1850 the Act for Better Protection of the Lands and Property of the Indians in Lower Canada defined indigenous peoples through "racial" and social criteria. It included the first official, legislated definition of an "Indian":

> First – All persons of Indian blood, reputed to belong to the particular Body or Tribe of Indians interested in such lands and their descendants.
>
> Secondly – All persons intermarried with any such Indians and residing amongst them, and the descendants of all such persons.
>
> Thirdly – All persons residing among such Indians, whose parents on either side were or are Indians of such Body or Tribe, or entitled to be considered as such: And
>
> Fourthly – All persons adopted in infancy by any such Indians, and residing in the village or upon the lands of such Tribe or Body of Indians and their Descendants. (1850 in Indian and Northern Affairs 1978:24-25)

A year later the residency condition was dropped; Europeans with indigenous wives were excluded from the category. In Britain, emigration propaganda focused on women as a means of "keeping Empire for the British race" (Mackenzie 1984:160), and eugenic ideas became popular from the late 1860s onward. As European women arrived, they brought with them heightened class-consciousness and a Protestantism that "tightened" the "colour-line" (Johnson 1969:350). These women were promoted as necessary to the "moral, religious and economic health" of the new country (Perry 1995:32). Their mission, most importantly, was to "tame the wild men" who had allowed themselves to slide dangerously close to a polluted state of "savagery" (32). The increasing presence of missionaries on the western frontier intensified standards of morality through religious sanctions. Members of the clergy publicly condemned marriages between indigenous women and European men (Van Kirk 1980:145-159).

These shifts reverberated in colonial legislation. In 1869 a "blood quantum" was added to the Indian Act: to be an "Indian" a person was required to "possess" one-quarter of this meaningful entity or to have one grandparent who was "Indian." At this time a significant stipulation was also made, reckoning ancestry only through the patriline. By 1876, "illegitimate children" and "half-breeds" were dropped from the status list.

The complex of ideas that constituted "race" had been bound, for some time, not only by physiological evidence, but also by questions of language and environment. American debates in the middle to latter part of the century raged between the "racial" theories of polygenists and the mostly environmentalist ideas of monogenists (Bieder 1986:11). Physical anthropology was already well accepted in academic circles.[23] By the mid-nineteenth century, monogenists and polygenists used Cuvier's approach towards biological "types" (Stocking 1968:39). He developed classifications based on precise measurement of skeletal and cranial differences. Theoretically, these measured differences corresponded to mental capacities that determined racial achievement. In explorers' journals, lengthy descriptions of the bodies of indigenous people are evidence of the flow of ideas around physical types. "Indian families" or "tribes" were categorized on the basis of language "stocks"; at this time philology was a certain science that scholars used in a quest for origins and diffusion (Poliakov 1974; Bieder 1986:155-160).[24] People were also classified according to culture areas. Groupings of Plains, Plateau, and Coastal peoples were based on environmental determinants. The environmental focus powered monogenist theories, which explained differences as a matter of adaptation and survival in varying ecosystems. A more generalized field of opinion held that levels of "civilization" could be measured through standards of economics, morality, and class (Stocking 1987:35). The blurring of economic and moral spheres was an essential element through which human development was judged.

Not surprisingly, amongst writers who were members of an intensely class-conscious society, social status was also noticed. Stations of "chief," "warrior," and "princess" reflected British reverence for monarchy and militarism. Age and occupation were also noted in a time where professionalization was overtaking Britain and rearranging the "occupational structure" (Kuklick 1991:27). Thus indigenous men were inscribed as "rude hunters and fishermen" (Dawson 1892:34), interpreters, traders, and guides. Henrika Kuklick (1991:31; see also Stocking 1987:32) notes that in the latter part of the nineteenth century there was, in Britain, the widespread assumption "that the moral basis of a society derives from its division of labour." As Elizabeth Povinelli (1995:507) outlines in her paper on Australian Aboriginal labour, a primary tenet of "colonial belief" was that indigenous people had "not sufficiently extracted themselves from or productively engaged their environment."

Implied in the categories of "savage" and "primitive" were popular representations of indigenous people as "paupers" and "wards or children of the State" (Dawson 1879:18, 31), who were "lazy," "superstitious," "degraded," and "deceitful" (Reserve Commissioner Peter O'Reilly 1885 in Schaeffer M1100/43:3). Knowledge, intellect, and religious belief became central markers of difference. The lynchpin of this complex was morality. Comparison of belief or "modes of thought" further reinforced "ideal versions of settlers and aborigines which excluded shared features" (Wolfe 1991:214). Belief had been a primary marker of difference between people for some time. Before the Enlightenment, with its emphasis on reason, scholars contemplated the origins of people of the New World through the story of the Old Testament, seeking similarities between Christian practices and those of contemporary tribal societies. Such theories of "degeneration," from an "earlier and purer faith" (Hodgen 1964:303), foreshadow nineteenth-century evolutionary perspectives.

Evolutionary Theory

The late nineteenth century was balancing on the edge of a sea change of social ideas about difference. It was the moment when "race" was about to be inextricably associated with evolution. Difference could still be measured through physical classifications, and now these classifications were used to naturalize conquest. Proponents of social Darwinism theorized about: "a struggle for survival amongst the different human 'races,' in the course of which those with lesser intelligence or capacity for 'civilization' would eventually disappear, their elimination being evidence of their natural inability to evolve" (Miles 1989:36-37).

Evolutionary theory combined "racial" classification with theories of intellectual development. In Britain, scholars sought "laws of nature," universal rules with which to evaluate the minds and physiologies of "peasants" and "primitives" (Tylor 1865:64). Robert Miles (1989:36) notes that in the United States, physical classifications of people included "human intelligence [as] a fixed and hereditary characteristic." Religion and ritual were examined within unilineal theories of evolution.[25] In "Sketches of ... the Indians of Canada," Dawson (1879:14, 23) noted the "curious mystic ceremonies" of Plains people and the "superstitious dread" of Coastal groups. Through the comparison of belief systems, indigenous people were rendered victims of irrational states of mind and the unrelenting need to respond to nature. Obviously, if indigenous cosmologies and technologies had been viewed as knowledge on par with science, the project of raising the "primitive" to a state of "civilization" would be moot. "In any social situation, established power relationships influence the identification of knowledge as such" (Kuklick 1991:30). According to many scholars at this time, language rather than technological knowledge provided the keys to intellectual evolutionary development.[26]

Cursing: Persistent Narratives and Legends

> Later they found out that white men were entering the valley and a lot of activity was going on. When the Chief found out what happened for sure, he called all the Kootenai together and at a large gathering [he] put a curse on the valley and all its inhabitants. This did not include Indians as they never went in the valley to stay anyway.
>
> This is the Curse as told to a group of us boys at South Fork by Johnny Long Time Start, who was a college trained Indian who had turned native after leaving school.
>
> "The valley and all its inhabitants would suffer from death, fire, hunger, all other human miseries and all would finally die by fire and water. This curse would stand for all time and could not be lifted by anyone."
>
> The whole original setup sounds like a modern day business deal with a few second class citizens talking through their hats.
> – Sydney Hutcheson, *The Curse and Other Stories from the Wella Board*

Cursing – the climax of the narrative – successfully incorporated the complex of colonial belief: normalized enmity between indigenous people and Europeans, erasure of indigenous economic interests, the essentialized mystical nature of indigenous peoples, and the ever-present threat of rebellion. The curse story evokes Michael Taussig's (1987:124-127) "culture of terror," "mediated through narration." I am asserting here that within the colonial context this story is a powerful political tool that reinforces an unequal relationship between indigenous and non-indigenous people.

Here and there in written histories of the East Kootenays, an image emerges of Ktunaxa people observing the massive European project of measuring, mapping, and surveying their lands. The image is potent. Within a very short period of time the social distance between Europeans and indigenous people became an enormous gulf enforced through colonial legislation that both defined Ktunaxa as wards of the state and attempted to spatially confine them to reserves. By the 1860s, intercultural intimacy had snapped. Miners in the East Kootenays did not socialize with Ktunaxa people in the same fluid ways that the fur traders had. They did, however, constitute a noticeable presence as they combed the country for minerals (Schaeffer M1100/42). The first settlers began to appear in Ktunaxa lands, and by the 1880s missionaries, surveyors, and the North West Mounted Police were part of the apparatus of control in the region. It is within this context that silence and cursing should be considered.

Ktunaxa people certainly recognized the importance of information flowing to colonial administrators. Following the survey of the international boundary, a "stricture of silence" was laid on the people by Michel, chief of the Windermere Band (Turney-High 1941:18). This was no passive act. Michel had his own territory surveyed and was outspoken about incompetent government interpreters.

Chief Isadore pulled up survey stakes intended to demarcate a reserve for the people of the St. Mary's Band (Schaeffer M1100/43). In an annual report to the Department of Indian Affairs, Indian Reserve Commissioner Peter O'Reilly detailed Isadore's explicit claim to ownership of territory: "The Chief stated, again and again, that he would not accept any limits to his reservation unless they included the whole valley of the Kootenay and Columbia Rivers (from the International Boundary line) ... follow[ing] the base of the Rocky Mountains to the boat landing on the Columbia River" (1885 in Schaeffer M1100/43:1-2). O'Reilly also noted Chief Isadore's refusal to "give the census of his people, the number of their stock, etc." Isadore later banished a government surveyor from the area, an act that ultimately led to the arrival of the North West Mounted Police in 1887 (Schaeffer M1100/43). O'Reilly's report cites the names of European settlers who "speak the language." It was largely through conversations with these men that he obtained information necessary to fulfill his bureaucratic duties.

While conversations among Europeans are accessible through published historical documents, the social discourse among indigenous people on the colonial frontier is often overlooked.[27] Peter Fidler's 1792 account of contact with members of the Tobacco Plains Band mentioned one man who was fluent in the Shoshoni, Flathead, Cree, Nez Percé, and Ktunaxa languages (in Schaeffer M1100/32). Clearly people of different nations travelled across territorial boundaries. They shared a social context and interacted through trade alliances, kinship networks, and episodes of conflict. Indigenous people, then, were also engaged in a larger dialogue about what they were witnessing and in their own attempts to gather information. David Thompson's journals (1807-1811) record an incident in which four men "who were waiting for us" offered food in exchange for information (in Schaeffer 1965:204). They wanted to know about the veracity of a story "that the white men ... have brought with them the Small Pox ... and two men of enormous size ... are on their way ... overturning the Ground, and burying all the Villages and Lodges" (204). O'Reilly's report noted Chief Isadore's total familiarity with the treaty arrangements of neighbouring groups in Alberta. Isadore was also informed about the conditions under which reservations were negotiated in American territories (1885 in Schaeffer M1100/43:1).

Oral accounts of colonial history in Ktunaxa communities appear here and there in the works of H.H. Turney-High (1941) and Claude Schaeffer (Schaeffer papers). A dialogue in 1887 between Chief David of the Tobacco Plains Band and Major O'Reilly is one such account. The conversation took place through Michael Phillipps, who was by then Chief David's son-in-law (Miller 1998:31). Chief David spoke to the establishment of the international boundary: "It runs through the middle of my house. My home is on both sides. Why should you, without asking me or considering me – divide my property in two and also divide my children? I have many people and where are they to hunt? If I came to your country and asked you to pick out land for a reserve you would not like it. You would refuse because you would know you were to pick out land that was already yours" (Chief David 1887 in Ktunaxa-Kinbasket Tribal Council 1992; see also Johnson 1969:344).

In this same year, Michael Phillipps was appointed Indian Agent at Tobacco Plains, and William Fernie submitted the first coal syndicate application to the British Columbia government. The creation of the Crow's Nest Coal and Mineral Company set into motion a flurry of industrial activities. A Canadian Pacific Railway route through the Crowsnest Pass, and the establishment of several communities, eventually opened up the area, with worker populations in the thousands.

When I interviewed a member of the Ktunaxa-Kinbasket Nation on 11 December 1997, she connected the curse to Phillipps, Fernie, and the coal company.

So what do you think of this tale of the maiden and the coal?
It's hogwash.
It's interesting how it's become something so important to people of that town.
Well, you can take that back to my great-grandfather, Michael Phillipps. He's the one that's credited with discovering Crowsnest Pass. He was also prospecting through there years and years ago with William Fernie, who Fernie is named for – he and his brother. They did discover the coal deposits and I think William Fernie was his superior at that time because he had gone to William Fernie to ask for money to build a trail through there. William Fernie had basically said there's no reason to go through there. My great-grandfather apparently had ideas in mind about making some money there with

this coal. And of course no money ever materialized. But William Fernie did go and stake out all the claims for the coal and made a hell of a lot of money out of it. If you want to talk about where [the curse] came from – well, she was his mother-in-law, so she understood the implications of her daughter and her son-in-law not being able to make any *ni'lko* [money] out of it. And that's the other one I've heard. That was the reason that she cursed the place. You know, they were going to rip the valleys and everything apart, to no benefit except to William Fernie and his company, whatever he was working for. That sounds a little more believable to me. You should take a picture of [her] and say this is the Indian princess that cursed the place and see what they say [laughing]. (Interview, 11 December 1997. Ktunaxa woman, born 1955.)

According to this woman, the act of cursing should be viewed through her ancestors' awareness of economic exploitation. Her interpretation jars with the simplistic representation of Ktunaxa motivations suggested by the legend. The curse story provides no clues as to the total context of violence, disease, and oppression during the period that it depicts. The vagueness extends to people known only as "Indians," who are portrayed as mystical rather than political figures. Silence is explained through superstition rather than a conscious strategy that acknowledges the power of information. The narrative also suggests that indigenous people possess little knowledge about natural resources and lack control over their technologies. Effectively, this complex of ideas distances them from any economic involvement with land, further depoliticizing and rationalizing the act of settlement.[28] As the woman below points out, the curse story also reinforces a narrative of fear that has served to naturalize enmity between Aboriginal and non-Aboriginal peoples.

I've heard different versions. I've never ever heard a version from a Native person, so I don't know who started it. [Laughing] ... At one time I heard that, a long, long time ago I was told that Ktunaxa people wouldn't camp in this valley because they thought it was bad. I don't know where that came from either, but I was told that ... I think it's fear on the white people's side. I think they're afraid. I think a lot of people have been taught that Native people were inferior and I think that Native people are beginning to show that they're not and it's creating fear. I don't remember reading in any of my history classes about the wonderful way that Native people lived! In reality they did because they survived totally on their own and they lived in this area for ten thousand years. They must have been super-intelligent and very, very hard-working to survive under the conditions they lived in. (Interview, 18 September 1997. English-Canadian woman, born ca. 1930.)

The curse legend is tenuously dated by the activities of two European men. In Hutcheson's rendition it is geographically located through a handful of place names. Many writers use the story of the curse as a preamble to the turbulent early history of the East Kootenays. More rigorous approaches to the narrative seek to confirm or deny its authenticity as an "Indian story." Ian Turner (1977a:11) cites Chief Red Eagle of the Tobacco Plains Band, who calls the narrative "slander in their mythology." The reference is to a traditional Ktunaxa story of Squirrel (see also Ratch 1998:10). Noel Ratch traces possible origins of the story to Father Coccola of St. Mary's Mission and even to the spare reference by Thomas Blackiston that the Elk Valley route "was a very bad road" (9-11). He asks why it is that this story has "such staying power to have survived all these years as common folklore." I suggest that images of indigenous and European people embedded in the narrative still resonate in the popular imagination.

Legacies

In British Columbia today, treaty negotiations have once again brought history to a public stage. Indigenous and non-indigenous individuals continue their negotiations of difference within several social and political contexts. When I sought permission to conduct this research, I was made aware of the legacies of this history through my discussions with Ktunaxa elders. On 28 August 1997 we met at the Ktunaxa-Kinbasket Tribal Administration Office on St. Mary's Reserve. The elders expressed concerns about control over information and outlined legacies of colonial inscription, legislation, and enforcement. Our conversations shaped the content of this chapter. What follows below is my fieldnote entry for that day.

I arrived at 11:45 to meet with the Elders Working Group of the Traditional Use Study Team [TUS].
"What tribe are you from?"
"I guess it would be a clan – the Robertson clan from Scotland."
The facilitator mentioned that a few days ago this group had signed a resolve that only Ktunaxa would represent Ktunaxa. He explained to the elders that what I am proposing would be dealt with in the same way as their control over information for the Treaty office. I spoke for a while to the nine men and women about my research – contemporary stories of difference, my work also with Europeans in Fernie, cooperative research – input in editing and writing-up.

Silence. A man told me that I was not to take the silence discouragingly: "You have to understand how we make decisions around here. We don't do it instantly."

A fantastic lunch was served – fish caught by members of the TUS Team, stuffing, rice, buns, fresh fruit, and juice. There was much joking and conversation in Ktunaxa. It was intriguing to hear a new language for the first time. Sometimes someone said something and others would turn and look at me. A woman working on the GIS [Geographic Information System] introduced herself and we chatted about university, her job, and cars. A yellow jacket was buzzing around the food. It had everyone reacting. Occasionally the woman sitting to my left (I had not been introduced to any of the elders by name) offered me juice or food. One of the elders said to a man next to her, "unexpected guest," then something in Ktunaxa. Towards the end of lunch an old woman had arrived and sat next to me. The food and dishes were taken away and there was silence again.

_____ asked if there were questions for me. The woman next to me wanted to know what it was all about. She was told that I was interested in stories from the "old days." This time he added that I wouldn't use anything without permission and that the university needed a letter to say I had approached them properly.

She replied: "This has happened to our people before. They take our knowledge and say it will just stay put and then they make a book! We give them our knowledge and then what do we have left?! Nothing! They take it away! [A writer] asked me a long time ago to tell him about things. I told him he should be speaking to my elders. He came back and asked me to write down everything I knew and he made a book. He used to come to my house. I didn't like him there – it gave me a bad feeling ... A man a long time ago came to work on our language. He said he wouldn't publish it; he'd just sit on it. Now it's a book – and what have we got?!"

The old woman turned slightly towards me and continued: "I'll tell you stories. When I was in residential school I used to get strapped for speaking my language. The strap was that thick [gesturing with her fingers] and it had a handle on it. They used to beat me, and I blame my kidney problems on them, the nuns ... I oppose this research but cannot tell anyone else to." She then told me of a recent trip to France, that she's never been to a colder place and that I should study my own.

Another woman said that the research should be about "the history of persecution and genocide that has been going on since whites came to this beautiful land." She also voted in opposition to the research, stating that that is what it should be about.

A man at the end of the table said: "Now you're hearing stories. These stories you can use." He continued, also speaking about residential schools and genocide. "There's an invisible line that's been drawn around reserves. That's how it is." He mentioned "Xs on blank cheques" and told me to turn around and look at the last few lines on a blackboard written in Ktunaxa. "What does it say?" I shrugged and said I didn't know. "That's what it was like for us! Those Xs on treaties – it's fraud!"

Another man also spoke about the Xs, about how they were all exactly the same on an important document of consent. "Xs are just like a signature. Everyone's is just a little different, eh?" He also voiced opposition to the research because he is writing his own book about his life. He said he had been told he "murders" the English language, said he believed that, until an elder told him: "That's not your first language!" He spoke of going to Germany and meeting a small child who knew he was an Indian but wasn't frightened of him. Then he said he had often been in white homes where children ran away screaming. "You can tell by children. Some aren't afraid." He spoke about Hitler and genocide, said he didn't like Belgium: "It was a racist place."

Another man talked about residential schools: "Persecution for speaking my language. Just being in those walls." He said when he went in there he wasn't told what he could be. "I wasn't told I could be a farmer, a carpenter – nothing. I wasn't told I could be anything." Then he spoke about being in jail. He said it was the easiest thing in the world for him because it was exactly the same as residential school. "Except you got treated better." There was laughter around the table.

The man who had spoken about the Xs spoke also about being in the army. He said people told him: "'There's absolutely no difference between you and anyone else.' But as soon as I took off the uniform I was an Indian!" He spoke of an incident with a woman and young boy. The boy looked up at him and pointed and said: "Indian." His mother took him by the hand and moved away. "But not when I was in uniform!"

Another woman spoke of an interaction with a white family. A girl asked her if she was an Indian. "Yes" she said.

"A real Indian?" the child asked.

"Yes. I'm a real Indian."

"Where are your feathers?"

The woman replied: "I'm an Indian, not a bird!" Again there was laughter around the table.

Alcohol was mentioned by a few people, jail because of it, and violence. One man said: "Now is the time we can begin to deal with all of this." He spoke a little about how he is a translator for treaty business.

How everything is in "yuppie" language – big words that not many people can understand. He said that consensus was one of the most difficult things because people can't understand the words. An interesting discussion of interpretation began around this. The man at the end of the table said that the Ktunaxa language uses the same words for interpreter and translator. A woman defined interpretation as "putting your own meanings on things – changing the meanings." The book writer said that he was asked by someone if he wanted help – they would co-author his book. He spoke again about his English and how he would write about it in his own "backwards" way. Silence – for a moment. The Xs man made a gesture towards me, but the book writer spoke: "So, we have a few opposed, how about anyone else?" ... Each of the elders present stated that they wouldn't speak for anyone else ...

[I told the elders]: "I respect your opposition to this research and the protection of your traditions. I hope you will consider it some more." (Fieldnotes, 28 August 1997)

Following the meeting there was a general agreement that the elders enjoyed the discussion and my attention to protocol. They opposed the research, however, on the principle of control over information. Later they sent me a letter of support stating: "While there was no formal resolution or decision ... there was consensus that it would be up to each individual community consultant to contribute to your research." Politics of information explicitly involve power relationships and histories of exploitation. Clearly there are legacies of ideas that continue to assert essentialized differences between people and justifications for historical acts.

Three months after my meeting with the Ktunaxa elders, I was sitting at a kitchen table in Fernie, interviewing a "Scotch" woman in her seventies. Our conversation stirred up the spectres of imperial propaganda, the normalization of conquest, and the continued discourse on morality.

But the Natives in North America, they had a hard time. Okay. There's a time in history when the world is going to change. And the time came. Somebody came to North America – things were going to change. So now, all we did was bad things. For the Natives. Everything was bad that we did – we took the land. We did this, we did that. They sold their land for a string of beads. Well if my great-grandfather sold his land for a string of beads, I couldn't fall back on anything! I think the time in history came when this was going to happen, no matter what. Whether it was to Australia. Whether it was to North America. It was going to happen. I don't think that everything was bad or everything was good. On either

side, for the immigrants or for the Natives. But I think when there
comes a popular thing in history or in government that we will fall
back, as human beings, on "Well the British did this to me" or "The
immigrants did this to me." And they'll make something out of it.
Is that a good way of putting what I think? In these schools, they
must have been horrible, they must have been dreadful! But there
was some good come of it. But we don't hear of any good. There
was a changing world where people lived as wild, free, and if you
want to call them savages, call them savages. You know what I mean.
Everybody has their own idea. But it was a changing world, and
where would they have fit in if there hadn't been something to
teach them a little bit of writing, a little bit of reading, a little bit
of wearing shoes. Where would they have been if they hadn't had
that? To guide them. Or pushed into them. Where would they
have been?

Presumably they would have lived here just fine as they had for thousands
of years!

I don't think they would have. I don't think they would have.
Because nobody lives the same. Nobody does.

People change, but this was an event of colonialism, this was war.

Yup, this was definitely conquest, but just like the Romans coming
to Britain. That was conquest too. And it's been the same throughout
history; there's been conquests in every land and everybody had to
change. As I say, I sound racist and I don't mean to. (Interview, 14
November 1997. Scottish-Canadian woman, born ca. 1920.)

I have discussed many forms of colonial inscription through which relationships between indigenous and European people were/are naturalized.
Scholarly theories of race, evolution, and blood have worked in harmony
with national narratives of empty and unknown lands. Images of the
"savage" and the "primitive" were instilled in the colonial imagination
through comparisons with "civilized" morality, economic structures, beliefs,
and mental capacities. Ideas were popularized through published memoirs, official correspondences among European men, and forms of frontier literature. Formal inscriptions based on indigenous knowledge and the
documentation of different histories played an official role in the imperial possession of lands. In this chapter about Europeans and the methods
used to rationalize and manage stories around conquest, I have briefly
traced the way in which relationships between European and indigenous
people shifted at the point of European settlement, and how theories and
legislation also reflected this shift. Colonialism is the backdrop for the
story of the curse. The legend renders the violence of colonialism invisible and natural.

This book is an attempt to map out imageries that people use to explain and negotiate human difference. In what follows I honour the concerns of elders with whom I met, and I do not seek to represent Ktunaxa traditions. I concentrate on Europeans in Fernie, the ways that they negotiate their diverse nationalities, and the stories they draw upon to speak about indigenous cultures.

2
Látkép ❧ Ansicht ❧ View ❧ ВИД: Constructing the "Foreign"

Not long after I arrived in Fernie, I was invited into the home of a couple who offered me coffee and conversation.

> I was introduced through my family. The man spoke about my great-grandfather in the mine at Coal Creek and how working there, "every day, it was like going into a totally different world." The woman enquired after my grandmother. I told them about my research, my interest in stories and in the cultural diversity of people living in Fernie. Without much ado the man recited his complicated work history as a tree feller, a mill worker, and then working in the coal mine. He said that "my people" were from the Russian border of Czechoslovakia. By this he meant his father's line. "I can understand Russian, so I guess my father spoke it."
> The woman asked: "Have you heard the story of Fernie yet?"
> "Do you mean the story of the curse?"
> "Yes."
> She began to recite the bare bones of it: how William Fernie came looking for coal, and he promised to marry the Indian princess. He ran off and left her – "Then there was fires." Her husband said: "He behaved like most men that way." He then spoke about how his grandfather had "bought" his wife from her father at age fifteen in Czechoslovakia – how unhappy she looked in her wedding photograph. "As far as I can figure out, she came over on a cattle ship." This led to a general discussion of the "ways of the old country" and the difficult marriages many women were part of. Another woman who was present was agreeing with him – "that's just the way it was." (Fieldnotes, 21 August 1997. Czech-Canadians, born ca. 1920.)

When speaking of the past, people in Fernie relate a series of historical events. The narrative of the curse folds into their experiential histories. It touches upon tragedy: fires, mine explosions – the identity-marking events of the early community. The conversation cited above was the first of many about the legend that explicitly dealt with gendered difference. It was also the first time I understood that the story was used to illustrate ideas from times and places now distant. The story of the curse *says* something about "the way it was." On this occasion it connects, in a meaningful way, to the photographed sadness in a grandmother's face on her wedding day.

I did not see the grandmother's photograph; nor do I know when she arrived in Canada, whether she came with her husband and a child already born, or where she landed. Was she raised in a village or perhaps in one of the cosmopolitan centres of Prague or Bratislava? Given the turbulence of late-nineteenth-century nationalism in eastern and central Europe, it is not even clear what nationality she may have described for herself. Depending upon when she arrived, officials may have designated her as Bukovenian, Bohemian, Ruthenian, Galician, Russian, or Austro-Hungarian. The term Slav would have been used informally, as would "foreigner," a popular term applied by those known as Anglo-Saxons. Almost certainly she was witness, in some way, to the displacement of agricultural workers, increasing industrialization, and the frequent movements of migrant labour typical of the period. Perhaps, like many, her husband had already left the turmoil of rising unemployment and was lured to the coal mines of Pennsylvania and then to Fernie at the close of the century. It is possible that through their shared kinship nexus, his and her photographs crossed the Atlantic and facilitated their marriage through brideprice. Or possibly, already married, he had been persuaded to leave by the "prospects of an El Dorado magnified through hearsay" (Böhning 1972:62-63 in Avery 1979:10). Maybe he met an emigration agent offering passage and railway travel, or, perchance, he saw advertisements of opportunity posted in a tavern or published in the local paper.

I am struck by the complex situations of people too easily homogenized under the category of "migrant labourer" and stereotyped in the image of "peasants" who suddenly find themselves in a bustling North American metropolis.

You know, the society they came from had been there for over a thousand years. Even though those people were held down as almost a serf style of society, still, that was a well-developed system. The trade! The trade was far reaching ... The things they could buy came from all over the world ... They could get DMC cotton in their village, but when they came to Canada they came to a primitive country. It was primitive ... They were illiterate. You know, all their language and all their stories were oral and largely supported by church, okay? But it was a defined society. It had lots

of sophistication to it. And then all of a sudden they were thrown
into this, this – what would you call it? This wilderness. Just
thrown into this wilderness. It was a matter of survival. (Interview,
4 November 1997. Ukrainian-Canadian woman, born 1925; father
arrived 1912, mother arrived 1922.)

To many, it was the New World that lacked "sophistication." This woman
compares the Old and New Worlds through access to transnational trade
networks. While she mentions illiteracy tied to religious authority and
an oppressive labour hierarchy, to her it is the availability of commodities that distinguishes the "primitive" from the "sophisticated," "defined
society" from "wilderness." Early immigrants were experienced industrial
workers who had already lived and laboured in some of Europe's most
cosmopolitan cities.

In Chapter 1, I discussed how the curse story normalizes a kind of racializing consciousness that justified colonialism. Here I present another representational era, when "the foreigner" became an object of social scrutiny.
People from remarkably diverse backgrounds came to be categorized under
this monolithic label, which is caught up in the establishment of ethnic
hierarchies in labour and society, and which appears with unrelenting
frequency in historical and modern treatments of the past. During the
era of colonial settlement, an abrupt social distinction arose between
indigenous and European peoples. Throughout the decades that followed,
another gulf developed between those people whom the Canadian state
defines as "immigrant" and those of the "charter" populations. Given the
complexity of people's locations and world events that surround the years
of early immigration, what follows is a pastiche of spoken memories,
excerpts from historical documents, and slices from popular social theories.

During the early part of the twentieth century, processes of citizen selection generated typologies of European peoples based largely on nationality
and class. Theories of human difference that were then current informed
immigration policy and were conspicuously grounded in the reconstruction of people's origins. Scientists used lineage in their investigations into
biological heredity and social Darwinism. Lineage was the cornerstone
of the eugenics movement, which came to be a central scientific approach
to difference in the early twentieth century. As a form of visual propaganda, the pedigree chart became the "ideal means for educating the public" in the "histories of families and classes" (Mazumdar 1992:77). These
diagrammatic charts of descent were effective in bridging the gap between
scientific knowledge and public understanding. Leon Poliakov (1975:3)
suggests that "the genealogical myth is ... the first form of historical thinking." He cites its value in nationalist projects where "primeval intuitions
of blood and soil" were used to create unique national identities and to

contest ideas of relatedness to other peoples. In Chapter 1 I discussed how bloodlines and genealogy are tools used in the colonial construction of categories of people. Social theories were later applied to questions of immigration in Canada, and they appear in popular culture, personal narratives, and official histories. I work with several forms of mass media that provide some sense of the popular ideas of human difference that were in circulation, including archival materials from the Fernie and District Historical Society (FDHS), personal correspondence and papers belonging to my family, and content appearing in the *Fernie Free Press* (*FFP*), the local newspaper established in 1898.

Throughout the early colonial period, information about the New World was transmitted by a contained and managed correspondence between European men. The subsequent era of settlement and mass immigration is characterized by what seems to be an unfettered flow of images, ideas, and people. John Mackenzie (1984:21) describes the period from 1898 to 1918 as one rocked by the "democratization of the visual image." Media boomed due to technical advances in photography, the ability to mass-produce printed matter, and increased efficiency in postal services. The Canadian postmaster general's report for 1897-1898 was printed on page four of the *Fernie Free Press* in April 1899. It stated that 28,153,000 postcards; 134,975,000 letters; 26,595,000 newspapers; and 3,372,000 photographs had been sent that year. By 1909 in Fernie there were "six mails daily" and ten passenger trains. For the immigrant, postcards, newspapers, and photographs were an accessible means of communication between new localities and homelands. They also contributed to the larger machinery of disseminating imperial and scientific ideas used to mobilize public opinion.

Amongst my grandmother's papers is a hand-coloured postcard of Budapest.[1] At the centre of the image are eight industrial stacks rising from a factory in the midst of a residential district. There are no dates or inscriptions on the card; the Maynar, German, English, and Cyrillic versions of the word "view" (which are reproduced in the title of this chapter) appear in the upper left corner.[2] They are languages that reflect reigning European powers and their dominating "view" of the world. The postcard evokes both a celebration of industry, broadcast transnationally, and my grandmother's acquaintance with a Hungarian miner.

Postcards in the Fernie museum archives depict local scenery, and some journalistically document important events. The early cards are printed by the local photographer, Joseph Spalding, or by Suddaby's Pharmacy. After the first decade of the twentieth century, Fernie postcards were also printed and distributed from Toronto, Montreal, Great Britain, and Germany. There is a collection of cards written to a woman in the Rhondda Valley of Wales – one depicts St. George's Cathedral in Cape Town. Many of the messages on those cards sent locally seem today to be the stuff of phone calls: a quick note to confirm arrival on that evening's train, a comment about the previous night's events, or news of getting home safely. Other cards in the museum commemorate military battalions or poems of parting, extending "Hands across the Sea." As one of the many forms of imperial propaganda, the postcard is described as "the supreme vehicle for ... the dissemination of news and views in images which heightened the actions of the age, pictures that encapsulated the world, and brought it into the humblest living room, the supreme expression of control through a particular type of slanted visual understanding" (Mackenzie 1984:21).

Themes disseminated on British postcards continued to assert the moral and political agenda of empire; they were used to aid in the recruitment of soldiers, to encourage emigration, and to promote a particular social ethos. Similarly, Fernie newspapers in the late 1800s were jammed with advertisements that linked imperial values to corporate products (see Figure 2). These materials drifted, perhaps unnoticed, through people's daily lives. It is the taken-for-granted assumptions of difference that I hope to be able to read from these materials of the past.

Immigration before the Turn of the Century

Amongst their descendants, details of first arrival and daily life of early immigrants are sparse. Inevitably, the further back the moment of arrival, the more vague the information. Many of the people with whom I worked speculated about small clues here and there. Visual materials anchor these puzzles of the past.

My dad was from Cosenza, Calabria ... He left at fifteen years old. He landed in Pittsburgh ... Well, he was born in 1870, so it would be 1885.
So he was, he came to work in the mines?
You know, that's the part I'm – it would be in Pittsburgh probably in the steel mill. Yeah, probably, but I'm guessing ... Well, 1898 he came over with the railroad one way or another. I don't even know if he worked on the railroad. And 1898 – you see that picture there? – 1898. So the railroad didn't get here until about [then] ... See those old buildings? You know where they were? Roughly where the swimming pool is now.
Oh, right. [The photo] says: "Coal Creek road looking north or west."
Well, they called it Coal Creek-Fernie in those days. That's Hosmer Mountain there. (Interview, 26 August 1998. Italian-Canadian man, born 1916; father arrived 1885.)

Hosmer Mountain is the site of the Ghostrider shadow. At the time the photograph this man referred to was taken, the town of Hosmer, eight miles north of Fernie, did not yet exist. There is a certainty in reading

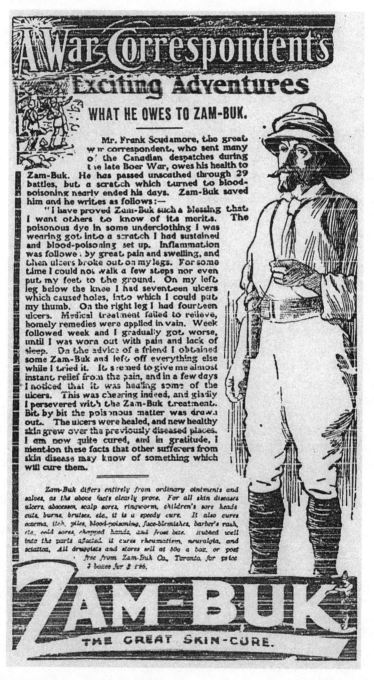

Figure 2 At the turn of the century, the imagery of British imperialism saturated popular media. In this 1909 advertisement, a Boer War veteran vividly describes a nasty case of blood poisoning alleviated by Zam-Buk – "the great skin-cure." *Fernie Free Press*, 5 March 1909.

the mountain ridges in old photos, a perspective that comes with the recognition of landscape. Certainly, without this clue, the rough clay roads and coarse buildings are outside of our contemporary realm of experience. As with oral histories, photographic images contribute to a memory of the past read through the present.

For Italians, unification in 1861 brought a rise in taxes, compulsory military service, and enormous stress on the agricultural households. Emigration from Calabria was well integrated into the social fibre of communities. Single men between the ages of twenty-five and thirty-five often became engaged before their departure, thus securing a dowry for their voyage and ensuring vital links to their home villages. In Calabria these young men were dubbed birds of passage: "a village by village study ... in Cosenza [showed] the percentage of those who returned for the period 1890 to 1905 amounted to about three quarters of those who had emigrated" (Arlacchi 1983:57-59, 60-61). An agricultural crisis in Italy in the 1870s meant that many sought work in Switzerland, Germany, the Austro-Hungarian territories, and France. Between 1861 and 1911 over four million Italians left their country to seek employment.

I interviewed twelve people whose predecessors arrived in North America before the turn of the twentieth century. Primary emigrating groups from this period include southern Italians, Ukrainians, Welsh, English, Scots, Doukhobors, Czechoslovakians, Poles, Hungarians, and northern Italians. These people's ancestors were miners, steel and mill workers, farm and construction labourers. Many took a circuitous route to Fernie, sometimes mining in Germany or Holland, then in Pennsylvania, Nova Scotia, Montana, Dakota, or Alberta. Some came to build the railway and then found steady work in the mines at Morrissey or Coal Creek. Others were farmers who cycled in and out of agricultural labour in Ontario, Saskatchewan, or southern Alberta. Only two of these families (one English and one Welsh) homesteaded near Fernie. The Dominion government had recruited Europeans who were, in most cases, too poor to "establish themselves directly on the land" (Avery 1979:17). Settlement policy pushed most people into wage labour with the eventual hope of homesteading.

Parents came from Russia. They were there – they lived in two, three different places too before they came to Canada. Different times, different places. There was big advertising in the papers and everything that there's lots of land in Canada. Good land and lots of it, cheap. People were poor then. A lot of them came. Mum and Dad, they came here, both unwed. They got married here in Saskatchewan. And now they're gone ...
Jews. Oh yes, Ukrainians, Doukhobors, and Jews. They come in bunches. Let's say somebody picked you and me to go and take a

look at the country first. If we think it's okay to move, we come back home, tell the people, and if they want to move, they move; if they don't, they don't ... Today [my people] are the minority. There is very little as they say "Doukhobor." They think Doukhobor [laughing], something made out of some different things. Doukhobor is a religion. Same as everybody else. (Interview, 12 December 1997. Duokhobor woman, born 1909; parents arrived 1899.)

This woman's parents arrived in Saskatchewan in 1899. From the standpoint of the Dominion government and its immigration agenda, Doukhobors met the demand for agricultural workers to settle the prairies. There is much detail in this brief quote that serves to introduce ideas about the period before the turn of the century. Perhaps more than other Old World people, Doukhobors were experiencing political strife in their homeland. For them, as for others across Europe, poverty and agricultural decline made the rigours of emigration more desirable. Before 1914 the Dominion of Canada openly recruited labourers from Russia, Poland, and the Ukraine. Invitations to settle the country were extended through newspapers, pamphlets, and lectures. The Dominion government entered into arrangements with businessmen who had shipping, railway, and land interests; the businessmen procured agents to act as middlemen, looking after the logistics of emigration. "Doukhobor representatives toured potential settlement sites," and 7,500 "refugees" were admitted to the prairies of Saskatchewan in 1899 (A. Scott 1997:121).[3] Such tours were commonplace, and the category of "refugee" was already instilled in official vocabulary.

Perhaps most striking in the above interview is this woman's understanding that her people were viewed as "something made out of some different things." Eric Wolf (1982:362) suggests that the most significant factor influencing the experience of an immigrant is "the position [she or he is] placed in, in relation to other groups, on arrival." Until 1900, people arriving in Canada were counted under the categories of British, American, and Other. The latter is an apt descriptor for those who came to be known later in the Dominion as "aliens" and "foreigners."

In 1896, Clifford Sifton, minister of the interior, stated: "I think a stalwart peasant in a sheep-skin coat, born on the soil, whose forebearers have been farmers for ten generations, with a stout wife and a dozen children, is good quality" (quoted in Avery 1979:19). The suggestion that agricultural abilities were inherited and connected to reproductive vigour evokes explanations of human difference that were then becoming increasingly biological.[4] Conservatives, labour unions, and Protestant clergy met Sifton's invitation to Poles, Russians, and Ukrainians with open hostility. In his research on immigration, Donald Avery (1979:41n8) notes that twenty-two daily newspapers in March and April 1899 had negative commentary on Ukrainian migrants. He quotes from the *Toronto Mail and Empire:* "[Sifton's immigration policy] is an attempt to make of the North-West a sort of anthropological garden ... to pick the waifs and strays of Europe, the lost tribes of mankind, and the freaks of creation" (10 April 1899 in Avery 1979:41). The reference to anthropology is testament to the popularization of the discipline. It appears strikingly close to two biblically based theories used to argue questions of human difference.

The theory of the lost tribes proposed that peoples of the Americas were descendants of Adam and Eve, who had "induced God's wrath" (Miles 1989:16), and therefore caused their progeny to be cursed with disfigurement and exile. The Book of Genesis has been used throughout European history to argue both the "divine unity" of humans and essential differences between what have been called "nations" and "races" (Bendyshe 1863:346). In early anthropological theorizing, the "degeneration" of humans from a state of pure faith constituted the primary model for change (Stocking 1989:12). During the waning years of the 1800s, scholars were well distanced from biblical explanations and now firmly entrenched in the scientific construction of classificatory schemes. Scientific knowledge, however, had to compete with more popular ideas for a foothold in the imagination.

During my first interview with a Ktunaxa woman, she was speaking about their language and the fact that it is an isolate, unrelated to any other in the world. Several years earlier she interviewed a Welsh pioneer in the South Country, that region between Fernie and the US border.

> There's a thing called the Kallispell Trail that used to come up from the Flathead Lake and along where the Kootenay River used to be, up into Fort Steele. The Kootenay people would make their journeys back and forth all the time and she used to trade stuff with them. She was Welsh and she swears she could converse with them. Not all words, but there were enough similarities that they could carry on a conversation or at least understand each other. She swore that that's the way it was. Of course I've never heard Welsh spoken myself, so I wouldn't know ... But she swears that she used to speak to them and have no problem and she swore that, I guess there was, just another one of those things that you hear – the Kootenays were supposedly called the White Indians or the Lost Tribe or something. She swore that must have been the ones they were talking about, that they must have been from Wales because she could speak to them. (Interview, 11 December 1997. Ktunaxa woman, born 1955.)

Before I began fieldwork, I was in Wales. Questions about my research led people to tell me about the "Welsh-speaking Red Indians." As Welsh nationalistic lore goes, these people were part of a colony established in the New World by their Prince Madoc, who had sailed to discover America in 1170. According to Welsh historian Gwyn Williams (1979), the Madoc legend transformed to include the "Welsh Indians" when it spread to the American continent in the last decades of the eighteenth century. "Contact," as a social experience, involves differing degrees of recognition or familiarity (Thomas 1994:52). Impressions are shaped not only through actual interaction, but also through images and ideas already instilled in the popular imagination.

While folklore carries representations of others, newspapers also provide an accessible avenue through which to gain a sense of popular, or at least widely disseminated, ideas of difference. At the turn of the century, Fernie papers drew stories from all over the world; they included excerpts from medical and scientific journals, explorers' accounts, royal speeches, and government reports. Throughout the March and April editions of 1899, Swiss, Russian, Japanese, Bavarian, Jewish, and "Servian" (Serbian) "Items of Interest" appear. Alongside these is news of the Turin International Exhibition, Delhi under British imperial rule, "The Wholesale Lynching" of "Negroes" in Arkansas, a "Violin made from Bones" of a South African chief, marriage ceremonies in Egypt, national culinary talents of Chinese male "peasants," a seventeenth-century Lithuanian women's petition, the Egyptian origins of the Cinderella story, a treatise on the state of "Culture," and updates on the US-Philippine War. There are glimpses here and there of the scientific ideas of the time: astronomy, Egyptology, and philology; "brain specialists" warn that "Red Causes Insanity"; and "hygiene" doctors discuss the risks of bicycle riding. Local editorials give detailed descriptions of the social landscape. A serialized novel appears weekly, featuring the exploits of women, cowboys, and Indians on the American frontier.

By the time the first immigrants arrived in the Dominion of Canada, Ktunaxa people saw their land pre-empted and fenced into reserves. Their communities had been ravaged by disease, and their rights to vote, buy land, move freely, and participate in forms of economic, political, and religious traditions were negated. By 1888, legislation required Ktunaxa children to attend St. Eugene's Mission, a residential school that attempted to sever the valuable links between generations. In April 1899, the *Free Press* published an article entitled "Canada's Indians: An Increase in Their Number, and Their Finances and Produce Also Have a Good Year" (8 April 1899:4). The article cited the population of indigenous "souls" as 100,093, with an increase of 27 for British Columbia. Dollar figures follow for farm produce and wages earned through fishing, hunting, and other industries. The article states confidently that the people "have settled down and been doing well on their reserves." That same month an announcement appeared in the paper: "Pathetic, dramatic, and quaintly humorous Indian stories [will be performed] by an Indian poetess in Indian costume" (*FFP* 2 April 1899). This was E. Pauline Johnson, admission fifty cents. The threat of "savagery," so preoccupying only years before, was now relieved by the confidence in state control and by a make-believe imagery that surrounded "Indians." In Britain, public concern had veered away from indigenous peoples and towards so-called dangerous classes.

"Dangerous Classes"

Mining and lumber operations had begun by the time the *Fernie Free Press* newspaper was in circulation. Two railways were under construction, and Catholic, Methodist, and Salvation Army personnel had commenced services in the mining camps (Mangan 1977a:41; Phillips 1977:71-73). A year later, in 1899, Catholic and Presbyterian schools opened and the Fernie Board of Trade was formed. An editorial appearing in March provides some insight into the experiential life of Fernie. Under the headline "Bacchus Rampant," the writer deplores "a certain state of affairs" in which "at least 17 whisky dives and about half that number of brothels" are making Fernie "the butt of the Province" and a "disgrace to any civilized community" (*FFP* 11 March 1899). The population is cited as 1,500, mostly "labouring men who remained in the country" after CPR construction moved west.[5] According to the writer: "It is too much to expect this class to be influenced by the sympathies and considerations which appeal to the average man." The article implores "intelligent citizens ... to effect by the irresistible force of public opinion what apparently cannot be done in any other way." This moral appeal to the standard of "civilization," combined with the social marking of labouring classes, highlights standard ideas at the time.

Across Europe, industrialization provoked mass movements of people away from the land and towards urban centres where wage labour could be found. During the 1840s, 2.5 million people emigrated from Ireland, evicted from the English-owned estates and reeling from the potato famine. German and English coal mining, steelwork, and textile industries had suffered in the late 1860s. By the 1890s, agricultural labourers from southern Italy, the Austro-Hungarian Empire, and the Balkan provinces were seeking employment throughout Europe and the Americas (Wolf 1982:364-371). In Poland, mining and factory work was booming until the late 1880s, but higher wages were to be found in Germany and Denmark, Buffalo, Chicago, and Philadelphia (Zaretsky 1996:7).

Britain's policy makers and scholars grappled with rising intensities of urban poverty. This was objectified in a discourse of "pauperism," which linked poverty to morality and crime. The most immediate and visible categories of difference coalesced around the "true industrials" and the "residuum." The latter were casual labourers seen to be entirely focused on the present, possessing little or no rational self-control, and destined to repeat mistakes. By the 1880s, evolutionary theorists revised an outlook on poverty now specifically dealing with casual labourers. They proposed a theory of degeneration, directly linked to standards of morality. Debates at this time circled around environmentalist theories and ideas of "natural law," which saw moral and physical traits as hereditary. Heredity theorists sounded alarms about rising populations of urban poor, then framed as a threat to national health. Unless some kind of intervention could be effected, the "direction of evolution of the human race [would be] reversed" (Mazumdar 1992:3). This basic logic of "degeneration" became the cornerstone of the eugenics movement, which determined that breeding should be encouraged in the "prudential classes" and discouraged in the "pauper class" (3). By 1901, Francis Galton, the founder of the movement (and the cousin of Charles Darwin), was calling for "segregation and sterilization of the undesirable" (McLaren 1990:23).

In Canada and the United States, class was collapsed with nationality, sparking debates over who, exactly, new citizens would be. Theories about hereditary causes of insanity and "national degeneration" were appearing in Canadian medical journals before the turn of the century (McLaren 1990:23-24).[6] Canadian scientists differed from the British in that their focus on heredity and degeneracy was also linked to immigration. These medical practitioners took their lead from Americans, who were also engaged in debates over immigration and the "improvement of the human race through judicious breeding" (18). During this period, medicine and psychology were professionalizing. Work in these fields became linked to questions of national health, and the practitioners were deemed indispensable in administering immigration policies. Opposition to the rising numbers of non-Anglo-European immigrants was voiced freely in the late nineteenth century. Public debates were shaped by the rallying cries of those known as Anglo-Saxons, a categorization of persons constructed from older ideas of superiority naturalized through conquest.

"Anglo-Saxons" and "Nordics"
In the *Fernie Free Press*, dated 18 March 1899, the warning "Anglo Saxons Beware" appears below the headline "Ontario's Birth Rate." The article cites 1897 statistics on births, deaths, and marriages, as well as "the total immigrants arriving by ocean steamers" that year.[7] It concludes with a strong warning to women about "advertisements of preventative medicines" decreasing the "productivity" of "Anglo Saxons."

> If the Anglo Saxon race is to fulfil its destiny on the American continent, and play the dominant part over inferior races in the march of progress ...

[women] will have to preach a gospel of patriotism to which today they seem singularly blind. Social degeneracy has always meant social decay, and it is the simple and moral citizens of today who will hold the supremacy of tomorrow.

Advertising through "the newspaper and the mails" was viewed as a potent force of persuasion offering women pharmaceutical options for birth control, thus "undo[ing] what nature has asserted."

The article goes on to cite a report by Dr. Peter Bryce, who, between 1904 and 1921, became the "chief medical officer of the Department of Immigration" (McLaren 1990:52).[8] It reveals the accessibility of scientific information and raises questions about who new Canadians will be. The article links reproduction with patriotism and, in referring to social degeneracy, employed "the argument that human intelligence was a fixed and hereditary characteristic" (Miles 1989:36). Regarding immigration, there were questions of assimilation to be answered. These questions had their starting place in basic assumptions about who these "inferior races" were. What was known then as Anglo-Saxonism arose in response to a new problem of settlement and evoked a much older set of debates about human difference.

Scientific explanations combined with philological studies and folklore to fuel imperialist and nation-building projects during this period. Anglo-Saxonism was a "form of racial nationalism" with conceptual roots that tapped into English assertions of superiority over Celtic peoples (Stocking 1987:62, 64). "Peasants" and "folk" had been the focus of scientific inquiry for some time. They were already well-objectified populations in the European and American popular imagination. In the terms of evolutionary theory, these people were viewed as "left-overs from an imagined agriculturally-serene past," whose lore was seen to consist of "vulgar errors which needed to be exposed and remedied" (Abrahams 1992:36). Just as the criteria of "civilization" had been imposed on so-called primitives, ideas regarding private property, laws, beliefs, and closeness to nature also figured into the negative descriptions of European "peasants." Stocking (1987:229) presents a list of stigmatized social categories: criminals, women and children, "peasants, rustics, labourers, beggars, paupers, madmen, and Irishmen all of whom were at times likened to savages or 'primitive' man." In the late nineteenth century, efforts were also under way to determine distinctions between British "races." Longstanding representations of the Irish, in particular, became the standard for European inferiority and the model for later primitivist imagery (Culhane 1998:39-40). Questions about European "races" revolved around hierarchical relationships that would explain conquest and the perceived potential for independent statehood. In the age of imperialism, conquest was a stable component of British propaganda that intensified during periods of military threat. Rhetorically, conquest was bound up with ideas about history, superiority, and homelands.

A ninety-year-old woman in Fernie showed me her elementary school writing book: *New Method Writing #7* (The Educational Book Company, Toronto, 1913). Inside, her assignments in composition and penmanship reveal the ubiquity of imperialist ideas. In 1919 she had written an essay about the explorer Captain John Smith, who was "saved by Pocahontas." Perfect rows of cursive filled other pages of her book, repeating the following lines, provided as writing exercises:

> The dominant races came from the region of the pines.
> The pines of Norway and Sweden sent out the Vikings, and out of the pinewoods of Northern Europe came the virile barbarian over running the effete southern countries.
> Wise men say nothing in dangerous times.
> History is philosophy teaching by examples.

Imperial propaganda was well-ingrained in school texts by this time.[9] "Race" was used here to distinguish between Europeans who occupied varying positions on a ladder of superiority based on conquest. Another recognizable tactic of othering also appears in these lines: the "feminization of the racial subaltern" (Linke 1997:561; see also Das 1998). Leon Poliakov (1974:253) notes "the symbolism of masculine and feminine races" was used often to contrast so-called masculine Germans and effeminate Latins and to distinguish Germans from "Slavs" and Celts, and Aryans from Semites. Scholars imagined Europeans through taxonomies constructed around northern and southern "types" that echoed the criteria used to describe labouring classes, peasants, and paupers.

By the closing years of the nineteenth century, biological explanations of difference through "racial purity" were common. Scientists speculated about the identity of the original conquerors of Europe, and they sought ways to delineate nations. In Britain, France, the United States, and Germany, comparative anatomy represented the scientific edge of modern investigation. These predecessors of physical anthropology focused on "racial achievement" based on "mental differences" that were apparent from skull and skeleton measurements (Stocking 1968:39; see also Miles 1989:36). Following the early work of German phrenologists, Anders Retzius developed the Cephalic Index, "a measurement of skulls which involved dividing the length of the skull by the breadth" (Miles 1989:34). Human "types" (read "races") were associated with "traits" of stature; skin, hair, and eye colour; and head shape. Thus, according to the Cephalic Index, "dominating, enterprizing and Protestant" Nordic "types" were long-headed, or

Dolichocephalic (Stocking 1968:60). These were the "Aryans," who hailed from Scandinavia, Germany, England, and France (1864 in Poliakov 1974:264).[10] In contrast, the Alpine, or broad-headed Brachycephalic, "type" was "plodding, conservative and Catholic" (Stocking 1968:60). Scientists viewed dark features and the shorter stature of Finns, Slavs, Bretons, and Lapps as evidence of separate origin from the taller, blonder Aryans. Thus, racialized distinctions arose between urban northern Europeans and rural central, southern, and eastern Europeans. Tying it all together was a growing certainty about the inheritance of moral, intellectual, and physical qualities.

Comparative anatomists from so-called Nordic nations shared an intellectual sphere. Russian theorists, on the other hand, were then dubbed "Slavophile" (Poliakov 1974:124-125). According to Leon Poliakov, Russians were seen to have no "pure" genealogy through which to construct a national identity. They were, in other words, "non-Aryan," the result of "cross-breeding between Slav, Asiatic, Indigenous Finn and Germanic" peoples.[11] In Italy, the "arts no less than science were imbued with patriotic passion" (Poliakov 1974:67-68). It was the ancient power of Rome to which anthropologists and philologists traced their new nation's origins. Italian scholars reversed the hypothesis of superiority; Aryans were seen as "unlettered primitives" who had rightly been held back in their attempts to invade Italy (Sergi 1897 in Poliakov 1974:68). Italian scholars' reaction to northern European scholarship is not surprising in an era where the third and lowest "type" of European was the "Mediterranean." Comparative anatomy seems to have played a greater role in Italy in the formation of what was to become the discipline of criminology (see Harrowitz 1994).

European scholars in the late nineteenth century were concerned about poverty and criminality. In the face of nationalism, these social issues were sometimes trapped within an idea of race that was now conceptually expanding to include class, gender, mental health, criminality, and nationality. Eugenics, in particular, took on local national concerns. French scholars were not taken by the enthusiasm over eugenics that seemed to preoccupy others; Roman Catholicism provided the base of resistance to interventionist policies of reproduction. While Britain struggled with its "feeble-minded" pauper class, Germany concentrated on "psychotics and psychopaths" (Mazumdar 1992:3-4). In North America, attention was focused on southern and eastern European immigrants, their high birth rate, and a perceived connection to criminality and insanity. Across continental Europe, America, and Britain, the pedigree chart became the new "scientific method of persuasion." It was both a scientific tool used to investigate hereditary lines of perceived deviance and an effective visual form of propaganda. It played a significant role in debates around immigration in the early years of the twentieth century.

Pedigrees

A puzzling article appeared in the *Fernie Free Press* on 13 May 1903. Puzzling, that is, until one reads about what German geneticists theorized as *Ahnenverlust* or "loss of ancestry" (Mazumdar 1992:92-94). The article, entitled "The Aristocracy of Birth," explains the dying out of royal classes through "laws of arithmetic, and ... the laws of physiology ... Arithmetic because it required that each individual or household should have a distinct line of ancestors ... It would be discovered in a few generations that there were not nearly enough to go around ... Physiology, as shown by the deterioration of one royal family after another in Europe ... having come to resemble those English race horses."[12]

There is a strong visual aspect to all of this. Scientists proposing "loss of ancestry" theory had only to refer to the pedigree chart to show the inbreeding of nobility. "Physiological laws" were discernible through physical appearance. Pauline Mazumdar (1992:58) suggests that for many there was little analysis of transmission; the pedigree supported the "simple fact that like produced like." German eugenists also looked at what they called the "zero family": "good German peasant stock" – "now the largest family of degenerates the world has ever known" (*Pall Mall Gazette* 1912 in Mazumdar 1992:94). In a similar fashion, British eugenists constructed charts of pauper families, sometimes across six generations, in order to show that pauperism is inherited. Pedigrees were used to prove the "interrelatedness of the whole pauper class," emphasizing large families and intermarriage between them.

In the United States, scientists used the pedigree to chart "single families traced to a unique defective ancestor." Canadian scientists followed, tracing family lines from inmates of asylums and prisons (Mazumdar 1992:4).[13] It was a small step to a correlation with immigrants: "Our asylums, jails, hospitals and other charitable institutions show an increasing percentage of men and women, emigrants from the older lands, who are handicapped by a bad heredity, and quite unfit to make their way in the new world" (Knight 1907 in McLaren 1990:52). Scientific pedigrees charted perceived social, physical, and economic deviance through the family lines of "peasants," paupers, and European immigrants. Theorists who used pedigrees identified the mode of transmission as heredity. It seems obvious, from the standpoint of the present, that the scientists were overlooking intensities that arise from clashes in culture and profound dislocation. In their zeal to prove heredity, they also overlooked kinship and social networks that bound people together through shared experience and through powerful ideas passed between generations.

Immigration after the Turn of the Century

They didn't dwell on the hardships. In any of their life, Mum and Daddy didn't dwell on their hardships. *We* learned history. We were very conscious of it, but it was never drilled into us. As I say, listen to the words in a song. They have meaning, you know. And this is how we learned it. Daddy would sing us a song and that one: "Firm as our native rock we have withstood the shock – of England and Denmark and Rome and the world." You know, there's something in that! There's something in "the birthplace of valour," the "country of worth" ... There is something in words like that, that tell you so much of where we came from. We came from people that were strong, that weren't whiners, that were willing to work for a living, to give up much of what they loved. (Interview, 14 November 1997. Scottish-Canadian woman, born ca. 1920; parents arrived ca. 1910.)

This woman, born in Canada, is filled with Scottish pride. Our interview brought to the surface some interesting ways that we all figure "where we came from." As part of our conversation about history she spoke about the Scottish clans.[14] Her comments traced an oral history of enmities between family groups. The nationalism carried through song is testament to the intergenerational transmission of powerful ideas. As with all expressions of identity, sentiments are fuelled by memories of interaction within and between groups.

It's a historical fact. Lord Sutherland, from somewhere in Scotland, of course he had a big estate. And they found out they could get more money raising sheep than they could bringing up children and families in their little crop cottages. They put people down on the beach to eat seaweed, and then the Canadian government said that they would bring them over to Canada ... There were never any arrangements made. They walked from Hudson Bay down to the Red River Valley, and the old mother brought a piece of heather tucked in her bosom to plant when she got to her new land. (Interview, 14 November 1997. Scottish-Canadian woman, born ca. 1920; parents arrived ca. 1910.)

By the time this woman's parents arrived in Canada, Scottish workers had been on the move for some time. In the late eighteenth century, Lowlanders relocated to Ulster and then to the United States. Highlanders also arrived by clans in North America around this time, "displaced by sheep or driven by rising rents" (Wolf 1982:363). Her narrative of displacement and struggle complicates simple distinctions between "foreigners" and "Anglo-Saxons" in Fernie. To non-Anglo-European people, Scottish, Irish, and Welsh are perceived as English as they too were able to attain better positions in labour and move through Canadian society with greater ease.

The woman who had shown me her schoolbook surprised me one afternoon when, over apple strudel, she exclaimed: "The British don't have a clue. They never experienced anything horrible! They were always right about everything!" She told me that books written on the area "missed the grist. They paint a nice veneer, but they miss everything lying underneath." As she said this, she gestured layers below layers with her arms. "They all write that everything's okay, but it isn't! It's not okay. Lots of people will tell you." Then she said: "These English people, they shouldn't be calling themselves immigrants! They have no idea what it was like!" She said her mother didn't speak about it much, but they had to travel six weeks on a cattle boat, and she carried a bedpan for the children. When they arrived in Quebec in 1903, they were "fumigated" on an island there. Her comments resonate with the words of others to whom I spoke. To her, an immigrant is someone whose origin is other than English and whose arrival experience was enormously different from that of charter peoples. Her remarks about the British suggest their privilege in history, the right to inscribe and define a particular, situated view.

Visual images also provide a view of the people "we came from." Postcards in my grandmother's collection mostly depict scenes of her parents' village in Northumberland. They show churches, halls, fields, and sometimes relatives standing outside rough stone houses.[15] On many of the cards it is the name of the house, not of the people, that is inscribed. On some of the cards, villages and relatives' names are marked with Xs. A note is scribbled on one: "the road home." My great-grandparents arrived from Northumberland in the first decade of the new century. In northern England my great-grandfather had worked as an agricultural labourer, as a stonewall builder, on bridge construction, and in and out of the local lead mines. Without doubt, his nationality contributed to his eventually obtaining the position of "stable boss" at the Coal Creek mines. During this era a pronounced ethnic hierarchy emerged, with English speakers obtaining more privileged positions.

People I interviewed whose relatives arrived after 1900 and before the First World War trace their origins to Czechoslovakia, Poland, the Ukraine, Bohemia, Russia, northern Italy, southern Italy, Ireland, Scotland, and the United States. While several were miners or coke loaders, others built the roads, waterworks, and buildings of early prairie cities. Service industries were also becoming established at this time; some people were tailors or bakers, grocers or shoemakers; they worked as hoteliers, pharmacists, or blacksmiths.

At this time, women and children began to arrive in numbers. A certain sense of melancholy was evoked when people spoke about their mothers and grandmothers.

[Husband] My mother's folks, it's a little different story. Her mother, was she sixteen when she came?
[Wife] Thirteen when she came to Canada from Czechoslovakia. Landed in New York. When she was sixteen she married _____'s grandfather and at nineteen she had two children and was a widow. Her husband was killed in a hunting accident. Of course in those days there was no kind of pension for women, so a year later she got married again and had thirteen more children [laughter]. (Interview, 5 September 1997. Czech-Canadian man, born ca. 1924; grandmother arrived early 1900s; English-Canadian woman, born ca. 1926; parents arrived 1920s.)

Women's well-being was crucially tied to marriage in the early years. There were few options for respectable independence outside of traditional unions; but the political landscape surrounding the "women's question" was, after the turn of the century, on the verge of change.

There is an odd dissonance in media representations of women at this time in Fernie. Advertising aimed at "weak, pain-wracked women" offered cures for "silent, secret suffering" (*FFP* 30 July 1909). Other material addressed to women appears in the form of platitudes for hysteria or commonsense advice on childrearing and dress. In contrast to these often-lengthy columns, more politicized topics occupy short blocks of objective commentary. Steven Seidman (1994:167) characterizes this period as one highly concerned with the "women's question." Until the First World War, "women's issues" were debated publically. Revolving around what is now known as "sexuality," they included "divorce, free-love, abortion, masturbation, homosexuality, prostitution, obscenity and sex education" (167).

Police records in Fernie for the year 1909 provide some insight into the gendered climate of the town. There were 188 charges of prostitution, 166 charges of drunk and disorderly, 32 charges of vagrancy, and 20 charges for assault. Amongst the fines that were levied, a Chinese launderer was given a fine of five dollars or fifteen days for spraying water from his mouth onto an article of clothing. A man was charged the same for assaulting a woman. Another man was fined twenty dollars or sentenced to two months for the assault of a man. Prostitutes were liable for a ten-dollar fine or one month in jail. In the 1911 records, all three charges for "seduction" had been dropped. In the records for 1917 there were thirty charges of "abduction." Apparently men were seizing women from their work in "houses of ill fame."

Many of the women I interviewed told of their mothers' and grand-mothers' struggles through a pragmatic discourse of survival and strength. Those who came from non-Anglo-European backgrounds were regarded as especially adept at managing large families in the face of poverty, cultural dislocation, and widowhood. People told me about complex circumstances where death left many women stranded in the new country. Most took in boarders, doing laundry and cooking for the large numbers of single, male workers. As the woman below explains, they were not passive observers.

Ukrainian women took control over their lives. I mean, they **used** the men in their lives.

In what way?

Well. For example, your husband only works three days a week, there isn't much coming in, so she takes in a boarder, okay? She takes in a boarder, she creates a nice living space for this boarder. Now you have two incomes coming in, right? The first thing you know, there are two or three children who look slightly different and they go right into old age with two men and one woman in a house and they're all happy together. She's the one who is controlling this situation ... It was quite common. There were more men than women. Because so many men had come and so many of the wives didn't come. Single women didn't come, not till much later. So there was a surplus of men. (Interview, 4 November 1997. Ukrainian-Canadian woman, born 1925; father arrived 1912, mother arrived 1922.)

Although some women had economic strategies to provide for their households, many were vulnerable participants in immigration. To schol-ars who write about "peasant" societies, women from central, southern, and eastern Europe are often viewed as important figures, holding together the institution of "familial solidarity."[16] These societies in particular have been theorized through their mode of production and their kinship net-works (Wolf 1966). Popular representations of non-Anglo Europeans were based largely on stereotypes of class that figured into official processes of citizen selection in Canada.

In his influential book on Canadian immigration, W.G. Smith (1920) quotes a passage from an earlier publication, which provides some sense of how the "Slavic world" was regarded by Anglo-Saxon officials in the early 1900s:

In ignorance and illiteracy, in the prevalence of superstition and priest-craft, in the harshness of Church and State, in the subservience of the common people to the upper classes, in the low position of women, in the subjection of the child to the parent, in coarseness of manner and speech, and in low standards of cleanliness and comfort, a large part of the Slavic world remains at the level of our English forefathers of the days of Henry VIII. (1910 in W.G. Smith 1920:383)

Recognizable categories of comparison arise here: belief systems, forms of governance, family and gender relations, ideas about pollution and temporality. In Canada after the turn of the century, anti-immigrant sentiment was unleashed on unskilled labourers and those perceived to be peasants.

[Husband] The British were terrible! I'm surprised they got to where they are now.
[Wife] Even when they came out here to work in the mines, they didn't want to bother with other people, other cultures.
What was the attitude?
[Husband] It was just arrogance.
[Wife] I think they thought they were better than everybody else because they came from England. This is what I think ... They were hard to, you know, the other nationalities all got along together, but the English didn't ... It was passed on to them I think. If you came from Europe, you were no good.
[Husband] No. You were either a Dago or a Bohunk. (Interview, 18 February 1998. Russian-Canadian man, born ca. 1914; mother arrived 1914; Polish-Canadian woman, born ca. 1915; mother arrived 1912.)

Selecting "Desirable" Citizens
In the early years of the twentieth century in the United States, immigration officials and scientists debated the question of "amalgamation" of non-Anglo Europeans (Boas 1908:203). They approached their concerns through scientific investigations of "the most important types of Europe": northern, southern, eastern, and central. The latter two were often collapsed within the all-encompassing category of Slav.

Emigration rhetoric in Britain from the late 1870s had become increasingly racialized. "Canada [is] subject to the same physical danger confronting the United States, namely, the actual physical submergence of the English stock by a flood of European people" (*FFP*, 27 November 1908:6). Immigration was promoted among three groups in Britain: women as agents of "feminine civilizing," children who were to assume "the natural heritage of the British race," and "gentlemen" who would increase the population of the "officer class" and "solve the younger son problem" (Avery 1979:160). This was a project of anglicizing the Dominion.[17] Doctors and immigration officials in Canada called for the need to weed out "defective immigrants" (McLaren 1990:51). Policy makers dictated rather vague categories of people.

Amendments in the Canadian Immigration Act between 1869 and 1908 barred entry to the following "classes of persons": "idiots, insane, feeble-minded, deaf and dumb, dumb, blind or infirm ...; persons with loath-some, contagious or infectious disease; paupers, destitutes, professional beggars, vagrants, or [those] likely to become a public charge" (W.G. Smith 1920:93).

"Feeble-mindedness" was seen to be the cause of problems like crime, prostitution, unemployment, and venereal disease in Canadian society.[18] This nebulous condition was equated with cultural incompetence, the inevitable difficulties people had in negotiating new cultural and linguistic terrains. It was determined that this was biological, an inherited trait in the immigrant population. After 1901, Canada imposed deportation regulations as a consequence of these classifications.[19] The Immigration Act of 1910 extended the list of "undesirables" to include: "imbeciles ... epileptics ... persons who have been insane within five years previous ... Persons who have been convicted of any crime involving moral turpitude. Prostitutes and women and girls coming to Canada for any immoral purpose, and pimps ... Immigrants to whom money has been given or loaned by any charitable organization" (W.G. Smith 1920:96-97).[20] Scientists collected family histories, then visually represented by the pedigree chart.[21] In addition to using family pedigrees, immigration specialists called for better medical examinations and "mental" testing at ports of arrival.

Arriving at Ellis Island after 1908, people may have been subjected to a rigorous battery of measurement and classification.[22] Procedures for those arriving in Canada may have been less intrusive. In 1908 railway and steamship lines were not cooperative partners in the push for stringent inspections. There were random medical checkups at Quebec, Halifax, Montreal, and Winnipeg, and at St. John's in Newfoundland. Into the 1920s, Canadian policy makers extolled the procedures at Ellis Island as the most effective example of such processes.

In 1920 W.G. Smith made an appeal for better means of "detecting defectives" as part of "the delicate task of selecting human beings for this country's citizens." He outlined the need for more interpreters, better facilities at ports of entry, and higher qualifications for examiners. He also described the logistics of arrival:

> But when the practice is to drop all third class passengers at Quebec, and then proceed to Montreal, no ingenuity of medical inspection can overcome the unavoidable difficulties. If the passengers remained with the ship to its final port, and then were examined in such numbers as could be scrutinized from nine to five, the remainder could stay on board ship and

await their turn, and this would not interfere with the process of unloading cargo. Such a system prevails at Ellis Island where, moreover, the immigration officials are provided with barges of their own. (1920:365-366)

Passengers travelling first class were exempted from medical inspection (McLaren 1990:56).

The lengthy process of arrival appeared to be intact into the 1920s.

We came in 1921. I knew how to read and write because the Italian government had put some schools – after the First World War, the government put schools on the farms ... We left my hometown by mules. From there we got the train ... We landed in Naples and had to wait for the boat to come in. We waited for ten days ... I was eleven ... I don't know why, but my father had made papers that we came through the States. So we landed in New York and I saw the Statue of Liberty. It's very nice. We stayed in this place where now it's a tourist attraction [Ellis Island]. We stayed in this place. They'd ring the bell for breakfast, ring the bell for lunch, ring the bell for supper. We stayed there for ten days because we had to wait for this woman that the company would send. She had to take us to Montreal. There was quite a few people. Every morning – it's not like it is now that they could just walk in. Every morning you get your face washed, everything. They check what's in your hair, if you've got anything. Everything was cleaned, not like it is now. There was Italians and there were other nationalities too. (Interview, 6 August 1998. Italian woman, born 1910; family arrived 1921.)

In 1920 Smith wrote:

The immigration of the people of Italy into the western world since the days when the Italian was known almost entirely as a wandering playwright whose troupe consisted of himself, a hurdy-gurdy organ and a monkey, has been one of phenomenal growth ... The same lack of knowledge of English which compels the Italian to work in gangs, also drives him into segregation in the large cities where he establishes a colony of his own people, with the retention of the language, customs and traditions of Italy. This of course produces overcrowding in a deplorable degree, and manifestly retards the Canadianization of the family. (1920:193, 196)

As early as 1911 in Canada there had been a public outcry that immigrants from southern Europe "constituted a serious menace to the community" (Avery 1979:28-29). After the turn of the century, "Italians were considered undesirable, racially" (26). Official views of non-Anglo Europeans hinged on ideas of conformity in language, residence, and customs. In Fernie at this time, "foreigners" were also represented through a perceived absence of social values in the face of peril.

Disaster and Foreignness

When your grandmother is a foreigner, you seem to be able to listen to other people. [She] would talk to me in Czech in a lot of cases, not steady. I would understand her pretty well. (Interview, 5 September 1997. Czech-Canadian man, born ca. 1924; grandmother arrived early 1900s.)

How do people narrate their entanglements with languages and customs now removed from their everyday experience? Language was often cited as an opening to other worlds. There was some regret about not fully learning and retaining this valuable way of knowing. Over a generation or so, many people speak about their predecessors through the seemingly self-explanatory label of "foreigner."

Media depictions of tragic events in Fernie are full of clues as to how "foreigners" were perceived. Modern publications continue to print excerpts from these historical, on-the-spot accounts. The litany begins with the horrible mine explosion at Coal Creek in 1902 that killed 128 men. A recent paper on that event discusses the political context, reflecting a current focus on ethnic politics and labour exploitation: "The accident would leave a complex legacy of sorrow, resentment, heroism and social division ... The mining disaster would test the emotional strength of next of kin, bring class relations to a breaking point, and lead to a riot" (Yarmie 1998:195).

The *Free Press* emphasized the non-participation of "foreigners" during rescue operations (*FFP* 24 May 1902:1). Newspapers printed letters accusing "foreigners" of sending their earnings home rather than spending them in the community (Yarmie 1998:202). Workers turned against the Crowsnest Pass Coal Company, in part blaming it for hiring cheaper, and what were perceived to be less-experienced, "foreign" workers (*FFP* 31 May 1902:1).[23] In the early years of the new century, a series of investigations began into both the mine conditions and the hiring of non-British labourers. Perhaps the most significant outcome of investigations into the disaster was the recommendation to exclude "all workmen who cannot intelligently understand others and instructions given in the English language" (1903 in Yarmie 1998:202).[24]

Five years later, another disaster struck. Newspaper coverage of the devastating fire in 1908 continues to spark bitterness amongst those who self-identify as foreigners. In 1994 the *Free Press* issued a limited-edition historical booklet to commemorate the city's ninetieth anniversary, which included reprinted accounts of the 1908 Fernie fire. There is an unmistakable edge of Anglo-Saxonism in the descriptions of this event:

> Here, again, all national lines were obliterated, and here was shown in bold contrast the serene indifference to danger of the Anglo-Saxons. The Italian, with his excitable nature and glib tongue, the Oriental, with his inherent dread of danger, and his equally great regard for personal safety, the stoic Slavonian, all fought and struggled for points of vantage ... in too many cases utterly regardless of the safety and comfort of the women and children. Not so ye Britons! (*FFP* 1908 in *FFP* 1994:no page)

The *Cranbrook Herald* reported the more grisly details of death by fire while also noting amongst the dead the name of "a colored resident of the restricted district," as well as "four foreigners found in Old Town, names unknown" (6 August 1908 in Turnbull 1983:81-83). Once again, non-Anglo Europeans were portrayed as failing in the midst of danger. Added to this was a judgment about standards of hygiene: "Much of the foreign element has imperfect ideas of modern sanitation and its necessity and the task before the authorities is a heavy one" (*FFP* 14 August 1908:2). The moral character of "foreigners" was also now linked to states of pollution, through the increasing authority of hygiene specialists.

News of the fire was carried not only by newspapers but also by postcards and rumours. The local photographer, Spalding, printed a series of cards; most of these scenes were inscribed with the efforts following "the Great Fire" (see Figure 3). They are grim black-and-white photos of people amongst the rubble. One image titled "Getting Supplies at Relief Stores" shows people lined up for food and supplies (see Figure 4). The postcards fed publicity that brought donations from across western Canada. Rumours were also unleashed. There was speculation about embezzlement of relief funds and theories about the cause of the fire. A writer for the *Nelson Daily News* suggested that members of the Italian Black Hand Society set it to divert attention from their jail escape (4 August 1908 in Scott and Hanic 1979:146). Correlations between nationality, poverty, unemployment, and criminality were sharpening. From 1909, police books in Fernie list the name of the offender, the date of the offence, and the penalty. Next to some names the words "Jap," "Hindoo," and "Chinaman" are written in brackets.[25]

During the first decade or so of the twentieth century, headlines in the *Fernie Free Press* specified Japs, Italians, Slavonians, Scotch, Orangemen, and Chinks. Coverage of local disturbances continued to include speculation about the activities of the Black Hand Society. While representational conventions surrounding foreigners were becoming established in

Canada, indigenous and Asian peoples were also described using recognizable conventions. The "Yellow Problem" surfaced as a new public
issue of "celestial immigration." Here "the Almond-eyed Man" was represented – through opium, gambling, and polygamy – as a threat to Canadian society. In contrast to the indigenous people, whose character was
seemingly known, Asians were represented as essentially other: "Some
white men think they know the Chinese and the Japs. As well might a
swimmer in the ocean imagine that the depth of his dive gave him to
know the secrets of its dark, unfathomed caves" (*FFP* 19 June 1908:4).

In 1900 the Canadian government legislated a "head tax" of $100 for
each Chinese immigrant; this rose to $500 in 1903. The legislation had
the effect of severing men from their families in China. It left a defined
male population with few options of incorporation into Canadian society. A story entitled "Chink Runs Amuck" in the *Fernie Free Press* of 17
June 1910 illustrates the vulnerability of these men:

> So far as can be learned the Chinaman was waiting on two miners in How
> Foon's restaurant and the guests had their servitor scared to a panic by
> threats and pretences of violence. During the performance one of the men
> made a pass at the Celestial with a table knife and scratched him on the
> forehead. The sight of blood sent him out on the street in a fit.

Figure 3   News of the "Great Fire at Fernie, BC" was broadcast through a series
of postcards. Titled "Weighing Meat for Relief Supplies," this is the only
photograph in the Fernie and District Historical Society archives that appears to
include the presence of an Asian man (seated, left, on the wagon). *Photograph by
Spalding, 1 August 1908. Courtesy of the Fernie and District Historical Society, 0168-a.*

There is a notable absence of stories about indigenous people in the *Free Press* after the turn of the twentieth century. It is particularly striking given that indigenous leaders at this time were formally organizing and presenting political demands to government officials in England and Canada (Culhane 1987:80). An advertisement for the Sells-Floto Circus provides some clues about the reasons for this oversight and the eventual placement of "Indians" in settler imagination (see Figure 5). "Buffalo Bill, his Indians, Ranch Girls, Cowboys want to see all the boys and girls" (*FFP* 7 July 1914). The poster shows a profile of the man himself, giraffes, an elephant, and Mme Ricardo reclining on a lion. The circus boasts "600 people of all Nations" and the opportunity to "see the only living 5 Hyneys." At the top and centre of the poster is the profile of a bonneted Plains Indian. By 1914 the Wild West Show was losing its allure, and Bill Cody was recovering from bankruptcy (Francis 1992:95). The vivid imagery of the short-lived frontier was now becoming the stuff of western films. Perhaps, like the enigmatic disappearing "hyneys," indigenous people were seen to be vanishing. It is likely that both were rendered unrecognizable by strange representations that fed a hunger for exotic entertainment and nostalgia for conquest. As Elizabeth Furniss (1999:167) notes, such representations fed into a developing national narrative: "Native Americans were not presented as static curiosities ... As Indians,

Figure 4 "Getting Supplies at Relief Stores after the Great Fire." Postcards such as this one, showing disaster in BC, led to a surge of relief supplies from across Canada. Many viewed the (now homeless) residents of Fernie as "refugees." *Photograph by Spalding, 1 August 1908. Courtesy of the Fernie and District Historical Society, 0167-a.*

Figure 5 In 1914 Buffalo Bill and the Sells-Floto Circus arrived to entertain Fernie residents. Although film was beginning to rise in popularity at this time, the advertisement provides a glimpse of popular public spectacles that included Wild West re-enactments, displays of "people of all nations," "untamed beasts," and a two-mile-long parade. *Fernie Free Press*, 7 July 1914.

they were critical to [the] colonial script: their exotic cultures represented the 'primitiveness' of the early inhabitants that would naturally give way to European 'civilization'; their resistance to the settlers was essential for the affirmation of a narrative of history as heroic conquest."

Like other colonized peoples across the world, indigenous peoples in Canada were rendered entirely knowable through staged appearances. Their imagery, dress, and customs became powerful symbols within new national identities. Interactions between Europeans and Ktunaxa people continued in the Elk Valley, but these were now shaped by the social and territorial segregation wrought by the Indian Act.

Opium appeared in police records around 1914, as did a new variety of criminal described then as "enemy alien." Further influence of the First World War was inscribed through penalties for having "no documents" or being in possession of "unlawful literature." This period was to bring a sudden closure to the seemingly unobstructed flow of images and ideas across the world.

"Enemy Aliens" and Bolsheviks

I am looking at a photograph of a young, serious man in a coarse uniform with shining buttons and belt buckle. He appears to be holding a riding crop or swagger stick (see Figure 6). On the back of the softened postcard, his mother, my great-grandmother's sister, wrote:

> Will got his photo taken the day before he joined the army. It is very like him. This is fairly good, he is going to be taken at South End sometime. They may be better.
> Hannah

There are the usual mysteries created by the passage of time – Who are "they"? What will be better? Throughout the First World War, letters from the trenches were published in the *Fernie Free Press*. They are vivid descriptions of the brutality of that war and of the perceived character of the enemy.

I juxtapose another photograph here. It is an image of a three-storey building. Its balconies and doorways bulge with people identified as enemy aliens. A high barbed-wire fence frames the foreground (see Figure 7). This image was not in circulation as a postcard.

The First World War marks a terrible height of military nationalisms. The reigning European powers at this time were Britain, Russia, France, Austro-Hungary, Germany, and Italy. From the Fernie area, 1,100 men enlisted for the Great War (Phillips 1977:81).

Ktunaxa men joined the forces to serve overseas and many Italians returned to fight in their own armies after Italy joined the Allied forces in 1915.

Figure 6 Portrait postcards were common during the First World War. This image of Will Nattrass was sent to the author's great-grandmother by her sister Hannah, ca. 1916. *Courtesy of Margaret Castle.*

ITALIANS PREPARE: ... your country calls you! The Motherland has sent the call ... all natives of Italy, of service age, whether naturalized ... or not. All are ordered to report to the Consul and to come up for medical examination as to fitness. Transportation will be paid home to Italy and back to this country after the war. (*FFP*, 18 June 1915)

Several people with whom I spoke told me about their fathers and grand-fathers whose lives were ravaged by the continuing effects of nerve gas and shell shock. At this time, psychologists and medical doctors were in high demand; mental health became the focus in many nations. For those of non-Allied nationalities, the war in Canada was fought mostly through public opinion. The War Measures Act of 1914 brought in censorship, deportations, detentions, and arrests. German and Austro-Hungarian language papers were banned; "enemy aliens" lost their jobs.

In 1915 six hundred men rallied at the Socialist Hall in Fernie. "The miners of British, Belgian, Russian, Italian and Montenegrin descent combined to demand that all German and Austrian miners be dismissed"[26] (Norton and Verkerk 1998:67; see also Avery 1979:67, 71). Leaders of the United Mine Workers of America stood with the Crows Nest Pass Coal Company in refusing these demands. A strike ensued. The attorney general of British Columbia responded by ordering the provincial police to

Figure 7   During the First World War, this hotel was converted into the Morrissey Internment Camp for "enemy aliens." The visibility of armed soldiers, dogs, and barbed wire leaves little doubt about the forced confinement of these people. *Photograph taken 19 August 1916. Courtesy of the Fernie and District Historical Society, 1184.*

intern the German and Austrian miners. Local men were deputized, and over the following month or so they arrested 306 "enemy aliens." These people were detained first at the ice rink (see Figure 8), and later in nearby Morrissey (B. Dawson 1995:78).

Men who were naturalized and married were permitted to continue working; however, they had to report daily to the police station. Unmarried miners who were citizens were basically laid off. Non-naturalized married men whose families were overseas were interned, as were single men (Avery 1979:67). "Aliens" became the inversion of "citizens" at this time. In his discussion of the Canadian Immigration Act (1910), W.G. Smith (1920:94-95) defined "citizen" as: "(a) A person born in Canada who has not become an alien. (b) A British subject who has Canadian domicile. (c) A person who has been naturalized under the laws of Canada ... 'Alien' means ... a person who is not a British subject."[27]

Some people I spoke with note a silence on the part of relatives whose parents underwent the trauma of internment. The silence reverberates also in text. There are few historical renderings of this episode in local history (B. Dawson 1995:78; Norton and Verkerk 1998:66-92).[28] The *Free Press*

Figure 8   Photographer Spalding was "on the spot" to document "Austrians and Germans" detained at the ice rink in Fernie. In contrast to the scene at the Morrissey Internment Camp, detainees and their lightly armed guards posed for the camera. *Photograph by Spalding. Courtesy of the Fernie and District Historical Society, 3248do.*

at the time seemed to oscillate between describing the serious threat of these "undesirables," some of whom "openly approve of the mad policy of the Kaiser and his brood," and downplaying the severity of arrest. "There was no disorder and the men whose liberty was being taken from them till the end of the war appeared to be undismayed by the prospect" (*FFP* 11 June 1915:1). "Dancing and card playing is the main amusement at the internment camp. The Colonel is very popular with the prisoners owing to his removing the ban placed on the tango" (*FFP* 16 July 1915).[29]

An elderly woman described for me vivid early memories:

> They called us aliens. I'm still a little bitter about that. They used to
> hit us, they were always after us. Aliens. They said we were Austrians,
> and when we told them we were Bohemians, they said that Bohemia
> belongs to the Austrian Empire. We had to line up every morning
> and we were always last. We couldn't be in the front or the middle,
> we had to be last. There were soldiers training there [at Morrissey]
> and they told us they were going to shoot us. They aimed their rifles
> at us every morning when we went past. (Interview, 30 August 1997.
> Bohemian woman, born 1907; parents arrived 1903.)

For others, this era is represented by seemingly innocuous memories.

> Both my parents were born in England. [My dad] has a lot of
> memories of the concentration camp. My uncle was a guard there.
> *That must have been a hard time for people here.*
> ... If what you do is normal, then it's not difficult, is it? ... My dad
> talks about actually being quite friendly with the German soldiers.
> I don't know if there was a lot of fear. I think they were treated
> quite well, so they – I know they had gardens because my dad told
> me once his rabbits got out and ate the garden. I imagine there's a
> lot of people other than myself [who could tell you more]. (Interview,
> 18 September 1997. English-Canadian woman, born ca. 1930; father
> arrived 1906.)

It is the sense of what is "normal" – taken for granted, understood – that interests me here. How were men who may have been fellow workers now transformed into "German soldiers"? How did people justify the seizure of their neighbours' valuables and lands, the censorship of mail, and the outlawing of social interaction? How was it that people could witness this scene of confinement and forced labour under the armed supervision of soldiers? At least six people died in the camp at Morrissey. Others were wounded, shot attempting to escape. Clearly there was questioning. Internees were recognized in the paper as "oldtimers ... held in the highest personal regard by people of Fernie" (*FFP* 11 June 1915:1) and "personal friends" of Mayor Uphill (*FFP* 20 August 1915:1). Early accounts of the internment situation discussed its fiscal sensibleness.[30]

By 1914, anti-immigration rhetoric in Canada was clearly fuelled by eugenic reasoning. "Feeble-minded" people were institutionalized by this time, which both prevented these people from reproducing and "protected" Canadian society.[31] The internment of "aliens" was also rationalized as a means of protection. An announcement about correspondence to British, Russian, French, or Belgian prisoners of war provides some clues as to the state of censorship during this period. It instructs people not to send newspapers "on any account" and says that postcards are better to send than letters and that "communications should be limited to private and family news" (*FFP* 4 June 1915).

Some people, whose origins deemed them aliens, managed to evade officials.

> My father, he's written a little piece. I have a little piece that he wrote about himself and it clarified some points for me ... What happened to my father was, 1914 hit and that was the world war. My father, being Ukrainian, coming from western Ukraine, was Austrian because the Ukraine was under the Austro-Hungarian Empire at that point ... So he was caught here. They were putting people who were of Austrian origin – it didn't much matter what their nationality was ... putting them in concentration camps. So my father, not being too dumb, he hid among farms. So he would do farm work and live in a little, whatever they might let him have there. And then he would move along to another community ... He moved among the farms where he was invisible ... Four years he did this! (Interview, 4 November 1997. Ukrainian-Canadian woman, born 1925; father arrived 1912, mother arrived 1922.)

At the time her father arrived in Canada (1912), the western Ukraine was a territory of the Austro-Hungarian Empire. By the end of the war, Poland had taken over the region. In 1925 this woman's brother was denied passage to Canada on the basis of a disability. Her mother arrived that year and the parents never saw their son again. He eventually became the leader on a *kolkhoz*, a collective farm in operation during Soviet socialism. The Iron Curtain dropped and for twenty-five years the family had no communication with him. This woman's history weaves in and out of several political regimes in what is now the Ukraine. The family felt the force of Canadian immigration policy, wartime classifications, and the abrupt loss of contact with relatives in Soviet territories. People's histories are intertwined with shifting national boundaries; their lives are touched in dramatic ways by the enforcement of official categories dictated by states.

Predictably, the "Enemy Alien Problem" became fused with debates around immigration and rising fears of labour unrest. Immigration into Canada ceased during the First World War. Along with conscription in 1917, this led to a dire shortage of workers. The Enemy Alien Act was put away so that prisoners of war could be hired out to industry on contract with the Canadian government. Even though these workers were not permitted to unionize, were paid a pittance, and worked in abysmal conditions, the *Fernie Free Press* decried their presence: "It is humiliating to think that we should owe any part of the production necessary to the war effort to enemy aliens in our midst, and yet that is one of the curses of the immigration policy which has prevailed in the past. We have invited citizens of every European clime to make their homes in our midst ... The warning should guide our future immigration policy into better channels and all coming efforts should be confined to selective immigration" (*FFP* 28 August 1918).

What the author above refers to as the "curses of immigration policy" were now exacerbated by the threat of Bolshevism. The familiar constellation of nationality, criminality, and mentality fused "aliens" and "foreigners" with what was to prevail as the Red Scare.

BOLSHEVISM IN ALBERTA MINES ... A large part of the mining population is foreign, and the condition of the public mind at present is such that there is neither sympathy for nor understanding of these people. Almost every public policy in the last twelve months has tended to alienate, exasperate and rouse the foreign population. They have been disenfranchised, suspected, and in some instances exploited; almost everything which could be done to alienate them has been done. (*FFP* 28 August 1918)

The stigma of socialism hovered over Europeans in the Crowsnest Pass. After the First World War, a newspaper known as *Soviet Russia* was in wide distribution. "RCMP scoured Alberta, after three months of hunting they ran the point of publication down to the office of the Fernie Ledger" (*FFP* 2 September 1954:7). There are no public archives of this paper available in Fernie; however, many people with whom I spoke had something to say about Communism.

But my father was from Russia. You know where the Black Sea is? Well that's where he come from. When the Russian Revolution took place, he and his brother, they fled. His brother ended up in South America, the Argentine, and he landed up in Calgary ... Oh yeah, he had land from there that when the Revolution came in, they burnt

everything they owned! They had stock – took the cattle and burnt
the buildings. Oh that Russian Revolution was terrible! ... But in our
place my dad spoke Russian, now that was hard Russian, the good
Russian, you know. *Belorusski* – that means White Russian. My mother
talked Polish. She was quite – without an education she spoke any
language, and she spoke it well too ... [Pause] I worked for the
Communist Party. "Workers of the world unite – you've got nothing
to lose but your chains." I used to paint their bloody signs for them
... They were quite strong here in town ... And they used to hold
dances every weekend because I know we used to sneak over that
way and get heck when we got home. (Interview, 18 February 1998.
Russian-Canadian man, born ca. 1914; mother arrived 1914.)

People's identities are complicated. Nationalisms and political ideologies are grounded in lived circumstance and in received social knowledge.
   Scholars presently concerned with rising xenophobia in nations of the
European Union are looking at "American rhetoric and sentiment" that
surrounded immigration at the turn of the twentieth century (Bendix
and Klein 1993:8; see also Stolcke 1995:2). Through "national political
repertoires" (Stolcke 1995:2) and their intersection with "expressive culture" (Bendix and Klein 1993:5), they identify discourses that constitute
commonsense images of the world. As in the context of colonial discovery and possession, procedures for the selection of immigrants generated
images and typologies through which to imagine non-Anglo Europeans.
Ideas that fuelled these representations may be traced through intellectual
genealogies shared by scholars across Europe. The construction of European "types," using comparative anatomy, social evolution, eugenics, and
philology, produced categories of Anglo-Saxon, Aryan, and Nordic in contrast to predominantly rural Alpine or Mediterranean peoples. Superiority
was constructed through histories of conquest. Class was emphasized in
pedigree charts to mark out "paupers," "peasants," and labouring migrants.
Throughout these regimes of difference, "race" proves to be a flexible concept. The events of the Second World War slammed shut explicit eugenic
scholarship. Collaborating efforts of western European eugenists seem to
have disappeared from public view, leaving Germans as the architects of
this science. By the end of the war, however, many of these ideas had
secured a position in the education and socialization of Canadians. Official categories of human difference are deeply implicated in the events
that mark our sense of the past. Ethnic boundaries were to shift again in
the course of further upheaval, but the category of "foreigner" remains a
potent site of looking sideways for non-Anglo Europeans in Fernie.

3

"The Story As I Know It"

As I know it? [Laughing] The story as I know it is:

William Fernie comes to this valley and he's looking for, he's
looking for riches. We're not sure if it's gold or if it's coal. He meets
the Natives and they treat him very kindly. As they are preparing an
evening meal for him, he notices one of the princesses is wearing a
necklace of coal diamonds. So he knows that the family knows where
the coal is – they must know where the coal is. So he stays some time
and he falls in love with the daughter.

And he tells the chief, he says: "I will marry your daughter if you
will tell me where the coal is." So he tells him where the coal is, he
finds the coal seam, and then he decides to tell. He jilts the girl and
leaves. Doesn't marry her. As I think about that I wonder, well! He
says: "I will marry your daughter." As if he's really offering her
something! [Laughing] "I will marry your daughter if you tell me" –
yeah, I think about that! So he leaves and she is angry. She feels
angry and so she climbs Fernie Mountain and she gets to the top of
the mountain and she says, she lays [a curse]: "This place will die
of fire three times. Three fires. There will be three floods. And it will
finally die of famine."

And that's the story. (Interview, 16 April 1998. Slovak-Canadian
woman, born ca. 1933.)

I return to the well-worn narrative of the curse, heard and recited countless times by this woman. Her rendition does not erase the humanity or
agency of "Native" characters. Here are the details of a domestic setting:
a stranger who meets and accepts the hospitality of a family. His meals
are prepared for him and he is treated "very kindly." The teller understands the young woman's anger. The story is set in "this valley" and the
curse cast from the summit of a mountain now, ironically, named after
the protagonist. The words of the curse itself are specific in their details

of demise. There is the suggestion that particular aspects of the story have been debated. During this interview, the narrator enters into a dialogue with the story; most notably, she critiques the currency of a marriage offer. Many women with whom I spoke had something to say about the gendered treachery portrayed in the story. It is as though we are discussing the affairs of people with whom we share a community, witnessing a social transgression and the inevitable repercussions that follow. In this respect, the curse story is a narrative of justice.

I have analyzed the curse narrative as a story reinforcing ideas about who indigenous people are in the context of early colonialism. Here I want to explore the story through beliefs and practices that constitute a particular kind of social knowledge. What I hope to achieve is the presentation of a social context that makes the idea of cursing credible.

After the turn of the twentieth century, residents of Fernie experienced an alarming sequence of events that drastically shaped historical consciousness into the present. It is during this period of time that I imagine the story of the curse gained its narrative power. In 1897, 1902, 1916, 1923, and 1948, rising river levels caused severe floods. Mud slides have always plagued the rough roads along the Crowsnest Pass. Outbreaks of typhoid (1897 and 1902), smallpox (1902), scarlet fever, measles, chicken pox, and influenza (1918) took many lives. Between 1902 and 1967, 226 men were killed in the mines at Coal Creek, Morrissey, and Michel-Natal.[1] In 1904 and 1908 fires ripped through the town. Residents of Fernie risked starvation in 1911 after a heavy snowfall cut off railway transport. The following year a rock slide killed six men at Coal Creek. Memories of these disasters continue to circulate through reminiscences and media.

Economically, Fernie was at the mercy of the fluctuating coal market. After the First World War, residents plunged into widespread unemployment due to the declining demand for coal and the return of hundreds of veterans. Prior to the Depression, miners had already taken drastic wage cuts, and many worked only for one or two days a week. The local situation was exacerbated in 1923 by the bankruptcy of the Home Bank of Canada – many lost their life savings, businesses floundered. Mine closures followed downturns in the world market, labour strife, and further disasters. Company towns were closed down, and residents of Morrissey, Coal Creek, and Michel-Natal were, sometimes reluctantly, relocated. The curse narrative was conceivably gaining momentum with each successive turn of events. Perhaps people engaged with this narrative to come to terms with such occurrences.

I am interested in the interpretive and emotional resonance of the curse story, the ways that people recognize and live with it as a form of situated, local knowledge. According to Mikhail Bakhtin (1981), "a story cannot be viewed in isolation, as a monologic static entity, but must be seen in a dialogic or interactive framework; that is, all stories are told in voices" (in Bruner and Gorfain 1984:57). It is a sense of meaning that I hope to get at here, the sense that, in any situated telling, the "air is already warm with names" (Holquist 1981:xx). I will suspend this woman's voice in textual dialogue for some distance here in order to highlight our analytical conversations about the veracity of this story.

So, as I'm growing up, I believe in fairies as a kid. I believe. There's one of the poems that was by Rose Fyleman, and our books were full of her poetry. And it said if you look really quickly back into the garden, you'll see them. [Laughing] So I would do this on the back porch. I would be looking this way and then I'd take a quick look – I did it forever! I couldn't see the fairies. So if I believe in fairies, I believe in the possibility of [the curse]. Because I believed in fairies, I believed that possibly this could happen. (Interview, 16 April 1998. Slovak-Canadian woman, born ca. 1933.)

In an academic work, belief is a problematic concept to be wrestled and pinned down through analytic ways of thinking. The story of the curse implicates a sphere of ideas and practices pejoratively classified as "superstition" or "folk belief," at best as "conventional wisdom" or "folk science" (Ward 1996:693). Phillips Stevens (1997:201) uses the term "primitive physics" to speak about "a sophisticated set of ideas about the way the cosmos works" and understandings of the effects of human actions on natural forces. Questions around belief preoccupy scholars who focus on legend as a distinct genre of folklore. I favour an ambiguous definition of legend:

A legend is a story or narrative that may not be a story or narrative at all; it is set in a recent or historical past that may be conceived to be remote or anti-historical or really not past at all; it is believed to be true by some, false by others, and both or neither by most. (Georges 1971:18)

"Legend" may not be useful at all. Some suggest "quasi-historical wonder tale"; "fantasy in the real world"; or the fabulate, "a poetic creation of the larger ... community. A story continually communally re-created."[2]

Do you have any idea where you might first have heard it?
This story? Who told it to me first? Probably, I think, in our kid-games. From other children in the Annex, yes. That's what it would have been, yes. So I hear this – I think that it's possible. And every time there's a forest fire – there was a huge fire in Michel in the 40s – the fall-out of the ash here was really tremendous and I worried

about it. I can remember thinking: "Oh! This is one of the fires that's
going to burn us out." Also we had this fear of the Fernie fire. The
Fernie fire story, and it coming back and what happened to people. It
was so quick and will we get out in time? Those kinds of things. And
I suppose the reality of the Fernie fire – because there were two fires –
there was a smaller one and then there was the Fernie fire. The large
Fernie fire in 1908, I guess it was. And then there was never the
third, all right? So that third would be hanging over you. If it was in
Michel, I was a young child thinking: "This could be the one coming
through." And the '48 flood was a very serious flood, but of course
everyone was flooded, you know? ... I understood there were two
floods, two floods and two fires, but there was never a third.

But a final dying of famine.

And each time the mines would close or the mines would only
work two or three days a week, I'd think: "Now is this it? Is this the
curse coming true?" And actually, I heard other people refer to it also
when things were depressed in the coal market. I would hear, I'd be
having coffee with a friend and she'd say: "I wonder if ... " just a
passing remark, you know, it's not, not that I really know or believe
it. But the remark would come through. Is this the time that we're
going to – is this the time that Fernie will die? Is this it? (Interview,
16 April 1998. Slovak-Canadian woman, born ca. 1933.)

We are all, undeniably, born into environments already adorned with
dangling stories. Some stories are anchored to events that have left their
residue in the memories of those who teach us about the world. "Each
word tastes of the context and contexts in which it has lived its socially
charged life" (Bruner and Gorfain 1984:57). This woman refers to the
"Fernie fire story," known and felt across time through oral and written
renditions. The story seems as real as the intense possibility of another
fire. The curse legend could perhaps be called etiological because of its
potential to explain and predict a tragic series of events; likewise, it could
be categorized as a specific place legend, relevant to those whose memories are enmeshed there. Obviously the curse narrative has been the object
of conversation for some time. Contested details include who cast the
curse, the correct formula of the words, and its power to actually affect
the physical world.

*Would you say that there is anything in your cultural belief system on
cursing?*
I've thought about that because my parents were not superstitious
at all. Not at all. In fact, I often heard my mother talk about
superstitions from the old country, and she really disliked them.

I don't know about any religious things either. There's nothing in my religion that would. I think it's just my own imagination. Young imagination. I think that's what it is. There's nothing in my religion, although I know of people who have taken, have been in the same classrooms that I was in, and I can't believe they heard what they've heard! It's nuts! They were in the same place I was and their belief system was completely different to mine. I don't know how that happened because I thought everyone believed what I believe. We all attended the Catholic school, we had the same teachers, the parents weren't – well, I don't know, I don't know what their parents were like. We didn't think they were that different. Those things amaze me – that classmates feel this way, you know? So it does happen. (Interview, 16 April 1998. Slovak-Canadian woman, born ca. 1933.)

We return to belief, sparked by my question about "culture," an occupational bias. Many Slavic-speaking people I interviewed told me of their family's rejection of "traditional" beliefs and imposed religions.[3] This woman suggests that "superstition" is an alternative to "religious things." What most interests me here is our common recognition of multiple meanings expressed through cultural lenses, religious belief, formal education, or family values. There is at base an understanding that knowledge is socially derived and meaning is negotiated in the spaces between everyday interaction and history.[4]

What do you see the function of that story – or stories in general – being? Well, I thought that story, I think the big stories mean you can do nothing about this. This valley is cursed, is going to die of famine, so why build anything! It's absolutely useless to do anything with this place. Did people actually believe that? Some people didn't believe it. Only when things went wrong ... When things were going wrong I would hear it. Not exactly blame, just a comment again. It's never that strong. No. And yet if it's never that strong, then why do I say that it's useless to do anything because the curse is here? I don't know. (Interview, 16 April 1998. Slovak-Canadian woman, born ca. 1933.)

There are several ways to approach "big stories." Our conversation, frozen here in text, shows the ambiguity on both our parts to fully apprehend how.

Thinking Supernaturally
Fernie's curse is what some would call a "serious categorical curse ... [a] declaration, [or] utterance automatically chang[ing] the world" (Danet and

Bogoch 1992:136). Many scholars view supernatural thinking through pragmatic lenses. Such beliefs are seen to be instructive; they carry lessons that protect individuals from harm. As explanation, beliefs offer reasons for unfortunate events. Supernatural phenomena may function to provide emotional comfort in dangerous times. Throughout my research, people expressed all of the above perspectives when asked about the curse story. The Ktunaxa woman, whose ancestor perhaps cast the curse, suggested the instructive role of supernatural thinking.

> Even today, you will hear people that are my mother's age from the reserve say: "You don't whistle at night." Okay, that's taboo. They don't tell you why lots of times. But it's: "Don't whistle at night – the bad spirits will get you, something will get you." But if you take that back not so many generations, if you were out in the dark and your enemy's around, if you're whistling, they know you're there. And there you go! It was designed as stories to tell children so that they could comprehend. Okay, don't whistle because something bad will happen to me. But the parents didn't go on to say: "Otherwise the Blackfeet are going to get you in the middle of the night or something. They're going to know where you are and get you."
> It's kind of a way of telling a story, but with a practical purpose of protecting your children. (Interview, 11 December 1997. Ktunaxa woman, born 1955.)

Most introductions to scholarly treatments of magical thought reverberate with the explanatory use of such beliefs. Particular oral traditions require investigation. The curse narrative may simply be something "good to think with" (Darnton 1984:4). I asked an Italian woman about the story.

> If I've learned anything, maybe in every story there's a grain of truth to it. What is so unbelievable about the fact that maybe this man was unscrupulous and that he did come here and he did make a promise and he did say, I mean, that is not unheard of. Men still do that today. Not for a coal seam, but for other things, right? They'll make promises just to get something ... I mean, perhaps the story is not really so much to do about coal but about other things, right? And yes, I believe that they could have put a curse because they were angry and upset. I mean, Italians will do that – they put curses, they send curses ... Oh yes, I remember hearing the older Italians saying: "Oh, you know, I cursed so and so. I hope they die tomorrow." I've heard stuff like that growing up over the years. Yes, I believe there is some grain of truth to it. (Interview, 28 July 1998. Italian woman, born 1945.)

Regardless of how people approach supernatural thinking, its veracity requires a context within which it is both useful and plausible.

I want to take seriously the idea of cursing. I will keep this idea turning, approach it through historical events, through ideas of belief, and through lenses of analytical traditions. I discuss cursing through the works of other scholars who have studied word magic, witchcraft, and sorcery as social acts. My analysis works outward from the ways that participants spoke about these ideas. Some people hesitated. Their caution has much to do with the social stigma attached to "superstition" – another tool in the construction of human difference. I situate the curse legend and the act of cursing within several contexts of social knowledge: cultural beliefs and rituals, coal-mining folklore, medical knowledge, and anxieties around war. Fernie is an intensely diverse setting. I do not wish to collapse the complexities of belief used by people, but I do suggest that through these diverse cultural lenses, similar concepts arise, albeit using different frames of reference. The cornerstone is a shared time and place, a present within which the same events are experienced.

Cursing as a Social Act

What if we take seriously the idea that our world is infused with symbols and forces outside of what we are able to prove, and which we are capable of affecting through thought, word, or action? The now taken-for-granted anthropological axiom of suspending disbelief comes into play. Cursing is categorized as a conversational genre that "attempts to influence social, natural, and supernatural phenomena through the bare power of the embodied and spoken word" (Abrahams 1976:201). The power rests in "magical beliefs concerning the effectiveness of the words which make up the curse" (Shai 1978:40). From a traditional anthropological perspective, this is the realm of sympathetic or word magic. Bronislaw Malinowski (1965:49-53) argued for recognition of magical language as "eminently intelligible" acts within particular social contexts.

Scholars interested in magical acts and beliefs focus on witchcraft and sorcery, although acknowledging the slippery terrain of definition.[5] Magic, witchcraft, and divination are "real in that they represent actual classes of actions and beliefs intimately related to the human problem of control in known cultures" (Lessa and Vogt 1979:332; see also Stevens 1997:199). Cursing may be viewed as an act that is "bound with concepts of justice" and used "to bring about changes in public opinion" (Shai 1978:39). The approach is alluring, as recent analyses of cursing show. All are grounded in the struggle for social control: to enforce adherence to religious doctrines (Brunvand 1971:202), to affect events in contexts where women have little public power (Shai 1978:45; Fiume 1996:122), to threaten those who contest the authority of dominating religious institutions (Gaudet

1988:207), or as a legitimate way for elderly persons to "vent anger" (Lehman 1997:142-143). All agree that cursing must be approached within the specific contexts of a social setting.

Many people with whom I worked expressed belief in curses, although few offered a detailed cosmology. I honour the wishes of Ktunaxa elders with whom I met and their concern to limit representation of their traditions; I did not, therefore, pursue this topic with them. Older people of Polish, Russian, and Czech backgrounds acknowledged cursing but see-sawed in their descriptions of the phenomenon. My questions about the curse story cued Italian women to speak with me about *mal'uocchiu,* translated as the "crooked eye." Their descriptions imply the coexistence of such beliefs with Roman Catholicism.

The evil eye was given to you even if it wasn't meant as an evil thing, they said. You could see a beautiful young woman walking down the street and saying: "My, isn't she beautiful," and you could put the mal'uocchiu on her. You could cause, you know, something bad to – it's almost like when Jesus said in the parables, he looked at the fig tree and it withered. It's almost like this is what they're talking about ... It's said and thought ... Some people were known to, could counteract the evil eye by prayers and utterances and, uh, things that are only known to them. (Interview, 28 July 1998. Italian woman, born 1945.)

Cursing appears frequently in the Old and New Testaments. In one bible under the index heading "Curses," I found the following references: Genesis 3:14 and 12:3; Leviticus 24:15; Job 2:9; Matthew 5:44 and 26:74; Mark 11:21 and 14:71; Luke 6:28. I was told that many people in Fernie adhere to practices surrounding the crooked eye that include enlisting the powers of old women who possess the knowledge to counteract it. According to those who spoke with me about mal'uocchiu, ill will, consciously propelled by jealousy, may be cast through spoken compliments or looks, or, when one is unaware of feelings of envy *(invidia),* through unconscious thoughts. Intention is ambiguous in explanations about mal'uocchiu and *affascinato,* translated as "fascination."

Many older Italian women were more comfortable speaking their own dialect, and I often worked with a translator.

She said with the *affascinato* or the mal'uocchiu or the curse, she said it's like even you have a beautiful house and I come and I'm envious of it, she said you can place a curse without even realizing ... I get jealous – she said that's where, even in this manner ... She said you could even get sick because someone will see your beautiful house and the jealousy can make you ill. Their jealousy can be transferred to you as an illness ... She says you usually have a feeling of who, an intuitive feeling of who might have done that to you.

So they don't even have to be conscious of it?

No.

And you don't have to speak it?

No. Just the thought.

I'm just asking how she takes the curse out.

She said ... even if somebody sees you and they like the way you're talking and the way you're looking, she said just by talking to you, by just thinking, they can, it can just hit you, you know, the way she just gestured. It can hit you just with their thought. (Translation during interview, 8 August 1998. Italian woman, born 1920.)

At this time, another Calabrian woman joined our kitchen conversation. They spoke with the voice of expert knowledge as they further elaborated the different forms of cursing. Mary, the translator, moved between the opinions of the women.

She believes that with curses, God intervenes ...

She believes in curses, but she believes that it works in reverse – that if you send a curse to someone, to their child say, that curse will come back on you ...

She believes that it's possible to send generational curses[6] ...

She doesn't really, really believe in that ... But for the *affascinato* for "e mal'uocchiu," she says everybody, they agree, everybody believes in that, but as far as cursing, one believes and one doesn't ...

She just feels that things that are considered curses by some people are just a destiny to the other person and that it really isn't sent by anyone in particular – it's just your destiny. Most of these Italians really believe in destiny ... She believes that destiny is something that's preordained for you in life by God ... Before birth, when you come on this earth, God says this is what your life is going to be like. This is going to happen to you and all these things that happened to you are preordained, predetermined. (Translation during interview, 8 August 1998. Italian women, born 1920 and 1918.)

Through their animated discussion, I understood that curses, destiny, and mal'uocchiu are relevant topics of conversation.

Scholarly analyses of the evil eye complex are intriguing. Most writers acknowledge the widespread appearance of this belief across the world, and they agree that vitality of belief depends to a large degree upon supportive mechanisms within dense social networks. For Italians who have stayed in Fernie, many of whom were sponsored by compatriots, immigration prolongs the life of such beliefs. In Scottish and English folklore, the evil eye was called "over-looking" (Jones 1981:151). Apparently this belief complex did not make the journey to nineteenth-century America. Eastern Europeans in Fernie spoke to me about their dwindling numbers and the impenetrable wall of Communism that blocked communication and travel. While some acknowledged their parents' belief in the evil eye, few adhered to any structured ideas surrounding it.

Initially, I was surprised by the willingness of people to speak on these topics. There appeared to be little self-consciousness about their actions and ideas. A sense of secrecy, however, hovered around certain topics that arose.

> Oh yeah, she remembers, but she doesn't want to say any of the words ...
> Oh, I'll tell you one of the bad things. If you didn't give [gifts to people coming to your door during a February festival in Italy], she said: "As many hairs as a donkey has, may you have lice on your hair."
> *It's like a curse?*
> Yes, yes, that's exactly what it was, a curse ... But she said if you gave them a really good gift, they would send you a blessing, they would say, "May your daughter become a queen or may your son become a prince." But if you didn't give them anything, they would curse you. (Translation during interview, 8 August 1998. Italian woman, born 1918.)

Some who spoke the words of curses did so only after qualifying the context (an ethnographic interview) in which we were speaking. The actual formulae of prayers and spells were never offered. "The act, in witchcraft, is the word ... Now, witchcraft is spoken words; but these spoken words are power, and not knowledge or information" (Favret-Saada 1977:9). When words are considered a form of power, the ethnographer herself is gaining not merely information, but also potential supernatural ability. This understanding calls for a turn away from an "ethnographic theory of language" towards the "language of magic" (Tambiah 1968:185). Reading over transcripts, I now recognize a frontier at which our dialogues stopped or were discreetly diverted. I did not pursue off-limit topics, but on several occasions people questioned my intentions before proceeding.

> *How do you protect yourself?*
> **She just wants to know why we wanted to know this, and I told her it was because you were studying.**
> *Yeah. It's okay if it's secret knowledge.*

Si tu non voglia parlare.
No. No. No. Ma io voglia sapere.
No. She just wanted to know – she said, why we were interested ...
È importante. È importante ... (Interview, 8 August 1998. Italian woman, born 1920.)

One evening an elderly woman, recognized for her abilities to *calma affascina,* or remove mal'uocchiu, looked into my eyes. She spoke through her daughter, saying that people with dark eyes were susceptible to, and capable of, the crooked eye. Her daughter said: "Only Italians do it." This statement drew an ethnic boundary, circumscribing expertise particular to Italians. Not all Italians with whom I spoke expressed belief in mal'uocchiu. The knowledge and authority to perform rituals was gender specific, confined to the world of older women. For the most part, first-generation Canadian men laughed it off as "superstition."

Superstition
"Superstition" is stigmatized in mainstream society, viewed with ridicule especially by religious, medical, and educational authorities. In Britain during the early 1800s, churches publicly targeted magical belief as "stupendous monument[s] of national weakness, ignorance and disgrace" (1808 in Davis 1999:46). Legislation followed; persons practising astrology, fortune-telling, and other "occult" arts were liable to prosecution under the British Vagrancy Act of 1824 (54-55). After the Education Act of 1870, the attack on superstitious practices turned away from rural people towards labouring classes. Education failed, however, as cases involving witchcraft continued to be heard in British courts well into the twentieth century. Science in particular has worked against ideas that are beyond the reach of its methodology. In James Frazer's (1922:11) nineteenth-century language: "Magic is a spurious system of natural law as well as a fallacious guide of conduct; it is a false science as well as an abortive art." Jeanne Favret-Saada (1977:5) critiques the endurance of intellectualist thinking and the prejudices it carries: "Do you really have to do thirty months of fieldwork to be in a position to say that country people are just as well able to cope with causal relations as anyone else, and to make the suggestion that witchcraft cannot be reduced to a physical theory, although it does indeed imply a certain kind of causality?"

Judgments about superstition were part of the complex of otherness aimed at "peasants" and "primitives." In present-day Fernie (and elsewhere), people continue to mark difference through the rituals and beliefs of others. Elderly people described cremation ceremonies of early Sikh residents. Some speculated about the men of Chinatown; "eerie" music and opium smoking seemed tied to exotic ritual in these accounts. In contrast to how they described their own practices, people dubbed the religious performances of others "hocus-pocus." The term arose frequently in discussions about the curse-lifting ceremony and about contemporary powwows. Some people used the word "superstition" pejoratively to mark out a "backwards" class of immigrants who have not fully assimilated "modern" Canadian values. Education seemed to be the critical defining point here.

During fieldwork, forms of magical and religious thinking were also described as expressions of self-identity. Words of blessing, hand gestures, charms, and the use of salt, herbs, and medicines were all offered as forms of protection. Holy images of saints hang in homes or appear on medallions and cards (see Figure 9). People use these images in practical pursuits. I was told about the power of prayers and blessings of persons, homes, and objects. Catholics told me about the "novena," special prayers said over a certain number of days to a saint or Jesus or the Madonna asking for a particular favour. Some expressed their belief in faith healing and miracles. Culinary and house magic were brought up often by people from British backgrounds: the stirring of a Christmas pudding or the yearly spiritual (and physical) cleansing of a house, the "first-footing" ceremony at New Year's, and the "shivaree" following weddings. Some people had rowan trees in their yards, originally planted to ward off witchcraft. People of all backgrounds offered personal dream narratives wrapped in stories predicting the death or illness of close friends or relatives and problems in childbirth. Many people of a certain generation, across nationalities, adhered to word taboos, particularly around the speaking of names of deceased persons and the devil. Alongside different cultural and religious cosmologies, people hail from different generations of shared social knowledge and experience. Mining, in particular, is embedded in supernatural lore.

The Miners' Mark

> I, Princess Nootka, say this place will always be a bad omen
> to all men, white or red. The earth will shake and explode.
> Water will cover its surface and fire will destroy all that is built
> upon it. This is my curse, and it shall be so until the burning
> rock is no longer taken from the earth. It shall be so until men
> fail to make profit from my betrayal.
> – David Scott and Edna Hanic, *East Kootenay Chronicle*

Yet another version of the curse itself. This curse reeks of a representational context loaded with recognizable imagery. Indigenous societies are

Figure 9 Born into a wealthy Portuguese family, St. Anthony of Padua (1195-
1231) later chose life as a poor Franciscan monk, working briefly as a missionary
in Morocco. Returning home, he was shipwrecked on the coast of Sicily, after
which he travelled widely in Italy and France. Speaker of many languages, he
was a popular preacher and is often shown, as here, carrying the Infant Jesus.
Renowned for his miracles, he is the patron saint of Native Americans, the
elderly, the oppressed, paupers, and animals. He is especially receptive to prayers
for lost objects. In Fernie, St. Anthony's image adorns the walls of many Italian
households. *Courtesy of Mrs. Rose Albo.*

collapsed into a single popular image of "Nootka," a name that passed into common use through mistaken cross-cultural translation. Phenotypic categories of white and red are a given. Details of calamity are almost biblical in their epic intensity. The utterance of this curse ends with its moral: greedy people who seek wealth through the exploitation of others will incur justified wrath for their wrongdoings.

A Ktunaxa participant in this research suggested that her ancestor cast the curse in response to the thievery she witnessed. As the sometimes grossly exploited labourers in the mining industry that followed, European residents in Fernie played a different role in economic expansion. The curse may be interpreted as a narrative used to contest, or critique, the authority of the coal company. In the face of further disaster, the story became a vital imaginative resource to Fernie residents.

"The date of May 22, 1902 is regarded as one of the grimmest in the mining annals of Canada. About 7 o'clock in the evening a tremendous blast shook the entire Coal Creek area, kindling a deep and suspicious fear in the hearts of the inhabitants. By the time the grisly evidence had been accumulated it was found that 128 men had met a premature end" (Mangan 1977a:35). Following and event a newspaper writer wrote: "Fernie is in a condition of gloom and resounds with the hopeless cries of widows and orphans" (*FFP* 1902 in Turnbull 1983:77). At the time of this terrible explosion, visual conventions allowed for the photographing of funerals. Gruesome descriptions abound in popular histories of the area. One work describes the preparation of corpses, the "stench of burnt flesh" along with the undertaker's "atomizer of perfume," and the need for quick burial and the observance of "old country" vigils (Scott and Hanic 1979:140-142). There is the suggestion that conflict arose between "foreigners," who insisted on proper (and time-consuming) rites of death, and Anglo Europeans, whose religious beliefs did not require such rituals. Funerals were conducted for four days following the explosion; many miners were never identified. Popular histories emphasize flourishing "superstitions" and "old country" customs of miners. Among these, the "miner's mark ... a smear of coal dust on the shoulder blade, was considered a very bad omen to accidentally remove" (140). Apparently women who washed the bodies took care to leave this mark intact, as did fellow miners who, after their shifts, scrubbed "each other's backs very carefully" (Hutcheson 1973:27-28).[7]

It is difficult to know how to approach an understanding of ideas in the air at this time. Given the intense fraternity of workers, occupational folklore or "industrial legend" may be a fruitful avenue through which to explore this past reality (E. Slotkin 1988:97). Writing about the anthracite mines in the US, George Korson (1938:149) remarks upon "how strikingly parallel were the superstitions and picturesque customs of English-speaking miners and those of the Germans and the Slavs."[8] Although specific beliefs were grounded in different religions, symbolic objects, and cultural imageries, all focus was on how to read a world infused with clues about how to stay alive.

Reminiscing about what he knew as a child in Fernie, Sydney Hutcheson (1973:26) writes: "I was familiar and practiced with every superstition that ever came out of Europe and Asia. We had large families from all over the world move into town to work in the coal mines and we boys were all able to understand one another's language, customs, games and superstitions to a certain degree ... Men that carried big knives were afraid of the devil and a woman that smoked cigarettes or cigars worked with the devil" (27). Iron and steel – particularly in the form of knives – were hung over beds, buried beneath thresholds, and carried to ward off witchcraft. Women took on various roles in beliefs regarding danger and pollution. Most insidious was the possibility that they were spell-casters or witches. In this case, women who smoked were targeted as agents of the devil. It is difficult not to impose a reading of this marking through the contemporary lens of gender politics and the patrolling of feminine traits. The curse narrative evokes gendered difference, constellations of belief, and ideas about inter-group intimacy.

It seems to me that Fernie is a place of a lot of legends and stories.
Oh yeah. There's lots of things going on! I'll tell you one about the curse that was put on Fernie, and this is as I know it. When William Fernie found the coal mines – this is the story – some Indian maid showed him where the coal was. And of course he left her. He was supposed to be going to marry her or something, and he left her, so the Indians put a curse on Fernie ...
When do you think you first heard that story?
From the day I was old enough to listen to it. It's been here all my life.
Who do you think started it?
I just finished telling you – the Indians started it. Supposedly. I told you old Fernie discovered the coal because this Indian maid showed him the way and he was going to marry her. And he didn't marry her. So the Indians put a curse on him. That was what happened, supposedly. I don't say it happened. That's the way it was told to me. That's the way it was told me, that's all I know. (Interview, 12 September 1997. English-Canadian man, born 1911.)

Once again there is hesitation – but there is also certainty. This man narrates a "supposed" chain of events in which a European man, "of course," does not follow through on his intent to marry an "Indian maid." The same story appeared in a newspaper article: "The curse of Fernie, according to Indian legend, came shortly after the town was born. Two brothers by the name of Fernie had married Indian women. One of the brothers later sent his wife back to her tribe. It was as a result of this insult that the girl's mother was said to have cursed the town. The long history of disaster and tragedy began shortly thereafter" (Kolfage 1967:11).

Legend, as a genre of narrative, begins with the breaking of some "taboo" or the "violation of a social norm" (Mullen 1971:411). According to many sources, William Fernie's act of abandonment has an air of common sense to it but jilting has dire resonance in the traditional value systems of all the people in Fernie.

Popular rituals and beliefs are infused with values that surround marriage and gender roles. My mother told me about one of them: the shivaree.

> Then there's the shivaree. It's an ancient, a medieval practice, I think, from France. It was spelt charivari. We called it shivaree. I didn't know anything about it, but the other kids did. They came by one day and told me to get ready, that we were going to do a shivaree that night. I guess someone was getting married. I don't remember who it was. We had pots and pans – we stood outside the gate – the lure was money. The idea was to annoy them, taunt them, yell at them until they threw money. I was maybe ten or eleven. (Interview, 12 May 1998. English-Canadian woman, born 1937.)

Originally the charivari was "used as an extralegal ritualized expression of disapproval that enforced community morality by publicly shaming transgressors" (M. Smith 1996:665-666). The actions were aimed at those who remarried too quickly, couples who broke rules of marriage between classes and age groups, adulterers, and "spouse beaters" (Darnton 1984:666).[9]

I had a conversation with my great-aunt about the curse story. She told me that, as a child, she was bothered by the description of coal diamonds around the neck of the princess. For years she had watched as her mother brought in coal from Lethbridge – shining anthracite coal. "Fernie coal," she said, "would just crumble into a mess if you wore it around your neck." Coal itself is surrounded by practices and beliefs thought to bring luck.

> Well I first-foot. I had to leave every bloody [New Year's] dance ... to go home before midnight to first-foot my mother and then I had to first-foot my Auntie ____ across the street and then my granddad's. They'd lock me out and I'd say: "Ma, they're shooting the guns. Can you hear the siren [signalling midnight]?"

"No. Just a minute, son. Not according to your father's clock. No."

And then she'd open the door and I'd have to walk in and give her a kiss and put a little piece of coal in her hand, and my father was waiting behind with a little shot of whiskey. "Down the hatch, Scotty." That's the only time he called me Scotty. And he'd give me a big hug and then he'd go in the kitchen and have a drink. (Interview, 8 July 1998. Italian-Canadian man, born 1936.)

I still like the idea of somebody coming in with something to wish you luck – food and warmth ... It's always supposed to be a tall, dark man that brings New Year's to you ... Basically, Mum always said to bring tea and coal. And that meant food for the year and warmth for the year. And "lang may yer lum reek" would be "long may your chimney smoke." If you get married, that's a saying they'd say and that meant warmth. (Interview, 14 November 1997. Scottish-Canadian woman, born ca. 1920.)

In *The Kingdom of Coal,* Donald Miller and Richard Sharpless (1985:9) outline themes of folklore circulating in mining communities. "Every important area of the coalfields had its own ... original folk-hero who supposedly first found coal in the vicinity." They cite the stories of several of these men who, after accidentally discovering coal, often end up "cheated and forlorn," then mysteriously disappear.

There used to be some details of what happened to William Fernie after as well. I can't remember. He never finds love, that's one of them. He never finds love. I can't remember what the others were. (Interview, 16 April 1998. Slovak-Canadian woman, born ca. 1933.)

That Mr. Fernie never did get married, eh? He died. We talked about it all the time. I remember. (Interview, 20 August 1998. Italian-Canadian woman, born 1930.)

As a narrative that speaks to gender inequality, the curse on William Fernie sentenced him to a life of loneliness and incomplete manhood that provides tellers with some sense of social justice.[10] As an industrial legend, the curse had the potential to explain death and disaster experienced by miners who were at the mercy of corporate interests.

William Fernie was not popular with the workers in Coal Creek. He symbolized the company that displayed little concern for its employees' housing and health. A series of circumstances following the 1902 mine explosion solidified anti-company sentiment. Impure drinking water led to an outbreak of typhoid; the company, which also owned housing, evicted ill tenants. Later that same year, miners went on strike for the first time in response to a lengthened workday. In January 1903, the *Free Press* ran an advertisement for one hundred miners to "get in on the ground floor" of the new Morrissey workings (*FFP* 10 January 1903). The danger and anxiety that surrounded underground mining is evident in participants' narratives.

> [Husband] It was like waiting for something to happen.
> [Wife] We were just, you know, we'd always wait for them to come home. My mother would hate to see him go. She never knew if he was coming back. You know, she'd just come over from Italy – it was so hard. It was a real nightmare and it was a panic sometimes ... I could always see that fearful look on her face and just hoping and watching by the door to see if they came home. Even in the winters, we used to have blizzards and they used to go and walk to the train [to Coal Creek] ... and you know, she'd never know if he got there. You could have been lost in a blizzard. The roads weren't ploughed. I always remember them talking about that, and it was real hard for them. (Interview, 9 September 1998. Italian-Canadian man and woman, born 1925 and 1928, respectively.)

Early mining communities were characterized by a sense of fatalism corresponding to the high incidence of injury and death. The volatile mines at Morrissey and Michel claimed the lives of twenty-five miners between 1902 and 1904. In 1916 and 1917 forty-six men were killed in Coal Creek and Michel.

> So you'd see the miners would get off ... [after] an explosion and they haven't got time to go into the wash house, so they came off [the train] with their hats and the black faces so you didn't know who was who. And waited and waited and waited to see if your father or brother or husband would come. I remember crying lots of times. And then my mother would look and she'd say: "Son, here comes your father." My sisters would be crying, whole families all over and then you'd see the stretchers come off, very discreetly covered with bradish cloth, eh. (Interview, July 8 1998. Italian-Canadian man, born 1936.)

Miners avoided work for several days after the funeral of a fellow worker.

The worst mine explosion in Canada's history occurred in 1914, when 189 men were killed in a methane gas explosion at Hillcrest, east of Fernie in the Crowsnest Pass. Within this climate of grieving and danger, it is important to take note of the imaginative resources at hand:

During the life of mines #1 east and #2, a continual struggle went on between the Curse and the miner's patron saint, Saint Barbara, with the Curse holding the upper hand at all times. (Hutcheson 1973:41)

The image is arresting. Two potent ways of knowing are intertwined. The saint is symbolic of protection.[11] She is locked in contest with the story of the curse, which represents eternal ill fortune.

In Fernie at this time, Methodist, Catholic, and Anglican churches were in operation. Many people of Greek and Russian Orthodoxy joined the Catholic parish. Organized religions have complicated histories in dealing with "superstition." In Britain, Anglicans blamed the persistence of beliefs on "survivals" of a Catholic past, thus evoking evolution (Davis 1999:13). Well into the twentieth century, Methodists were known to have strong supernaturalist leanings (13-18). Catholicism approaches supernatural phenomena with some flexibility.[12]

Set into the walls of Holy Family Catholic Church in Fernie (established 1912) are colourful stained-glass windows inscribed with dates and the names of individual and group donators. The likeness of St. Nicholas was donated by Russian Catholics, the Black Madonna by Polish members of the parish, and individuals presented the church with donations to pay for images of St. Patrick and St. Agnes. St. Barbara is not memorialized here. She is associated with storms and is also the traditional patron saint of artillery. That miners would choose this saint is understandable. They had frequent and intimate contact with dynamite. A woman told me about early days living in Hosmer, when they used to take in boarders who brought home dynamite that had frozen during the day. They kept the oven door open to thaw it at night. "One night – maybe someone slammed the door? I don't know. There was a big explosion. Up at the house we still have a piece of bone from [my brother's] head!" It is important to acknowledge the fine lines between life and death for people in early mining communities. Miners' narratives provide powerful images of the danger they faced.

Mind you, when it bumped[13] like that it was easy coal. You didn't have to dig it, you just had to shovel it. But this day it bumped so goddamned bad that we figured we were stuck in there. Holy God, well the goddamned roof come down – the floor came to meet the roof and just on the side, on the wall, there was a little space left, eh ... We got out of that one, but some of the guys wouldn't go back in the mine again ...
   But you went back in?
Oh yeah. Why not? If it's your time you're gonna go whether you're in or out, it don't matter. (Interview, 2 November 1998. Italian-Canadian man, born 1923.)

In Fernie a kind of pessimism surrounded the landscape itself:

> Lots of times when I was there I said: "Those mountains are going to
> fall down on everybody one of these days." I just know it. It's going
> to happen. I mean, it's, uh, flooding and everything, the fires and
> the coal mine explosions. It's just a matter of time before those
> mountains come down. In Coal Creek, even when I was a kid, in the
> one mountain when you're driving along, they had an explosion, it
> was, oh hell, probably before my mother was even born. You know,
> once you get something like that – a fire burning in a coal seam –
> you don't put it out. And that whole mountain is full of coal. So it
> just continues to burn. (Interview, 11 December 1997. Ktunaxa
> woman, born 1955.)

On one occasion on the road to Coal Creek, I was guided to a mountain
and told to look carefully at the northeast ridge. We waited silently for
some time until a defined plume of smoke spewed briefly from an unseen
opening into the winter air. It is another physical anchor in this landscape
that cues the story of the curse and connects it to coal-mining activity.

A Regional Curse

> In a cafe in [the South Country] ... an old man sat at an adjacent table,
> chain-smoking and drinking coffee. He began telling dirty jokes. Women
> ... politely avoided his addresses. He shouted to them by name – they
> gently told him they would listen to him another time. He asked me if
> I was married. Said it was a shame [that I wasn't]. Asked where I live.
> Fernie. "Oh," he said, "Fernie's a terrible place!" Said he had a friend
> who moved there because he was too elderly to stay [on his land]. His
> friend told him that Fernie is doomed. "The sky is falling there – you
> watch out, the sky is falling!" (Fieldnotes, 25 November 1997)

Themes of disaster and tragedy resound in published histories of the
Crowsnest Pass. A written account

> cannot be regarded as a mirror image of what actually happened ... [It]
> should be read as [a] version of a happening ... Like all storytelling, it
> sets the action in a frame of reference; it assumes a certain repertory of
> associations and responses on the part of its audience; and it provides
> meaningful shape to the raw stuff of experience. (Darnton 1984:78)

In 1997 yet another version of the curse appeared in a brochure
(Real Rockies Travel Planner and Vacation Guide 1997) advertising the Rocky

Mountain area: "The valley will suffer from fire, flood, strife and discord; all will finally die from fire and water!" This is a regional curse. Many miners worked, travelled, and lived in several different communities throughout the Crowsnest Pass. As Noel Ratch (1998:14) states: "'The Pass' and 'The [Elk] Valley' are often seen as one continuous region," bounded on the east by the prairies and to the west by the Kootenay River.

In 1903 calamity occurred, not in Fernie, but in another town of "the Pass": "Early Wednesday morning wild rumours of a dreadful disaster at Frank went flying over Fernie ... One of the most terrible rock slides known to civilization took place this morning when almost half our peaceful mining town was buried under millions of tons of rock from the summit of Turtle Mountain" (*FFP* 2 May 1903). The disaster struck near dawn on 29 April 1903. There were fantastic narratives arising from this event. Survivors' accounts of the Frank Slide are filled with strange coincidences and fortuitous circumstances. The disaster was blamed on earthquakes, gas explosions, and volcanic eruption. It was popular opinion that the slide was caused by "robbing that coal seam that was being operated" beneath it (Personal letter by Pearce, mines inspector 1915, in Kerr 1980:60). In Fernie, newspapers eagerly covered the event, anxious about the welfare of former residents now living in Frank. Amongst the stories told about the slide is "an old Indian legend that the mountain moved ... [this] discouraged the Indians from camping at its base" (Crowsnest Pass Historical Society 1980:12).[14]

One year later to the day, Fernie became the site of a "Terrible Conflagration" (*FFP* 29 April 1904:1). The fire, which took no lives but razed Fernie's commercial district, was the subject of front-page coverage for weeks. It was duly noted that the "Ire" had descended on "the anniversary of the Frank Slide" (*FFP* 29 April 1904): "The event abounded in tragic scenes, heroic efforts to check the demon's onward march and in scenes of plundering and debauchery that clearly brought out the varied traits of the human race" (*FFP* 6 May 1904:1). The personification of fire as an angry "demon" provides more than just a glimpse at rhetorical conventions. I think it worth considering that it also summons the imagery used to imagine such uncontrollable forces.

There is an interesting aside to be made here. During this year (1904), the Oblate Father Coccola became a priest in Fernie (Holy Family Church 1988:8). The parish had been troubled by "ethnic differences ... amongst Poles, Slavs, Italians and others who could not speak English" (8). Coccola, a Sicilian, "learned sufficient Slavonic language to hear confessions and bless homes" (8). He had worked at St. Mary's Mission with Ktunaxa people. Noel Ratch (1998:9) suggests that one of the likely sources for the story of the curse is this priest's chronicle, which inscribed details of "Indians" accidentally discovering the "black rock in the fire" and informing Mr.

Fernie. In the written history of the Fernie Parish, Coccola is described as "diplomatic." He mediated between the CPR and Ktunaxa authorities when conflict arose around the building of the railway. Certainly cursing would have been part of his cultural framework, if not also his religious one.[15]

Under the headline "Antiquity of the Oath," the following appeared in the *Free Press:*

> The oath is practically as old as history. As far back as we can go we find some form of appeal to the forces that are stronger than man. The oath calling God to witness is of course much later than that made in the name of the powers of nature, fire, flood and tempest or the ferocity of wild beasts or the terror of the pestilence. (*FFP* 3 July 1908:6)

This article is not proof of a belief in cursing or word power; however, it appears now as if to foreshadow the explanation of events about to occur.

On 31 July 1908, three miners were killed and twenty others "imprisoned" in a "bump" at Coal Creek. Two days later a fire totally devastated the city, leaving over six thousand people homeless and ten people dead. A second, more devastating, fire was added to the burden of disaster already carried by residents in the area. I have heard stories about the family who boiled in their well and about others who took refuge in the Elk River and in the coke ovens. Immediately following the fire, fear of disease and exposure were paramount. Accusations of sorcery, witchcraft, and magic abound in communities following disasters, plagues, and serial tragedies (Stephen 2000).

I came across a historical postcard in the archives of the Fernie museum. Postmarked 16 July 1909, the black-and-white image portrays a familiar form. Inscribed below the image are the words "Cave Mtn Fernie BC" (see Figure 10). It is a grainy portrait of Hosmer Mountain, signed by photographers Stant and Boddis. The cave on the mountain face appears as a smudge – not yet translated by mass media into the evocative Ghostrider. Nearly one year after the fire that devastated the city of Fernie, it is difficult to say whether the story of the curse was circulating. The Ghostrider was certainly not conceptualized at this time.

> We had fires and floods and when anything happened, well, it was the Indian curse. But they had the same Indian curse in Oklahoma too! And a few other places! [Laughing] When the Depression came, well, that was the Indians who put a curse on us of course. And when Coal Creek burned and we were kicked out of the town at midnight [1928], that was the Indian curse too. And of course the famine, well, just something that was there.
> *Is that a story you've heard since you were little?*

Yeah, we've always known there was a curse around here, always ...
It's just something people knew about. We maybe read it or maybe
heard somebody talk about it, and it just flits from place to place.
And I tell you, and you go home to Trail and tell it to somebody else.
But we always knew about it. We didn't really fear it. You know, this
and that.

Did you believe it?

Oh no. I believe more about a black cat walking in front of you being
bad luck than that! Or walking under a ladder – you didn't do that!
Those were my superstitions [laughing]. (Interview, 14 November
1997. Scottish-Canadian woman, born ca. 1920.)

The curse appears here as a form of knowledge "always known ...
always." This woman recognizes the promiscuity of stories, how they "flit"
from place to place. I imagine the Crowsnest Pass as a corridor where
passing rumours and legends brushed against each other, becoming inter-
mingled with the phantasmagoria derived from mobile imaginations.

In this rich narrative environment it is reasonable to speculate that the
curse story may have its origins in the oral traditions that made their way
across the Atlantic. According to Roger Absalom (1999:34), Italian "peasants" generate folklore that embraces themes of "real or supposed cata-
clysm" (plague, drought, famine, etc.). Their stories emphasize "struggle for

Figure 10   Postmarked 16 July 1909, this postcard of Cave Mountain (now
Hosmer) is the earliest photograph of the landmark in the Fernie and District
Historical Society archives. An older image appeared on eBay recently; the
historical society was unable to match the bid. *Photograph by Stant and Boddis.*
Courtesy of the Fernie and District Historical Society, #P-356.

an archetypal justice" within "apocalyptic transformations." There are other forms of social knowledge used by people in contexts of grief and disaster.

Medical Knowledge

In March 1902, the *Fernie Free Press* announced that "Rheo! Celebrated palmist" had arrived in Fernie: "Palmistry is a science as old as the world itself. It is recognized as an interesting and instructive study by the greatest scholars. It has nothing whatsoever to do with fortune-telling ... Reads your character, telling you your faults and virtues, tells you what business or profession you will be most successful in, the length of your life and the condition of your health, whether you will have changes or not, and if you will travel" (*FFP* 8 March 1902).

Notably, science is the authority called upon to grant legitimacy to the arts of the palmist. Advertisements for curative tonics and medicinal sodas began to appear in Fernie papers, sporting images of learned men lecturing with pointers or leaning over microscopes. Professional medical knowledge emerged in public arenas in the first decade of the twentieth century, competing with superstition for a hold on the social imagination.

> FORTUNE TELLING does not take into consideration the one essential to women's happiness – womanly health. The woman who is neglecting her health is neglecting the very foundation of good fortune. (*FFP* 30 July 1909)

> AFRAID OF GHOSTS: Many people are afraid of ghosts. Few people are afraid of germs. Yet the ghost is a fancy and the germ is a fact. If the germ could be magnified to a size equal to its terrors it would appear more terrible than any fire-breathing dragon ... They are in the air we breathe, the water we drink. (*FFP* 6 August 1909)

Authorities made new claims about causality and identified entities not visible to the human eye. What better avenue through which to represent the invisible realm of disease and to confer authority in medicine than by ideas and images already associated with another known world? After the turn of the century, the question was how to make this knowledge accessible. Medical authority was competing with several well-instilled forms of social knowledge.

> Oh God, yeah there was old Mrs. _____ [an Italian], she'd always pick wild plants and she'd treat all kinds of people. Do you know _____? His grandmother, that woman, she always wore dark clothes. It was her and Mrs. ____ [a Bohemian]. Christ, we'd wonder if they were old witches or what, you know. Bent old women with a sack on their back. They were either picking coal along the tracks or picking herbs

or weeds or whatever you want to call it, eh? And if you were sick you'd go to either [of them]. And they either gave you something to drink or a poultice or something. And by God it worked! (Interview, 2 November 1998. Italian-Canadian man, born 1923.)

During an interview with a Calabrian woman, I was shown a diverse array of objects and images in her home. Above pictures of Jesus hung a horseshoe; in the living room, Buddha sat below a crucifix; St. Anthony appeared both on a calendar sent from Italy and framed and hung above the doorway to her kitchen. The objects in her home resonate with meanings accumulated from relationships to people and places both near and distant. Many objects are enlisted for protection and the prevention of illnesses. Charms used to ward off ill forces are prolific. The jeweller in Fernie sells several that are used to deflect the crooked eye: the *mani cornuta* (a hand); the *cornetta* (a twisted horn); and *chiavi masculini* (an old-style metal key) (see images in Migliore 1997:48-49).

There's certain symbols that Italians wear to ward off evil, like, for instance, they'll wear a little horn, which is a total contradiction because the horn represents the devil. You're wearing it as a good-luck charm. So tell me, how does that work if you're wearing the little horn or the little hand that in Italy everybody wears? ... The little finger and the index finger held up so that it makes horns, right? ... You're supposed to put these horns behind you over your shoulder to say: "Satan get behind me!" But wearing them on your chest ... It's really a paradox of our beliefs ...
  Or like the symbol of the snakes. Just about everybody in Fernie I know, when they dress up, has a snakehead ring. I always just thought it was a fun thing to wear ... I wore it once and the nun saw me and said: "What are you wearing? You can't wear that!" And so I sold it ... She made me aware that that was a sign of Satan ... I thought, I won't give credence to anything to do with Satan including wearing his rings or his horns or his hands.
  Interesting that people use them to ward off evil.
Or to give them, to give them strength with the devil ... A lot of us poor unsuspecting Italians just wore them because it was considered a good-luck charm. Don't ask where all this came from. It's just superstition. (Interview, 28 July 1998. Italian woman, born 1945.)

In the extended care wing at the hospital, an elderly Italian woman repeatedly used the gesture of the mani cornuta towards me. It was accompanied by the softly repeated word "Benedicta." She was warding off the crooked eye through gesture and the uttering of a blessing.

My mother used to calma the *affasciana* ... I remember some of the
Italian people, if the kids were sick, too sick to bring up, they used
to send a stocking or a shoe or a little sock and she'd say this little
prayer over it, and if she yawned that baby was in a state of
affascinato. But she used to know all the prayers. I remember all the –
not the prayers, I shouldn't say that – all the wordings ... She'd close
herself in the bedroom and you know, we knew what was going on ...
She sends the article [of clothing] back and she tells the parents:
"Yes, è stata affascinato" or "No he's not affascinato" if they were
sick. (Interview, 9 September 1998. Italian-Canadian woman, born
ca. 1928.)

Women from many cultural groups in Fernie performed curing and mid-
wifery duties. Most acknowledged that their mothers and grandmothers
had learned these skills from their female predecessors. Rituals and prayers
used to *calma affascina* were traditionally learned from a maternal grandmother, as prescribed, on Christmas Eve.

The historical struggle between medical authority and "folk" medicine
involved a search for images and metaphors with a resonance powerful
enough to replace faith in older ways of knowing. In 1882, tuberculosis
was identified as a bacterial infection. Under the headline "War on White
Plague," a *Free Press* article reported on a tuberculosis exhibition in Montreal that, along with scientific lectures, *showed* "ravages caused by the
disease and methods by which to fight its progress" (*FFP* 27 November
1908:6). Like fire, disease was personified through familiar forms held
in the popular imagination – as an extraordinary entity or as an enemy
at war.

War and Cursing

I have another example of the slipperiness of past imagery. It is a postcard
of a black cat on a rooftop, sent to my grandmother by her grandmother
sometime during the First World War (see Figure 11). The inscription reads:

A black cat brings luck
So the old legends say
Let this be your mascot
For ever and aye.

The insane reality of the war exacerbated what was considered to be yet
another social problem. "Troubled waters created by the war have favored
the operations of those who dangle the dazzling bait of 'magic' before
the less wary fish of the human shoal" (1917 in Davis 1999:266). Fortune
tellers, spiritualists, and astrologers became the focus, during wartime, of

Figure 11 Periods of warfare generate a resurgence of "superstitious" beliefs. This card, sent to the author's grandmother during the First World War, depicts symbols that now have little resonance for younger generations. *Courtesy of Margaret Castle.*

state authorities who sought to control "their effect on public morale." These practitioners began to professionalize at a time when they were popular with soldiers of every rank and their family members of every class.

The imagery on the postcard intrigues me. It represents the gap in meaning that can occur in the space of one or two generations. Within the context of the First World War, it provides an example of a charm in circulation during the conflict. I showed this postcard to a scholar who had recently arrived in Canada from a nation in the throes of civil war. She suggested that the context of war generates resurgence in "superstitious" beliefs.

From the standpoint of the present, the black cat, crescent moon, and horseshoes are familiar symbols; it is their arrangement that puzzles me. The inscription tells us that this menacing-looking, almost totally black cat is the subject, in legends, of luck. In my view, the horseshoes, likewise, are inverted; they are positioned to allow for the draining of this elusive substance. The crescent moon, although familiar as a symbol, does not evoke a precise meaning for me. There is a kind of everyday knowledge at work here, a social world of symbols once understood, but now elusive.

The black cat is, at base, equated with witches – it is the preferred form of these shape-shifting persons. In spite of this (or perhaps because of it), black cats are perceived as "lucky"; although they represent the devil, the owner has a "talisman," and they are good "mascots."[16] In sixteenth- and seventeenth-century Europe, cats were tied to the domestic household, to women, and to sexuality. Most dramatically, they were important elements in community-wide "witch hunts" (Darnton 1984:83-101). Public rituals pivoted on the incinerations of cats in bonfires.[17] As an omen, black cats crossing one's path are generally bad luck, particularly on one's wedding day and for men in dangerous occupations on their way to the workplace. "There are conflicting beliefs regarding the influence of black cats. Some consider them a sure sign of good luck, others regard them with dread and awe" (Cielo 1918:70). Complicated distinctions arise between completely black cats and those with other tints. It is, perhaps, not without meaning that the cat in this image has white feet!

Horseshoes, likewise, are powerful symbols. "If hung with horns up, talisman against ill-luck ... to prevent the power of witches. A survival of the belief that elk horns guard against evil; also derived from the crescent moon" (Jobes 1962:791). The shape of the horseshoe is said to "cause evil to return back upon" witches (Opie and Tatem 1990:203). Iron, in general, was associated with warding off witchcraft; the shape also evokes the "two-finger gesture" of the mani cornuta, used to repel the devil and the crooked eye. Middle-class observers in late-nineteenth-century Britain saw the downturned horseshoe as a reflection of class. The suggestion was that, even in matters of "superstition," people in the countryside (mostly Scottish, Welsh, and Irish) were intellectually lacking. Clearly superstition was a public problem that occupied the minds of several observers.

> One reason why superstition has not yet died out among intelligent people is because it is contagious ... It was in the very air [in Salem]. It is the hardest thing to shake off superstitious prejudices. They are sucked, as it were, with our mother's milk, and become so interwoven with our thoughts that a very strong mind is required to shake them off. They become a sort of religion, semi-sacred in their appeal. No wonder that the lower classes cannot abandon them and that even men of intellect cling to them. (Cielo 1918:3)

Ideas of contagion and heredity of belief are not surprising in an era of eugenic policies linked to class distinctions. Late in the nineteenth century, belief was linked to ideas of degeneration and a fear of "a popular relapse into idolatry and paganism" (Davis 1999:46, 54). Perhaps predictably, superstition came to be seen as "a disease of the mind as fever or smallpox is a disease of the body" (1858 in Davis 1999:53). The metaphor is powerful.

During the First World War there was also a form of word magic afoot:

> A QUEER WHISTLE: ... celebrated war correspondent, describes a peculiar whistle carried by a number of the ambulance men in the German army ... the latest Germanic war machine; this particular invention of the devil is worked by compressed air. Put in a glass case in a museum with label of origin this little weapon would damn the German without further evidence ... A given German soldier lying helpless on the field of battle is of no further use to the state ... [The whistle is applied] to temple and heart or other vital spot. There is practically no noise and the work is always done at night. (*FFP* 4 June 1915)

Atrocity stories must be included as powerful emotional phenomena that mobilize hatred towards one's enemies and erase their suffering. Such "myths" transform humans into animals, demons, madmen, or other monstrous entities that appear during periods of warfare. According to Veena Das (1998:110), "panic-laden rumour" signals a breakdown in communication; it animates collective "memory composed of incomplete or interrupted social stories." The stories arise in surprisingly similar forms during different eras and amongst different national and cultural groups. Participants who lived in Europe during the Second World War spoke about rumours of the enemy in circulation at that time.

We had Germans look after us. I guess it was the Russians that they were, no, the Americans were coming and bombing. It was the American people and the Russian – they wanted to take over Italy I guess, and the Germans didn't want that. So the Germans were helping us fight ... But we were scared of the Russians. The Russians, they were telling us – they were coming to do bad things to us, you know, and people built some, like, little caves and stuff like that to hide the young people. (Interview, 25 August 1998. Italian woman, born ca. 1930.)

And then the first Americans came. And I bet you there was Canadians too. Oh, I tell you, we were so scared! Everybody was in their nightgowns. We had to stand in [gesturing a line]. We didn't know what he was saying. He had this [gesturing firing a rifle] bop, bop, bop, bop, bop – you know, this rifle. We don't know. And my mom, before they came in she bought some coffee in the black market for 120 marks, one pound. She put it in the toilet because she thought they were looking for coffee. And it was not even true – they were looking for guns. And we had no guns! ... Oh my God, we were scared ... Lots of women had kids from the Negroes. Oh I was scared! Everyone says: "They'll kill you, they'll cut your throat." And we believed it, you know. There was big, big trucks with all of those Negroes on top of them, and of course they talked to us and we didn't understand. So we ran like this. [Laughing] We were afraid they would come up behind us! Oh my God – at the time! (Interview, 22 June 1998. German woman, born 1920.)

Writing during Hitler's rise, Jacques Barzun (1937:171-189) identified "race fictions" that "carried meaning and satisfied emotions because they called up familiar ideas." He cited Nordic and Aryan myths, a mystification of "blood," "spirit," "soil," and forms of worship around dead war heroes. What he called a "hypnotizing reiteration" of "verbose mysticism" (177) was central to propaganda techniques used by Hitler, Mussolini, and the Allied leaders. Barzun is quick to point out that "wartime racism is only an extension of the normal thing" (170). In Canada, racialized people were also the subject of atrocity myths.

There was an old Chinese man – we called him Gopher. There were myths that he drank gopher's blood, that's why he's got that big wart on his head. At night after the curfew would go at nine o'clock, "Don't go past Gopher's place." So we'd get off the sidewalk and go the other way. (Interview, 8 July 1998. Italian-Scottish-Canadian man, born 1936.)

Gl' indiani? O siamo morte!

She said she nearly died when she saw them here. When she first saw them.

Why?

Oh, she said because she had heard that the Indians – like the Native Indians – would kill people. So she was frightened.

Was that something you heard in Italy or in Canada?

No qua – here ...

She said in Italy there was none so there was no such thing.

Neanche nero c'era à Italia.

She never saw blacks in Italy either. (Translation during interview, 8 August 1998. Italian woman, born 1920.)

The curse legend is an important element of local identity that cues particular kinds of social knowledge. It is bound to place through its association with historical events and local landscape. As a form of popular narrative, the story describes a formidable act of censure that summons ideas of justice. It may be seen as a kind of resistance narrative critiquing gender transgression. Likewise, it has been used to highlight greed and exploitation on the part of the coal companies. Different renditions also explain local tragedies. In the context of early coal mining, the narrative evokes experiential struggles of past generations in a language of images and symbols once commonly understood. "Superstition" has been used by dominant authorities, both as an avenue for introducing ideas and as a trait of "primitiveness" or "backwardness."

Throughout Part One I have examined narratives and ideas in circulation during particular historical contexts. These discourses transmit ideas about people; like curses, they affect the social world and the ways that people imagine their relationships. What I call the politics of cursing involves the transmission of powerful stories as political tools used to contest and maintain dominant ideas. Typologies of people are constructed through the social power of words inscribed in official documents and memoirs, transmitted through mass media, or embedded in popular narrative. Accusations of supernatural hostility and dehumanizing descriptions fill spaces in the vast distances between groups of people separated by war, colonialism, or the social barriers of class and language.

Part Two
Imagining Difference

No matter at what point one chooses to begin a story, there is always a prior story waiting to be activated, one that has been lying inert or circulating within only limited zones.

– Veena Das, *Specificities*

One morning in October 1997 I received a phone call from my friend across the street. She was concerned; neighbours were asking what was going on at Margaret's house. They saw a car, but they didn't see anyone coming or going. Worried that I was ill, she invited me for lunch. We had borscht and homemade rye bread. An old, cut-paged book sat on her table, a historical novel about the Enlightenment. Opening it to the front page, to an illustration of Voltaire, she spoke about the power that priests once held and about a Bohemian woman burned as a witch. She then pointed to a paragraph she had highlighted in a Jehovah's Witnesses *Watchtower*. It was the story of a Bohemian queen who, in the 1380s, had married an English king, translated the bible, and facilitated student exchanges between England and Prague. Her case was building towards a statement as she referenced another book detailing the history of Bohemians who came to America after they were run out of their own country. "You don't hear anything about it!" she exclaimed. Our conversation covered centuries of Czech history, religious oppression, and gender persecution.

She mentioned watching a television show about "Indians." "They were immaculately dressed," she said. "Like premiers and doctors with starched white shirts and suits. And those people *were* doctors and lawyers. They were talking about their future." She said she didn't think Aboriginal people would have had so many problems if they had not been put on reserves, in separate schools and places. "Like the immigrants that come from Europe," she said. "And now, they're giving all this money to people who come to the country. They land here and they get a cheque. It just makes me feel for the Indians!"

Her remarks about new immigrants receiving money prompted me to ask if she was speaking about the Roma people in Czechoslovakia, then the subject of much media attention.[1] She wasn't, but then she said: "Gypsies are people without a nation." She was confused about what makes them "a people," and we talked about language and belief and custom. Her parents spoke often about the Roma. "They stole children, and you had to be careful or else they would steal your goose!" (from Fieldnotes, 11 October 1997).

Images and ideas flew across that kitchen table; it was as lively a conversation as any I have had in academia. What distinguished this context, however, was the way experience was brought to bear on social theory. Notably, her understandings about people were derived both from her own social location and from her parents' narrated experiences.

In the following weeks I had several conversations about Czech Roma that summoned up popular discourses of difference, albeit from many perspectives. These people are stigmatized through atrocity myths as child-stealers, branded by poverty and criminality and by their absence of affiliation to a nation. Their history of persecution renders them easy targets for official propaganda in the Czech Republic and in North America.[2] I was surprised by the certainty in people's voices as they spoke about who Roma people are.

> An Austrian-Canadian woman contrasted the arrival of Roma to the plight of "enemy alien" miners during the First World War. "No one would hire them, they lost their jobs. English-speaking miners said they wouldn't work with them – they were afraid they would blow up the mines. There was no welfare in those days. And now you see all those Gypsies coming to Canada and getting right on welfare! By the droves! You see them [in Europe] when you get off the train. They're all over you. A woman with her baby: 'Please, my baby needs food.'" I spoke about the campaign of propaganda in Czechoslovakia enticing Roma people to leave for Canada – she finished my sentence, "to get them out, they want them to leave, and it's true – you see them."
> (Fieldnotes, 25 August 1997)

Not all descriptions were negative. Other people told stories about the resilience of Roma peoples in the face of absolute power, understandings that came from their parents and from the memory of distant places.

A Slovakian woman said her father's stories of Tzigan people honoured their strategies of resistance and their traditional knowledge. "Gypsies were able to eat diseased animal carcasses even after they were buried and poison was poured over them. The Gypsies ate it and they were fine." Her father told her how Roma begged for food scraps – fat or whatever was left over – and how these were used in ingenious ways. She said his stories always emphasized their exuberant music, their elaborate oratory, and their freedom. Her parents danced in the kitchen to Roma music, told stories about their actions during the Austro-Hungarian reign and the ensuing oppression by the church. Most of the stories praised these people for their cunning resistance to priests and military officers. The Tzigan who lived near her parents' town, she was told, had the foresight to leave when the communists came. These narratives trace the political history of her Slovakian parents, their views towards state and religious power. She mentioned to me that younger generations currently feel disdain for Roma people. Following the rise of the Iron Curtain, her relatives came to Canada. On one occasion they asked her if she would swim in the same water after "Indians" had swum there. She replied that she would. Their response was that they would not do that with Tzigan.

There are parallels here in the ideas about social pollution and segregation that brand Roma and indigenous peoples.

Imaginative resources are malleable. Contemporary events activate social knowledge derived from informal histories passed on through families and through official discourses generated by state authorities. In Part One I identified historical processes and hegemonic discourses that continue to exert an influence in people's lives. Throughout Part Two I discuss discourses and categories of difference people summon during periods of intense nationalism, contemporary colonialism, regionalism, and globalization. My intention is to highlight structures and discourses of power that take different shapes in different places, but operate in similar ways to assert a common-sense view of the world. Participants speak from diverse positions of age, locality, nationality, gender, religion, class, sexuality, and "race." They express strong, albeit diverging, opinions about the social power of words.

I spent most of my time in Fernie with members of the eldest generations, many of whom are well acquainted with my family. Through our extended dialogues I became aware of the ideological and experiential distances between different generations of people. We are all socialized within successive eras of ideas and structures of power that give meaning to what the social landscape looks like. Amongst younger people, cursing has lost the edge of relevance necessary for vivid transmission of legend, and other forms of folklore have been generated in step with changing ideas of community. I break my discussion into three primary areas of analysis: the transmission of ideas, narrative maps, and social spectacles.

Flows of information between people are mediated by different forms and by social sanctions that govern acceptable "talk." Ideas about human difference move across generations; they are learned in school, reinforced through political institutions, and broadcast by mass media. They inform our sense of social recognition and they inhabit our bodies, inspiring small acts of self-censorship. New forms of transmission are now appearing in the immediacy of cyberspace and the unlocatable somewheres of video games. Traditional belief in curses may now be the dominion of older generations and particular cultural groups; however, ideas about gossip and political correctness suggest that speech acts remain a potent social force.

Mountains and Fernie neighbourhoods

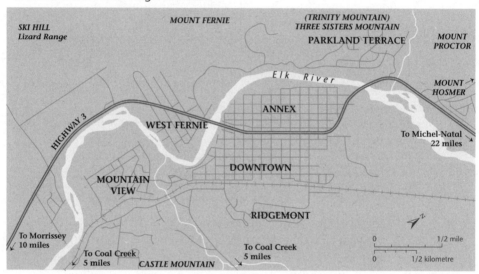

Old-timer's map

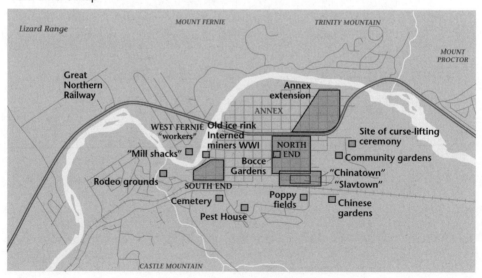

Middle-ager's map – Socio-economic

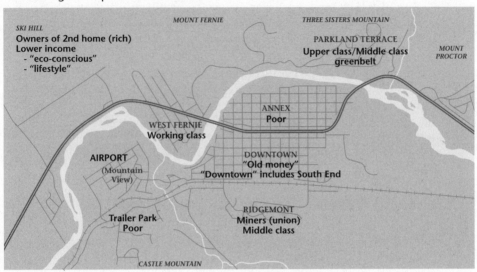

Teenager's map

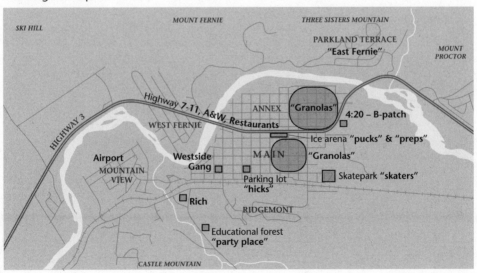

Difference has a spatial expression as well. I brought maps of the town with me to some interviews. People marked areas delineated by ethnicity, neighbourhood boundaries, occupation, and specific activities. During the mapping sessions, events and individuals came suddenly to mind. Spatially short distances were widened as people identified social categories seemingly worlds apart. Different age groups in Fernie narrate changing landscapes of people and places. Landmarks have shifted between generations, a sign of physical changes in the landscape but also in the social relevance of place as it relates to identity. Stories overlay conceptualizations of place, vibrantly providing access to the past through memories of shifting populations and social categories. How people narrate place and space brings attention to patterns of mobility, separateness, sociality, and belonging.

Across the axis of time and space, public performances are held at a particular place on a particular occasion. Embedded in shared understandings about the symbolic and social world, successful rituals, ceremonies, or entertainment events require some degree of meaningful display. They highlight imageries that resonate with the individual and collective expectations of particular audiences, and they legitimate social positions within a community. As such, social performances enact sometimes subtle taxonomies of difference. Ethnographically, public spectacles provide a view of imaginative displays that reproduce central tenets of social reality.

4
A Moment of Silence

So before you came to Canada, what were your ideas about America?
I never thought anything about it.
Did you ever read any Karl May?
No. My husband did. I didn't. I was afraid of the Indians anyways.
[Whispering] I was afraid. Oh yeah. They were out to kill us. That's
what you heard, you know! You heard it, everybody talked about it,
the Indians, they kill, they kill everybody, you know! They scalp!
Was that here or in Germany?
In Germany, you know. [Pause] They don't even bother you!
Do you know the story of the curse?
Curse?
Of William Fernie, the Ghostrider – that story.
Ah, this is nice when I see the Ghostrider. This is really lovely.
Can you tell me that story?
No. I don't know anything about it. I never heard a story. I just
know there is a rider – a horse and a rider, that's all. Nobody told me
a story.
*You don't know the story of the curse – with the fires and the floods and
the princess with her coal necklace?*
No. No. Never. How could we find out? I couldn't read, you know.
How can somebody tell me? They are all not born here. Nobody
practically was born here ... We never had friends, you know –
Canadian friends or so. When we moved into town, oh you should
have seen this place! (Interview, 22 June 1998. German woman,
born 1920.)

This woman has lived in Fernie for nearly fifty years. Her explanation for
not knowing the curse story has to do with her exclusion from a language
community. She makes a connection between birthplace and social knowledge, suggesting that this excludes her. I do not know why she has not

heard the legend of the curse, so spontaneously narrated by many of her age. This rupture in the flow of a seemingly well-known narrative raises questions about story-sharing communities and public knowledge. Perhaps it is the brand of "superstition" that limits her speech. While she does not know the story of the curse, she is familiar with the Ghostrider of Hosmer Mountain, and she shares with her peers an appreciation for the evening shadow on the rock face. The eldest generations in Fernie do not associate what they call "the Rider" with the curse story; it is a notable distinction between people of different ages. Old-timers told me over and over that the Rider was never representative of the legend. Many suggest that the Chamber of Commerce initiated this link sometime after the curse-lifting ceremony in order to entice tourists. At stores throughout Fernie, the familiar jagged outline of Hosmer Mountain draws attention to postcard stands. Amongst the eldest generations there is a sharp awareness of this image, now transformed into a fetish for "culture" and "history."

Each day, the Ghostrider is invisible until the sun reaches the right place in the sky. Some struggle to see the figure as it emerges from the rock in the late afternoon, a reminder that we are not always able to see what is ever-present. It is an illusion of depth and distance that is visible only from a particular angle, and then only when you know what you are looking for. Once you see it, you become constantly aware of its presence; it is unshakable, inscribed in the landscape. The shadow attests to the power of strong images.

During a later visit with the woman whose excerpt appears here, she showed me, and allowed me to copy, postcards that had been sent to her during the war (see Figures 12 and 13). In these potent images, the Mercedes-Benz symbolizes Germany. The context in each is conquest: in Libya, where an *Araberjunge* (Arab boy) is posed by the hood ornament; and in Naples (1938), where a shining Mercedes turns onto a street lit up by Nazi monoliths. People between the ages of sixty and one hundred are well versed in the sleight of hand orchestrated through official propaganda. It is not surprising that some are skeptical of the Ghostrider image and its recent connection to the curse legend. They witnessed the political manipulation of symbols and images that resonate with popular history, reinforcing ideas of national identity and raising the spectres of old enmities.

Like the Ghostrider, the expressive worlds of the eldest generations in Fernie move between light and shadow, between what is said and what remains silent. When these people speak about difference, they draw from experiences that are, to some extent, shared. Everyone in these generations lived though an era of mass warfare and the accompanying sanctions on speech and action. Following Luisa Passerini (1992:7-10), I approach "totalitarianism in mentalities" comparatively – looking at their similarities and

Figure 12 This German postcard shows the streets of Naples in May 1938, when monoliths were erected to celebrate the arrival of Adolf Hitler. The Mercedes-Benz was a common symbol of German imperialism. Postcard inscription: "Festschmuck in Neapel beim Empfang des Führers Adolf Hitler in Italien, Mai 1938." *Photograph by Erich Bauer Karlsruhe. Courtesy of research participant.*

Figure 13 The inscription on this German postcard translates as: "Arab boy in Tripoli in front of the star of conquest." As Libya was an Italian colony, the image signifies the "Pact of Steel" between Mussolini and Hitler; the use of the Mercedes-Benz to portray imperial power is explicit. Postcard inscription: "Araberjunge in Tripolis vor dem Stern der Siege," ca. Second World War. *Photograph by H. v. Stwolinski. Courtesy of research participant.*

the kinds of social knowledge that are instilled through them. The cornerstone here is "a cult of consensus and authority" that applies not only to Fascism, Nazism, or Stalinism, but also to colonial relationships in democratic regimes. During periods of war *and* peace, these generations of people have learned and unlearned ways of marking others that are cued by images and stories. All have experienced, to varying degrees, political climates where human difference had dire consequences.

During our conversation, the woman who spoke with me acknowledged the gap between what is heard and how things really are. Her comments about "Indians" illustrate a kind of social knowledge circulating in distant places, not derived from any experience of interaction. Karl May (1842-1912) was a popular writer whose books revolved around a German superhero and his Apache sidekick, a "civilized, noble savage."[1] Perhaps the fear of "Indians" she once felt reflects how a regime wielded the imagery of Native American peoples. Hitler's National Socialist Reich at first promoted themes from May's work as part of its apparatus to indoctrinate youth. Karl May festivals began in 1934, sponsored by the regime. Characters were used to instill in boys notions of the self-sacrificing warrior with unfaltering obedience to one leader and loyalty to a nation rather than the individual. By 1936, Nazi race theory was well elaborated, and May's works were then seen to instill "a false idea about the nature of mankind" (Usadel 1936 in Kamenetsky 1984:148). The ministries of propaganda and education publicly discouraged reading these materials, which officials judged falsely ennobled a non-Aryan "race."

I interviewed a younger woman from Germany who arrived in Fernie very recently but has lived in Canada since the late 1950s. We also spoke about Karl May. She told me about attending the summer plays of his work, still performed in calcium caves near her home in Germany. "There," she said, "they would re-enact cowboys and Indians." I also asked her about "the Fernie story."

Well, yeah, the Ghostrider story. Everyone loves to talk about that.
My version of it? Well, that Mr. Fernie cheated on this chief and did
not marry the daughter after he'd been shown the coal mines. Black
gold. And that the chief and the daughter were banned from the tribe
and their ghosts are visible. What have you heard? A different story?
 Do you know the story of the curse?
Oh yes, the curse. Always the floods and the fires which have
happened. In [1964] the curse was lifted. But we had a flood since
then, so ...
 How did you hear about the story?
I read it in the brochures from the Chamber of Commerce, the
tourist information. Not from people that I've met. Just wanting to

know about Fernie. (Interview, 9 January 1999. German woman, born 1938.)

In this rendition, Fernie's story *is* the "Ghostrider story"; the curse narrative is secondary to the explanation of the shadow. This woman has also not "heard" the story, but knows it through promotional brochures. Both women are outside the oral transmission of the curse narrative. While they are both German, their different perspectives on local lore point to important distinctions. They represent the two edges of the generations who experienced the Second World War. The first came into adulthood during the war in Germany; the younger woman was a child during Hitler's regime. Within that space of time, ideas and experiences shifted enormously. The women's respective levels of education and their fluency in English also separate them. They arrived in Fernie at different points in time, and ideas in Canada towards and between Germans had changed greatly.

You know, there was so many Germans we never bothered with Canadians. Mind you, we couldn't speak much English, you know, you are afraid to speak it because you thought you would say something wrong ... Before the war I can't say [what it was like here], but I think they're for [different nationalities] now. Because they don't kick about it anymore. Before, they said: "Ah! What do you want? He's a, whatever, Polish" or something like this. Now they don't bother. (Interview, 22 June 1998. German woman, born 1920.)

Do you know other people from Germany here in town?
No ... Germans have had to hide in the First and Second World War in North America – from each other. They were not to be seen together and did not want to be identified as Germans ... So, compared to Italians, Chinese, and Jewish people, Germans don't tend to be bounded to one another in a group ... I really never have felt comfortable with other Germans. [Laughing] We have a saying in German ... "God protect us of storm and wind and Germans who we meet in our foreign countries." I've yet to find out where that came from and why. And other Germans who I've met will know this. (Interview, 9 January 1999. German woman, born 1938.)

I place these narratives at the beginning of the chapter because I hope to discourage an easy tendency to read participants' words as representative of their nationalities. They are not. The excerpts I include reflect only my acquaintances during fieldwork with those individuals who were interested in participating. My interpretations are shaped by the diverse locations from which people remember and narrate what is a troubling period in their past.

Experiencing War

Regardless of nationality, people over the age of sixty grew up in the midst of intense nationalistic activities that were tied inextricably to important symbols of identity: peoplehood, religion, monarchy, or class struggle. Participation in youth groups and military service instilled values of allegiance, authority, and obedience. They lived through an era of official propaganda focused largely on national character, where the everyday was shot through with small acts of compliance and rituals that reinforced these values. My aim is not to argue people's complicity with certain ideologies or to suggest that everyone occupies equal positions. They do not. I found no consensus from people of any nationality when it came to opinions about wartime ideology or leaders. I heard many comments about Mussolini and Hitler. Some people argued that these leaders elevated the status of their nations and represented the interests of poor people. To others they were hated figures, responsible for the deaths of sons and the destruction of their ways of life. One man spoke about Churchill:

> I was in the army for four years and I was discharged as a captain, but I never claimed any of my bloody campaign ribbons or anything else because I am anti-monarchist to begin with. I didn't want a bloody foreign monarchy. I didn't want to wear them, and the ribbons are still, and the medals are still in Ottawa. I never claimed them. That was the reason. Then Churchill gets up and says he wasn't up to disbanding the British Empire. You know. In other words, he fought the war to keep India and everybody else.
> (Interview, 26 August 1998. Italian-Canadian man, born 1916.)[2]

It is important to keep in mind that no regime was entirely successful in eradicating dissenting views. People who have experienced war express an acute awareness of control over the flow of information. One woman said to me: "Don't read the headlines on the newspaper. Flick through to the small stories on the back pages. That's where the real news is. They don't tell you anything they don't want you to know!" I heard warnings passed on to others by people who had lived through Austro-Hungarian rule: "Pay attention to what is happening now. There is so much information, yet it all provides only one image. It's all the same. That's the beginning."

During the Second World War, political regimes were actively engaged in the social production of ideology. Within different nations, people witnessed an era of totalitarian rule that sought to "completely control political, social and intellectual life" (Passerini 1992:7). Italy was under the

Fascist reign of Mussolini and the Blackshirts, or squadristri, for twenty years (1922-1942). In Germany, Hitler's National Socialist Reich held power for over ten years (1933-1945) and also imposed Nazification on protectorates of Czechoslovakia (1939-1944) and Poland (1939-1944). Marxism-Leninism lasted seventy years (1917-1987) and eventually extended to Poland, Czechoslovakia, and the Ukraine. I worked with people whose lives were affected by all of these regimes. Many from Eastern Europe whom I interviewed lost contact with their relatives during the Communist era. When the regimes fell from power, people visited their relatives in Fernie, where they were reminded of the songs and stories officially banned from public performance.

> They couldn't sing their own national anthem. When we had our cousins here, I remember them all singing it and they just wept as they were singing it. Imagine, they had to come to Canada to sing this song! They still sing [Slovakian songs in the Czech Republic] on occasion, but they would be sure about who was present. (Interview, 16 April 1998. Slovak-Canadian woman, born 1933.)

Totalitarian power constructs worldviews in part by controlling flows of information through propaganda or censorship. Officially sanctioned images, ideas, and actions are enforced by various forms of threat; surveillance and violence lead people to practise self-censorship in their public activities. Totalitarian regimes were "obliged to possess a truth, whether it [was] placed in the laws of history, as in Marxism-Leninism, or in biology and race, as in Hitlerism, or the State, as in Fascism" (Passerini 1992:5).

In my description of an official state ceremony in Fernie, the sacrifices of "Allied" troops are commemorated. I hope to show that the form of the ritual itself has resonance for everyone who experienced the world wars. I am suggesting that particular kinds of social knowledge and experience, shaped most especially by nationalism and war, are shared by people of the eldest generations.

National Spectacle: Commemoration

Remembrance Day

> I decide not to wear my coat with the red AIDS ribbon as well as the poppy. People are gathering outside the Legion. Some stand on the sidewalk pointing to their fathers, sisters, brothers, and grandparents assembling in formation on the street. It is sunny but cold. Uniforms, wreaths, and regalia. I ask who the men are with white feathers in their purple hats, black capes, tuxedos, glinting swords at their sides.

A woman standing in a doorway says, "The Knights of Columbus."
A police car pulls to the front. The man shouting orders yells the
procession to order. (Fieldnotes, 11 November 1997)

My attendance at the Remembrance Day ceremony in 1997 is preceded
by an act of self-censorship. The red poppy of Flanders signifies the unknown soldier, the importance of keeping alive the public memory of those
who sacrificed themselves in warfare. The AIDS ribbon is the symbol of
the Red Campaign, also a reminder of loss and a fundraising strategy for
medical research. Both are socially recognizable. On this occasion I had
a sense of these symbols colliding. I highlight this because it flags both
my perceptions of this age group and the small negotiations of symbol
and action we engage in every day. Many people whose stories appear here
have felt the official censure of symbols. All have experienced war in some
form or another – as "Allies," "enemies," "POWs," "aliens," "DPs," "heroes,"
or "civilians" on the home front.

The brass band begins. All of the pipers and drummers are girls and
young women. Behind the pipers march the RCMP in their red serge,
followed by flag bearers – Canada, the United States, the Union Jack,
and the Legion Branch 36. Young cadets make up the honour guard.
Veterans follow in uniformed clusters; some wear only caps, medals glint
on chests. Women also march here, some carry wreaths. Following the
vets, the Knights of Columbus walk regally in their red-lined capes. They
are followed by the fire brigade and merchant veterans. Members of
the Ghostriders hockey team march next in their named and numbered
playing jerseys. Some wear toques. Brownies, Girl Guides, and Boy
Scouts follow, brandishing their flags. The parade marches down the
main street – most of the businesses are closed, people line the
sidewalks.

The suspension of economic activity by merchants and workers signifies a move from the daily routine to ceremonial time. The Remembrance
Day parade is led by a kilted band of pipers, a reminder of the legacy of
Scottish regiments in Canada, whose placement in the procession is perhaps indicative of the role they played on the battlefields. Brass bands hail
from a long tradition in Britain, where they were used as a form of recruitment for the armed forces and were vital to the youth movements of the
1930s. National flags are official emblems of sovereignty.[3] There is an uncomfortable absence of non-Anglo-European flags, given the number of
men who enlisted in "foreign" allied forces in Fernie. Perhaps this absence
signifies the shifting alliances of nations between wars; certainly it affirms
the official character of the state ceremony. The presence of young cadets

marks the ongoing transmission of military traditions across generations. Cadet groups were established in Canada after 1896 under the name "Boys Brigade" (Mackenzie 1984:242). It is apt that they form the honour guard for veterans whose sacrifices fuel that tradition.

Uniforms evoke another era when insignia could be read to outline social networks and to recall the places where people trained and their paths of combat. Some of the medals that men wear dangle from differently coloured ribbons; their meanings are obscure to many of us. One or two of the women wear caps that signify their service with medical corps and service organizations. The Knights of Columbus represent the Catholic Church, evoking an era when male societies based on religion and occupation were socially commonplace.[4] I find the presence of the uniformed Ghostriders interesting. These are young male athletes who represent Fernie in regional competitions, members of a team from which the National Hockey League "drafts" players. Youth groups march behind the hockey team; their uniforms and banners echo the militarism of the occasion. The RCMP, military forces, and fire brigade reflect rank and respect for civil authority. Each adheres to traditions based on service to the nation, instilled through disciplined training.

As a procession of social categories, the actors in the parade reflect membership in the institutions that have played a significant role in people's lives. Across nationalities, young people belonged to groups modelled on militarism, through which they learned state narratives and were taught to respect authority. Under Marxism-Leninism, the Communist League of Youth *(Komsomol)* was established in 1917. Organized according to age, its members camped, travelled to politically important sites, performed community service, and learned stories about the lives of leaders and martyrs (Pauley 1997:118). In Italy, members of the coed *Opera Nazionale Balilla* ranged in age from six to eighteen years. This organization largely excluded the "peasant" and working classes and was not focused on political indoctrination. Germany's youth movements date to 1810 and were renowned for their discipline and national spirit. Across the British Empire, youth groups were based on the philosophy of "rational recreation," viewed as the "most successful system of social discipline" (Mackenzie 1984:257). Young people throughout Europe were involved in youth organizations where sports, singing, and drilling formed the basics of their premilitary training.

Early newspapers in Fernie are stamped with the symbols of fraternal lodges: Masons, Eagles, Oddfellows, Woodmen, Owls, Elks, and Lions. My great-grandfather was a member of the Ancient Order of Foresters. All these organizations use(d) regalia and participate(d) in some form of secret ritual. In Fernie, Italian benevolent societies included the *Order Independent Fior Di Italia Cooperativa*, Christopher Columbo and Marconi lodges.

Some people told me about the Slav Benevolent Society, the Canadian Slovak League, and other societies of Polish and Ukrainian people. All of these orders had separate societies for women as spouses of the members. People celebrated their respective traditions. Most of the societies provided some form of financial support to their members, assisting families with health care, or widows and orphans with funeral expenses and ritual duties.

> Orders are shouted at each turn until the procession reaches the courthouse and the cenotaph, where four motionless cadets stand on pedestals at the four directions of the monument. Their rifles, like their faces are downturned. People line the driveway and the lawns of the courthouse. The band shouts itself to the front and then kneels. One by one, the units of the parade take their positions around the monument. Flags are lowered. Other flags are inverted. There is one minute of silence. Everyone sings the national anthem. A young, uniformed woman arrives in a rush. Another shouted order: "Sound the Last Post." Her lone trumpet sounds. The flags are raised. (Fieldnotes, 11 November 1997)

In front of the château-style courthouse, the cenotaph bears the names of local men who lost their lives in warfare.[5] Inside, the courthouse floor is tiled in a stylized swastika mosaic, a symbol intending well-being.[6] On the lawn outside stands the white stone monument of a man in First World War uniform; his hat hangs from one shoulder, and his face is lowered. One hand rests on the peak of a planted cross. Motionless cadets mirror the statue; they breathe life into the monument. On this occasion their stance evokes mourning and humility. There is a moment when flags and rifles are inverted, when silence is enacted, breaking the preoccupation with everyday thought.

What Patrizia Dogliani (1999:13-14) calls the "cult of the unknown soldier" began in Italy shortly after the First World War. Bodies of fallen soldiers were relocated from battlefields to central monuments and borderlands. The intense project of recording their names also began at this time. Mussolini created a series of monuments and sites where these names were inscribed and where he delivered speeches. Hitler also introduced "elaborate ceremonies dedicated to Nazi martyrs"; on these occasions he replaced hymns with marching songs (Pauley 1997:105). Every political regime participates in some form of public commemoration. During the twentieth century, the "sacraria" of war was commonplace across Europe.

> A Salvation Army representative announces the intention of the ceremony to remember those who served in the two world wars, but also in the Persian Gulf and in other places of conflict where Canadian peacekeepers are stationed. She speaks about the people who have died

in warfare, "Local boys, young adult men and women," and reminds everyone of their ordinariness: as boys next door, newly married men and hairdressers. Those who entered "an exciting but terrifying world ... Some returned with deep emotional scars, for all the innocence of youth had completely dissolved. We stand today and pause to reflect and remember all those brave comrades who never returned. They shall not grow old as we that are left grow old. Age shall not worry them nor the years condemn ... At the going down of the sun and in the morning, we will remember them."

Psalm 46 is read and a prayer offered. The crowd sings "God Save the Queen." To the tense roll of drums the master of ceremonies calls for wreaths to be placed below the cenotaph. Most of the men salute and then return to their positions. Civilians are called forward to bring their wreaths last. As I look around, I see none of the faces of the men I have interviewed who fought in wars.

The band, RCMP, and flags march out. Everyone else is commanded to reassemble on the street in resumed formation. They march back to the Legion Hall.

The address vividly acknowledges the horrors of war. There is a blessing of eternal youth bestowed upon men who died in battle; those who returned are cursed by the loss of youthful innocence. Everyone taking part in an official state ceremony anticipates the songs of nation and monarchy, prayers, and scriptural readings. Nation, God, and Queen are brought together in a familiar cluster of oral traditions performed throughout people's lives in many nations. The Salvation Army represents both militarism and an interdenominational Christianity.[7]

Political regimes maintained various distances from religion. Under Mussolini, "children were taught that they owed the same loyalty to fascism as they did to God" (Pauley 1997:115). What Patrizia Dogliani (1999:16) calls "Fascist political religion" was evidenced in schools where roll calls of the dead were performed regularly and classes were named after fallen soldiers. Fascists in Italy maintained a fairly stable relationship with the Roman Catholic Church. The Vatican approved many of the anti-communist policies of the regime, and some religious feasts remained state holidays under Mussolini. In the USSR, religion was officially and unequivocally divorced from state aims. Communism held that "religious beliefs were socially destructive superstitions that had to be fought" (Pauley 1997:140). Ideologically, Hitler's party set itself up as "defending Christianity against Communist atheism" (143). Hitler replaced religious holidays with festivals commemorating important events in his party's history. German nationalism tapped into fundamentalist notions of "Aryan spirituality."

As the veterans lay their wreaths at the base of the monument, they step back and enact the embodied gesture of salute. Their marching precision is a reminder of their years of military drilling – they are still in step after all these years. The ceremonial order of the actors mimics their distance from the direct horrors of war. Civilians are asked to come forward last. For many of them, the war evokes grief and loneliness, air-raid drills, and the constant press to buy war savings bonds or tend a Victory garden. As witnesses, spectators are spatially separate from those whose uniforms symbolize sacrifice through battle or service. When the crowd thins, many people return to business; others gather at the Legion Hall to participate in a more intimate service. Their numbers will again be reduced when people meet later for the "Smoker."

Inside the Hall, cigarettes are lit. There are moves towards the coffee maker. The scarlet-dressed RCMP officers assume their positions at the back of the hall. A bingo sign is dark; someone opens the piano. This hall is lined with dartboards; there is a photograph of a young Queen Elizabeth and her husband, Philip. The Salvation Army captain and his wife conduct the service – she is also a captain I am told. The person sitting next to me asks what a "Smoker" is. A man tells her it is for the vets – when they get together and smoke and drink free beer ...

Flags are marched up the aisle to begin the ceremony. "Onward Christian Soldiers" is followed by "Oh Canada," the colour party is shouted into place, and a prayer of invocation is cited.

There are readings from the Old and New Testaments. The sermon is based on the poem about the poppies of Flanders Fields. The captain notes that this work is recited and memorized for those who have died in war. He stresses the importance of commemorative acts given "the fear that death will be forgotten." A prayer asks the Lord for help in remembering those who died and those who are still suffering in wartorn places. The Lord's Prayer is followed by a poem written by a girl in Fernie who has won a prize for her "awareness of remembering." We are asked to stand for a hymn. "Lest we forget, Lest we forget." ...

"God Save the Queen." The colours are returned, signalling that the public ceremonials are over.

Prayers offered on this occasion take in the past, the present, and hopes for the future. The Lord's Prayer evokes a general community of faith, and the closing hymn depicts the melding of political acts with religion. The Legion Hall is a social space filled with the symbols of nation. On this occasion the space contains a palpable tension fuelled by the fear that young people will forget the ultimate sacrifice of warfare. Poems and hymns are viewed as forms essential to the real problem of transmitting social memory in the absence of direct experience with war.

> Veterans and their spouses, Legion members, and staff wait for the "Smoker" to begin. I am asked if I would like to attend as the "guest" of a young man who talks about the silence surrounding the war. "Most of them are very private," he says. He places his card in the slot of the door. We buzz through and are met by two women sitting at the entrance table. They are surprised to see me. "Sorry. Only members and their spouses are allowed." Tables are set with large beer glasses. It is already very smoky, and the room is alive with laughter and talk ...
>
> Later that day an elderly man tells me about "Zombies," the name given by First World War veterans to men in service who never saw combat. "They wanted the Legion to die with them, the World War I vets." I am told that silence is the mark of a true soldier. "They don't even talk to each other about it. You can tell the ones who never saw [battle]. They talk about it all the time!" (Fieldnotes, 11 November 1997)

The Smoker is a space reserved for veterans and their spouses. It recognizes their fellowship, awarding privacy to the reminiscences of soldiers publicly marked by silence. To be a member of the Legion requires a blood or marriage bond to a veteran. There are notable exclusions. Until 1951 the Indian Act forbade returning Aboriginal veterans from drinking in the Legion. I do not know who attended the Smoker, whether men who fought for Italy or Germany or the Union of Soviet Socialist Republics were there. I was not allowed entrance to this event. But these people do reside in Fernie, as do the women and children whose lives were also embroiled in these wars.

Other Relationships to Remembering
In any performance of public ceremony it is important to notice not only who participates, but also who is absent. I interviewed people who experienced the Second World War from diverse geographical and ideological locations. Many women I spoke with described to me the physical and emotional exhaustion caused by the dropping of Allied bombs. One woman is still unable to attend Canada Day celebrations because of the fireworks; she quakes in embodied terror at the sound of what were known as "Christmas tree" bombs. One Italian woman spoke about her physical scars.

> Oh, I don't want to remember. I was in a bombing. I've got a scar on my foot. Me and my mum were in a train station to catch a train

home. A bomb dropped right at that time. Me and my mum were
split up in the blast. My mum went one way and I went the other.
One lady who had a stand selling oranges, she was dead. I was right
there. I was so scared. In school they taught us, in case of a bombing,
go lie down on the floor. I remember I went down. But this lady was
dying, it was a mess ... Disaster! I was fourteen ... April 13, 1943.
I couldn't sleep in my bed for many years. I was too scared. I went
underneath the bed. They came a few times to Cosenza – there was
the sound of the plane, the siren. (Interview, 10 September 1998.
Italian woman, born 1929.)

Women whose husbands had been prisoners of war described the lingering emotional effects. One man was a German soldier captured in Africa
and held in Canada over the war. Later he decided to immigrate because
of his experience here. Another woman told me that her husband had
been in the Italian military but was imprisoned in Germany. He died
not long after immigrating to Canada at a young age. I interviewed an
Italian man who was captured in Africa by the Allies, shipped to Australia,
incarcerated in South Africa, and eventually sent to a work camp in
Scotland. People spoke about occupations by different armies, starvation,
distrust, and the many acts of intentional cruelty. All have complicated
relationships to the Canadian state in the context of official commemo-
rations of war.

Different generations of immigrants also distinguish themselves through
war and the ensuing complications of nationality. After the First World
War, Italians who enlisted in overseas forces returned with the status of
veteran. These men were not subject to wartime restrictions imposed on
other Italians during the Second World War. I heard from people in town
about first-generation Canadians who enlisted and found themselves
facing their cousins on enemy lines. Others had difficulties enlisting in
Canadian forces. One man stated clearly that it was his nationality, read
through his surname, that prompted military recruiters to scorn his initial attempts to enlist. For a Welsh-Canadian man it was his social class
that barred access to the armed forces. He was turned down several times
on the basis of his grade eight education. "If you wanted to become an
officer, you had to speak with a British accent! We were patriotic as hell!"
He was eventually ordered to work in the coal mines to contribute to the
war effort.

Another story I heard from several people referred to the frustrated
attempts of one veteran's family to secure for him a military salute at his
funeral. The request was refused by a Canadian Legion, and the decorated
Ktunaxa man, who had twice been wounded, was buried by a Legion from
the United States. The story echoes the words of an elder who spoke about

his social standing while in uniform, and the stripping away of respect when he returned to his civilian (read racialized) status. Ktunaxa people with whom I spoke had great reverence for their fallen ancestors and returned soldiers. I came to understand that, for many, the position of the "warrior" resonates with continuity to their past.

I attended the Yaqan Nukiy Pow Wow held in Creston in May 1998. The grand entry procession was led by members of the Veterans' Warrior Society of the Ktunaxa Nation. They bore the flags of Canada, the United States, and the Salish-Kootenay Federated Tribes, as well as the Eagle Staff – a potent symbol of indigeneity. The master of ceremonies for the event was a Cree man from the United States who was also an ex-Marine. Throughout the powwow he joked with veterans from various tribes who were present, some of whom also served in the US Marine Corps. At one point he spoke about the British flag and how Americans had succeeded in driving the British north into Canada. "That's just something you may want to think about," he said. Several humorous references were made to Christopher Columbus. At one point he urged people to "speak Indian" so that Japanese exchange students would understand how it felt for Columbus when he arrived in the "so-called New World" (from Fieldnotes 16 May 1998).

A year almost to the day after attending the Remembrance Day ceremony, I went to a powwow at the Fernie ski hill. The event was held to mark a new beginning in the treaty relationship between Ktunaxa people and residents in the Elk Valley. There was a small local turnout. Ktunaxa veterans again led the grand entry parade. The master of ceremonies called upon everyone to observe a minute of silence in respect for lost soldiers. He introduced the Warrior Society and spoke about how he had lost his Aboriginal status when he enlisted in the military. "I wasn't an Indian anymore. I was a Canadian and I didn't even know it." He then spoke about the various twists wrought upon his official identity vis-à-vis the Canadian state, about *not* being an "Indian" – that is, he was not from India; about his name *not* being the one given to him in and through his own language, but an English name that he was christened with at the age of two. "I'm not Canadian, I'm not American." "I'm Ktunaxa," he said (from Fieldnotes, 14 May 1998). In the *Fernie Free Press* his status as a "warrior" was noted: "Today, we're all warriors yet ... We're talking about the non-existence of a treaty in BC. Technically, we're still at war with the government" (*FFP* 17 November 1998:2). Remembering is a political act for many people at the margins of national boundaries.

While nation is a salient concept for members of the eldest generations, it carries meanings that reflect different relationships to the Canadian state. Official state ceremonies celebrate national narratives through symbols and expressions imbued with nationalistic values. They legitimate particular organizations of people, reinforce official histories, and ensure the transmission of powerful ideas.

Transmission: The Journey of Ideas

Between Generations

Participants' stories move in and out of official histories and personal memory. Some people revive their parents' stories, and their accounts attest to the potency of intergenerational transmission. Knowledge of social categories runs through family networks; old animosities from far-off places pass on to children in new contexts. A first-generation Ukrainian-Canadian woman spoke with me about this haunting process. Her narrative includes a comparison of different political regimes.

> [My mother] would tell me about how it was [in the Ukraine] under the Polish regime. Under the Austrian regime the men had to go in the army, serve in the army for three years and that was it. That was what you owed the Austrian government; otherwise they left them alone, they planted their crops and they sold their land and they bought land and things went on. But under the Polish regime, things became [pause] oppressive and suppressed. She said that in order to keep people down, they decided the way to do it was to use religion. So they closed the Greek Orthodox churches, imposed Roman Catholicism on the people, and if they didn't go to the Catholic Church they were imprisoned. They used the priests as controls over the people ...

Political regimes leave their mark in the oral histories of citizens. Through her mother, this woman is able to narrate the differing strategies of Austro-Hungarian and Polish authorities in what is now the Ukraine. I asked her about the weight of her mother's words.

> *So how did [your mother's] stories about Poland – or what became Poland – affect you?*
> That was the strangest part of it. My mother never actually, never actually denigrated those people. They lived in our neighbourhood, she bought milk from our Polish neighbours, she visited with them when necessary I guess. YET ... There was that feeling that she actually transposed into something that I picked up. I could feel that she hated them – not as neighbours, but because they were Polish. There was a lot of this union stuff going on, and the Polish were typically, at this point, not union. The Ukrainians and the Russians

were union. The Polish tended to be the scabs ... So there were lots of reasons to be resentful of them. I remember them driving by in trucks that had all the sides boarded in. They would pick up the Polish men and drive them to work in these trucks so they'd be hidden. And other people throwing rocks at these trucks. [Laughing] So there were many reasons to be angry with these people. That anger that she had brought with her. That anger ... somehow or another, it was something that was – I must have got it by osmosis because she never actually said anything. It was just – just that. To this day, you know, I will hold back – Polish? I will hold back, I'll reserve judgment – to this day! It's an awful thing. I mean, what did it come from? It came from very little, but I can really understand how countries like Ireland and what is going on in Israel – I can understand how this will go from generation to generation. And never end. I believe it will never end. (Interview, 4 November 1997. Ukrainian-Canadian woman, born 1925.)

In our conversation, this woman grappled with the embodiment of prejudice. She provided a powerful description of a kind of "osmosis" whereby her mother's antipathy towards Poles was transmitted to her. In Canada, interactions with Polish neighbours resumed the uneasy tension experienced in Europe, and the union strife reinforced these sentiments. I heard many people essentialize other nationalities, based on parents' accounts of transgression in their homelands.

One woman's parents came from Bohemia in 1903. She told me that her father spoke often about having to leave their country because "Germans were encroaching on farm lands." Czech regions were administrated from Vienna and closely tied to the German sector of Austro-Hungarian rule. Since the turn of the century, Czech nationalism revolved around a pan-Slavic movement in which ideas of German encroachment were central (Leff 1988:27). This woman's description of Germans was reinforced by an image of post–Second World War "refugees," their perceived wealth, and the information now coming to light about the Holocaust. Not unlike the example of the women above, this evaluation of nationality drew from later events in a new setting.

During the 1930s the Communist Party was popular in the Crowsnest Pass. In response to a series of strikes, authorities deputized police and began a campaign against what they called the "Communist push." People described to me door-to-door interrogations where they were questioned about their neighbours. Union membership corresponded with nationality for many people from Europe. To a Slovakian woman whose parents arrived in 1931, communism was the most significant social boundary learned through family stories.

We knew who the communists were. Mind you, the only ones we knew were the Slavic ones ... But our family was anti-communist ... My father had fought in the First World War, joined at seventeen, was only in the army, I think, six months or something like this. After the war, they had kept the communists out of Czechoslovakia and so he felt very good about it ... It was 1918, of course that's when Czechoslovakia was formed ...

They had been under Austro-Hungarian rule, and my parents were both, their education was in Hungarian, although they spoke Slovak as well[8] ... There was a song they sang at this time. My parents sang it until the '40s because it was a song of freedom. Something like: "It may look like the ice has frozen over the water, but underneath it the water still runs – the fresh water still runs." ... What this leaves you with is the fact that you can do anything politically, you can do something with the union, you can **do** something! You can form a country. (Interview, 16 April 1998. Slovak-Canadian woman, born ca. 1933.)

This woman speaks about the power of song as an expression of national identity, family history, and individual empowerment. She speaks the dialect of her region in Slovakia and notes how language was imposed by different regimes. As the child of a man and woman who witnessed the birth of a nation, she nurtures the corpus of traditions that celebrates resistance and freedom. As a member of an "anti-communist" family, she is part of a social hierarchy that marks communists as "other."

These interview excerpts reveal the resilience in ideas of human difference generated through eras of conquest and empire building. They also suggest the diverse histories of Polish, Ukrainian, Czech, Russian, and Slovak peoples, known in North America under the monolithic category "Slav," which erases complicated alignments in history. Ideas about difference have intricate genealogies involving interesting journeys between different times and places. Narratives also reveal political discourses used to delineate particular populations and to perpetuate social hierarchies. Political imagery is instilled through real or perceived threat.

Embodiment and Repetition

I have already touched upon atrocity myths perpetuated during times of warfare and imperial conquest. Here I am interested in the construction of images forged through repetitive, imposed, everyday actions. In all political regimes there was/is a "model of race in which images of difference were not [always] visibly written on the skin but had rather to be carefully constructed in order to identify the other" (Linke 1997:560). Through theoretical links between "race," disease, contagion, and pathology, political regimes have marked ethnicity, disability, sexuality, class, and ideology. Taxonomies of difference created in the 1930s drew upon eugenic theories then well accepted across Europe and North America. In scientific journals, German scholars rationalized their theories of race by citing miscegenation laws in the United States (Pauley 1997:160). To them, "race" was "derived from a typology of blood ... evoked through genealogy" (Linke 1997:560).[9] During the 1930s, in reaction to Hitler's application of scientific discourses, scholars focused their attentions for the first time *critically* on the concept of race. The term "ethnicity" emerged at this time; however, it too reproduced the idea of distinct groups and spawned debates amongst scholars around distinctions between science and dogma. At issue was an enormous body of works by scholars across disciplines and nations in which "race" as a scientific fact was central.

On the ground, wartime racism was/is fuelled by popular expressions of xenophobia. In Italy, the word *"allogeni"* designated "people of another kind" (Sluga 1999:179). In Germany, *ausländer* was used for those from other lands (Linke 1997:565). In Canada it was the term *alien,* meaning "not one's own ... differing in nature" (OED 1982:23). Xenophobia and anti-Semitism had been commonplace in European nations since the nineteenth century. Given the ubiquity of anti-Semitism, it is interesting that I encountered silence surrounding Jewish people in Fernie – a silence broken by my persistent prompting. I asked several people if there were Jewish immigrants who came to Fernie. The reply was usually negative. Many told me anecdotes about Jews in the old country that their parents had passed on to them. In some of these accounts, difference was re-marked through music and dress or through perceptions of abusive gender relationships – yet another common form of othering.[10] Nobody, it seemed, knew anyone in Fernie who was Jewish. One day a woman with whom I had spoken a good deal told me of a recent realization. Her parents mentioned a man who lived in the Annex; his name came up in passing here and there. She realized that what she had assumed to be his surname was really the word for Jew in her parents' language. Naming is a powerful way to reinforce public forms of recognition.[11]

I was told one other story. An elderly woman who was in need of medical attention required some persuasion to come in to see a young female doctor. After the doctor left the room, someone said to the patient: "Now, that wasn't too bad was it? She's a nice young doctor." The woman, who is eastern European, said only: "She's a Jew."[12] What is important here is how "political fantasy" comes to inhabit the individual (Linke 1997:560). Recognition of otherness draws upon an older history of images and ideas already embedded in our imaginations.

Knowledge about one's own people is also constructed through familiar images and ideas. The National Socialists worked from a cluster of theories bound together by ideas of race, social evolution, and eugenics. Their image of Germanness derived largely from the phantasmagoria of Norse mythology (Kamenetsky 1984:85-102). Mussolini invoked the image of the Roman Empire and its nineteenth-century rebirth in the form of the Risorgimento to instill Fascism as the "divine civilizing mission of Italy" (Pauley 1997:116). What John Mackenzie (1984:253) calls British "Imperial Nationalism" had its widest propagation after the First World War and into the 1950s. The familiar cluster of monarchism, militarism, and social Darwinism propelled wartime actions and ideas while justifying the subordination of colonized peoples. Eric Hobsbawm (1994:121) suggests that within democratic nations it was the hegemony of "revolutionary traditions" symbolized by "Liberty, Equality and Fraternity" that both prevented fascism from taking a foothold and mobilized populations against fascist ideology.

Religion, class-consciousness, nationalism, and xenophobia provide emotional symbols effectively activated during periods of warfare. All political regimes accomplish their aims through powerful messages and enforced compliance to small rituals that come to inhabit the body.

> *Can you tell us about some of the political beliefs in the earlier days around here?*
> Well, everything was around the bloody monarchy then, aye? George the Sixth, you know, you saluted the bloody flag, eh, the British flag, and then in the officers' mess – you always ended up in there – you had brandy and good Rocco cheese and a salute to the monarchy, a toast. That was the last thing you had every mess dinner. And then the regiments were all tied to the British, so you got their traditions, eh? Even the Rocky Mountain Rangers here, you know, would have been a Canadian unit – they got bumped by Canadian Scottish ...
> You got all this propaganda in those days, and I don't have to tell you about propaganda! ... I mean, you owed your allegiance to the Queen, God, and Country, in that order. And, you know, at that time, all the thinking and everything else, all the actions at the time [were about this]. (Interview, 26 August 1998. Italian-Canadian man, born 1916.)

For those who served in the armed forces, such rituals are part of a defined tradition of rank and patriotism. For civilians, wartime events and the roles they may have played in them occupy an ambiguous and sometimes uncomfortable place in their memories.

We had a doctor, he was a Jew. He was a beautiful guy. You called him, he was there. He was so nice and all of a sudden he didn't show up anymore. So we thought that maybe he went to Canada or some place. We didn't know! And then after we found out – I don't know if he got killed or whatever. It is sad! They shouldn't have done it! But we had a good time when Hitler was in. We could go on holiday. We could go with the *braen* – a few pennies. And we could sleep in a place – what was it called? *Yugentabagger* – you wouldn't know. You could go there for fifty cents a night. You could sleep there. Mind you, I never went there.

Were you a member of the Hitler youth movements?
No. I'm glad I wasn't! You were practically forced into it! ... These were young guys who had to go in, just like here you have Brownies or so. But they had to go, you know? They marched and things, just like they do here, like cadets. Something like this ... BDM it was called for girls. *Bundt Deutsche Maidens*, I think, "A group of German girls." Do you think I remember? ... We had gymnastics and we had to sing there too and we went all over the place dancing and shouting. And the soldiers were looking and they were clapping. You had to do it when you belonged to this ... I mean, you can't make us suffer from it, there's nothing we could have done! And the *"Heil Hitler, Heil Hitler"* – sure, and when you say it you had to put your hand up like this [gesturing]. (Interview, 22 June 1998. German woman, born 1920.)

There is little sense of personal choice in this woman's descriptions of Germany at war. How do people overcome the dissonance between experience and history? Hitler's time in office signalled better conditions for poorer citizens and the sudden availability of travel. As a member of the BDM, this woman was able to leave her agricultural household and travel to entertain German soldiers. "There's nothing we could have done!" she stated, and her final comment about the salute solidified her conveyance of powerlessness.

In Italy, too, the creeping obedience to total authority was a social norm. One woman, born in Canada to Italian parents, told me about their return to Italy during the rise of Fascism.

We went back to Italy in 1923 and I was in school there until 1928, when we came back.
How did it feel as a Canadian going to school there?
We weren't accepted, you know, at first. No, we weren't accepted because my father must have taken the Canadian citizenship, so in those years, you know, when the Blackshirts came in to power, we were called traitors ... The bigwigs – I call them the bigwigs, eh, the doctor and the mayor – whatever in this town, when they passed by we had to salute them. Yeah, we had to salute them in the fascist

way there ... We put our hand out like that. I know we put our hand out like that. Even the doctor's wife, she'd growl if you didn't. She said: "Where's your manners?" She'd stop, and here I'd be carrying the milk from the co-op home, a bucket of milk ... and I'd have to put the bucket down and, you know.

Who were the Blackshirts?

It must have been the first Fascists working with Mussolini there, but he said he wasn't bad. The people didn't call him bad. It was just the Blackshirts they hated. They disliked them because you couldn't wear anything red, not even a flower on your [dress], just a corsage. And if they had suspicion you were a communist, they'd raid your house to look for papers, eh? I guess a lot of them were put in jail, and I know our next-door neighbour there, there was a lot of raids at his house, and for many days he'd be hiding in the fields.

And you were saying they publicly punished people?

Oh yeah, the ones they found papers, they suspected them of being communist, and they'd come with a bus. They gathered them up, they put them in the town square, and they tied their hands to the bottom and they give them a drink of oil. So you can imagine what went on. Punished them all, and some were incarcerated too ... I have to tell you, I won't mention names. (Interview, 2 September 1998. Italian-Canadian woman, born 1918.)

In the case of many who experienced totalitarian regimes, there was a lingering self-censorship that translated into hesitation or silence. Performed salutes, dances and songs, the censure of personal symbols, and public demonstrations of state violence are all examples of the enforcement of particular rituals of authority. Leaders tapped into popular social issues to rationalize their actions; most made appeals to the improvement of the economic, physical, and moral health of their nations. Both Hitler and Mussolini were anti-communist, stressing their defence of Christianity against atheism. Hitler used the term "Jewish Bolshevism" at a time when anti-communist sentiment was widespread (Pauley 1997:163). Both leaders promised to crack down on criminality, prostitution, pornography, and homosexuality. State propaganda was infused with family values and gender virtues, also instilled through compulsory membership in youth organizations. In Italy, education was made available to everyone, and the age of leaving school rose to fourteen. Health care and affordable transportation improved under all of the totalitarian regimes. During this period, people learned particular categories of difference, and these categories were enforced by the threat of absolute power.

In Fernie, where the potent sting of "foreigner" and "alien" still hung in the air, new designations of otherness accompanied the Second World

War. "Enemy aliens" was revived again and this time included Italians. Regardless of their citizenship status, those people identified as enemy aliens had to register and report weekly to the local police.

> Italy was against [the Allies], but they treated the Italians good. Maybe it's because it was a small town. Maybe in a big city it was different. But the Italians, they never bothered us – we never bothered them ... I remember I went to the police station. I had to go and get my fingerprints taken and that's about it. I did have to go sign in ... All the Italians did, when it came to Mussolini sticking his nose in. They weren't too strict, even with the Germans they weren't too strict ... You're English, why should I hate you for it? It's not your fault that the nation's at war. It's the big shots that want the war, not the working class. The working class doesn't want no war! (Interview, 6 August 1998. Italian woman, born 1910.)

> Well, I need to tell you that. I still have a gripe on that! I married an Italian, my first husband was an Italian, and during the war I had to go and register. I was born here [and] I lost my citizenship because I married him ... So naturally, I was out, and born in Canada I had to go and register every week ... Just sign, report where I was, at the police station. To this day I can't understand the government. I was born here and I can't even call myself a Canadian ... The English were bad to us. We couldn't even talk Italian – they'd stop us on the road: "You speak your language, you speak English here" ... During the war they were worse. Especially the women, they were bad. (Interview, 2 September 1998. Italian-Canadian woman, born 1918.)

One of these women downplays the distance between nationalities during the events of the Second World War. To her it is one's class position that defines sentiment about the war. The second woman, a first-generation Canadian, speaks about her marriage to an Italian, the loss of her status as citizen, and the requirement to register. Both address the social distance between themselves and the English. One woman describes how enmity was fuelled by the actions of ordinary people meeting "on the road."

Powerful ideas radiate from the designation of nationality, lingering in the oral histories shared by families and collective memories forged through experience. They are generated in contexts of enmity; fuelled by popular, nationalistic narratives; and imposed by structures of authority. These ideas come to inhabit bodies; they colonize gesture and speech in everyday interactions between people. Those who experienced eras of mass warfare have witnessed a sea change in social consciousness.

After the War
My mother told me about the end of the war.

> I can remember that the first victory was the victory in Europe.
> So everyone knew that the wars were ending. VE Day – I don't
> remember the date. VJ Day, which was Victory over Japan, it was
> the last, you know, the end of the Second World War. It must have
> happened in either July or August because I was in Fernie on
> holiday. We were all playing, a bunch of kids at _____'s house,
> which was uptown. I think people had expected that the war was
> going to end. All of a sudden the bell started to ring from the fire-
> house. Of course it rang all over town. This was the signal in town,
> by the way, that something was going wrong or something – they
> would ring the bell. It rang and rang and I remember all of us as a
> group, little kids, ran downtown. I'm a little vague on it except that
> I know I got split up from my friends. I joined into a conga line.
> [Laughing] Holding hands, stretched out. I must have been eight
> years old and I can remember going through – in this long conga
> line – through the theatre, which is not where it is today. That was
> beside the Diamond Grill. We went in through the theatre with the
> show on. We went in and out of restaurants and bars and all over
> town, and this went on for a long time. I can't remember what
> happened after that. Of course everyone was yelling and hooting and
> screaming and dancing. (Interview, 12 May 1998. English-Canadian
> woman, born 1937.)

Immediately following the Second World War there was a huge re-
arrangement of populations that sent social ripples across the world.

> The '40s. I remember one thing that happened that really, really
> devastated me. A girl who, I'm not sure if she was German or not,
> but I remember a whole gang of kids chasing her home and calling
> her awful names because she was of this – I can't remember what
> race it was, but it had something to do with the war. I couldn't
> believe it! And this girl was screaming and running down the street
> with all these kids running after her, throwing rocks and calling her
> names. I think that's when I began to notice difference in races. It
> all of the sudden seemed to become important to people. It hadn't
> mattered before. (Interview, 18 September 1997. English-Canadian
> woman, born ca. 1930.)

This woman was born at the beginning of the war years in Europe when
"race" still meant nationality. Her awareness of difference awoke during

yet another huge reconfiguration of the social imagination after the war. She describes feeling "devastated" by the event she witnessed. By the 1950s, new ideas of anti-racism were competing with well-instilled wartime repertoires. Following the war, people arrived in Fernie from wartorn places. Officially, they were called "DPs" or "displaced persons." People were forced to negotiate new relationships with those whom they had been socialized to fear. The usual misunderstandings of language and arrival were exacerbated by sentiments of wartime enmity.

> *Do you remember when racism started to become an issue?*
> I would think since the 40s. I think we were conscious of it when
> the DPs came, the displaced persons from Europe. They were Italians,
> they were Germans, they were Austrians ... I think we noticed a big
> difference in the attitude towards people then. And some of them
> deserved it. Just as we might deserve something ... For instance, if
> there were a group of – and I won't mention any definite nationality
> – a group of DPs come in, and you were pushing a buggy down the
> street, those are maybe twenty-eight-year-old, thirty-five-year-old
> people. They would not get off the street to let you push that baby
> buggy through. And common courtesy, in any nationality, would let
> a woman with a baby, they'd step aside and let them pass! That was
> one of the things ... And then of course "They're going to come and
> take our jobs." There's this, but I don't think it was that bad when
> it came to the jobs ... I think things boiled up at times. I think it
> would be a natural thing to do ... They have learned, and we think
> nothing of these people now. (Interview, 14 November 1997. Scottish-
> Canadian woman, born ca. 1920.)

This woman's awareness of racism also began when she experienced the arrival of DPs. Her description, however, naturalizes the difference between nationalities and renders wartime racism invisible. The list of nationalities she cites includes only those who were wartime enemies. She acknowledges the false threat of job loss, thus identifying a popular xenophobic discourse. It is the face-to-face interactions that are mentioned, collisions between social understandings recast in the context of wartime conditioning.

Some people welcomed these newcomers, who revitalized traditions that had become frozen during the voluntary exile of immigration.

> *Were there different points in time in the town's history when ...*
> *different people moved in and out? I think about after the war especially.*
> Yes, I do remember that ... yes, they were called DPs and it was a
> disparaging term ... I think it's disparaging because it sounds like
> they're stupid. Stupid is the word. I think that's it, that they wouldn't

know very much. Of course you can't tell what they know because
the language is different. The reason I had to pause with that word is
because – something in my own family, that we can tolerate anything
but there is no tolerance for that ... For not having the common
sense or not having the wherewithal to handle a thing properly ...
My mother had a word for it – it was *kosa belava* and all it meant
was blue goat. "You're really not being sensible about this" ... They
were hard-working people. And I suppose I also made a connection
between them and my own family. I could see their problems and
imagine this is what must have happened with my older brothers and
sisters ... [Displaced persons] weren't entirely accepted. I'm thinking
of, there were Polish and Ukrainian DPs, those are the ones I'm
thinking of. There were some Germans also ... They actually revived a
lot of our culture. It's the same thing that happened with the Italians.
When they came there were a lot of parties, and weddings ... A good
deal of the music and the storytelling was revived when they came ...
they would be invited to our parties ... Of course there were fewer
and fewer Slavic people by that time. (Interview, 16 April 1998.
Slovak-Canadian woman, born ca. 1933.)

The conversion of an official category into a "disparaging term" hints
at the social processes that forge national narratives and identities. Once
again, intelligence is the critical marker of human difference. This woman
speaks from her identity as a non-Anglo-European immigrant. She compares the experience of postwar refugees with her family's experience of
immigration. In her case, displaced persons were welcomed into their
social network, credited with refreshing the "culture" of her community.

For many of the people with whom I spoke, the concept of racism
entered their vocabulary sometime during the years following the Second
World War. Within the academic community a significant shift had
occurred; "race" was no longer regarded as a neutral scientific concept. It
was recognized as a powerful political tool in Nazi ideology. During a
series of meetings that spanned the 1950s and '60s, UNESCO brought
together international scholars "who were asked to summarize the scientific evidence concerning the nature of 'race'" (Miles 1989:46). Their final
statement provided the first scholarly definition of racism: "Racism falsely
claims that there is a scientific basis for arranging groups hierarchically
in terms of psychological and cultural characteristics that are immutable
and innate" (Montagu 1972:158 in Miles 1989:46). I draw a boundary at
this ideological juncture, where new sanctions on speech and social interaction were mediated through the creation of structures dedicated to political freedom and the promise of ethnic equality. This new consciousness,
however, initially applied only to European peoples and was not extended

to include members of racialized communities until much later. The United Nations and its declaration of human rights (1948) competed with the well-rehearsed repertoires of wartime difference. A gulf opened between generations; many people were embarrassed by the rigid categorical thinking of their parents. For the eldest generations, this ideological turn forced people to re-evaluate their language and their ideas about who people are. The shift foreshadowed a contemporary phenomenon known in its current form as "political correctness." Social sanctions around everyday speech are, perhaps, most evident through silences.

Silences

Silence emerged consistently throughout my research as an enigma both between and within generations. Regarding certain subjects, the rationale for silence is not at all clear. The pervasiveness of silence around war was brought home to me during an interview with two brothers and then, often, through the words of people from subsequent generations.

> Well, what's his name, who the hell is that guy from North Vancouver, the writer? Oh yeah, [Doug] Collins.[13] You know. [He is a Holocaust denier], and there's a great number of people who don't believe that, you know.
> [His brother interrupts him sharply] Well I happened to be there! Not in the Holocaust. I haven't got a tattoo, but no! I saw all those refugees going here and there and everywhere! ... Concocted, eh? They've got footage! (Interview, 26 August 1998. Italian-Canadian men, born 1916 and 1919.)

As with current dialogues about British colonialism, interpretive struggles are now being waged around the events of the Second World War. During this interview, two brothers clashed in their understanding of the veracity of events during the Holocaust. Remarkably, they had never spoken about the eldest brother's experience. I am reminded of the line that veterans draw between themselves and "zombies," and of the silence of soldiers. One woman's father had been among British troops who freed prisoners from Dachau. She found this out many years after his death. "Why didn't they speak? Why didn't they tell us? My son and grandson know nothing. They wouldn't go to war now! It doesn't mean anything to them!" While war has instilled categories of human difference that maintain a stubborn hold, the experiential memory of soldiers is tightly contained. Perhaps the silence around real warfare contributes to the resentment people feel when their speech is subject to social sanction. Without a rationale for soldiers' silences, connections between words and discriminatory actions in the world remain invisible.

Many people of the eldest generations view government as the enforcing agent of speech. Now, in the 1990s, some participants preface their comments by declaring their awareness of "political correctness" and new protocols for speaking about "race" or "culture."

What do you think about political correctness?
I think it's the awfullest thing in the world. I really do. I think it's taking away our natural thought. And I think when we can't express ourselves, we'll be worse than the Nazis ... But they are making me feel as though the government doesn't think I have the sense to make my own judgment ... Now, do I have a mind of my own?! ... I think it's terrible that we can't say truthfully that – how can I put this? If we had said ... "Mrs. ___ is a terrible housekeeper," it wouldn't be because she was Scotch or Polish; it was because she was a terrible housekeeper! And it was the truth ... But we can't say that now because it's a slur on their nationality! We can't be natural in our speech without meaning to be racist. There are many things said that aren't racist. That could be taken as racist. And I think it's a very, very pathetic thing that you can't express yourself in your own manner. (Interview, 14 November 1997. Scottish-Canadian woman, born ca. 1920.)

This woman draws a parallel between political correctness and the control over expression enforced by the Nazi regime. For her, categorical thinking is not dangerous; it is the intention that counts. The danger lies "now" in who controls expression in a social climate where speech conventions have changed. She views current ideological sanctions as infringements on her "right" to free speech and thought. Once again, the idea of what is "natural" emerges here in the link between people's behaviour and their nationality. Everyone I spoke with in the eldest generations was upset about what they perceived to be a regime of judgment on forms of expression that are, to them, quite everyday.

I get so mad when I hear all the fuss they make over this "N" word in the States. You know, to say "niggers" is an offence as heck now. When we were growing up, if somebody called you a Wop, that would really make you feel bad ... But by the same token, the Irish were called Micks, the English were called Limeys. The Slavic were called Bohunks, the French were called Pea Soups. We grew up with this and it was a common – it was a slur, but never meant so that it was a cutthroat deal with a knife coming out unless some were very serious and were born totally void of a sense of humour. Like my father, when he heard the word Dago, oh, his hair would stand up. (Interview, 8 July 1998. Italian-Canadian man, born 1936.)

The many ethnic slurs recited here are derived from an Anglo-European idiom that marks national and language groups. This man identifies humour as a strategy of interpretation not shared by his Italian-born father. Everyone I spoke with recognized personal consequences of speech acts. Shaped by their distance from dominant privilege, they rationalized these acts differently. What really stands out in these remarks is the ubiquity of habits of speech associated with human difference. Human difference is "traditionalized" in vocabularies through ethnic slurs (Bendix and Klein 1993:7; see also Dundes 1971b:187). As members of nations, we are aware of the cargo of past generations, their language and imagery. We are also subject to contemporary social processes whereby information is filtered and restricted.

Structural power was often evoked when people addressed the sanctions surrounding public expression. While some participants hesitated to speak about political regimes, others identified the potential repercussions of talking about mining and immigration. Many children of early immigrants did not know the stories of hardship faced by their parents. The perceived threat of deportation or job loss fuels some of these acts of self-censorship. Parents have also resolved to protect their children from the conflict they experienced in another age. Certain groups and organizations are surrounded by silence. I heard whispered, "off-the-record" statements about the Masons and their control over employment. Because of the secrecy surrounding their rituals and symbols, Masons have a noted place in the realm of rumour.[14] Membership in fraternal societies corresponded with religion, which often also correlated with nationality. During the wars, secrecy was part of an intensive public awareness campaign. It fuelled much of the suspicion towards "enemy aliens." Public service advertising was prolific on this front: "Watch every word you say! ... If you know anything, keep it to yourself!" (in *FFP* 4 June 1945).

Some silences are "traditional" acts that ensure protection from mal'uocchiu or preserve the secret nature of sacred knowledge. While we were conducting the Italian Oral History project, I came to understand that refusal to participate reflected a belief in the dangers of making information public. The more someone knows, the more power he or she has to inflict the eye. While mal'uocchiu revolves around the public display of wealth and prosperity, harmful gossip also ties into a class discourse. Secrecy and silence should be viewed as ways of preserving particular bodies of social knowledge and circumscribing the boundaries of their transmission.

Those who chose not to speak said that they were protecting others – usually their children, whose futures do not need to be stained by the past, or sometimes families whose reputations could be affected. I met an elderly man whose comments illustrated the power of old families in Fernie and perceptions about the slipping force of authority and morality. "Young people don't know how to work. It's all the marijuana." He spoke about being a leader for a youth group and mentioned the importance of discipline. "You know what broke it all up? It was the homosexuals! ... Some say they're born that way. Some say they're made. It don't matter – it's not natural, it's not right, it's dirty." What followed was a description of the actions of a local pedophile. He conflated the sexual abuse perpetrated by this person with homosexuality. I asked him if he reported the man to the police. He had not. He said he had known this man's parents since before they were married. A woman who was present agreed: "It's a hard situation when you've known the parents that long." Intergenerational tension is evident here in values of discipline, loyalty to other families, and ideas about yet another category of persons – the "homosexual." Steven Seidman (1994:169) notes: "From the early 1900s through the 1950s, a psychiatric discourse that figured the homosexual as a pathological personality, a perverse, abnormal human type, dominated public discussion." In most interviews around who and what to speak about, authority was mentioned and the spectre of social repercussions was evoked.

To people in the eldest generations, complex taxonomies translate into perceptions of place. Their maps suggest social distances that correspond with changing relationships between people in Fernie.

Narrative Maps: Neighbourhoods

So what do you think is so different today about cultures?
[Wife] Well, the immigrants that come out now, you find, have money. You find they can go out and buy themselves a home and they can go and buy themselves a car. Where the immigrants in those days had nothing when they came here. They had to build right from the bottom up. And I think it made a big difference. And now they have everything. Especially these people that came out after the war ... At least that's the way I see it.
I was going to ask you about religion.
[Husband] Well, this town is predominantly Catholic. It always was.
Were most of the Slavic-speaking people Catholic?
[Wife] Most of them were. Well, the church helped the people quite a bit when they first came out here, to get their citizenship and things like that. The church helped them.
[Husband] The kids got along. There was no enmity amongst the younger generation. If there was any enmity it was amongst the older ones. I never saw much among the older ones either!

[Wife] This is what we were brought up with, and I say, "If it can work then, why can't it work now?"

[Husband] Where's the problem now? With the Hindus and Chinese? East Indians?

[Wife] Well, we had East Indians here! They worked in the mills.

[Husband] Yeah, but they didn't live among us, they –

[Wife] No, they sort of lived on the outskirts of the town.

[Husband] They lived in country shacks.

Where?

[Husband] The Hindus? We had Hindus here in West Fernie, worked in the mill.

[Wife] You see, it was men. Just men. There were no women. Just like the Chinese that came out. The men came out but the women didn't come. And then we only had one dark family in Fernie that I can remember.

[Husband] Coloured.

[Wife] Yeah, the Negros ...

[Husband] In Fernie you can't divide the areas into ethnic groups because we're a cosmopolitan area. That is, every area had a mixture of everything. And they got along wonderfully well.

So divisions were maybe about class? Were there richer areas?

[Wife] South End. That's where they lived. This went on for quite a while. When I married [someone from outside West Fernie], Mrs. _____ [a merchant], she says to me one time at a church meeting: "I don't know why you and _____ don't move up to the South End." She says: "You live among the peasants."

Meaning West Fernie?

West Fernie. This is where we lived. And I turned around to her and I said: "Listen. If it wasn't for people like my dad that work in the mines – that keep your business going – you wouldn't be anywhere!" And I said: "I'm not going to come and live up here!" I said: "I'm happy where I'm at." I thought, uh-oh, and she never mentioned it again after she had mentioned it several times ... We could never afford to live up that end of town.

Peasants though, hey?

Yeah, peasants. "Why do you live among the peasants?" (Interview, 18 February 1998. Russian-Canadian man, born ca. 1914; Polish-Canadian woman, born ca. 1915. West Fernie.)

At my prompting this couple narrated a dizzying list of social categories based on gender, age, nationality, religion, class, and phenotype. Previous generations of Asian immigrants are marked as male populations. Nationality is associated with language and religious affiliations. They spoke about changing configurations of enmity between younger and older generations in Fernie. Ideas about social class riddle all of these categories. They made distinctions between pre- and postwar immigrants, education, and wealth. At times this couple suggested that class was the great equalizer between European groups. Finally it appears as the great barrier that defines and separates people through a labour hierarchy suggested by the term "peasants." Ideas of physical proximity and social distance are central in these interpretations.

During this interview, we sat with a map and marked out the shifting social landscape across the years in Fernie. Alongside the categories of human difference generated through war, there are others that appear in the narrative maps of the eldest generations: "Hindu," "Chinese," "Catholic-ers," "Public-ers" (referring to students who attended Catholic or public school, respectively), "workers," "bosses," "old-timers," and "youth." Geographical landmarks and homes served as important points of orientation. In this sense, perceptions of place are very much about a social history of families in town. Gardens are also common landmarks. Invariably, talking about these led to discussions of food as a marker of difference. Mobility also emerged as central to gender and to patterns of interaction between different communities of people. In this section, alongside the ages and nationalities of speakers, I also include their neighbourhood – another location that further complicates the social landscape in Fernie.

Everyone in the eldest generations identified distinct neighbourhoods: West Fernie, the South End, the North End, the Annex, and the Annex Extension. These areas are linked to personal identities; each had its own schools and its own community halls. Rivalry was rife.

I think the North End of Fernie were lots of Italians.
[Husband] Yeah. That was the tough end. [Laughing] I can remember slingshot fights across the Elk River between the South End and West Fernie.
[Wife] It's a wonder they didn't kill each other!
[Husband] And each area had their own football team ... what they call soccer. West Fernie had a team, Coal Creek, the North End.
   Who lived in the Annex?
[Husband] Pretty much a mixture. Europeans. From what I recall, West Fernie was mostly English. I don't recall too many foreigners. I think the same would go for the South End – mostly English-speaking people. (Interview, 5 September 1997. Czech-Canadian man, born ca. 1924; English-Canadian woman, born ca. 1926. West Fernie.)

Accounts of who lived where varied greatly. Many Anglo Europeans told me that people in the North End were mostly Italian; others stated that this neighbourhood was mixed and that this was where "miners" lived. One woman recalled "Slavtown," consisting of two blocks facing the CPR line. Frenchmen who were lumberjacks lived in the North End; those who were shopkeepers lived in the Annex. Class distinctions are far more revealing. Those who lived in West Fernie were often called "workers." There is some stigma attached to this district. Some see the district as the poorest in Fernie.

> I think the North End was kind of ethnic. A lot of the Italian people lived there. We lived right in the middle of an Italian community in the Annex ... West Fernie was kind of off-limits. It was kind of a different place. You have to remember, too, that there was a curfew in Fernie. Any kids that were on the street at nine o'clock were, the police used to actually patrol ... So West Fernie was a long ways away. So we very seldom went to West Fernie. (Interview, 18 September 1997. English-Canadian woman, born ca. 1930. Annex.)

Someone pointed out the simple houses in an area of West Fernie by the river, near where the mill shacks used to be, and told me that "DPs" had built them. It is interesting that the distinction between pre- and postwar immigrants also takes on an architectural dimension. In early days the Annex Extension was marked by its darkness. For some time there were no streetlights beyond the border to the Annex proper. The South End, or "uptown," was where the "moneybags" lived, an area of large brick houses with generous verandahs – also called "bosses' row" by some. Mining and railroad managers, merchants, and utilities executives lived here. Some places separated by negligible distances seem far away through narrative.

> I know more about the town than most people because I lived uptown most of my life. I never lived anywhere else. Most of these other people didn't live in town. They lived ... most of them lived in West Fernie, the Annex, or various places, but I lived in the main area of town all my life ... You know where the English Church is? The Anglican church is? (Interview, 12 September 1997. English-Canadian man, born 1911. South End.)

Churches were common landmarks as schools and meeting places, and identification of the Anglican Church as English was widespread. Religion translated often into one social category or another. Some identified those who had been Greek Orthodox in their home countries as "communists." Others used the wealth of the Vatican to suggest that Catholics were "rich." People drew on their own and their parents' experiences to speak about Catholics as collaborators with the Nazis. Others stated clearly that Protestants were members of the Masons and Shriners, who also had higher positions in labour and discriminated against Catholics. On a map, one woman marked out the trail she followed from her home, across the GNR tracks, to the Catholic school. This was a time when two school systems existed and the children from the public and Catholic schools were rivals. I asked her about religion in Fernie.

> I felt the difference being Catholic. I felt that. Yes. We had gone to Catholic school, I had gone for eight years. So just being in a separate building ... [A long-time acquaintance in town] apologized to me a couple of years ago about a comment she had made when we went past her house to go to school. She says: "Do you remember when I called you a [pause]?" I've forgotten what it was. There was Catholic-ers and Public-ers ... I would hear talk that you probably wouldn't get a job because you were Catholic. Things like this. But that didn't happen ... Older Catholics would say this ... I think it's old Protestant-Catholic differences ... There were some English-speaking Catholics, but most of them were – I couldn't even say most because there were many Irish Catholics ... Many of the Irish, and the Irish Catholics had very good positions with the mines ... I think within our own religion there was a class difference ... Was it based on nationality? Yes it was: English-speaking and non-English-speaking, that's right. (Interview, 16 April 1998. Slovak-Canadian woman, born ca. 1933. Annex.)

Ethnicity (here figured through language) and class are not the only markers of religion. One day I gave a woman a ride from the hospital to her church. As I dropped her off she said: "This isn't my church, you know." She belonged to the Congregational Church. "We broke away from the United – it's made up of Methodist and Anglican too." They split over the inclusion of gays and lesbians in the ministry. "At first," she told me, "there used to be only eight members. Now there's over ninety, because of this. It's not about homosexuals per se; it's about them being in positions of teaching children."

During the 1940s and into the 1950s, children were members of neighbourhood gangs. I heard about the "West Fernie Gang," the "Annex Bunch," the Fairy Creek Gang" (whose place was the Annex Extension), and the "North End Gang." People laughed as they spoke about throwing rocks and the creative rivalry around building rafts, constructing Ferris wheels, and raiding gardens. They emphasized a sense of neighbourhood that existed then, and the way that older children took responsibility for the young ones. They used to toboggan on the cemetery hill and roast potatoes in bonfires where the Ridgemont suburb is now.

> The North End Gang – I remember that gang. We lived in the
> Annex and there was the South End people, who we used to think
> of as snobs because they were the people who worked for the coal
> company. All those big houses up there. It was kind of like they lived
> in a different world. (Interview, 18 September 1997. English-Canadian
> woman, born ca. 1930. Annex.)

Again, in terms of real distance, the different worlds coexisted in close
proximity. It is class, defined largely through occupational positions, that
defines space and distance most clearly among Europeans in Fernie. People
mark Ridgemont as the old pasture grounds for coal company horses and
the location of the "Pest House."[14] Now it is also associated with the Kaiser
Steel takeover of what was then called Crowsnest Industries in 1977.[15]
Industrial history translates into a sense of class solidarity grounded in
neighbourhoods. It is what Italian, Polish, Ukrainian, Russian, Czech,
Slovak, Welsh, Scottish, and English "workers" evoke when they say they
were "all the same," "there were no differences or problems." In reference
to space and place, these people were united in their poverty, working
conditions, and recognition of the abyss separating them from "bosses."
To borrow the most commonly expressed phrase, they were "all in the
same boat." Most people who arrived in Fernie before the Second World
War have experienced dire poverty in Fernie and in their home regions.
Many who arrived after also told me about the hunger and struggles of
living in occupied territories. While there is an acute awareness of nationality, old-timers for the most part "look sideways" based on the experience of "being poor" and "working class."

> Nobody had nothing, nobody had anything, because that seems to
> be the problem nowadays. You know, everybody's trying to get what
> everybody else has. That wasn't like that when we were growing up.
> If we had nothing, we didn't care if somebody else got something ...
> It didn't bother us. (Interview, 9 September 1998. Italian-Canadian
> man, born 1925. North End.)

I heard about working-class pride and its repercussions on families.
One woman's father refused to take strike pay; another's was "blacklisted"
from mining because he refused to retract his political stance. I heard
about eating cabbages for whole winters, getting sick eating grain stolen
from barns, sleeping in coarse bleached sugar sacks, and making high
heels out of tin cans or costumes out of rhubarb leaves. Nostalgia for
these hard days pivots on ideas of sociality that are seen to be very different now. The death of people from the eldest age groups exacerbates
the sense of estrangement.

Narrative Maps: Outskirts

Social distance was evoked when people spoke about particular areas that were clearly geographically central. In the conversation with which I began the last section, the "Hindu" mill workers "living on the outskirts" were really only at the end of these people's street. This, in itself, is worth considering as a kind of apartheid thinking, where a great social abyss between people becomes transformed into *real* physical distance. Others called the small area where Sikh mill workers lived "Hindu Town." The Elk Lumber Company in West Fernie employed these men. After the mill burnt down in 1908, they moved west, following the lumber industry. One story I heard repeated over and over was the description of a cremation held not in Fernie, but at a sawmill in Elko. People commented on the "trancing and dancing" and the funeral pyre that burnt the frozen corpse of a fellow worker.

I was guided to many sites that are infused with knowledge and memories of persecution, work, relocation, or childhood happiness. I stood by weathered ruins while my guides conjured life back into abandoned structures and uneven topography. I was solemnly shown the overgrown graves of "enemy aliens," hidden away in thick brush. "Place-making" is a "universal tool of historical imagination ... a way of constructing the past ... social traditions and, personal and social identities" (Basso 1996:5, 7; see also Stewart 1996; Gupta and Ferguson 1997). The demarcation of certain areas through practices and beliefs sets apart places that were, in many cases, well positioned in the midst of things.

Everybody pointed out "Chinatown," a four-block area that included laundries, restaurants, and stores. People who remember this district do so through the eyes of childhood. Their descriptions combine fascination with a sense of distance.

I was born right in the middle of Chinatown – and New Year's Eve was out of this world! They had their own firecracker shows, and they'd bring a dragon out into the snowbanks for us kids. Yeah, and then have us for Chinese tea ... They did all of the laundry for the lawyers and doctors – you could see the stiff white shirts – and a lot of the hospital laundry, all of the major hotels, and there were eleven major hotels, all the linen sheets, tablecloths for the dining room. The Chinamen all did that ... and the gambling ... Oh yeah, and I know what opium smells like. I grew up with that smell ... We used to have opium fields over here, down the tracks from where the sawmill was. (Interview, 8 July 1998. Italian-Canadian man, born 1936. North End.)

Many followed up their descriptions of Chinatown by saying that "they" (Chinese men) were the only people who frequented the gambling and

opium dens. People remember these men living in Fernie until late in the
1930s and into the 1940s. Another "Chinese" area remembered by participants is the vegetable garden that was located "across the tracks."

> Like I said, we weren't allowed to come down here [pointing to the
> map] ... When we came we came with our parents and we'd always
> listen to Chinese music ... it was very weird and scary and we could
> always smell that aroma of soap and water and pressing ... They were
> old and scary and real Chinese, real Oriental, you know? But they
> were nice; I mean, they wouldn't hurt a fly.
> *Why do you think you were scared of them?*
> Because of their appearance ... they were very, like, primitive sort of,
> they very seldom went out, stayed right in their uh ... Nice people,
> really nice. Like if you went by they gave you a big smile, and they
> were very old. I remember a lot of them didn't even have their
> teeth ... Louis Bing had a veggie garden ... They lived behind and
> they used to deliver vegetables ... We never bought because we had
> our own gardens, but they used to deliver uptown to all the people
> who didn't have gardens. (Interview, 9 September 1998. Italian-
> Canadian woman, born 1928. North End.)

Through the eyes of children, these old men were exotic and "scary."
They were marked by their social apartness. Interactions with the larger
community were well circumscribed within the tight frames of economics. Communities of racialized people were always identified and named
along sharp lines. In this excerpt, the familiar evolutionary frame of primitivism is used.

Class designations often marked areas where Europeans met and worked.
On a strip of land owned by the coal company, people tended a large
community garden. Plots were rented for a dollar a year. This area, associated with labour, was also roughly bound by ethnicity.

> Where the Tom Uphill Home is, and the Isabella Dicken School,
> that was all allotted to miners, whether you were Slavic or Italian,
> but it was predominantly Italian because they were the premier of
> gardeners. So they were all given plots ... We raided gardens, but lots
> of the old fellows would sleep at night between the spuds. (Interview,
> 8 July 1998. Italian-Canadian man, born 1936. North End.)

Food pride crept into narratives when people spoke about their own
identities. Sometimes I was told how culinary customs were targeted by
political and civil authorities. A Polish-Canadian woman told me about a
time in the 1950s when the police came to destroy the poppy gardens of

the "Slav races." She was laughing as she described asking the officer to explain the reasons why her poppy-seed pastries were dangerous.

Food is a major marker of authenticity and difference used by people in Fernie. An Anglo-European man told me about working on a chicken farm. Every Friday he killed thirty chickens. "The girl with the crutches plucked them, the mother eviscerated them, the father folded the legs up underneath them and put them in bags." He said: "The Italians came for ten every week – alive. They like the blood." I asked him how they used it. He had no idea. "But the Bohemians made blood soup." He spoke about eating it one time and how it had fat floating on the surface. Then he said that was why he had to have heart surgery.

Food is a potent symbol of human difference that evokes yet another regime of commonsense knowledge.

> We never ate sauerkraut! [Mother] never allowed us to pick mushrooms because there were poison ones. And poppy seed – you don't eat poppy seed! ... But there were some things that Mother just, "You don't know what a mushroom is, so don't eat it!" And that was that ... The Europeans all did. I don't remember the English people going for mushrooms ... I never remember them picking mushrooms or dandelions. So that's another part of our culture that was so different. *We* went picking blueberries and chokecherries and saskatoons and wild strawberries, but not mushrooms. We didn't pick those or dandelions ... It was the Italians that picked those. (Interview, 14 November 1997. Scottish-Canadian woman, born ca. 1920. Annex.)

What is most striking about my many conversations about food is the way that people emphasized knowledge. Many especially acknowledged medicinal wisdom of particular national groups. I heard non-Anglo Europeans speak about the British in terms of a perceived lack of knowledge about gardening. Good-humoured comments were dropped here and there about their inability to survive for themselves by growing their own food and tending animals. When talking about relationships between different ethnic groups, people spoke of food and language in similar ways. Being invited into a home meant sharing strange foods and conversing with older people in other languages. They often responded to my questions about multiculturalism with these proofs that showed how "natural" these interactions were. Sharing food and language revolves around proximity.

North from the "Park," upriver from the rodeo grounds, in a clearing below the large houses of the South End is another "outskirt." This is the place where internees were held and processed during the First World War before internment at the Morrissey Camp. There are other places important to the eldest generations that carry their own memories of relocation, stigma, and community. These are the mining towns that have now disappeared: Corbin, Coal Creek, Morrissey, Michel, and Natal. Many of these places included within them "towns" named through national and language groups. When I listen to people speak about these places, I understand that the layers of marking otherness also translate into maps of mobility, especially for women. One Italian woman I spoke with was warned by her parents to stay away from the areas where Hungarian (read fascist) men were boarding. Young Anglo-European women were forbidden to visit areas where "foreigners" lived: "across the creek," "across the track," Middletown, and, in the case of Michel-Natal, "behind the coke ovens," were considered "alien."

There is no unified voice here; perspectives hail from diverse national histories, periods of immigration, and personal experiences of war. I hope that I have shown the complex categories of difference employed by these people, and their connections to scholarly and political discourses. Nationality, gender, sexual orientation, religion, class, age, and "race" constitute sites of solidarity and divergence. People's recognition of difference is selective, comparative, and, in many cases, essentialist. In varying degrees, old-timers express an understanding of absolute power through structures of authority. Ideas may be imposed politically; they are transmitted between generations and controlled in different ideological contexts. While some people acquire knowledge about others across vast distances, many take their cues from interactions of face-to-face sociality. Physical space is a component here in the real or imagined distances between people.

5
Getting Rid of the Story

Do you remember any First Nations people when you were growing up here?

You mean Injuns? Well, you know the story about the Injuns, eh?

What's that?

Well, William Fernie, when he found coal, the Indians showed it to him. And the story goes something like this: Fernie promised to marry this Indian's daughter. But he never, he reneged. So they put a curse on Fernie. And the curse was that every seven years we would be burnt out, flooded out, or some catastrophe would happen.

And it did too! Don't ever kid yourself! And then they had the curse-lifting ceremony. And the Indians stayed away from Fernie – they never came to Fernie at all. Then they lifted the curse. But it didn't make any difference.

So that's a story you've heard all your life?

Pretty well.

Do people believe it?

Oh yes. You bet your life they believe it ... There's no mistake about it. Boy, we've really been burnt out, flooded out.

[Wife] Do you want a teacup or a mug?

Oh, just whatever you have.

[Husband] Give her a tin cup [laughing].

[Wife] There are people who just want tea in a teacup.

[Husband] What is your second name?

Robertson.

[Husband] Robertson. You're not married?

No.

[Husband] How come?

[Wife] Well, she's been in school! (Interview, 18 February 1998. Russian-Canadian man, born ca. 1914; Polish-Canadian woman, born ca. 1915.)

I visited these people often. On this occasion we sat in their kitchen surrounded by boxes in various stages of packing. They had sold their home and were sorting their belongings in preparation to move into a facility for elderly residents. We drank tea (from mugs) and they generously shared with me their knowledge of Fernie, as well as their histories and ideas. This old-timer responded to my question about "First Nations" people in Fernie with the curse legend. It is, to him, "the story about the Injuns" that explains why these people "never came to Fernie at all." Again, the context for the act of cursing follows from "Indians" revealing the coal fields to William Fernie and the broken promise of marriage that ensued. Like other renditions of the curse story, this version highlights historical events: the fires and floods that have shaped the identity of this place. The formula of this curse is grounded in time, stipulating "catastrophe" every seventh year. In previous renditions the chief, the princess, or her mother proclaimed the curse of fires, floods, earthquakes, or famine. In this telling it is a generalized "they" who cast it. No particular cultural group is identified – only "Injuns," the quintessential filmic representation of indigenous people. This man mentions another episode in the legend, not yet touched upon. Ktunaxa traditionalists ceremonially lifted the curse in Fernie in 1964. According to this narrator, "it didn't make any difference."

Several people who participated in my research witnessed the curse-lifting ceremony. Their accounts reveal attitudes towards ritual, perceptions of affiliation or estrangement, and the imaginative incorporation of further events into the story-realm of the legend. Spectacles in the form of ritual, ceremony, and powwows are important sites where indigenous people are visible to Europeans. In the current context of land claims in BC, Ktunaxa representatives are using these occasions to re-educate the public. New representational conventions are eerily reminiscent of older ideas. Discourses of blood, race, and Nordic superiority are entangled with "special rights" talk. Most significant is the narrative of the empty land resounding in participants' refrain: "There are no Indians in Fernie." Perceptions of distance – real or imagined – are complicated.

> People who stay apart have few channels of communication. They easily exaggerate the degrees of difference between groups, and readily understand the grounds for it. And, perhaps most important of all, the separateness may lead to genuine conflict of interest, as well as to many imaginary conflicts. (Allport 1979:19 in Ryan 1996:150)

I heard repeatedly that the curse legend explains the perceived absence of indigenous people in the Elk Valley. In this sense, the story is also a narrative of social distance. A Ktunaxa woman provided an intergenerational perspective.

But even when I was younger, I remember when some of the old
people used to come from Grasmere to stay with us. They wouldn't
stay overnight [in Fernie]. Even ____'s mother ... not so long ago
[they] were driving through there ... and her mother was just clicking
her tongue and shaking her head and saying: "Why do these silly
people keep building here? Don't they know?" So.
   So that's an old thing?
It's old.
   Some accounts say that there was a band of Ktunaxa that lived at
   Michel Prairie.
I don't know if they lived there so much as travelled through there.
I think where [the story came] from is that the area there through
Elko all the way to the Pass was so overgrown with thick brush that
you couldn't get through there ... I think that's probably where it
came from, that it was just such a horrible area to get through that
nobody tried after a while. When the Indians used to travel over the
Pass and into Alberta, they went up though the Corbin area, through
there. If you go up through Coal Creek and up there you run into
Corbin. That's the way they used to go. Not directly through the
Fernie area. And of course it flooded out all the time, and you've got
big mountains on both sides – what do you do? ... So it's just like I
say – for practical purposes, it could have been: "Just don't go that
way because it's no good." (Interview, 11 December 1997. Ktunaxa
woman, born 1955.)

She suggests that the curse narrative fulfilled the practical purpose of
warning people about the rigours of travel through the Fernie area. Her
comments evoke Thomas Blackiston's inscription that the pass through
that region was "a very bad road." As a colonial narrative, the legend
provides a malleable form through which to explain difference and normalize enmity. I return to the management of colonial narratives and contexts within which they are negotiated or symbolically erased.

And then I mentioned to you, when the curse-lifting ceremony
happened, within a year Kaiser Coal was here and everything
changed within a year. One year! And there was a difference.
   And did people also talk about it as being a result?
No. Not too much. Once in a while. [Pause]
I do though. I say: "The curse is lifted." Yes ...
   What's your general opinion about how people reacted to that ceremony?
Some said: "Well, you know there was no truth to it anyway!" Or:
"No. It had no power anyway!" And said it was just something to do.
Others were saying: "Well, this is going to get rid of that whole idea

that there's nothing here and we'll die of famine." You know? "This will get rid of that story. This will be the end of that story." Those were the two reactions. (Interview, 16 April 1998. Slovak-Canadian woman, born ca. 1933.)

The resurrection of the legend in 1964 and its resolution through public ritual is here associated with symbolic and economic renewal in the coal industry. A month before the curse-lifting, the United Mine Workers of America had negotiated a "breakthrough contract" with the Crowsnest Pass Coal Company (Langford 1998:56). In 1965 the corporation changed its name to Crowsnest Industries Ltd. and adopted a new corporate symbol (Mangan 1977a:43-44). One year later, Kaiser Steel took over its coal operations. For workers and industry, the ceremony ushered in an era of prosperity. As this woman states, the efficacy of the curse-lifting is a subject of discussion amongst older generations in Fernie. There is the suggestion that the story itself is a force to contend with, and the ritual was a means of "get[ting] rid of that story."

I am interested in what the curse-lifting ceremony meant both in the political context of the mid-1960s, and through the interpretive frames of the present. Internationally, early struggles for decolonization were widespread throughout the 1960s. Aboriginal title was argued around this time in British Columbia courtrooms. Until 1951 it was illegal under the Indian Act for Aboriginal groups to solicit funds for the purpose of pursuing a land claims case. Those classified as Indians received the right to vote in federal elections in 1960. While the government proposed assimilation, indigenous leaders argued for recognition of Aboriginal sovereignty. Dara Culhane (1998:74) marks 1963 as the beginning of an important series of legal cases concerning Aboriginal rights. Precedent for Aboriginal rights at this time was drawn from cases across the British Empire. In *R. v. White & Bob* (1965), lawyers representing the British Columbia government argued social evolutionary theory at the base of Rhodesian precedent. They also used eighteenth-century British maps to argue that the Royal Proclamation of 1763 could not apply to peoples whose territories were not mapped at that time (75-77). Since aboriginal title was upheld in the 1973 decision of *Calder*, a series of court cases have come to define the way in which indigenous people of BC assert their rights to land.

I draw parallels between popular discourses in the 1960s and the current context of land claims in the late 1990s. "Aboriginal peoples have never accepted assimilation. Indeed, their unique cultures, traditions and languages remain an integral part of the Canadian mosaic" (Canada DIAND 1995:3). This is a state narrative that seeks eventually to "replace the Indian Act with a modern partnership" (4). Marcia Crosby (1997:28) views "political partnerships" as a "euphemism for an old agenda." Although discursive conventions have changed, colonial narratives remain essentially intact.

Cross-Cultural Spectacle

Lifting the Curse

On 14 August 1964, Ktunaxa traditionalists were invited by Fernie city council and Rotarians to perform the ceremony to lift the curse. For weeks leading up to the event, advertisements appeared in the local paper inviting visitors and residents to attend.[1] The ceremony took place before a largely local audience and included the participation of the mayor. His first duty was to officially welcome the traditionalists and set the context for the ritual.

> On behalf of the City of Fernie it is my pleasure today to welcome the members of the Kootenay Indians. This is the 60th anniversary of its incorporation as a city ... it is most fitting indeed that your people, the real natives of this country should participate with us at this time – as an immigrant to your country and having travelled from Nova Scotia to British Columbia, I have formed the personal opinion that the native Indians of the country were not fairly dealt with by the early white settlers. The land allotted to them seems to me to be the most unproductive in the country. According to the legend, similar treatment to your forefathers brought upon our community a curse which has been hanging over our heads for many years. During these years many misfortunes have befallen us and by many, it is believed that your curse brought these about. However, it is very pleasant to know that you are here today to perform the ceremonial of removing this curse and which we hope will bring prosperity to yourselves as well as the remainder of the community. (Speech by Mayor James White, 14 August 1964, FDHS Archives P747B)

In his speech, the mayor draws a parallel between William Fernie's act of betrayal and larger forces of colonial incursion, most notably the loss of traditional lands and access to resources. White identifies himself as an "immigrant" and uses the term "real natives" in reference to indigenous peoples. He is highlighting a distinction between these people and those Europeans then popularly known in political discourse as "native born." According to Howard Palmer (1982:13), the term was in common use until the 1940s. Rhetorically, it bolstered an anti-immigrant discourse that was primarily Anglo-Saxon and Canadian-born. There is an element of nation-to-nation protocol in the mayor's invocation of a break from the "misfortunes" of the past and the forging of a new relationship in the future. When asked by a newspaper reporter about his own belief in the curse, White "indicated that he believes many people, since all are superstitious to a degree, have no other explanation for the series of tragedies" (*FFP* 20 August 1964:1).

Thirty-four years later, Mayor White's granddaughter revived the story of the curse and its ceremonial resolution in an installation piece titled *Fold It Up and Put It Away: Fernie's Curse*, at the Southern Alberta Art Gallery in Lethbridge, Alberta (MacGregor 1997). Through film, video, and audio she constructed a dialogue between members of her family and Ktunaxa descendants of Tobacco Plains ceremonialists. In the dark gallery, a large screen shone with blurry images of gardens, airplanes, scenes of the ceremony, and excerpts from parades – cuts from her grandmother's home movies. Voices sounded from two sides of the room. Regarding the ceremony, a Ktunaxa man stated: "It was kind of a goodwill ambassador thing from both sides."

It is difficult to assess the state of public awareness about Aboriginal issues during the 1960s. In 1969 Harold Cardinal (1969/1999:3) wrote: "There is little knowledge of native circumstances in Canada and even less interest. To the native one fact is apparent – the average Canadian does not give a damn." Media across the world was focused on South African apartheid and struggles for civil rights. Internationally, Canada was criticized for what was perceived outside the nation as apartheid.[2] In response, Prime Minister Pierre Trudeau released the controversial White Paper of 1969. The White Paper policy called for the dissolution of the Department of Indian Affairs. "Indians" were to assimilate into larger Canadian society, the Indian Act would be abolished, treaty obligations terminated, and Aboriginal rights dismissed. Cardinal (1969/1999:1) called the policy "a thinly disguised programme of extermination through assimilation." In response to the proposal, "First Nations organized themselves on a Canada-wide basis, mobilizing their members to present a united front in defence of their cultural and political survival" (Culhane 1998:84).

The episode served to solidify indigenous organizations and signalled a major shift in Aboriginal-government relations.[3] It is significant to note the turn in literary and scholarly realms towards representation at this juncture. Indigenous authors publicly criticized state policy (Cardinal 1969/1999) and ways that "Indians" were inscribed by anthropology (Deloria 1969). From the 1970s onward, "the idea that indigenous people should represent themselves (rather than be represented by others, such as anthropologists)" signalled a major shift in public discourse (Cruikshank 1998:139). The period corresponds with what Nicholas Thomas (1994:189) has named the era of the "new ethnicity," when class, age, gender, and political consciousness ruptured the entity of "ethnic group." The 1960s mark a turn towards explicitly "racialized politics" in Canada, where difference was framed not though biology but through "culture" and the politics of group rights (Kirkham 1998:246).

To some of the people with whom I spoke, it was the media coverage of desegregation in the United States that signalled a shift in consciousness. I asked one woman when she first heard about the idea of human rights.

I suppose it was the thing in Mississippi. Yes. It wasn't here. That was probably in the '60s. Integration, the integration laws. I was surprised that the blacks couldn't drink from the same fountain, and yet at the same time I didn't hear about the Natives not being allowed into Fernie unless they had permission. Now I didn't hear about that until the last, say, fifteen years. As I look back on it now, I wonder why we didn't, why I knew about black difference before I knew about our own ... Probably what happened with integration in the '60s is what is probably happening for us now. (Interview, 16 April 1998. Slovak-Canadian woman, born ca. 1933.)

While decolonization efforts in other places were well publicized, this woman suggests a silence surrounding colonialism in BC. Perhaps this silence is the most potent product of colonial narratives. At the time of the curse-lifting ritual, a popular primitivism overshadowed the under-publicized struggles for recognition of indigenous land rights.

It is difficult to state with any confidence exactly what the curse-lifting ceremony meant to residents in Fernie in 1964. The occasions on which certain stories are retrieved or recited deserve detailed attention. The ceremony marked the city's sixtieth anniversary, when it was on the threshold of a new era of corporate prosperity. At this time, cultural tourism was in a state of germination. The stigma of superstition was, however, still acute.

When the subject was first broached, there were some local people who objected on the grounds it would make Fernie look "foolish" ... There were others who really took it to heart. They did not look on it as something which would attract tourists, something which would be entertaining, something definitely unusual. No visitor who attended the "curse-lifting" gives a hoot whether you or I or everyone believes in the curse or not. No visitor looking for a glimpse of the Ogopogo or the Loch Ness Monster really cares what the local people think ... A few decided it has publicity value ... as well as being a kind of morale-builder for those who half believe in it. That it has publicity value is proven. We haven't done any psychology on the local morale lately, so we can't answer the second question. (Editorial *FFP* 20 August 1964:2)

This writer makes a distinction between "visitor[s]" and "local people." The former, drawn to Fernie by publicity, are in pursuit of spectacle. According to the writer, they care little about local interpretations. "Local people" have a more intimate connection to the curse-lifting ritual. Having lived with the legend, residents assess its meaning through local knowledge. The participation of Ktunaxa traditionalists is not mentioned here, only the "publicity value" of the event.

> Saturday's parade began with an indifferent parade of too few Indians. The parade, thrown in as a kind of last minute bonus to the afternoon program, started about 30 minutes after its scheduled 11 a.m. time ... mainly because of the hectic last minute scramble to make the parade presentable ... Spectators expected to see Indians, they weren't satisfied with what they got. (*FFP* 20 August 1964:1)

> I remember when they had the, the chief came to, uh, lift the curse – that sort of thing.
> *Did you go?*
> No. Because I didn't take this seriously. I didn't take the chief seriously. I didn't take the curse seriously. Maybe I'm as practical as my mother was. No. I should think about it I think. But at this point it doesn't influence how I feel about this community. (Interview, 4 November 1997. Ukrainian-Canadian woman, born 1925.)

Interpretations of the curse-lifting ceremony include understandings of who the ritualists were and what they were doing. They betray a popular politic of spectacle in which audiences have certain expectations of what they will see and what it should look like. Those who witnessed the event re-create it from varying positions of acquaintance and distance.

> To the sombre, sometimes eerie beat of the tom-tom, the gaily-costumed Indians gave their war cry and danced wildly but rhythmically around the seated drummers. For the spectators it was a unique sight. For the Indians it looked war-like at times but they seemed to enjoy it ... The crowd of 600 or more applauded enthusiastically. (*FFP* 20 August 1964:1, 7)

> There were maybe one hundred spectators who attended the event. It was interesting to see the mayor a Scotch Presbyterian, smoking the peace pipe. The ceremony called for smoke to be blown in the four directions. The wind was so strong that day that it would only go in one direction. I thought he was going to choke! He never smoked a day in his life! (Interview, 20 May 1998. Welsh-Canadian man, born ca. 1928.)

The ritual of the curse lifting began. As the dance grew wilder and the Indians screamed their ancient imprecation in their own guttural tongue, Chief Red Eagle and Big Crane consulted in whispers, heads together as Big Crane, for the first time, revealed details of the ceremony. The 200 year old peace pipe, handed down from chief to chief, was dragged from its pouch. Big Crane lit it as he intoned the ritual. Mayor White was called from his seat in the stand and was seated between Big Crane and the chief. Big Crane reached the end of his ritual the tom-tom sounded louder. (*FFP* 20 August 1964:1, 7)

I was there when they lifted it. I thought it was really interesting. But I thought it was kind of hokey too. I think the Indian people knew that it was just a game. They did what they were asked to do, but I'm not so sure they really thought that they had lifted the curse. I think they kind of giggled about it behind their hands. I remember the pipe going out before the ceremony was over, and they were laughing and saying that maybe the curse wasn't lifted after all because the pipe was going out before the ceremony was over. But it was a big occasion. (Interview, 18 September 1997. English-Canadian woman, born ca. 1930.)

The pipe was passed to Chief Red Eagle, who puffed once, then passed it on to Mayor White. Then it went out. More incantations were called down as the pipe was lit once more. The mayor puffed nervously from the long stem. The curse had been lifted. (*FFP* 20 August 1964:1, 7)

Tension builds in the published description of the curse-lifting ritual. The pipe is extinguished, the mayor is nervous, and the drums are getting louder and louder. Images of "war-like" people who "danced wildly," "scream[ing] their ancient imprecation" to the "eerie beat of the tom-tom" evoke the terrifying narrations circulating in earlier colonial contexts. In contrast to this is another image of "gaily-costumed" performers, and spectators who applaud the "unique sight." The coexistence of primitivism and entertainment was well established by this time through popular forms of representation. Certainly, media representations were still based on images from the Wild West. In the *Fernie Free Press* during July 1958, television listings included *The Lone Ranger, Last of the Mohicans, Wild Bill Hickock, Have Gun Will Travel, The Cisco Kid*, and *Frontier Justice*. An Italian woman who immigrated to Canada in the late 1960s spoke about popular media in Italy:

I remember *Tarzan*, that was my favourite movie. Then they came with those Hercules shows, they were very interesting. And then they start to show American movies too – westerns and romances ... In early 1960, they start those spaghetti westerns and they were very popular! They became very, very popular. They were Italian-made – cowboys and Indians and everything like [that], but we had our own Italian actors ... They gave you the wrong impression in those movie. Always – especially those old, old [movies] where always the Indian were the bad people. (Interview, 22 September 1998. Italian woman, born 1946.)

A photograph taken at the curse-lifting depicts two men at the centre of the ritual (see Figure 14). Perhaps because his attire was not explicitly "Indian," the man at left, Chief Red Eagle, was not initially identified on the image. The ritual was performed by members of a culture whose traditions are understood by many Euro-Canadians only through popularized imagery that extends into the present. People speak about procedures surrounding the "peace pipe" with an air of familiarity. It is an assumed understanding of ritual between indigenous and European people that evokes the small ceremonies of oratory and exchange described in explorers' memoirs.

Figure 14   Traditionalists Chief Red Eagle (Ambrose Gravelle) at left and former chief Big Crane (Joe Dennis) confer at the curse-lifting ceremony in Fernie, 14 August 1964. *Photographer unknown. Courtesy of the Fernie and District Historical Society, 1086-03.*

Ritualism is taken to be a concern that efficacious symbols be correctly manipulated and that the right words be pronounced in the right order. (Douglas 1973:28)

On that August day in Fernie, few observers understood the symbolic lexicon of the Ktunaxa traditionalists.

Many of those who witnessed the ritual base their observations on their social relationships to the actors in the ceremony. Perhaps because of the pejorative view of superstition, people waver on the truth-value or their personal belief in the curse. They draw from different bodies of social and traditional knowledge to assess the effectiveness of the ritual.

You can't lift it but you can change the flow of it. (Ktunaxa woman in MacGregor 1997)

Well, the curse was on Fernie right through until old Jimmy White, he got to be mayor of Fernie. He decided it would be a good idea one year ... to take the curse off Fernie. This is just a pile of crap you know, but this was going to be a big celebration. So they had this big celebration, you know. I didn't go to it. But they had it down there and the Indians came ... and they went through their "Kay aye" and all the rest of it. Took the curse off Fernie. A month later old Jimmy White dropped dead. I says they took it off Fernie and stuck it on him! He dropped dead in his office. That was, nobody thinks that's what did happen – it actually happened! It sounded just like that's what happened, took it off Fernie and put it on him. I thought about it ... I started thinking ... they put a curse on him! (Interview, 12 September 1997. English-Canadian man, born 1911.)

MAYOR WHITE SUCCUMBS TO HEART ATTACK: ... Mayor White who had a serious heart attack just over a year ago, had not been completely well since that time ... Recently in Fernie's famous curse-lifting ceremony, the mayor was made a blood brother of the Kootenay Indian Tribe with the tribal name, Chief Big Eagle. (*FFP* 10 September 1964:1, 8)

I was told over and over that the only one who could ever take a curse – if they cursed you, if something was, it's called bad medicine – is the person who originally did it. She's long gone. She's never going to that place. (Interview, 11 December 1997. Ktunaxa woman, born 1955.)

Interpretation of meaning occurs through an individual's "own world of observation and knowledge" (Siikala 1992:202-203). Ktunaxa statements about cursing suggest culture-specific knowledge of ritual and belief. I heard speculation about the death of the mayor from many non-indigenous people. The association of this untimely death with the curse legend evokes ideas of sympathetic or contagious magic, where the effect is associated with close contact to a cause. In the context of cross-cultural relations, such beliefs fuel atrocity myths and perpetuate ideas of enmity.

Older generations of people continue to speculate about the curse-lifting ceremony. Their often conflicting interpretations are rife with ideas about power and belief that implicate colonial taxonomies of difference. Cultural performances are riddled with the "contesting of views and of power" (Bruner and Gorfain 1984:57; see also Cruikshank 1998:138-159). Some people use imaginative resources circulating in local contexts to speak about unequal power relations.

> People say it was put back on because the Indians weren't looked after. They were just left in town with no way to get home and no one to put them up! I think they just used them. They just used them so the curse was put back on. (Fieldnotes, 12 January 1998. Czech-Canadian woman, born 1909.)

> Maybe people of Fernie should remember not to get us mad [laughing] remember us when they are signing treaties. (Ktunaxa man in MacGregor 1997)

The curse legend is used here to address social and political inequalities between indigenous and non-indigenous people. Clearly the curse-lifting ceremony presents an opportunity to speak about this history of interaction into the present context of treaty making. Historically, "nationhood ... [is] asserted within and between First Nations through the traditional display of material culture and ritual," practices that are "still inextricably bound up with lands, rights and resources" (Crosby 1997:23). As a formal performance between members of dominant society and colonized peoples, the curse-lifting ritual reflects a long history of symbolic exchanges that mark new relationships between nations.

In the late 1990s, interpretations of curse-lifting are offered within a context of re-evaluation of past actions. Currently the idea of "reconciliation" is widespread. It is used in reference to resolution of colonial relations between indigenous peoples and imperial governments, the recovery of nations from totalitarian regimes, and the righting of injustices during periods of warfare. For scholars of oral history, it is a time for looking at the past in the present and examining official forms of memory.

On 7 January 1998, Jane Stewart, Canada's minister of Indian Affairs and Northern Development delivered a "Statement of Reconciliation." After thanking elders for their "guidance and spiritual blessings," Jane Stewart proceeded to address "the negative impacts that certain historical decisions continue to have in our society today." Through official oratory imbued with symbolic gesture, she spoke to the fallacy of the empty land discourse, acknowledging the "thousands of years" through which Aboriginal peoples maintained their "own forms of government" as well as their position as "custodians of lands, waters and resources of their homelands." The minister also offered thanks for, and acknowledgment of, Aboriginal "contributions to Canada's development" that began with "welcoming newcomers to the continent":

> We must recognize the impact of these actions on the once self-sustaining nations that were disaggregated, disrupted, limited or even destroyed by the dispossession of traditional territory, by the relocation of Aboriginal people, and by some provisions of the Indian Act ... The Government of Canada today formally expresses to all Aboriginal people in Canada our profound regret for past actions of the federal government which have contributed to these difficult pages in the history of our relationship together. (Canada DIAND 1998)

Mayor White's speech and the government's statement of reconciliation both acknowledge past injustices. The ceremonies address the history of Aboriginal and non-Aboriginal relations. One speaks about the curse on Europeans, the other about "negative impacts ... historical decisions" have wrought upon First Nations peoples. Both ceremonies are symbolically staged to get rid of the story of colonialism. My conversations with European and indigenous people are situated at this juncture of historical re-evaluation.

I spoke with an elderly woman about the speech of apology to Aboriginal people. She became agitated and said: "Nothing will take away the damage that's been done. I know! It was exactly the same with us!" She said she knows what it means to be "treated like nothing," and "nobody can fix that." She said: "Treaties won't fix that. Taking people's land won't change things." I talked about the redistribution of wealth, mostly from corporate hands, and that treaties don't involve private lands. She said that's why it won't work (from Fieldnotes, 17 January 1998. Czech-Canadian, born 1912).

This woman parallels her experience as an "enemy alien" with the persecution of indigenous peoples. Many people in the eldest generations approached the treaty process in BC through European examples. They spoke about invasions and occupations by enemy armies in Europe or the downfall of Soviet Communism and its failed project. Some invoked the failure of wartime treaties and pacts in order to condemn the land claims process in BC.[4]

> Well, women were not created as human beings until when? When were we put into the Constitution, recognized as beings? And we don't hold that against them. We forget it and go on ... Every step you take forward. You don't dwell on the fact that we didn't, you go forward and you make sure that it doesn't happen again.
>   *I was just reading an article about the prisoner of war camps in Morrissey.*
> The First World War – that's where my father would have been if he hadn't run away. Most of the people there were Ukrainians.
>   *That's what the article was saying, and the Ukrainian community is demanding an apology and compensation. That's similar to what's happening all over.*
> I don't believe in the word compensation. I don't believe that our children should pay for our fathers' sins. I don't believe in compensation, but I like the word reconciliation. I like the words, yes, we did it, and we were wrong. The gesture is important. Compensation becomes as bad as the sin. There may have been cases, but – who is paying the compensation? People who did not commit the sin. But to admit that it was wrong is important. (Interview, 4 November 1997. Ukrainian-Canadian woman, born 1925.)

What emerged most often from my conversations with Europeans was a naturalized notion of conquest as a simple, but unfair, fact of human behaviour. People showed me poems describing the destruction of their villages and cities, photographs and postcards that memorialize their loss of places. They emphasized the importance of "moving on" and the impossibility of righting past wrongs.

Ritual, Spectacle, and Cross-Cultural Perceptions

One afternoon in the Fernie library, as I was photocopying newspaper descriptions of the curse-lifting, a man in his seventies began speaking with me about the "early days." He told me some entertaining stories about my grandfather and great-grandfather and asked what I was doing. A smile broke across his face as he told me that "Fernie-ites" living in Vancouver gathered together every year for a reunion in the Waldorf Hotel – an establishment built after its namesake in Fernie had burnt down. He told me that they had their own curse-lifting ceremony there; that there were so many people you "couldn't seat everyone." I asked if they had invited indigenous ceremonialists. He said: "We just had a guy dressed up like an Indian" (from Fieldnotes, 13 January 1998).

The simultaneous enactment of a curse-lifting in Vancouver attests to the power of the legend as a symbol of community identity. It is important to interrogate the role that fantasy plays in our configurations of belonging and estrangement.

On the occasion of the curse-lifting ceremony, a reporter asked the Ktunaxa traditionalists to comment on the curse legend:

> Elders of the tribe believe heartily in the existence of the age-old curse ... but neither holds any stock in the whiteman's version. As far as they are concerned, the legend of William Fernie and the broken agreement to marry an Indian Princess ... is poppycock. They believed in the story that a greedy squirrel ... took control of the valley from Elko to Frank where the squirrel's uppity wife guarded the entrance to the valley. As the Indian youth toppled the rocks of the first Frank Slide onto the expiring lady squirrel, he intoned the mighty curse ... This curse ... goes back to the days when the valley was recovering from the glacial lake under which it had been submerged. (*FFP* 20 August 1964:1)

The Ktunaxa narrative is grounded in traditional knowledge. Characters and their motives evoke meanings that are embedded in a particular symbolic universe not easily accessible to outsiders. Despite this disavowal of the "whiteman's version" on public record, the narrative continued to be scripted as an Indian story. The image of the betrayed Indian princess endures. Three years after the curse-lifting ceremony, a writer for the *Nelson Daily News* wrote: "The Indian woman crouched before the small fire of twigs muttering incantations. As she spoke, she tossed a few handfuls of unknown substances into the flames. As her ceremony concluded, she arose and walked into her tepee, her black work concluded. The curse on Fernie had been born" (Kolfage 1967:11).

Non-Aboriginal people of every age group discuss their perceptions of indigenous people through spectacle and ceremony, contexts where they are culturally visible. Spectacle provides a frame through which non-indigenous people imagine Native Americans; the Wild West shows were perhaps the best example of performances that reified people in a timeless past of normalized conflict. It is as though the caricature of the Indian has become traditionalized in European thought and performance – what bell hooks (1992:133) might refer to as imperialist nostalgia in mass culture, "re-enacting and reritualizing in different ways the imperialist, colonizing journey as narrative fantasy of power and desire."

Social and cultural boundaries separating different belief systems become visible through various interpretations of the curse-lifting ritual. To Roy

Rappaport (1992:249), ritual is, most importantly, a "sequence of formal acts and utterances," communicating and "bringing into being" "enduring messages" drawn from "the social and cosmological order." The question of interpretation across epistemological boundaries is enigmatic. Italian women with whom I work straddled this abyss by recognizing the form of communication itself: ritual and the knowledge required for its performance.

> I don't think the Indians would have done it if they thought it was just being done for fun. At least, I don't think they would have, 'cause I think they took that pretty seriously ... And really, if you're going to believe in religion, if you're going to have any faith belief, then you have to believe that there could be curses as well, I think. So I think a curse could be like a death by prayer, and obviously the ceremony was some form of prayer. It had to be a form of prayer to remove it. (Interview, 28 July 1998. Italian woman, born 1945.)

> She said she did hear the story of the curse-lifting ... She said she heard that Fernie belonged to the Indians. That's what she heard, and they lifted the curse, but that's all. She's not really familiar with it ... She feels that the Indians are really knowledgeable on weather, and she said if they tell you, if they say: "This fall, this winter is going to be a bad winter," she feels that they know and it will happen. She feels they are knowledgeable in these things. She has heard this and she says she has great respect for the Natives 'cause she said they are also very knowledgeable on medicines.
>   Questa è true yeah. Yeah è true [it's true]. (Translated during interview, 8 August 1998. Italian woman, born 1920.)

Italian women look sideways at Ktunaxa people, expressing their affinity based on a shared reverence for ritual and religious belief. As devout Catholics and practitioners of traditional knowledge, these women participate daily in ritual and adhere to a complex of beliefs around cursing. Like the woman above, most Italians acknowledged the politics of land. Many were reluctant to offer any authoritative opinions about the truth of the curse or the actual details of the story. While some were new arrivals to Fernie, others had been residents for several decades. I view these silences within the realm of traditional knowledge and sanctions around dangerous talk.

Ritual is surrounded by proscriptions on behaviour, presentational conventions, and roles and obligations of witnesses. It is also a flexible performance that creates meaning within particular social and political contexts. An English-Canadian woman who is married to a Ktunaxa man told me about her exclusion from a ritual she was previously sanctioned to attend.

> That's the difference too, you know. A long time ago I went to the Black Tail Dance [at the New Year], and now I'm told I shouldn't have gone because I shouldn't have been allowed – but I was invited ... I think the old people didn't have the, I don't know what it is. It's an entirely different feeling. I can see a lot of reasons behind it, but I don't understand why people say "This is the old way" when it wasn't the old way when I was with the old people. (Interview, 18 September 1997. English-Canadian woman, born ca. 1930.)

To Ktunaxa elders with whom I spoke, this shift reflects a long struggle for control over traditional knowledge and the contexts of interaction between themselves and non-indigenous people. Several old-timers in Fernie mentioned attending the yearly "powwow" (Sun Dance) at Edwards Lake and their eventual exclusion from this event.[5] Many of these people suggest that it is indigenous people who have *essentially* changed rather than the politics shaping interactions between people. Ktunaxa people participated in Labour Day parades until sometime in the late 1950s.

> They'd be in the Labour Day parade, their regalia is beautiful – the feathers, the horses. The women were plainer, of course it was the chiefs who were completely in dress ... But they must have felt like a spectacle [with] people watching. They finally refused to come; they were invited but didn't want to come. (Interview 16 April 1998. Slovak-Canadian woman b. 1933.)

I viewed home movies of Labour Day processions in the 1960s. Euro-Canadian children dressed in feathers and headbands often formed the last dangling edges of the parade. Up until the 1960s, images of the "de-politicized Indian subject" were ubiquitous in popular culture (Crosby 1997:25). In the context of self-representation, imagery and performance are now "re-invested with contemporary political meanings" (25).

Indigenous peoples in British Columbia have a long history of organized struggle against colonial oppression. As I have discussed, strategies include control over flows of information necessary to the administration of colonial policies. Indigenous groups use their distinct cultures and traditions as important ideological tools for internal mobilization and external recognition. Powwows and festivals are recognized occasions for dialogues about cultural differences. "Public performances of indigenous culture should be understood as tangible forms of social action rather than as texts or representations standing outside the real activity of participants"

(Cruikshank 1998:138-139). In the present context of treaty making in BC, indigenous speakers are using these sites to make colonial history visible through the politics of land.

People of younger generations in Fernie (aged twenty to fifty) attend a yearly event known as the "Gathering," which has been held since 1996. Each summer, five hundred people camp or drop in at Island Lake for a "music and wilderness festival" (*Mountain Fresh [MF]* July 1998). It was variously described to me as a temporary "community within nature," "a powwow without Indians," "a beer ad." After paying $50 for a weekend pass to this alpine event in 1998, you could rent a tipi for $300 over the weekend and listen to a member of one of Mali's "ancient 'griot' families" or an East Kootenay marimba band playing Zimbabwean music. Professional hoop and grass dancers from prairie Aboriginal communities also perform at the Gathering. Most years the master of ceremonies is an indigenous "storyteller."

> You go up there to listen to some good music, relax in a beautiful place and some guy gets up and starts telling you about how all of the land belongs to them and how you stole it and how bad we are. But *I* can't shoot a moose out of season! (Fieldnotes, 20 August 1998. Euro-Canadian man, born ca. 1960)

These comments suggest a dis-ease with the explicitly political comments of the Cree orator. The Gathering draws audience members who share an ethic for wilderness as symbolic property belonging to all of humanity. In contrast, the orator speaks about sovereignty over traditional lands and the violence of colonial incursion. People who oppose land claims call upon the popular discourse of "special rights." In this case there is a perceived inequality between peoples' rights to hunt. The argument of special rights disregards traditional Aboriginal resource use and ignores the history of economic marginalization.[6] There is a sense that we coexist on a level playing field. Special rights discourse takes place through the idiom of "rights," in which "there is no more effective way to deny the right of others than to say they are denying your own" (Ignatieff 2000:5). This "alternative hegemonic project" (Kirkham 1998:245-261) is based in the premise that inequalities have been reconciled during the last thirty or so years of human rights initiatives, affirmative action legislation, and multicultural policies (245-261). There is a harshness in special rights talk that serves to erase the history of colonialism and structural inequalities. Unlike the discourses of conquest used by older generations, special rights talk does not acknowledge the horrors of nation-to-nation conflict. While new nationalisms are unsettling historical representations of indigenous and non-indigenous people, older regimes of imagery remain intact.

During an interview with three teenagers (aged sixteen to eighteen) in Fernie, the question of Aboriginal presence was again answered through the context of spectacle.

> *What about First Nations people?*
> b: What's First Nations people?
> a: The Natives.
> c: All the First Nations people – Black Diamond, Calgary, um, Longview, Grasmere, that reserve out by Cranbrook, Hosmer – there's a whole bunch, like, all around here.
> *And in Fernie?*
> c: Well they come in for that one powwow.
> *Do you go to school with Native kids?*
> a: Yeah. We've got friends. They go to powwows all the time and we go with them ... they set up these big tipis.
> c: I had to dance. It was embarrassing!
> *Do you know the name of the cultural group who live on the Tobacco Plains or Grasmere or St. Mary's at Cranbrook?*
> a: There was, like, eight of them that came that one time. But I don't remember. The Sweetgrass or something? (Interview, 24 February 1998. Young Fernie women, born ca. 1980-1982.)

Although they acknowledge their schoolmates, there is some ambiguity in the young women's responses as to whether or not there are "First Nations" people in Fernie. It is interesting that indigenous people are identified by towns rather than cultural, tribal, or band names. Like these teenagers, people in the middle generation were also unable to specifically name the Ktunaxa, Kootenai, or Kutenai. Most old-timers used the anglicized names of nations. Several people were either uncomfortable or unfamiliar with the use of the term First Nations.

I had a glimpse of a grade five Social Studies test on Aboriginal cultures given in 1998. The students were asked to define the following words: heritage, history, ancestor, totem pole, Haida, tipi, igloo, culture, belief. The imagery conjured by these words and objects makes indigenous peoples visible through symbols that have changed very little in the last hundred years. It is not surprising that many in the youngest generation recognize these people only at powwows. I wonder at the definitions of "history," "culture," "heritage," and "belief," whether they include "land" or "treaties" or "colonialism" or "racism." The test called for students to write a story using the following words: ritual, shaman, pride, courage, harpoon, soul, chant. It makes me think about descriptions of the curse-lifting ceremony, the availability of stories about indigenous people using these words. At best there is a demystification of Aboriginal religious rites occurring in this classroom. Indigeneity is still, however, approached through belief and ritual, areas of knowledge now guarded by Aboriginal traditionalists. Under the word "Ktunaxa" there were two statements – What I know about them; What I want to know – and a space for comments. It raises the question: How are these children supposed to "know" "them" given the actual contexts within which Aboriginal people are made visible? Local media in Fernie often print photographs of dancers in their regalia performing at the Gathering or at powwows or school exhibitions.

Social performances are conventional sites of intercultural communication. Boundaries of inclusion that surround ritual have shifted over time. Ktunaxa people now control the contexts through which their traditional expressions are accessible to non-Aboriginal audiences. Spectacle continues, although now the discursive and representational contexts are highly politicized. In 1997 I arrived in town shortly after a powwow held to promote "cultural awareness" and "understanding" (*FFP* 3 June 1997:12). A Ktunaxa spokesperson stated the goal was to show an Aboriginal presence "in the valley because we are here." The event was spoken about as the first shared celebration since the curse-lifting ceremony, thirty-three years earlier.

Narrative Maps: Social Apartheid

While many Europeans learn about who indigenous people are from social performances, there are other contexts of interaction shaping perceptions of proximity between people. Distance may be constructed and reinforced through popular taxonomies of difference or through perceptions of economic and social marginalization. Distance may also be actual, determined by geography, patterns of mobility, or imposed segregation. The current context of map-making conjures the spectre of public information management during the early colonial era. Perceptions of difference have shifted dramatically across generations, reflecting movements of people and services. These shifts also suggest subtle differences in the ways that different generations recognize each other socially. People of all ages in Fernie express the idea that there are no indigenous people there.

Social and Spatial Proximity

Old-timers told me that Blackfoot and Ktunaxa people travelled regularly through Fernie until sometime in the 1950s. They came from the prairies in southern Alberta and from other parts of the East Kootenays. At this time railway travel was accessible and frequent.[7]

I used to know a lot of people [from the Tobacco Plains]. But I don't know any of them now. My wife used to know them better than I did because they used to come and get [government services] off her.

I used to know the old guys and now they're all gone. I used to meet them hunting and meet them in Elko. They were everywhere. They used to come into town. In fact, down here [gesturing west] was our racetrack. They used to have a half-mile racetrack down here. We used to have a sports day on the first of July. The Indians used to come in and set up their tipis right where those houses are down here. And they brought their horses. They'd be racehorses. (Interview, 12 September 1997. English-Canadian man, born 1911.)

In Fernie, the area called "the Park" seems to have been the circum-scribed place for regional competitions. It was where the rodeo grounds and racetrack were. During the Labour Day parades it was also where Ktunaxa people set up their camps.

There are significant differences in the ways that men and women of the eldest generation describe their involvements with Aboriginal people. Patterns of mobility are important here. Men spoke often about meeting Ktunaxa people in neighbouring towns while they were working, hunt-ing, or fishing. Economic transactions revolved around game, produce, and horse business. The high quality of Ktunaxa horses was praised often. Some men mentioned social get-togethers "in the bush," as Aboriginal people were forbidden to enter drinking establishments, the common place for male socializing. Women, on the other hand, mentioned individuals in town with whom they had some acquaintance. They worked with women in cafés or shops. Some Aboriginal young people boarded in Fernie rather than attend the mission schools. Many of these friendships ceased when people returned to their communities. Families travelled in and out of town selling berries, meat, vegetables, moccasins, and gloves. Between some fam-ilies there were relationships of reciprocity.

The women wanted me to eat again. In a foil bowl they have cracked open a chocolate Easter bunny. Each time they offer it: "Take the head – it's the best part! Indians say the head's the best, the head and the front [gesturing down her chest], then the flanks last." I asked her how she knew this. She spoke about Paul Luke, a Ktunaxa man whose family they were well acquainted with. How they camped nearby, shared meals, and hunted together. (Fieldnotes, 12 April 1998. Czech-Canadian women, born ca. 1909)

These women grew up on homestead property at the outskirts of town. As Bohemians during the First World War they were subject to the sting of the term "alien." They express a strong sense of marginalization from dominant institutions. Throughout their lives they hunted, trapped, tended livestock, and grew vegetable gardens. Their strategies of subsistence were dependent on knowledge of wild foods and animals that was, in part, shared with them by the Ktunaxa families they came to know. These women spoke often about their relationships with Ktunaxa individuals that continued into their adult lives. They feel that poverty was the equalizer; hunger built strong ties of reciprocity between these families in the early decades of the 1900s. These families, and others like them, look sideways as they shared in the struggles for subsistence.

I heard from many old-timers: "There are no more Indians." To those people who had frequent interactions with Ktunaxa families, "Indians" are marked by knowledge of animals, trekking, hunting, tanning, and wild foods. Visually they are people clothed in tanned skin jackets and moccasins. Some old-timers suggest that indigenous people are now "white." By this they do not mean phenotype. The designation refers to the trucks indigenous people now drive, the suits they wear, the education they acquire, and houses they live in that are no different from those of the non-indigenous people. Indigenous people, it seems, have dropped out of these people's repertoire of social recognition because of their increasing involvement in mainstream institutions.

During my first meeting with a Ktunaxa woman of a younger generation, she led me through her photo album. One image of her relatives was already familiar to me. In it a Ktunaxa man, his wife, and a child stand side by side. The child is holding two large cabbages under his arms. It is an image of a Ktunaxa man and his family that also appears in the photo album of one of the sisters above. Their father had taken the photograph at their homestead property during one of the many visits between these families. This sociality is difficult to reconcile with the impression of physical and social separateness between indigenous and European peoples.

To this Ktunaxa woman raised in Fernie, physical space is implicated in the social distances between people. Her assessment of space includes the idea of ethnic enclaves that largely determined their patterns of sociality as children. She draws a line of affiliation to Italians in Fernie. Looking sideways here is not based solely on economic marginalization. It is also based on her experience of racialization during the 1960s.

They seemed, they just seemed closer to us ... The area we lived was called the North End, and that was where all the Italians lived. I guess you kind of gather a kinship with people that have been, you know, that have kind of had to go through the same struggles as you. That happened a lot with the Italian community. Just the prejudices and their having to be in the same area. Of course, one of the main blocks is that if you don't speak perfect Queen's English, you must be stupid or something. So you've got an Italian accent or you don't

speak English at all, you must be stupid or something. It's just the
way people seem to look at things. So we grew up in the North End
with all the Italian people, and my brother could speak quite a bit of
Italian. [Laughing] ... I swear they thought he was Italian!
   What about Slavic people?
I think there were maybe – the only groups I distinguished between
when I was there was "us," meaning my own family because there
was nobody else, uh, Caucasian people, and Italians. That was about
it. I didn't know any differences. Czechoslovakian people or Polish
people or Scottish people or whatever. They were all lumped together.
You were either white or you weren't.
   And Italians weren't white?
Well. No. Not really. [Laughing] I guess that's the way I compre-
hended it at the time. You know, they were Italians. They seemed
to be the only ones that really kind of held on to their culture and
their language. (Interview, 11 December 1997. Ktunaxa woman, born
1955.)

There is a sense here of limited opportunity for hospitality confined to
Italian homes in the North End. According to this woman, her family was
welcomed in those homes where people "held on to their culture and their
language" in the face of similar "struggles" with "prejudice." The idea of
affiliation based on a shared experience of discrimination collapsed almost
immediately during our conversation. This woman described a neighbour
screaming at them from across the street. She was yelling: "Go back to
the reserve where you belong!" Notably, the neighbour was a person who
not long before was subject to prejudice following the Second World War.
While older Italians expressed their affiliation with indigenous people on
the basis of expressions of traditional knowledge, to this Ktunaxa woman
in her forties, the sideways glance is based on the experience of racialization by dominant "Caucasian" or "white" society.
   Across generations, distance from "whiteness" seems to be the defining
criterion for comparison. The eldest generation had frequent social and
economic interactions with Ktunaxa people. They recognize indigenous
people through traditional knowledge and through their informal economic interactions. To others, distance is marked by "race," defined
through language, culture, and the experience of discrimination and ethnic segregation. The visual pathology of racism is evident in perceptions
of difference expressed by all ages in Fernie.

Separateness
The seemingly inevitable comparison to "white" hegemony raises questions about how ideas of dominant power are enforced on personal and

societal levels. British colonialism in Canada employs various strategies through which the image of racialized others is managed. Here and there in participants' narratives are mentions of small acts of self-censorship that hint at the social distance between people and the potential consequences of transgression.

_____ told me about travelling to Chicago by train with her mother and toddler sister. Her sister was restless, crying and wriggling around on her mother's lap. Across from them sat two "old Indian ladies." She recalled that the train was moving across the flats where bright pumpkins were growing. The old women were pointing out the window at them and speaking quietly in their own language. The toddler wanted down, her mother loosened her hold. The girl went straight for the old ladies, "tugged at their leather dresses and stretched out her arms to be picked up." The old women spoke with each other and looked at the child smiling. ____ said she told her mother to tell them it was okay to pick her up. Her mother said: "Do you think I should?" She told them that it was all right. "Well, they just loved her up! She didn't want to get out of their arms!" (Fieldnotes, 22 April 1998. Polish-Canadian woman, born 1914.)

[Speaking about her work as a chambermaid at one of the hotels] When you went to a door you had to knock first before you went in to clean it. This one day she knocked on the door, and when the door opened this black man came up and shocked her so much. That's when she yelled: "Mamma Mia!" Never, ever had she seen a black man before. She said that he went down to the owner and said to the owner: "I didn't do a thing to this lady." Because she let out such an exclamation. The poor man was just frightened that – she said he just took his suitcase and left. The owner tried to say to the man that she probably hadn't seen a black man before. She said he was so black. He was blacker than the machine. She had never seen anything, anybody so black. He told the man: "I didn't do anything to her." But making beds is hard. (Translation of interview, 8 August 1998. Italian woman, born 1920.)

She told me a story from her childhood about a "Chinaman" who sold vegetables in town. It was a sport for the children to climb up on his wagon when he was in front of a house and to steal a carrot. One day he saw her and chased after her. She ran to a house but the door was locked, so she cowered down into a corner of the verandah, screaming. He saw she was frightened "out of [her] mind" and just warned her. "To this day I still have dreams about that Chinaman. I shouldn't say

"Chinaman" – Chi-nese man. I still dream about him today." (Fieldnotes, 29 August 1997. Austrian-Canadian woman, born ca. 1927.)

These situations unfolded, respectively, in the 1920s, the 1950s, and the 1930s. The hesitations, screams, and retreats described here reveal a fear that fuels essentializing discourses. They also portray how members of racialized communities – indigenous, African Canadian, and Chinese – anticipated reactions by the dominant power. The scenarios serve to high-light the backdrop of mainstream racism, lending a sense of ordinariness to these interactions and pointing to the institutionalization of these ideas (see Blee 1993:606). Hierarchies of difference are perpetuated through organized structures that reinforce separateness.

Colonialism administers social and spatial exile through structures of segregation. A Ktunaxa woman used the violent struggles of decolonization in South Africa to speak about tensions surrounding land claims in BC.

When you can have stuff like the apartheid that was going on in South Africa in this day and age – [Europeans] are going to be fearful, of course you're going to be fearful. The thing is that they modelled their black townships after what the government was doing here with the, with *their Indians.* "What do we do with these people?" "Well, go home and stick them all by themselves together and don't let them do anything. Don't give them any legal rights and it'll take care of it." ... Well, you know. You put animals on a reserve. You don't put people on a reserve! (Interview, 11 December 1997. Ktunaxa woman, born 1955.)

Comparing systems of colonial control de-emphasizes ideas of enmity, instead focusing on political structures and ideologies that generate these ideas. Ktunaxa people often expressed their perceptions of social and phys-ical segregation. They share a kind of embodied knowledge of separateness. Under the Indian Act, indigenous people are subject to different laws, they have been legislated to separate educational, health, and social services.

Like structural barriers, discursive acts also reinforce ideas of separate-ness between people.

Do you know much about the treaties that are being negotiated right now?
b: Treaties?
a: Uh, no [laughing].
c: ... For them to be treaty, they have to work in the band office and they don't have to pay for the, they get to stay in the house, they don't have to pay for it. Some appliances they don't have to

pay for. (Interview, 24 February 1998. Young Fernie women, born ca. 1980-1982.)

Special rights discourse appears to have successfully made the leap to the youngest generation. It is no longer ideas of primitivism or savagery that separate indigenous and European people. In the realm of public information, special rights talk promotes a discourse on perceived privilege that erases the history of imposed inequalities. Perceptions of separateness were expressed by people of all ages with whom I spoke, albeit from different perspectives. Idioms of "race," colonial oppression, or special rights each constitute a social knowledge rationalizing difference.

Map-Making
Maps have reappeared on the stage of public information in British Columbia. In the 1800s they were used as tools to bolster public support for empire and provide evidence of territorial claims. European discovery and conquest are not the focus of current media attention. In BC at present, the locations and movements of Aboriginal peoples are part of a new regime of proof making.

I could just die every time I think of this! The office of Native claims said you can't submit a claim to the office in Ottawa unless you have your boundaries drawn for your traditional territory, right? Okay, so it never worked that way, [where] you go to point B and, that's it, man, you're Kootenay, you don't go any further than that! There was intermingling! You know, you got together and you basically knew where you could go without getting killed. Just like the Blackfeet coming over to steal horses – we knew where we could go there too. But there used to be a lot of battles. So the government says to us: "You send us a map, complete with lines of your territory." So we send it to them and everybody else is doing the same thing at the same time, so of course the territories all overlap! And *then* they throw it to the public and say: "Look what these stupid Indians are doing now! They're claiming territory that's this big!" That's not to say that this territory was used twelve months of the year – it was to say we used that territory, we used to pick *ngumsu* there or this type of berry there. Or we used to go over there and kill a buffalo or we hunt here for elk. You know? We moved around. Okay, that was basically your territory, and of course it overlaps with the Okanagans and it overlaps with the Blackfeet ... So the government then throws it up for public consumption! "They have claimed more area than even exists in British Columbia!" ... Nobody knew when they were submitting their claims. "This is how you apply, A, B, C, D, okay, go ahead." Then they toss it out to make everybody look like total idiots! Of course these territories are going to overlap . They asked for those boundary lines. We didn't come up with that. They've got strategists, I'm sure ... to sway public opinion against Native people and land claims and make everybody totally paranoid that we're going to steal everybody's houses. I tell you, sometimes! Who **is** in control here!? It's just so ludicrous! (Interview, 11 December 1997. Ktunaxa woman, born 1955.)

As this woman points out, the delineation of territorial boundaries is an administrative requirement of the treaty process. "In order to be eligible, a claimant group would have to prove that their ancestors were members of an organized society who had occupied and used specific lands and resources before Europeans arrived" (Culhane 1998:90). Many Canadians are unfamiliar with the specialized channels through which Aboriginal claims are made, yet public opinion has become a key element in "the new politics of 'special status'" (Dyck 1986:32). The management of public opinion is taking on the many forms of identity politics. Demands for democratic participation in the process, calls of "one law for all," and publicizing the claims to urban real estate are some conservative manifestations in public discourse. The headline of the *Vancouver Sun* on 2 February 1998 read: "B.C. Indian Chiefs Lay Claim to Entire Province, Resources." The opening paragraph states: "BC's Native Indians are laying claim to every tree, every rock, every fish and every animal in the province" (Ouston 1998:1). The maps and their accompanying messages are reminiscent of the early colonial management of appearances. Instead of empty (read uncivilized) territories, lands are now known to be fully inhabited. Anti-treaty rhetoric represents Aboriginal people, once again, as a threat to the institution of private property. The perceived threat activates a kind of panic driven by rumour.

I went to the local pub with a neighbour. Someone joined us; he described himself as a "case of beer and bucket of chicken man." He asked me what I do. I told him about my research and he became agitated and started to speak about "special rights." He felt that the Nisga'a treaty would actually "change the body of laws in favour of the Indians. I can't go there and buy land and start a business. It's not a free world when that happens. It's a double standard – there should be one law for all."

I asked: "Do you think there is one law for all now?" (Fieldnotes, 14 August 1997. Euro-Canadian man, born ca. 1955.)

It is ironic that non-Aboriginal people are now protesting land claims through rhetoric of space and a perceived infringement on their rights to mobility and ownership of property. "The Indian Act from 1876 up to the present still controls Indian lands and property, local government, money and Indian status" (Teneese 1997:6). Aboriginal people in Canada do not own reserve lands. The Crown holds these lands in trust for the use of "Indians." While residents on reserves pay for their houses, personal property "may not be mortgaged and [is] not subject to seizure, hence cannot be used as security for loans" (Duff 1969:72). This man's plea of "one law for all" ignores the history of colonial legislation that has effectively prevented indigenous people from having full participation in mainstream economies. He imagines bounded territories to which access will be limited, based on his ethnicity.

In 1998 the public school curriculum was revamped to include "BC Aboriginal Content" for kindergarten to grade ten. In grades four to seven, students using the "Shared Learnings" booklet will be taught about "stereotyping of Aboriginal people in the media." They will also learn about "the Indian Act: an historical perspective" (BC Ministry of Education 1998). It is interesting that a significant element of the new school curriculum focuses on locality: "Since all schools are located on a traditional Aboriginal territory, that area should be the first focus of study" (ibid.). I asked three teenagers about what they were studying in their classes.

Do you learn about First Nations people in school?
a: You do in grade nine Social [Studies].
b: I'm learning about Indians right now. The Plains Indians and
hunters, northern hunters and stuff.
c: I'm learning the history from, like, Laurier and Macdonald and all
those guys.
b: They don't really give you enough time to learn anything.
a: Yeah. Like, we did our reports and we just chose one culture. So
we didn't really. I did the Blackfoot, but I don't really know things
about the Cree or, like, anybody else like that.
So you had a section on the Kootenai?
a: We, like, learned about it, but they didn't go into great detail.
(Interview, 24 February 1998. Young Fernie women, born ca.
1980-1982.)

Old anthropological categories are evident here in the partitioning of people. Indigenous groups have been classified through categories of subsistence as hunters, fishers, foragers, horticulturists, and pastoralists. The "culture area" concept also classifies people based on their geographical locations as Great Plains, Plateau, Northwest Coast, Woodlands, Sub-Arctic, and Arctic peoples.

Maps are important symbolic tools through which places and peoples are imagined. In Fernie, narrative maps of proximity reveal a spectrum of relationships between people. To many it is the distance from "white" hegemony that defines perceptions. Maps delimit political and social territories that become powerful hooks in public discourses. Perceptions of distance between people reflect patterns of mobility and social recognition that are tied to political structures and to scientific theories of human difference.

Transmission: Ideas Reactivated

Taxonomies of human difference are transmitted between generations, popularized through mass media, and reinforced by authoritative institutions. Participants' narratives reveal old ideas that remain salient and are easily incorporated into new discourses of human difference. As I have shown, different generations are socialized within eras of particular ideas that constitute popular forms of knowledge. Scholarly concepts of "race" and blood emerged alongside political discourses of discovery and special rights, during discussions about European-indigenous relations.

During a conversation with two elderly women in Fernie, Nordic superiority was drawn into our dialogue, recalling older regimes of racial construction.

One of the women was speaking about the British: "They were Limeys, it was an attitude, they were soft!" Another said: "They were the Vikings, warriors." The other woman disagreed entirely, although admitting they fought many wars. "And what about the Irish! They were at the bottom of the heap of all white people!" The other woman was fascinated with Australia and the convicts who built a country. She spoke about the women coming over in those prison ships. Then ____ asked if we had heard about the human remains found in the USA recently. "They were Danish," she said, "and they were there long before the Indians!" The other woman asked how she knew they were Danish. "From their bone structure," she replied, moving her hands across her cheekbones down to her chin. They both agreed that there would soon be proof that other people were here long before "Indians." They conjectured about sea voyages, the ships of the Vikings, and their "spirit" for exploration. (Fieldnotes, 9 November 1997)

For these eighty-year-olds, conjecture about Kennewick Man involved old stories of exploration and conquest.[8] They cited "proof" in the form of comparative anatomy; however, they were clearly interested in the historical voyages of Northern peoples and their natural, dominant "spirit," invoking the theory of Nordic superiority through which they were educated. Successive generations learned other ways of reckoning difference.

> I guess when we got old enough to realize we were different, I guess you hear enough from other people about the dirty, stereotypical, lazy-Indian-thing that you start to believe it yourself. It didn't do very much for our self-esteem, that's for sure ... Then, even with the school curriculum that we've integrated into the schools here ... You learn about Indians period. You don't learn that their cultures are all different, their languages are all different. I can remember being in grade seven and being so embarrassed. We were studying North American Indians and the teacher was drawing a diagram on the blackboard and telling us the difference between Caucasoids, Mongoloids, and Negroids. But then he went on to describe the physical characteristics of a North American Indian person. [Laughing] "Their legs are shorter than a Caucasian person in relation to the torso," and things like that. Everyone in the class was turning around, looking at me, just to see. Is that the way they really look? ... It was very painful for me, I'll tell ya. It's almost like I can still feel everybody's eyes on me. (Interview, 11 December 1997. Ktunaxa woman, born 1955.)

This scenario unfolded in the late 1960s in a schoolroom in Fernie. Children's education about Aboriginal peoples proceeded through the nineteenth-century categories of race theory. In professional journals in 1964, cultural anthropologists were challenging colleagues in physical anthropology to debate the veracity of the race concept. The textual dialogues reveal a struggle for proofs through the language of science. In one article, scholars argued for the term "cline" to replace "race" as a measure of variation of traits in particular populations. A shift from racial typology to population studies was also criticized, as "population traits grade into one another" (Brace 1964:313). Importantly, the traits in question were blood, phenotype, and "ontogenetic development." Finally it was asserted that scientific attention must focus on "process – ultimately the mechanics of evolution."

The debate around the race concept sharpened distinctions between anthropologists. "I do not believe that the specialized biological scientists are, by virtue of their training, necessarily in a position to evaluate or understand cultural behaviour, and the problem of making judgements about 'racial' capacity is, technically defined, precisely a problem of recognizing and interpreting cultural behaviour" (Diamond 1964:108).

A Polish anthropologist was unable to agree with American views, stating that they were "agnostic conclusions about taxonomy" (Wiercinski 1964:318). Some went so far as to suggest that scientists were being led by "accepted dogma" rather than by "objective information." "If there are any real group differences in temperament and aptitude, it cannot be concealed forever; and if there are not, it cannot be proved if we suppress impartial investigations in the field" (Brues 1964:107).

A scholar writing from Britain agreed with Americans in their use of the term "ethnic group as neutral" and "scientifically the most respectable designation" (Huxley 1964:316). Semantics surrounding "race" unleashed debates about the power of words, their connection to everyday acts of bigotry, and the responsibilities of social scientists. "The terms Mediterranean, Negroid, Nordic and others are formally nothing more than pure mnemotypical devices for given combinations of a larger set of phenotypical traits" (Wiercinski 1964:319). These dialogues foreshadow theoretical debates in the 1990s about the relationship between discourse and action.

Racial categories continue to assert a commonsense hold on the social imagination. Presently these regimes of classification are bound up with special rights discourse.

The man began a list of categories: Caucasian, Mongoloid – he couldn't remember others. I spoke about the construction of "race." He said to me: "Do you mean to tell me that if my bones and a black man's bones were found somewhere, they couldn't tell our races?" I spoke about variability, environmental and cultural factors. He asked about craniums. I said that these theories have a life of their own and are used to oppress certain groups of people. "Up North," he exclaimed, "whites can't get a job now, discrimination because of race. We don't want that here!" (Fieldnotes, 13 December 1997. English-Canadian man, born ca. 1950.)

Our conversation circled around the proofs of science: "race" and comparative anatomy. The speed with which this man leapt from "race" to comments about special rights is worth noting. According to the logic of special rights, treaties "set up racially based territorial enclaves," thus dividing Canadians and undermining democracy (Furniss 1999:141). The veracity of this discourse depends on its "claims to be race-neutral" and its ability to "disguise racial issues" (Kirkham 1998:247, 255). "Race" has historically been used to justify colonialism. It is rendered invisible in the new discourse of special rights.

The tone of these conversations differed radically from those I had with older people. It is not that older people do not share these views, but they discussed the issues differently. There is harshness in the discourse of special rights that erases ideas of sociality and history between indigenous and non-indigenous peoples. Where older people drew upon their memories of wartime pacts and historical voyages to speak about treaties in BC, special rights discourse does not evoke an idea of nation. It is a hard line about the past without direct experience of nation-to-nation conflict. For people who have experienced this history of racialization, hegemonic concepts are explicitly bound up with the politics of land and colonial policies of assimilation. Indigenous people are deeply affected by histories that special rights discourse seeks to erase.

Blood

> In the early days when I came, my father told me one time. He says: "The Indians don't stay in town because the town is cursed." So when the Indians came, they used to go by the old brewery, way down there, to camp. He used to tell me that. He said: "Because the Indians believe in that curse, they wouldn't stay in town, they went out of town." But now they come, they stay. It doesn't make no difference. They're more, I think they're more civilized now. And then, I think most of them are, they have white blood in them. (Interview, 6 August 1998. Italian woman, born 1910.)

This woman's comments describe the power of ideas transmitted between generations. Her father's explanation provided her with a kind of social knowledge about who Aboriginal people are. It is interesting that the story is used to illustrate why Ktunaxa people camped at the outskirts of town, by the brewery near the old restricted district. She mentions belief as an important marker of difference, here entangled with the idea of being civilized. Not unlike the early colonial officials, this woman in her late eighties speaks about blood as a commonsense entity that explains the shift in belief and, consequently, in people's movements.

I heard talk about "miscegenation" amongst members of every generation I spoke with.[9] Most people used the term "intermarriage." Old-timers told me about the tribulations faced by people wishing to marry outside the Catholic or Protestant communities in their parents' generation. These unions were simply forbidden. In their own time, marriage between European women and Chinese men was unheard of. Some women who married indigenous men moved to reserve communities and were disowned by their parents. While social class was an issue for the wealthy, many people in the oldest generation successfully managed marriages between classes and different ethnic groups. Working-class people were permitted to marry outside their language groups, crossing the boundary between

Anglo European and "foreigner." English people expressed the most rigid views against intermarriage in this generation.

For the middle generation, people who fell in love across boundaries of "race" also faced great hardship. I heard about the disapproval of both sets of parents when it came to marriage between Chinese and European partners. English-indigenous unions provoked wrath from previous generations. Many of the people wishing to marry across this ethnic boundary were forced to elope; some were permanently disenfranchised from their families. Marriage with an indigenous person was most accepted by Italian and Slavic families, perhaps because of their shared Catholicism.

> I never belonged in Fernie because there was a lot of prejudice there and we were really put down. But then you find out, say with people my age, [mixed heritage] is not so bad, but with a lot of elders it's a real sore spot. You don't, when the egg and sperm are coming together, you don't say: "Hold off here – you're the wrong race!" [Laughing] You can't help who you are. But a lot of Native people, especially the elders, the full bloods, they don't like that ... I decided I was just going to be a human being! [Laughing] I had to for the sake of my sanity. When do you cease being a Native person or an Indian person? And do you want them to – I don't know, there we go again, just wiping ourselves out. And that's what the government wanted all along. So pretty soon maybe you're going to have the reserve and the reserve lands, but it's just going to be all white people on there ... There are a lot of, say, children of mixed marriages, or there's a lot of Native children who were sent off to foster homes and things like that. They're just coming back now. They either take pride in it and really get into their culture or they blow their heads off! I've seen that happen an awful lot. An awful lot! (Interview, 11 December 1997. Ktunaxa woman, born 1955.)

This woman describes both her experiences of prejudice in Fernie as an indigenous woman and the stigma she feels as a person who is "part white." The idea of blood remains salient. Intermarriage and intergenerational tensions are situated in a critique of colonial policies that seek political and economic assimilation. Her question: "When do you cease being a Native person?" evokes colonial taxonomies that have shifted between blood, "race," and legal criteria.

When People speak about differences between Europeans and indigenous peoples they use the language of concepts and images available to them. The social power of words pivots on group memory – shared symbolic imagery that stirs sentiment and opinion. Popular discourses surrounding land claims depend to some extent on the recognition of older concepts cast into circulation during the early colonial period. Ideologically, this falls within what Verona Stolcke calls "cultural fundamentalism" (1995:7). Central to the rhetoric is a "heightened sense of primordial identity, cultural difference and exclusiveness" (2-8). Essentialist discourses should be viewed as "ambiguous and mutable instruments" that acquire value only in context (Thomas 1994:188).

Ideas initially generated by structures and ideologies of early colonialism persist in popular narratives. Contexts within which indigenous people are visible to Euro-Canadians include spectacle, ceremony, and ritual where difference is perceived through belief and conventions of intercultural performance. These arenas are now important sites where ideas of history and land are renegotiated through oratory. People explain relationships between Aboriginals and non-Aboriginals from varying perceptions of spatial and political proximity. Some express affiliation with others based on their religious practices, their economic marginalization, or similar experiences of racism. It is the distance from dominant institutions that emerges here. At the same time, many participants use belief, economic practices, and taxonomies of "race" to explain irreconcilable differences between people. Early colonial narratives attempted to erase indigenous economic, political, and cultural institutions. The latest incarnation of colonial discourse leaves this cluster of ideas essentially intact. Special rights talk attempts to sidestep colonial history and the impact of legislated inequality in Canada. In effect, the discourse is a means of "getting rid of the story" of colonialism in Canada.

6
Development, Discovery, and Disguise

CURSED! The Ghost in the Mountain: The Legend of Fernie's
Ghost Rider

A shadow perpetrates [sic] the legend of a Ghost Rider in the
cliffs on the South side of Hosmer Mountain ... The legend arose
after the prospector William Fernie came to the Elk River Valley.
Apparently, Fernie saw that the native people wore beads of
coal. He demanded they show him where they found the
valuable substance. They agreed to show him only if he
promised to marry the chief's daughter. Yet, after obtaining
access to the coal mine, Fernie refused to marry the woman.
The natives revenged the deception and put a curse on the
valley ... Recently, Native Elders removed the curse ... but the
Ghost Rider remains on Mount Hosmer. The Ghost Rider
reminds people of the power of a promise and the strength
of a betrayal.

– Janice Strong, "Cursed!"

So begins an article in the "Outdoors" section of the *East Kootenay Weekly*,
a regional newspaper distributed door to door in Fernie. This brief outline of the curse story lacks the detail of earlier written versions. Strong
mentions that "Native Elders" removed the curse "recently." In her version,
"the natives" asked Fernie to marry the woman; his strategy to acquire
knowledge is entirely erased. There are no details of the content of the
curse formula, who cast it, and from where. The only landmark is Hosmer
Mountain, the site of this writer's hiking destination. At the article's con-
clusion, an editor's note refers readers to a published hiking guide in which
the "legend of the Ghost Rider" may be found.

Strong writes: "It was the unstable weather that betrayed our initial hiking adventure to Mount Hosmer, when in July of last year, the mountains
sent us snow squalls ... Still, I longed to see the shadow ... hidden in the
faults of that dynamic limestone" (1998:11). The shadow is now a sight
to see on a hiker's trek, a tantalizing product in the flourishing market of
outdoor recreation. Brochures use both legend and image as an opening
to history, but also to introduce the maze of backcountry trails to wilderness enthusiasts. Fernie has become a "lifestyle" destination. In this moment
of pilgrimage, local knowledge is an important commodity that fuels new
discourses of discovery.

Returning to the writer's quest to see the "locally famous shadow," upon receiving instructions from a resident, she is finally able to make it out from a restaurant window: "All the features I heard described about the illusion jumped out from the rocks ... Shadows of skinny horse legs held a three-quarter view of the huge horse ... The rider cloaked in a face mask with oppressive cut outs for his white eyes, rode the horse while aggressively standing forward in the stirrups. A faint shadow of a person walked to the right of the horse. All the embellishments of a legend stood timeless on that rock face. The image hung there for almost half an hour and with each minute the structure looked more fierce" (1998:11).

What is now the Ghostrider legend provides no clue to the identities of the figures in the evening light. This description is particularly menacing; it jars against other interpretations I have heard. To older generations, the Rider is a nameless sojourner travelling the country sometimes, leading a packhorse. I asked one woman if the shadow was connected to the curse legend:

> Not at all. But I understand it is now. That was just a picture [then]. It wasn't connected and it wasn't the Ghostrider, it was called "the Rider on the mountain," just the Rider. It probably is a Chamber of Commerce thing. (Interview, 16 April 1988. Annex woman, born 1933.)

Some paid little attention to the shadow.

> As a kid I never heard anything about the Ghostrider. We never paid any attention to it. I don't even know if you can see it from West Fernie. (Interview, 5 September 1997. West Fernie man, born ca. 1927.)

A 1966 photograph of the Shadow on Hosmer Mountain (see Figure 15) has no inscription; there are no clues here as to its explanation.

I am interested in the transformation of meaning taking place regarding this old legend, and now its manifestation in the Ghostrider shadow. It is difficult not to view recent imagery as a disguise of a far richer past. As the emphasis in interpretations of the curse story shifts away from social relations to the landscape itself, a new regime of meaning-making takes form.

In 1998 another incarnation of the Ghostrider image appeared on a postcard.[1] This card reads: "The Ghostrider of Hosmer Mountain. Fernie British Columbia. The Canadian Rockies" (see Figure 16). Now the Rider has entered an international arena located by a well-recognized geographical feature – the Rocky Mountains. It is apt that the transformation occurs at a time when Fernie is being sculpted into a world-class ski resort. Hal Rothman (1998:11-17) describes tourism as an "extractive industry" that generates new forms of information and spectacle. The natural resources here are "authentic visions" of history, the environment, and local character.

In the new postcard, viewing windows decrypt the illusion of the shadow. One zooms in, providing a close-up; the other translates the image into three defined figures: a faceless rider galloping out of the rock face away from two other figures, one of whom is wearing a headdress, the other draped in a feminine cloak. The designer-photographer told me she used a computer effect called "Romantic Vision." The images are a soft ochre colour, reminiscent of cave paintings. They evoke a recognizable association with a prehistoric past. Small print on the card identifies them respectively as Fernie's ghost, the chief, and his daughter. No longer is the illusion malleable by individual imagination. The Ghostrider shadow is now reified, wrapped in a compact bundle of information on local

Figure 15   There is no caption on this photograph dated August 1966. Fernie old-timers knew the shadow on Hosmer Mountain as "the Rider." In their day, it was not connected to the curse legend; its meaning was open to interpretation. *Photographer unknown. Courtesy of Ivy Haile and the Fernie and District Historical Society, 2458 do.*

Figure 16 A 1998 postcard leaves little to the imagination. Here, the Ghostrider shadow clearly depicts William Fernie galloping away from the princess and her father, the chief. *Postcard photograph, design, and copyright by Alice Thompson. Illustrated by Nola Johnston.*

history and location. At the core of tourism is a "process of scripting space, both physically and psychically" (Rothman 1998:12).

There are significant representational shifts to be read on the new post-card. It provides detailed historical references to two fires, a flood, a mine explosion, and the curse-lifting ceremony. The "Kootenai" are now plural-ized, recognizing political diversity within the Ktunaxa-Kinbasket Nation. The ceremonialist "who smoked the pipe of peace" with Fernie's mayor is acknowledged by his English name and by his anglicized Ktunaxa name. A directional star appears on the postcard, along with the elevations of the City of Fernie and Hosmer Mountain, and degrees of latitude and longitude. What remains recognizable representationally is the association of indigenous peoples with the sense of prehistory and the "Romantic Vision" effect of cross-cultural imagining. The designer told me about another legacy of the curse. Anyone using the name of the protagonist in order to make money will suffer. She said: "You notice that there are no businesses or buildings with his full name on them!" William Fernie has faded into the background of popular iconography in town, while the Ghostrider has now become a commercial logo.

Just as the shadow was gradually reduced into one readable image, cur-rent interpretations of human difference are also narrowing. Recurring themes highlight transformations of older categories, recast in the current context of identity politics. With a few exceptions, the familiar tags of nationality, religion, or neighbourhood do not mark social positions. Many people in the age groups from twenty to fifty years are second- or third-generation Canadians who identify themselves through the regions or cities they hail from. Within the context of resort development, ideas about place and local identity are at the centre of public dialogues. At the time I was doing my research, Fernie was becoming inscribed nationally and internationally through a new discourse of discovery. Its identity was re-negotiated as it transformed from a predominantly working-class, resource-based town to a destination resort. The initial pangs of transformation spawned intense regionalism that coalesced in public tensions between those identified as "locals" or as "granolas." Class figures greatly in this conflict, now disguised in essentialized images of the rural and the urban. Unlike the complex locations of the eldest generations, new vocabularies of difference orbit uncertainly around identity politics and "lifestyle choices" that confound the stuff of class and "race." Some statements on difference are thinly disguised appropriations of voice, as local knowledge is now pulled and shaped to fit the advertising needs of the ski industry.

Spectacle: Sacrificial Rites
An older body of lore and ritual is now undergoing elaboration to fit the current moment of economic expansion in Fernie. This new folklore is

derived from the ethos of the ski industry, made local through the rescripting of place for an international clientele. Stories pivot on the seasonal anxiety around snowfall that is of increasing economic interest to Fernie residents. Figures drawn from Norse mythology meld into the developing narrative of the Griz, a local lumberjack/abominable snowman who inhabits the Lizard Range. Social rituals such as the Mogul Smoker, described below, dominate the seasonal calendar. New legends generated by the ski industry are used to both promote and contest current development processes.

The Mogul Smoker

In 1997 I saw no written announcements for the annual Mogul Smoker party. News about its location and date flitted through town by word of mouth. Attendance was free and everyone was welcome. Four years later, a sign erected by the old Fernie High School advertised the event. Tickets now cost three dollars, and identification was required for entry. "An estimated 1,000 people from the 20 something age group plus, and from all parts of the globe" attended the event on 13 January 2001 (*FFP* 17 January 2001). In 1997 there were perhaps half that number, and people were already lamenting the incursion of outsiders.

> This year the party is being held on a property a ten-minute drive outside of Fernie. There is some talk in town preceding this event. I hear that it is "for the older crowd," meaning those who are now in their forties or thereabouts. I hear comments here and there about how the "yung-uns" now attend and just "drink until they get sick." "It ain't what it used to be!" "It's gone too commercial." "It's gotten too big." As I arrive I see that special mugs are on sale and there is a mixed drink served especially for this occasion. (Fieldnotes, 11 December 1997)

In his history of tourism, Hal Rothman (1998:169-178) discusses the "regional" character of ski hills and how "local symbols" are eventually colonized by outside interests. What started in Fernie in 1964 as a weekend operation for local families now attracts outside capital and seasonal newcomers. People who consider themselves to be the "older crowd" suggest that the "yung-uns" are unable to either hold their liquor or fully appreciate the occasion of the Mogul Smoker. These veterans grumble about the commercialization of their event, the change in meaning that has occurred since the first Mogul Smoker took place in 1976.

> At the time it was more of a staff party on the mountain ... At first it was a house party. It's a drink, eh? The Mogul Smoker ... coffee, Kahlua, white rum, and hot chocolate. It began for staff at the ski hill, people who worked somewhere at the base too, in the equipment

shops or on maintenance. We were all geared up for the season, but there was no snow yet. In the mid-'70s there was a staff of fifteen to twenty people. Once you got their spouses and friends there were maybe forty to fifty people, and these people had known each other for eight years or so. They were friends who were all working or associated with the ski business. It was a family. People returned every winter to work at the hill, seasonal employment. Now there's hundreds of staff and they don't get it. In the '90s [the Mogul Smoker] grew into a public thing, so lots of us don't go anymore. I don't go anymore. [Laughing] When you have maybe three hundred people and there's a local bus every forty-five minutes to the site! (Interview, 20 November 2000. Maritime-Canadian man, born ca. 1955.)

I am reminded of the Smoker for veterans on Remembrance Day, another informal event to which access is restricted to members and their spouses. What this man calls "family" was a seasonal group of workers at the ski hill, a small enough number to ensure familiarity. What he laments is the loss of this spirit of acquaintance, perhaps inevitable given the rising numbers of staff and the increased popularity of skiing. In his work on "invented traditions," Eric Hobsbawm (1989:287-291) briefly discusses "unofficial" social performances that express class solidarity. There is little at the Mogul Smoker that resonates with the nostalgia of industrial workers. People in the eldest age groups spoke about May Day parades and union marches, political rallies and miners' picnics. These social occasions were also organized around workers and their families, specified by industry. Fernie is currently engaged in an awkward transition from what Donald Avery (1979:57) calls an "occupational community" of resource-based employment to one of service industries. The Mogul Smoker provides one window through which to view shifts in class-consciousness among members of different age and social groups.

I arrive around 10:30 and make my way directly to the largest bonfire, around which stand clusters of visually well-defined groups. I met people from Japan, Australia, Sweden, New Zealand, Quebec, Nova Scotia, and Austria. The "older" ski crowd stood in more bounded spatial circles ... Conversations around the fire range between highly technical equipment talk about mountain bikes or snowboards to tales of past adventures, usually with high degrees of physical risk. Visual styles of dress correspond with different activity groups. Many of the "older crowd" wear less-costumed clothing. Long thin ski jackets and high toques are worn by snowboarders. Some people wear ski goggles and Dr. Seuss-like hats. (Fieldnotes, 11 December 1997)

The number of people from different parts of the world attests to the international character of the ski crowd. Immediately I assumed that privilege enabled these young adults to travel across the world in pursuit of their leisure activities. Skiing has always "maintained important class distinctions" (Rothman 1998:168). The activity requires freedom of mobility; it expresses a kind of individualism and celebrates new engineering and equipment technologies. On several occasions I asked skiers about their perception of social class. Most were reluctant to acknowledge its salience, stating that they occupy all class positions.[2] One man said: "There are those who buy condos and houses and fly in and out, and then there are the skiers that have no money who work at the very bottom of the hierarchy." The latter are people Hal Rothman (1998:189) calls "neo-natives," "incoming workers who accept the constructed ethos of a place and generally are willing to be under-employed there." Another man offered an opinion about the economic vitality of the community. "It's like mutual funds," he said. "It has to do with stability through diversity. It's the same with ranching. If you have wheat and cattle, when the price of wheat drops, cattle are up." He identified three industries here: skiing, mining, and forestry. "Miners are probably the most consistent in their class."

The Mogul Smoker has shifted from a celebration for those most intimately involved in ski-hill operations to a public social gathering of various activity groups. Snowboarders are socially distinct from telemark, cross-country, backcountry, racing, powder, or mogul skiers. I did not analyze the different groups and their idiosyncrasies of dress and activity; however, equipment and styles of clothing vary for each. Not unlike the uniforms of a previous generation, clothes functions as social markers for people who are part of the ski crowd in Fernie and elsewhere.

I was in time to see a man walk into the red embers at the edge of the fire and thrust a pair of skis, tip up, into the flaming pile. Throughout the night this was repeated with different articles of equipment. Some shouted or made guttural sounds as they did this. Each time the action set off a roar from the crowd. Throughout the night about fifteen pairs of skis, poles, and a few snowboards were ceremoniously staked into the fire. The smoke was black, putrid – everyone stepped back when skis were planted. The steel edges glowed red in the fire, all that remained after the fibreglass and other elements melted away. I asked several people about this. Most said they found it a bit extreme. Some commented on the noxious smoke and damage to the environment. I asked what it meant. Everyone knew that this action is meant to entice and encourage the "snow god," variously called "Griz" or "Ullr, son of Zeus."[3] (Fieldnotes, 11 December 1997)

On this occasion I saw only men participate in the performance of in-
cineration. Their shouts were not intelligible to me. Environmentalism is
deeply implicated in the phantasmagoria developed by skiers. I found a
certain dissonance in the space between the collective roar that swept
through the party-goers and the individually expressed environmentalism.
Four years later these collisions were discussed in public forums where the
Mogul Smoker is now being inscribed into local tradition: "Some time in
the early 1950s, we began to see plastics (especially P-Tex and ABS) introduced to our skis ... So ... we've been burning plastics at these offerings,
releasing dioxins and PCBs into our atmosphere, ultimately poisoning our
environment, our food chain and ourselves" (Letter to the Editor in *FFP*
23 January 2001:5).

The origins of the Mogul Smoker are also being authenticated. "The ritual started some 150 years ago in Norway. When locals there had insuffi-
cient snow for their ... travels between work, school and social visits ...
the best built (wood) skis" were burned (Letter to the Editor in *FFP* 23
January 2001:5). A write-up in the *Free Press* on "these sacrificial ceremonies" suggests that they derive from "ski mecca rituals in other locales"
(*FFP* 17 January 2001). "We probably have 2000 or so ski towns around
the world, each one holding a similar ritual yearly" (Letter to the Editor
in *FFP* 23 January 2001:5). In Fernie the ritual is explained through a collage of cosmologies, associating elements of different traditions with the
thrills of skiing.

> It was to pay homage to the snow gods. When you pay homage you
> have to sacrifice something. In ancient times that would have been
> the heart of a person, or it could be a pair of old skis. So everyone
> was obligated to bring an old piece of equipment ... You know, it
> used to be, everyone had a saying before they threw their skis in –
> something about that piece of equipment, how those skis had
> mistreated you or something. There was more [pause] reverence.
> We considered it spiritual, not unlike our Native friends doing a
> rain dance. (Interview, 20 November 2000. Maritime-Canadian man,
> born ca. 1955.)

Gods, sacrifice, and homage are invoked here to explain the meaning
of this ritual performed at the physical and social centre of the Mogul
Smoker. The reference to "ancient times" conjures popular understandings
of the past that are both placeless and peopleless. Anthropologically, the
performance suggests knowledge of weather magic used in agricultural
societies, seasonal rituals of renewal and thanksgiving. The parallel drawn
between "the heart of a person" and reverence for "an old piece of equipment" is interesting. Sacrifice of equipment was originally accompanied

by a "saying" that was somehow representative of the relationship between the individual and the article. Presumably these sayings were expressions of one's skills and misadventures on the slopes. The performance takes place before an audience of peers, people who share knowledge of the snow-covered terrain and an understanding of what it means to descend runs, each named and designated a degree of difficulty.[4] The "obligation" to bring equipment to sacrifice in the bonfire has now dropped away. In the past, this stricture perhaps limited attendance to the hard-core skiers. This man speaks about the burning of equipment as a "spiritual" act performed with "reverence."

Perhaps predictably, indigenous people are cited as a point of reference through which to understand the ritual for persuading the "snow god." According to Aboriginal filmmaker Loretta Todd (1992:72): "We have become the source of spiritual merit badges for the politically correct, and conduits to the cosmos for the instant shamans of the New Age." The analogy to the "rain dance" of "our Native friends" serves to both legitimate the ritual and erase the complex cosmologies of a huge diversity of Native American peoples. Not unlike understandings about smoking the peace pipe, those associated with the rain dance have transformed it into an artifact in the popular imagination that requires little explanation. What is missing is the recognition that ritual is encased within systems of knowledge and faith, borne through tradition, its rules for transmission, and the use of symbolic codes. Environmentalism cloaked many of the discussions I had with the middle generations about Aboriginal land rights. They emphasize cosmological harmony with nature, ecology rather than the politics of land. The commercial interests of those whose business is wilderness remain largely undiscussed and unmarked. A critique of the ski industry has been taken up in the local media; it coalesces around new repertoires of legend.

The Snow Gods

For those who participate in the Mogul Smoker, the meaning of the event is to encourage the snow gods to usher in the beginning of a new ski season. Ullr is a marginal figure in Norse mythology.[5] He is identified variously as the "archer among the gods" (Branston 1980:143), the "God of Winter" and hunting (Guerber 1912:139), and the "god of skis" most probably worshipped during the Viking Age (Davidson 1993:58, 93). H.R. Davidson (58) stresses that much of what is known about "Ull" is conjecture drawn from scant references in the Icelandic *Eddas*.[6] The most detailed description is provided by H.A. Guerber (1912:139-140), who scripts "Uller" as a "parsimonious" god, clad in thick furs, who travels swiftly by snowshoe and skates, hunting across the frozen lands and taking refuge in the high Alps during the summer months.[7] Regarding worship, Guerber writes: "The people visited Uller's shrine, especially during the months of November and December, to entreat him to send a thick covering of snow over their lands, as earnest of a good harvest" (141). Branston (1980:143) adds that Ullr is "fair of face and has great power as a warrior. You should pray for his help in single combat." According to these sources, Ullr or Ull or Uller was associated with popular rituals that involved offerings of personal belongings, tools, weapons, and animals (Davidson 1993:131).

I provide some detail here because of the resonance between this body of myth and the figure of Griz, described to me as "a quasi abominable-lumberjack-rifleman-logger who lives on the mountain." Like Ullr, Griz is responsible for snowmaking; he is clad in furs, carries a weapon, and is designated supernatural by the term "abominable." Unlike Ullr, Griz is described here through his occupation as a logger. Like many potent figures of legend, Griz leaves telltale signs on the landscape – his tracks are seen in the fault lines where snow is about to avalanche. The image of Griz is everywhere in Fernie. When I first arrived it was on signs, brochures, and T-shirts. Buildings at the ski hill are named after him, and the only remaining community-wide festival is called Griz Days.

> Griz Days began in the 1970s. You know, in various places you had Woodsmen-Logger Days or Black Powder people, where they dressed in period costumes and celebrated festivals. Griz Days started as Winterfest. We held it one year and then Kimberley got in a knot – they had a Winterfest and objected to us using it.[8] This evolved into Griz Days and mountain-man costume ... There was axe throwing, leg wrestling, black powder.
> *What is black powder?*
> That's the ancient rifle with a ball and cap. You use a powder horn and flint. They had shooting competitions and hunting. We still have a black powder shoot at Griz Days, and there's a mock holdup on main street where people dress in their buckskins. It's about a whole way of life, about early exploration, mountain men, Indians, and trade goods. (Interview, 20 November 2000. Maritime-Canadian man, born ca. 1955.)

The resuscitation of this familiar constellation of characters evokes the popular Wild West shows of the past and the frontier mythology within which they figure. At the centre of this mythology is the "strong, ambitious, self-reliant individual" who courts the dangers of a "wide-open land of unlimited possibilities" (R. Slotkin 1973:5). Gone are the cavalrymen and cowboys, the transculturated traders of past eras. The "mountain man" melds familiar motifs of intercultural enmity, lawlessness, and discovery with a new environmentalism centred on wilderness and survival. In the context of the tourism industry, Griz is a valuable commodity whose image evokes the "mythic American west" within a larger "romantic vision" of Rocky Mountain wilderness (Rothman 1998:13-14).

What Legends Are Made Of

... As the legend goes, a baby boy was born back in the year 1879 in the midst of a cruel and bitter winter. It is said that that baby was born in a Grizzly bear's cave high in the mountains above our fine alpine town. Sometime later the resident bear awoke ... A terrible battle ensued between the two, one fighting for his life, the other for his dinner. Well, as the story continues, the people went into the mountains ... They looked high and low on the mountain now known as Fernie Alpine Resort [FAR] ...

Just recently, some of our avid ski tourers were ascending the peaks above the FAR area ... There on the very summit stood the most fantastic sight ... This man has shoulders six feet wide and carried an enormous powder musket. The bulk of [his] 300 pounds was made to look even more awesome by the bristly Grizzly coat he wore. A bear hat was pulled down shadowing his eyes. As the skiers watched he stood shooting that giant musket into the clouds and still more snow fell ... Some of the town's elders remembered the sighting of the little Grizzly clad boy so long ago, and the discovery of massive barefooted tracks ... In recognition and admiration of the man who became known as Griz, the town's people held a festival all week ...

This winter you owe it to yourself; come and experience excellent ski conditions. Come and experience a local legend! (*FFP* 2 January 2001:12)

There are several interesting places to touch down in this article/advertisement. The anonymous writer makes no attempt at historical accuracy. When baby Griz was born, Europeans had cleared only a rudimentary trail through the Crowsnest Pass. Michael Phillipps and Ktunaxa chief Isadore completed the trail in 1881, and the first coal syndicate application was not filed for another eight years. Griz has interesting resonance with the Norse figure of Ullr: dubious parentage, his fur-clad figure, and the emphasis on hand-to-hand combat.

As I have discussed elsewhere, the truth-value of legend is not important. What is potent is the way in which a narrative is authenticated and socially useful. Here the "town's elders" are called upon to lend authority to this legend. As an advertisement, the story performs a role similar to that of the Ghostrider; it is a narrative lure, part of a new strategy that sells ideas of place. If the curse story may be viewed as an origin myth of sorts for the Crowsnest Pass Coal Company, the legend of Griz is surely the counterpart for Fernie Alpine Resort. It is another example of industrial legend, this one unfolding in an era of information technologies.

Given the social tensions surrounding development in Fernie, it is interesting to consider how Griz has become an emblem of conflict.

Tensions around Snow

The Griz legend and the Mogul Smoker ritual are, first and foremost, expressions about the anxieties regarding snowfall. Development of the ski industry in Fernie has spawned investments in property and development by locals and non-residents. "Here is what [BC's] ski industry represents in economic terms. Total assets: $500 million; direct annual sales: $300 million; jobs: 7,900 full-time and part-time; annual payroll $82 million" (*FFP* 2 January 2001:4). In Fernie, Griz has become the mascot for this enormous economic shift. Alberta entrepreneur Charlie Locke took over Fernie Snow Valley in 1997, expanding facilities and ski runs. He also renamed the ski hill Fernie Alpine Resort. Humorous editorials appeared in the *Free Press* at this time.

Under the headline "Is the Griz Mad or Is It All Locke's Fault There's No Snow?" an article debated "reasons why there is a noticeable lack of the white stuff" (*FFP* 9 December 1997:4). Local knowledge was harnessed to suggest that the dryness was not climatologically unusual. The wrath of the "Mountain Man Griz" was also invoked; perhaps he was "upset at being taken down from the big signs that used to let people know there was a ski hill around Fernie." The magical power of words was evoked in 1997: "Rumour has it that when the new owners of the ski hill took the 'snow' out of 'Snow Valley,' they made their own bed. Well, it's now written in stone with these new signs" (*FFP* 16 December 1997:3). Three years later, Griz was still a valuable trope in public opinion pieces: "Angst among powder-hungry, depraved skiers continues to grow daily in proportion to the snow drought – most reliable sources say the lack of the white stuff is an indication The Griz is furious about a new lift, put in at the ski hill this year, destroying his fabled cave" (*FFP* 17 January 2001).

A Mogul Smoker participant saw the lack of snow as the result of a "lack of faith" – "we have to appease the snow gods" (*FFP* 17 January 2001). Griz and all that surrounds him are approached ironically, through poles of truth and fantasy. Gone is the awkward silence that once surrounded ideas of superstition. Now stripped of connotations of backwardness, "folk belief" has been commodified into a vital marketing strategy.

Folkloric devices are potent vehicles for critique (see Figure 17). Griz represents the tension felt in town when the new owner restructured and erased symbols associated with the local character of place. There has been much debate about logging the slopes of the Lizard Range in order to open new runs and build roads for heavy machinery. While Griz has emerged from a new cornucopia of myth and symbolism, his social power is similar to that wielded by the curse legend. Called into service in vastly different contexts to speak about inequalities wrought by industry, both these narrative resources were appropriated by corporate powers to promote their own interests.

Mogul Smoker Postscript

The day after the Mogul Smoker party I visited an elderly woman over instant coffee and warm cinnamon buns. Under her clear plastic table cover was a new handwritten note: "Nature recognizes no State boundaries. Winds, clouds and rivers do not need visas." She is an environmentalist of another age. I told her about the Mogul Smoker and she asked me if it was new. I said I thought not, that it had been held annually for some time. She was surprised she had "never heard anything about it!" Then she said: "Exclusive. It must be exclusive I guess." I told her about the burning of skis. "Why don't they give them to somebody who can't afford skis at all? They would be happy to have somebody's beat-up skis!" She told me about homemade snowshoes, sleds, and skis from her youth; said she would have liked to teach her grandchildren these skills and that

On The Street

What do you think about the lack of snow this year?

"Personally, we'd like to be draped in the stuff. It keeps most of those pesky hikers away. I wonder if they make Raid for humans."
The Three Sisters

"Personally, I don't care. Just like the snowbirds, I'm heading south."
The Ghostrider

"Let it snow, let it snow, let it snow. November in Fernie without snow is downright depressing."
The Griz

Figure 17   As the lack of snowfall led to mounting tensions in November 1998, *Fernie Free Press* writers took the attitudes "on the street" and channelled them through three characters representing the new faces of local lore: The Three Sisters, the Ghostrider, and the Griz. "On the Street," *FFP*, 17 November 1998.

she could never afford the pricey equipment. "They're saying those skiers who live all around line up in the supermarket and just buy one tomato or something. And they all own dogs, they get welfare for their dogs! They're all living on welfare, but then you go up to the ski hill and they all have the most expensive ski equipment! I wonder if some of them are tree planting in the summer, but they say they're on welfare all year round." I asked from whom she hears this. "People who know them," she replied (from Fieldnotes, 11 January 1998).

Over and over I heard elderly people comment on money as a marker between generations. To many, the seemingly disposable income of skiers is representative of this vital shift. This woman's comments about welfare reminded me of stories about pride told by people of her generation. They evoke a time of going into the bush to hunt rather than accepting strike pay, or living on the mining "blacklist" rather than capitulating and abandoning a political stance. I also recalled the elder generation's perceptions of postwar newcomers as wealthy. What have shifted most dramatically are the demographics of class. Those who would once have proudly described themselves as "working class" have joined the ranks of the middle classes, now the unmarked majority in Fernie. And unlike the eldest generations, younger people do not identify themselves through explicit class categories. The shift is evident in the ways that younger generations speak about the "suburbs" of town. Miners and union men live at the Airport and in Ridgemont, places now designated middle class by the middle-age groups. It seems that class currently has "no language"; it is "hidden," "displaced," "spoken through other languages of social difference – through race, ethnicity and gender" (Ortner 1998:8-9). According to Sherry Ortner (8): "The plain 'middle class' is the most slippery category ... At the same time, the 'middle class' is the most inclusive social category; indeed it is almost a national category ... It is everybody except the very rich and the very poor."

Stories of poverty are no longer a source of solidarity. "Low income" is a label with a barb. It is associated with people who are seen to be personally lacking. Conversations about social class take place through veiled commentary around locals and newcomers. Perceptions move between idealized types of urban and rural; they also evoke older ideas of foreignness. In the context of development for tourism, "the very identity of place becomes its economic sustenance" (Rothman 1998:22-23). Ideas of locality, like identity, unfold through time.

Narrative Maps: Suburbia

Fernie is discussed by younger generations of people using a new list of suburbs: the trailer park, Parkland Terrace, Ridgemont, and the ski hill. Although I did not hear people speak of it, there is a new subdivision named after the Ghostrider. Residents at the ski hill are described as "rich"; many own a second home. Others at the ski hill are categorized by their lifestyle and their environmentalism. Downtown remains the area of "old money." Parkland Terrace is the home of middle-class residents.[9] Across the tracks, near the city yards, in an area near where the Chinese vegetable gardens once were, the city recently built housing for low-income earners. "Low income" was also used to describe residents of the Annex and West Fernie.

Debates about access to housing and the affordability of residential property are intensifying in town. So too is the public problem of poverty, phrased largely in terms of locals and newcomers. Between 1997 and 2001, real estate prices in Fernie more than doubled. Notice boards were peppered with requests for winter rentals. Applicants qualify appeals through their self-descriptions as "hard-working," "reliable," "older," "local," or "professional." Stories move through town about young skiers who live by the dozens in small houses that are "gutted" by the end of the season. One newspaper article described people living in their vehicles and defecating in garbage bags. There are photos of campsites in the bush where people squat illegally on the outskirts of town. Another story featured the discovery of two young men who had set up an elaborate home in the closed-down Fernie High School.[10] Transience is central in representations of squatters and welfare recipients. Fernie's history as a town of immigrant workers is being drawn into debates that define locality and outsiderness.

Locality

Ideas about outsiders appear to have shifted little. My great-grandfather spoke about "strangers" and "friends," terms still used by elderly people who state that they now feel like strangers in their own town. Tensions between locals and newcomers are often framed by implicit class markers.[11] Urban professionals have arrived seeking a permanent "lifestyle" change. Seasonal labourers, tree planters, or fruit pickers come to ski. Young "travellers" arrive from across the world.[12] Professionals are greatly involved in the structures of community; they work in the hospitals and schools, are lawyers, and run for city council or manage many of the businesses in town. During the last fifteen to twenty years, "educated" South Africans and Rhodesians moved into the community. Some people who work in the service industry refer to Australian men as the latest "wave of immigrants," whose gender values and ignorance of tipping practices create some tension. For the most part, however, the arrival of other Canadians is perceived to be unsettling the community. Expressions of locality are grounded in birthright and genealogy, in rural and urban identities, and in the perceived ideological distance separating these positions.

During my fieldwork, people in the middle generations greeted me in two ways. Their responses reveal perceptions of outsiders and locals. Often

I was asked why I was in Fernie. I told people about my research. Many locals employed by mine and forest companies were defensive when I met them. They anticipated criticism about the environmental impact of their industries, mentioning the "tree-hugging" perspective that they obviously expected from an urban academic. When I told people about my family history, I was met with immediate silence by those who are not "of" Fernie. I came to realize that the discourse of genealogy is still very much alive and is part of local ways to privilege particular voices. Locals proceeded with the usual reconstruction of my family line, working out from West Fernie where my great-grandparents lived. Many younger people had difficulty placing my family. They said they would have to ask their parents. I received different responses from newcomers.

Not long after I arrived in Fernie I went into a local business and spoke with the young woman working there. She asked me the usual identifying questions: "Where are you from?" "What are you doing here?" I told her about my research. She said: "Ah. You're studying white trash. I would love to do a study on white trash here." I was surprised and asked her what she meant by the term. She said there were many people in Fernie who had never had money before, but who now suddenly had it and didn't know how to deal with it. She identified herself as being from a large city in Ontario. She had lived in Fernie for two years. This interaction was not typical of the ways in which newcomers spoke with me about Fernie. However, it confirms a suspicion of outsiders shared by many locals.

"White trash" evokes yet another typology of difference branded in the space between centre and margin, between the "bourgeois imaginary" and the "hillbilly" (Stewart 1996:116-139). Kathleen Stewart (119) outlines stereotypes associated with popular representations of "white trash," now conceived as a "culture":

> People in the hills were friendly and suspicious, talkative and taciturn, fatalistic and individualist, religious and anti-religious, pathologically dependent and utterly self-sufficient, pathetic and heroic, loving and violent, and above all capable of living with contradiction ... it became the site of a culture that was irredeemably white, poor, rural, male, racist, illiterate, fundamentalist, inbred, alcoholic, violent, and given to all forms of excess, degradation and decay.

While Stewart is describing the enormous burden of ascription carried by people in Appalachia, these markers appear in hostile exchanges between locals and outsiders in Fernie. The discourse resounds with ideas of "peasantry," which also evoke general descriptions of poverty. Many locals view young city people as new arrivals who discredit and look down on them. Others are leaving Fernie:

GETTING OUT WHILE THE GETTING'S GOOD ... As a resource town for many years the trades that plied to the blue collar families prospered and withered with the fortunes of that crazy cycle we all used to take for granted ... Soon there will be a Tim Horton's, Marriott Hotel, more condos, freaks, rich people, poor people, thieves, lunatics, more franchises, more franchises, and yes, more franchises ... The cosmopolitan feeling of downtown is beginning to make me want to heave my cookies ... So I am leaving ... [to a place that is] real pretty and is quieter and not a cosmopolitan lunatic in sight ... Adieu Fernie. (Letter to the Editor in *FFP* 5 August 1997:4)

It is ironic that this man is leaving Fernie for the same reason that so many "cosmopolitans" are seeking it out: a better quality of life.[13] The list of people he mentions touches on well-worn typologies of criminality, poverty, and insanity – the stereotypes of dangerous cities. Class critique is explicit. Fernie is changing from a "blue collar," family-oriented resource town to a commercial, service-oriented place of "freaks [and] rich people." As a resource-based community, the population of Fernie has always grown and shrunk in response to processes affecting the marketplace. What is different now is the perception of newcomers as transient property owners or absentee residents.

We knew every single person in Fernie at one time. Where they lived. But now I don't know anybody. 'Course, I'm getting old now too ... It's a big change for us; let's say that. When Kaiser came in, that was a big change, but it seemed like you knew those families right away. But now it seems like it's going tourist and it's, they're not families. Its just people coming and going all the time ... When Kaiser came in we were in our prime, in our forties. I don't know anybody anymore ... You've got to go with progress, that's what I say. It's good for our children. For us older people it just seems like Fernie isn't what it used to be. (Interview, 20 August 1998. North End woman, born 1930.)

In "traditional industries" of mining or forestry, incoming workers settle within the social fabric of a community (Rothman 1998:26). Tourism opens places to semi-permanent labourers, managers, and supervisors who "embrace a fixed moment in local time" (26) and who have no memory of the local community. Their impressions are formed within the present context of development. People of the eldest generations spoke about having to lock their doors for the first time in their lives, about houses that sit empty until the weekends, and about the increasing expense of food and clothing. Their statements about current development reveal older strategies used to negotiate conflict. One man joked about segregation.

I just wish they would build a whole bunch of condominiums up on the ski hill and put a big fence around it. They can keep all the skiers up there, and they could have an escort from the north end bridge directly up there – and they stay there until the weekend is over and they are escorted back. (Interview, 5 September 1997. West Fernie man, born ca. 1924.)

Supernaturalism appeared here and there in conversations with old-timers about development. In June 1998 there was an article in the paper extolling the friendliness of "newcomers." An elderly woman read it aloud to me. Then she said: "Don't look into newcomers' eyes. They say the eyes are the most powerful part, be careful." Another man invoked cursing:

We're cursed in the other direction.
What do you mean?
Too much bloody prosperity. Well, I mean all this development is what I'm getting at. That's another argument for an old-timer! (Interview, 26 August 1998. North End man, born 1916.)

Discovery

> Ironized and modernized ... vivid imperial rhetoric endures
> today in the writings of ... postcolonial heirs, for whom there is
> little left on the planet to pretend to conquer.
> – Mary-Louise Pratt, "From the Victoria Nyanza to the
>   Sheraton San Salvador"

Knowledge about the backcountry constitutes an important element of identity for many locals. They visit their parents' berry-picking sites, fish, hike the old trails, and picnic at places now a part of family tradition. Processes of discovery and appropriation have led many locals to guard their knowledge of place and space. For those employed in the promotion of recreational tourism, this knowledge is a valuable commodity. Published guidebooks, with their images of tucked-away places, constitute one genre of discovery in Fernie. Other materials are generated for an international audience of readers; they function to entice visitors who will come to "Discover Fernie." As is common to processes of discovery, outsiders are now inscribing the community from faraway perches; in effect, they are putting Fernie on the tourist map. Authentic images of local character sell these views.

Snow Dream

Fernie Snow Valley is steep, deep and cheap.

Should I stare at the scenery or ski 2,400 feet of untracked powder? ... The scene is surreal and legends surround it. Preparing to marry, an ancient Indian Chief couldn't decide between three equally beautiful sisters. Distraught, he sought the advice of the gods, which, it turned out, was a mistake, because the gods detested indecision. They promptly turned him into a mountain. Heart-broken, and with a rather extravagant display of martyrdom, the three sisters pleaded with the gods to turn them into mountains as well. The gods complied and ever since Chief Mountain stares longingly at the Three Sisters. (*Missoulian* 14 February 1998)

The story of the Three Sisters is yet another legend bound in the unusual contours of a mountain ridge. We return to recognizable motifs of chiefs and princesses, marriage and supernatural disapproval. There is a seemingly obligatory nod to "the gods" within an "ancient" setting. The writer misidentifies the "longing" mountain; to locals this is Mount Proctor. The eldest generations in Fernie call the Three Sisters, Trinity Mountain. They shake their heads as they speak about the renaming of places traversed throughout their lives. Outside representations of Fernie complicate the shifts in social knowledge they have witnessed.

Missoula, Montana, is a five-hour drive south into the United States, yet this writer uses all of the tropes of imperial discovery common to transnational contact. According to the article, Fernie is "little known by others" except "hard-core powder skiers." It is a place "destined to go on hiding in plain sight." "The town of Fernie should be experienced. A turn-of-the-century coal mining settlement turned ski town, downtown Fernie is all red brick and sandstone ... Local accents seem to be an amalgam of Scottish and deep-woods trapper, which adds to the illusion that you're far away from home" (*Missoulian* 14 February 1998).

I don't know what "deep-woods trapper" sounds like, but it may be how Griz speaks. The newspaper article hangs framed in the barroom of a local hotel amid old skis, traps, snowshoes, historical photographs, iron tools, moccasins, and bridles. Like restaurant reviews, it serves to reassure visitors that they are in the right place: "Tourist space is especially scripted to keep visitors at the centre of the picture while simultaneously cloaking, manipulating and even deceiving them into believing that their experience is the locals' life, reality and view of the world" (Rothman 1998:12).

In 1997 articles on Fernie began to appear in international outdoor and lifestyle magazines. Gradually, locals and their histories have faded into a scenic backdrop. Skiers are at the centre of new representations, and Fernie is their "Mecca." One American magazine inscribed Fernie as a "Dream Town." The manager of the Chamber of Commerce explained that he had worked with the journalist "to ensure the right image of Fernie was being painted – that being an image of being a really natural type of town" (*FFP* 19 August 1997:12). In the bars and the bakery, at gas stations and grocery checkouts, it was the pros and cons of international recognition that were debated that summer.

By 1999 the new owners of Fernie Alpine Resort had more than doubled the size of the ski area, and international magazines published more articles. On 9 January 1999 the *Globe and Mail* declared that "Fernie and the Lizard Range are famous." "Close to the Alberta border is the skiing town of Fernie, home to aging hippies, good-natured rednecks and one of the most snow-blessed mountains in Western Canada. In the eyes of many aficionados, Fernie is ... a nicely priced skiers' mecca waiting to be discovered by the outside world" (Dafoe 1999:A15).

Fernie is now a "skiing town," where "hippies" and "rednecks" are fixtures of the environment. This writer also mentions the legend of Griz and offers the website address for snow reports, "trail maps and links to other Fernie sites." One of these sites is "a bulletin board where local issues get hashed out in the overheated atmosphere of the Web."

Locals and Granolas
In what follows I work from messages posted between January and February 1999 on a public electronic chat line called "Fernie Talk." It is interesting that people participating in textual discussion use speech to define what it is they are doing. Virtual reality is the quintessential arena for disguises, where writers are without identifying locations – names, genders, or ages. Their conversations, called "threads," occur in that no-place of electronic circuitry. Readers are given only the information writers choose to disclose, the date, and exact time of "posting." Comments are titled, and many messages in these difficult exchanges appear under the headings "Granolas" or "Locals."

LOCALS
At any given time there are 500 Fernie locals in receipt of welfare who have little else to do than: 1) get drunk at the Northern. 2) Complaining about how the Ministries of Families seized their children for neglect and/or abuse. 3) Drinking and driving. 4) Beating their spouses. 5) Complaining how "the mine" hasn't hired them back. 6) Poaching ... (28 January 1999 at 3:44 p.m.)

GRANOLA
Just a message to all granolas:
1) Soap is a good thing. 2) Shampoo and conditioner are your friends. 3) Brushes, Combs, and pick are used to comb hair! 4) Skiing/Snowboarding

is not a job! 5) Dreadlocks is not a fashion statement. 6) Deodorant is that white clear stuff for under the arm to prevent that odour you carry around! For all you trying to smoke hemp necklaces, get a life ... Sincerely, Concerned Citizens. (30 January 1999, 9:38 p.m.)

These messages present the clearest list of essentialized views of the other, including perceptions of job loss to newcomers, increasing gaps between wealthy and poor, the takeover of community identity by people who know nothing about its values, and the perceived degradation of Fernie's social environment. Just as in the struggles of other generations, difference is enforced through derogatory assumptions. Ideas of pollution surround granolas; they are carried in negative descriptions of work ethic, personal hygiene, drug use, and social politeness. Locals are denigrated through class and work. Negative stereotypes of intelligence and family degradation long associated with rural poverty are evident. These are difficult dialogues around identity groups that take on old patterns of animosity. They echo criteria used by earlier generations to mark immigrants, poor people, and racialized others. One writer explicitly acknowledged one of these continuities: "It's amazing that a group of 'real locals' believe that there are others of the same country that should not travel, move or settle in a town they truly love" (8 February 1999, 9:55 a.m.).

In these exchanges, there are glimpses of what people perceive to be the social climate in Fernie.

I can't believe there are so many "hate-mongers" in the area ... I am sure all of you have gone to other towns at one point or another. Do they shun and publicly insult you? (29 January 1999, 1:14 p.m.)

Maybe all this should end and maybe this town would not be so bitter about the different kinds of PEOPLE here! I have lived here all my life ... there are more locals with jobs than granolas ... As the saying goes it is who you know! (25 January 1999, 7:52 p.m.)

A subtext around local knowledge was evident in these dialogues. Local defensiveness was continually expressed in response to newcomers, on the basis that they simply do not know about the way things work in Fernie. An elderly man I spoke with connected social knowledge to one's length of residency. I asked him if people used the curse story to speak about bad things that happened.

No. They usually don't talk about it. Nobody knows about it. These people here don't know anything. Ninety percent of the people in Fernie don't know nothing about Fernie! They all came in here in the last twenty-five years. Why would they know anything about Fernie? (Interview, 12 September 1997. South End man, born 1911.)

His comments draw a boundary, set at twenty-five years of residence, between those who know about Fernie and those who do not. The relationship between knowledge and tenure of residency highlights "place" as a point of perspective.

Besides locals and granolas, there are other categories of persons mentioned throughout these threads: citizens, ancestors, Fernie-borns, tourists, welfare recipients, business people, new residents, ski bums, teens, real locals, retailers, and rednecks. Many locals posting messages qualify their comments by stating they are "born and raised" in Fernie or they are "life-long residents." Responses from new residents or granolas often critique this genealogical privilege. One person wrote: "Fernie locals seem to want it all, the revenue the ski hill brings and a closed community where only those whose ancestors were born here are welcome" (21 January 1999, 2:59 p.m.).

Other messages are attempts at mediation. Some argue through economics that the influx of people is good for local businesses and property owners; that, proportionally, locals do not seek employment at the ski hill, nor do they tend to spend as much money in town. One person made an appeal for "tolerance of difference"; another asked people to "search their hearts for compassion." The two approaches echo larger discourses of coexistence through rational economic argument and humanistic appeals.

While the conversations in these threads appear to be between residents in Fernie, an awareness of outside observers gradually leaks into the exchanges. It is a further reminder of the trickiness of the electronic medium, which brings the local into a boundless and uncertain space. Writers who may – or may not – have local connections with the community used shame.

Do any of you realize that the whole world can see this (all the other 4 999 995 001 or so people). We have to make a good impression of our small town ... With the growing number of people using the Internet for planning trips/vacations, I think it's "our" responsibility to make a good impression. (29 January 1999, 1:14 p.m.)

I am one of those peoples from another part of the world. Here in Russia we read Fernie talk every day and wonder. It is interesting to watch a family argue and determine who are the articulate ones ... I propose that all incoming granolas be required to wear a patch on the left shoulder so they may be readily identified! (Slavomir, 31 January 1999, 4:39 a.m.)

These appeals work from a standpoint outside the local. Writers invite discussants to step outside of their immediate context and view their "talk" through the eyes of vacationers and through shared understandings about brutal regimes that have historically marked human difference and targeted particular populations.

I have discussed earlier periods in Fernie when the arrival of different groups created conflict, but other clashes also resonate with the current discord between locals and granolas. During the 1960s, important intergenerational shifts occurred. Pacifists led protests against authoritarian structures. Youth subcultures emerged alongside struggles for civil rights and ethnic and sexual liberation movements.[14] As an ideal type, the "hippie" was the manifestation of these changes.

> Let's see, [my son] came home with this kid. He went to university in '63-'64 ... It was really funny. Christmas. White shirt, narrow black tie – Dad, everybody. Everybody in town. Everybody wears a narrow black tie ... The second year he was still in the black-tie mentality of course, and this boy came on vacation ... wearing the jeans and a flannel shirt, a plaid flannel shirt, guitar on his back, long hair, right? No one in Fernie had ever seen that! I mean, it was the talk of the town. The talk of the town ...
> *How was he talked about?*
> They wouldn't tell *me!* The talk was around us! ... They don't tell you because they're shocked. But that was the first hippie to come into Fernie. There was more after that, but they were never quite accepted ... Very strange, the hippies. I remember this boy sitting at the table for breakfast and he was, he had this thing in front of him and he was going [she gestures with her fingers in front of her downturned head]. I thought: I wonder what religion that is? [Laughing] ... I had no idea. I remember asking [my son] and he laughed and laughed, he nearly killed himself laughing. "Ma!" he said. "He's just putting in his contacts!" (Interview, 4 November 1997. Crowsnest Pass woman, born 1925.)

Hippies were visually distinguished through dress and, in the scenario above, through perceptions of difference based on religion. The woman's comment that they were "never quite accepted" is telling. Stereotypes of granolas seem frozen in this crossfire of ideas between generations.

> I remember the first man to walk through Fernie in a skirt! So I'm at [the supermarket], I spot this tall, blonde, bearded man wearing a long, velvet, patchwork skirt. And suddenly I feel safer in Fernie! [Laughing] People can barely contain themselves! They're almost

walking into stacks of beans! People are making eye contact that
have never made eye contact before when they're shopping. This
man leaves the store; as soon as the door shuts the place explodes
with laughter. They're uncomfortable. Incredibly uncomfortable.
They're making really sexist jokes about cross-dressing. He was
definitely identified as a granola by the comments they were
making. So I say, in a really loud Scottish brogue: "Have ye nay seen
a man in a kilt before?" I was hoping it would make them think
another way. (Interview, 4 September 1998. Crowsnest Pass woman,
born 1959.)

The skirt-clad man is labelled "granola," which is apparently also a
convenient category for those who express alternative images of gender.
Just as descriptions of spousal abuse are attributed to racialized others,
sexuality has entered into current negotiations between locals and outsiders. Central here are the closely guarded images of community, still
defined through morality.

The Closet

In August 2000, Fernie city council was approached to proclaim an official Lesbian, Gay, Bisexual, and Transgender Pride Day (*FFP* 1 August
2000:1). The front-page headline read: "City Reluctant to Endorse People's
Sexual Preferences." Council members refused this "controversial" request,
stating that they would "hold off on declaring proclamations" altogether
"until they receive[d] an opinion from the Union of BC Municipalities
regarding their protocol." According to the mayor: "If it's a free will choice
and if it's something the community we feel wouldn't support, it may not
even reach an agenda item ... Where do we stand? Where would we wind
up as a community?" (1-2).

The mayor is discussing the moral integrity of the community here. In
an editorial one week later, signed by six writers, there is a suggestion that
"the gay rights steamroller" could be responsible for wiping out proclamations altogether. At risk, according to these writers, were the civic mechanisms that support awareness for Alzheimer's, cancer, and Mining Week
(*FFP* 8 August 2000:4). Special rights discourse is implicit in the commentary; it emerged more clearly in the debate about same-sex benefits
that were then under corporate and legal consideration. People in Fernie
speculated about who the gay miners might be and how difficult it must
be for them to work in that environment.

Like it or not, [homosexuality] is a legitimate lifestyle that exists in most
if not all communities, and, ideally, should get no more attention than
a heterosexual relationship ... While sexuality should remain a private

matter, the issue of homosexuality has been a target for hate and discrimination. (*FFP* 8 August 2000:4)

The writers acknowledge that "most if not all communities" harbour people with homosexual "lifestyles" and that these people have been targets "for hate and discrimination." The general discussion takes place through the idea of community, but there is no acknowledgment that gay and lesbian people are residents in Fernie. This invisibility evokes the idea of "the closet" as a location enforced through discourses of otherness: "The very notion of the 'closet' (as well as the metaphor of 'coming out of the closet,' now somewhat widely diffused) reflects the influence of the homosexual/heterosexual dichotomy on broader perceptions of public and private, or secrecy and disclosure" (Epstein 1994:196).[15] The closet circumscribes a safe area of public silence amid speculation about causes of homosexuality.

Right now everyone's really trying hard to find a scientific authority so that the AIDS epidemic – trying to explain what makes somebody homosexual. There's two ideas I hear discussed around here. One is genetic, which is scientific, and the other is kind of social psychological, this idea that if somebody's been abused it will make them homosexual. (Interview, 4 September 1998. Crowsnest Pass woman, born 1959.)

These ethno-theories parallel essentialist views of gender and "race." They serve to "naturalize" sexual categories through scientific typologies or through the stigma of social deviance. The biological explanation of homosexuality was/is promulgated not only by heterosexual experts, but also by activists in the gay and lesbian community. "It was intended to legitimate homosexuality ... by asserting [its] naturalness and normality" (Seidman 1994:170). Like the essentialism expressed by indigenous activists, these arguments are politically strategic. Opponents of gay rights contest them through special rights discourses.

Special rights arguments depend on the invisibility of dominant ideas and the unequal power relations they create. What is made visible is a perceived threat from minorities whose claims for equality appear to unsettle the status quo. To mark one's "cultural" background is, according to special rights rhetoric, now a matter of "personal choice." Homosexuality is likewise a "lifestyle" alternative. Regarding class, each individual is expected to demonstrate "fiscal responsibility." According to the backlash discourse, the victims of the new injustices are all those people whose privilege has now been upset. The argument ignores "political consequences that in turn reflect certain structural barriers to achieving ...

equality" (Kirkham 1998:258). The screen onto which these ideas are projected is one where actions or statements exhibiting overt racism, sexism, classism, ageism, ableism, or homophobia are subject to legal and social sanctions. Some individuals are currently sidestepping these codes of speech and behaviour using voices not their own. In the context of development, these appropriations illustrate how outsiders use authentic visions of community.

Transmission and Ventriloquism

In town there are specialized networks through which information flows to intended audiences. Elderly people go to a bulletin board on the side of the old post office. Here they read funeral notices that may or may not appear in the newspaper. Bulletin boards for ski equipment, house rentals, and rides are located in other areas that serve a younger clientele. Telephone poles are plastered with notices of visiting performers, club meetings, bake sales, and lost animals.

Other modes are less direct. Like cyberspace exchanges between locals and granolas, some forms of public media involve the intentional or unintentional use of disguises. Given current sanctions on speech about difference, it is revealing that younger writers use disguises to present perspectives on age, class, gender, ethnicity, and locality associated with older generations. In the context of development and the reification of local authenticity, two writers have appropriated voices of local authority. They are both young people from elsewhere, engaged in the project of "imitating locals" (Rothman 1998:26). In the process, they contribute to a reification of locality expressed through stereotyped voices of old-timers and immigrants.

An erupting market for tourism has spawned media in the form of "lifestyle" newspapers, brochures, and magazines conceived and scripted by professional newcomers. One such local paper is *Mountain Fresh* (*MF*), described by its editor as a "free lifestyle/cultural magazine with stuff on the great outdoors, on music festivals, the arts and the sometimes polarized politics – all with a personal voice. A publication that defies age group, but deals in mindset instead" (*MF* June/July 1999).

Odd Einarsson writes a column called "Odd Missives." He describes himself as "a 90-something pensioner living at the Lodge." Einarsson wears a visual mask, presenting himself through a computer-generated image of an elderly man with unruly white hair – a disguise that has much to do with current sanctions on public expression. The column focuses largely on tensions between locals and newcomers:

> Jack Turnbraugh is that old crony you see every Remembrance Day, dragging his leg and snarking about the dwindling attendance ... He is dying

now ... he thought he could keep the outsiders out, and the insiders in line, by the sheer volume of his rants about the good old days and the good old ways. (Einarsson *MF* October 1998)

Einarsson appropriates the voice of an elderly man to lend insider authority to his critique of those who he calls "pig-ignorant xenophobes" (*MF* January 1998). In the process he crosses representational and social boundaries. For the most part, the column presents criticism of Fernie council decisions, advocates the need for economic development, and provides commentary on various situations of enmity as they arise in the community. Einarsson describes Fernie as "this goddamned smug valley and its narrow minds" (*MF* November 1997), "inbred" (*MF* January 1998), "this forgotten corner of the province" in a "Valley of Doom" (*MF* March 1998), and "the one hundred year old whore called Fernie" (*MF* July 1998). Like young male skiers he also refers to Fernie as "Sausage Town"[16] (*MF* July 1998). Woven throughout Einarsson's articles are remarks about genetics, performance-enhancing pharmaceuticals, alcohol, hip-replacement surgery, strokes, computer technology, global warming, science, death, dementia, depression, and, of course, skiing.

Einarsson's columns focus on the sometimes violent clashes between locals and newcomers.[17] Terms used to describe locals include "truck-brains" and "political dolts," "down-vested beer-swilling lougans" (*MF* November 1997), who are "ignorant," "cowardly," and "apathetic" (*MF* January 1998). In one column he honours the historical script of Fernie. Referring to wars, mine disasters, and fires, he calls residents a "heroic" "loving family ... of folk" (*MF* October 1998). Newcomers are described as "rings-in-their-noses-and-bells-on-their-rears-types," "out-of-towners," "intruders" (*MF* November 1997), "young people and new arrivals" (*MF* July 1998), "drifting and demented young," "transient," "strange and unusual," "weak and defenceless" "strangers," who arrive with "new genes" (*MF* October 1998). More affluent newcomers are seldom mentioned. He uses the history of immigration in Fernie to shame locals who are critical of new development (*MF* July 1998). There is more than a hint of the stereotypical representation of rural people by urban outsiders. While Einarsson uses irony to critique xenophobia and violence in the community, he seems unmoved by his own marking of difference that reinforces older, essentialist ideas.

At the height of political correctness, it was difficult not to read Einarsson's opinion pieces as a way to sidestep current sanctions around speaking. Through the voice of an elderly man, this young man also presents sexist views. A shifting list of characters who surround him "at the Lodge" include "Gunella Gunderson," a widow of "Icelandic/Norwegian stock," with whom he has regular sexual relations and skis at FAR (*MF*

July 1998). Gunella is sexually objectified through descriptions of their relations and the decrepit state of her failing body. The ageism Einarsson propagates would surely also be subject to social sanction were he to reveal his "real" age.

A subtext throughout this series of editorials speaks to "hatred" between young and old (*MF* November 1997). He mentioned by name the two facilities in Fernie where elderly people are accommodated. I took a copy of this paper to a woman who lives in one of these facilities. She described it as "bizarre," said she doesn't understand it at all and that whoever was writing it is a "Kook. Why are they doing it!? They don't know what they're doing! It sounds like they have a screw loose! I just don't understand!" She said she thought it was "one of those skiers. They speak in a whole different language, a whole different way." She continued, pointing out her window: "They come here running away from somewhere else and they don't think they have to abide by any rules here – they refuse." She said she sees them looking over towards the Lodge, and she thinks they are sizing up the property because there is some space out front and they think they should have it. On her television, a small calendar with sayings is open to this day. It reads: "Blessed are the hard of hearing for they miss much small-talk" (from Fieldnotes, 12 April 1998. North End woman, born 1909).

This woman analyzes Einarsson's column through the language of skiers and a perceived disregard for local norms. Property infringement is central. What she calls "rules" include sanctions around speech and authority. She acknowledges the power of these words; however, she interprets the writer's transgression as an indication of mental incompetence. Members of the eldest generations do not agree with what is called political correctness, yet they do take issue with false information and unjust representations. Ironically, younger generations are using the elders' voices to present essentialist discourses.

Under the headline "Canada is a Good Place," an opinion piece appeared in the *Free Press* on 28 October 1997. A photograph of the writer, "Holga," shows a woman with curly dark hair and large glasses (see Figure 18). The lower part of her face is obscured by a long scarf worn about her head and shoulders in babushka style. The column begins: "I just come here from the old country. I love this place Canada – I can't believe it to see it. I don't speak too gooda English, but this is what I was seeing" (*FFP* 28 October 1997). Holga uses broken English throughout the piece, the first of what was intended to be a monthly column.

Several disguises are donned here. First, she is visually camouflaged. Linguistically, she employs the stereotypical voice of an immigrant whose constant point of comparison is an unlocatable "old country." Perhaps the greatest irony is that the highly stigmatized language of an older

Figure 18 In reaction to Holga's column, local artist J.F. van Delft initiated the poster campaign "Who is Holga?" *Photograph by L. Robertson.*

woman is used here to authenticate views that are politically conservative and socially exclusionary. The vocabulary carries a brand that so many have struggled to overcome. Her chosen issues form a predictable neo-conservative cluster: welfare, the health care system, old-age pensions, and treaties:

> I never seened a country where peoples get money for not working ... This is a joke, yes? In my country you have to work your l'il pushka off to get enough money to buy some food ... I was been hearing there is some pensioning plan for old people. Holy Shootska ... In my country they go live with other family peoples and help with the work and chil-drens. (*FFP* 28 October 1997)

The writer wields a vocabulary of cross-cultural and intergenerational comparison. She uses an "ethnic" voice to critique liberal social policies of the Canadian government that are seen to threaten traditional forms of family and work ethics. Her rhetoric works through a commonsense understanding of place, unnecessary to name or specify through history or location. In the "old country," poverty is natural, life is hard, and there is no free ride. Finally, the writer known as Holga evokes land:

> But I was been hearing they give muchka money to some natives peoples who say dish is dere land and the government owes them. In my coun-try it is our land too but we don't be getting special treatments. Why is that they get special treats? What are they been doing for this? (*FFP* 28 October 1997)

History is sidestepped once again in this special rights commentary. Holga assumes this is the rhetoric of a previous generation of immigrants who settled in Canada. She seems to be working from hollow impressions. While elderly immigrants spoke with me about land, they did not use the avenue of special rights. Their analyses were grounded in ideas of conquest and the inevitability of loss. Eldest generations of non-Anglo-European immigrants did not erase colonialism or the experience of mil-itary dispossession.

"I'm not being famous like Princess Diana or Mother Teresa, but Holga is here to stay and to help. Tank you from Holga from the old country" (*FFP* 28 October 1997). Holga was not "here to stay." This column was the first of two. It generated local controversy in town. Many elderly people said that they refused to read it after the first few lines. It was simply not worth the time. One woman, a daughter of Ukrainian immigrants, rec-ognized the genre and was somewhat receptive to her message.

I thought that was intriguing. I thought, Now can she keep this up? ... Let's see what this person has to say next. *But.* I also think that whoever is saying this thing is hiding behind a name and I think, my feeling about things like this is, stand up and be counted ... Stand up and be counted, "This is what I am, this is what I believe." Well that person's hiding. I've seen so much of this, I'm immune to it. The Ukrainians do it most of all about themselves. I get so angry with them! ... They use the accents of their parents for humour. I don't appreciate it ... That's the only part that bothers me.
    Not the use of that immigrant voice?
No. That doesn't bother me. I guess it should. It should but it doesn't. It should but it doesn't. I'd have to think about that. But it didn't irritate me. Now, you see, you know why it didn't irritate me? Because I don't come from a generation of politically correct people. My generation didn't know about political correctness. (Interview, 4 November 1997. Crowsnest Pass woman, born 1925.)

This woman's critique is not phrased in the language of appropriation of voice, representation, political correctness, or the power of words. Instead there are values about standing by one's opinions, regardless of what they are. As she points out, Holga has tapped into a well-known genre of ethnic humour that she feels is disparaging. A younger immigrant woman raised in the Crowsnest Pass had this to say.

There were things about [the Holga article] that really disturbed me. One was, basically, it was a hidden voice for a right-wing agenda. It was given validity through the voice of an aging Eastern European immigrant ... It was a complete lie. It was someone who was young and rich and white wanting to spew a Reform Party line ... A lot of people hadn't read Holga and wanted to understand what it was about. (Interview, 4 September 1998. Crowsnest Pass woman, born 1959.)

This woman exposes the disguises of age, class, and ethnicity donned by Holga. To her it is the "hidden voice," the appropriation of identity, that constitutes transgression.
    Holga and Odd each dip into worlds not their own in order to have some licence to speak in ways that have been considered socially unacceptable. They work against a fading backdrop of identity politics, where self-representation was once key. The voices through which their ventriloquism occurs were chosen because of the assumed privilege they carry. Ironically, these voices belong to people who do not share these assumptions of privilege but who have, rather, borne the burden of stigma. Currently, sanctions around public discourse are being challenged. Like

the turn from essentialism to inclusion following the Second World War, the shift is evidenced in social sanctions around what you can say. In March 1999, *Fernie Talk* was shut down when the site's operator was threatened with legal action after "negative and sexual comments about a pair of local girls" were posted (*FFP* 23 March 1999:3). In a face-to-face community such as Fernie, social sanction is swiftly administered for slanderous acts against individuals. More generalized "curses" against marked groups blur into a background of normalized opinion.

Tourism has generated new conflicts in a setting already riddled with social complexity. Skiers represent the latest social category; their legends and rituals have become the new visions of authenticity representing Fernie to the outside world. To some locals, young skiers are perceived as threats to community identity. People use many of the discourses once aimed at foreigners and immigrants. Perceptions of granolas summon old ideas of animosity – social pollution, economic incursion, and sexual deviance. Despite shifts in identification, social class remains a vital category of difference to younger generations in Fernie. It is now disguised by the vocabulary of lifestyle and rural and urban identities. Cosmopolitans and locals replace foreigners and Anglo Europeans in expressions of regionalism and outsiderness. Fernie's identity as a place is now being inscribed through new processes of discovery, and the construction of new visions of place confounds originals with replicas. Just as the postcard designer can click the mouse and apply the "Romantic Vision" effect, social complexity is being reduced to available and marketable homogenizing images. People and place are rescripted to suit the needs of an industry that relies upon local knowledge and idealized visions.

In December 2000, Canadian Pacific Rail's "Holiday Train" arrived in Fernie as one stop in its journey to raise awareness and funds to alleviate hunger in Canada. Tom Jackson, an indigenous singer-songwriter, actor, and Order of Canada recipient, stepped out onto the platform. "I hear I should be looking for a wife here ... It's something to do with that mountain over there," he said, gesturing to Mount Hosmer (*FFP* 26 December 2000:1).

7
One Step Beyond

Do you know the story of the curse?
a: The story of the what?
b: Oh – Ghostrider?
c: Yeah. Do you want the Ghostrider one, or the fires?
Whichever one.
c: There was two fires and two floods – or two fires and one flood, something like that?
b: Yeah. That Fernie guy, I forgot his first name.
c: William Fernie.
b: Yeah. He had this plan to get gold or something. No. He wanted to marry the Indian chief's daughter so that he could get the plan for the gold, but once he got the plan for the gold he, like, ran off, so that the picture of the Ghostrider –
a: He ran into the little hole in the mountain.
b: Yeah, yeah, like on the Ghostrider, that's the Indian chief riding on his horse with his daughter and because William Fernie stole the plans for the gold mine, he put a curse on Fernie.
a: So they had to get it, like, taken off in the '60s. And then we had a flood again in '95 ...
So, the curse, what do you reckon about it? Did you grow up hearing that story?
a: Not really. No one really knows it.
b: My grandma.
a: Yeah, and when it flooded it kinda came up again.
b: Yeah, people were just talking. (Interview, 24 February 1998. Young women, born ca. 1980-1982.)

We were sitting in a fast-food restaurant. Electronic beeps from video machines punctured the air, interrupting the more familiar sound of pool balls in collision. The young men we had invited hadn't shown up. Other boys hovered at the edge of our conversation, hands thrust deeply into the pockets of their jackets. Our table was strewn with tape recorder, map, and French fries. At the time of this interview, these young women were between sixteen and eighteen years of age. As they spoke with me, another world of story and social location materialized. The years are beginning to show in the erosion of the curse story. Is it gold? Who was "that Fernie guy"? According to these teenagers there are now two stories: the Ghostrider and the "one" about the "fires." Like many in previous generations, they are well aware of the number of fires that swept through Fernie. Once again it is the number of floods that is in doubt. Different renditions pronounce an alternative series of disasters depending on which curse formula is adhered to. The narrative's resolution hinges on such details, which pump vitality through the heart of local legend. In the version told to me here, the link between Hosmer Mountain and the curse legend is finally made explicit. "He ran into that little hole in the mountain." Perhaps most interesting is the comment "People were just talking." The teenagers tell me that the curse story is no longer really "known," but leaks out now and then when it floods. A grandmother is one person's link to the narrative. The legend appears to have slipped from the realm of oral tradition. Or has it?

I asked a group of girls in grades two to seven if they could tell me about the Ghostrider. A six-year-old said: "This father didn't want any of his daughters to date this man. He got turned into Mount Fernie and the daughters were turned into the Three Sisters so they would have to look at him forever." She was almost interrupted by her seven-year-old friend: "No, the chief wouldn't allow Fernie – who discovered Fernie – to marry his youngest, most beautiful daughter. He gave him the ugly one. But the young one still was seeing Fernie behind the chief's back. They all got turned into mountains." At this time an eleven-year-old spoke: "It's impossible to discover Fernie – it was made!" Then the eldest of the children, a new teenager, said: "That's not what I heard. I heard about Mount Hosmer, that that's the Indian Princess riding towards Fernie on the mountain." (Fieldnotes, 7 November 1998)

Here the Ghostrider legend converges with the story of the Three Sisters and with motifs of European fairy tales. Marriage and gender politics remain at the centre of the narrative. The comment on "discovery" illustrates an awareness of processes of inscription.

In May 1999 I was again visiting this household when the youngest sister arrived home from school. In her grade two class they had been given a photocopy of "The Legend of Hosmer Mountain." At the bottom of the page was a handwritten instruction from the teacher, "Read 1 Time," and below this a note to the parent to "sign please." And so it goes. The narrative that once dangled enticingly, spreading dread for some people and sheer imaginative delight for others, is now delivered in text as an institutional assignment to be read once. In the reading there are the recognizable details of the legend: the necklace of coal worn by the "dark-eyed Indian girl," a "tribal secret," marriage to the "maid in the Indian way," and finally "a Princess shamed for all to see!" The story then takes a sudden shift. Fernie flees with the tribe in pursuit. "Strength near gone and almost dead," he arrives at Hosmer Mountain and climbs into the cave on its face.

> But Fernie could not believe his ears
> The yelping faded, as did his fears.
> The Indians passed by his hiding place.
> So he never did pay for the girl's disgrace.
>> But Hosmer Mountain still tells the tale.
>> When the Indian Princess rides the trail.
>> The old chief walking by her side.
>> Their heads bowed low in wounded pride.[1]

The act of cursing has been erased from the Ghostrider legend. Perhaps negative representations of indigenous-European relations have been acknowledged. The "Indians" remain culturally indistinguishable, identified through phenotype, kinship, warpath pursuit, and noble pride. Perhaps the act of cursing is no longer recognizable to younger generations, or maybe it has new associations not encouraged by their educators. I do not know. Clearly William Fernie remains the transgressor in this rendition. He is described as "cool and conniving," a "fortune hunter? Gambling man?" His infamy revolves around the princess's "despair." Gender transgression, exploitation, and greed are the lessons that remain intact.

In 1997 members of the Fernie Junior "A" Ghostriders painted their "logo" on the side of the ice arena. It is an image of a Plains warrior galloping forward on a horse. Feathers from his headdress stream behind him; in one hand he grasps a coup stick (see Figure 1 in Preface). The Ghostrider image was stylized during the time I was in Fernie, apparently because the first one included too much detail and the hockey uniforms were difficult to read. The new logo, reduced to a headshot of horse, rider, and mountain, appears on the official program for the Rocky Mountain Junior "A" Hockey League (see Figure 19). The stencilled outline of a chesspiece-like horse head appears below a grimacing skull wearing a stylized headdress. Figuratively, the contour of Hosmer Mountain represents the rider's shoulders. It is an artifact of now ubiquitous computerized imagery.

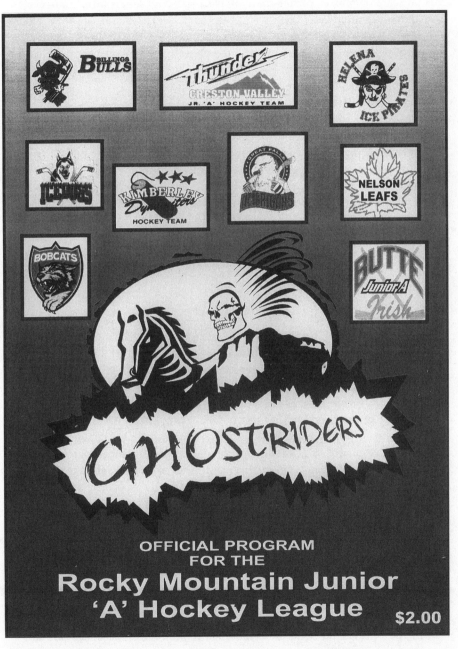

Figure 19 Hockey players' uniforms were difficult to read because of the detail in the original Ghostrider image. In 1998 the team redesigned its logo, generating stylized imagery with computer graphics.

Just as people of their parents' and grandparents' generations created postcards, younger people share a visual sphere through images of popular culture that are relevant and familiar. Social knowledge generated through new technologies resonates with "historically powerful themes" (Provenzo 1991:17) that echo old storylines informing our sense of who we, and others, are.

Interactive Spectacle

Most people in the youngest age groups spend six hours each day, five days per week, in elementary school and in high school, where they work through a provincial curriculum. At school there is a clear hierarchy of adults: daytime and nighttime custodians, substitute teachers, lunchtime supervisors, teachers, counsellors, vice-principal, and principal. The school bell divides hours and days. Each morning the national anthem emanates from the speaker cone, followed by announcements from administrators. This is the physical setting for the performance of a visiting hypnotist, described below. It is the everyday turf of children and teenagers, now rid of daytime authority.

A Visiting Hypnotist

The show was posted to begin at 7 p.m. I arrived shortly before, bought my ticket and a root beer, and took a seat on a chair in the middle of the gymnasium floor. It is a standard high-school gym: banners on the high brick walls for girls' volleyball, boys' basketball; an honour roll of students' names; the Canadian flag; a Terry Fox flag; trophy cases; a poster of the Canadian Olympic hockey team; a clock encased in wire; a speaker cone; the red bell on the wall. Young people ranging in age from about twelve to twenty dribble in. They greet their friends enthusiastically. Some girls walk in shyly and take their seats without greetings. The boys seated in the front row on the right side are gregarious. They each wear baseball caps – within half an hour their caps are turned backwards. Visually, another group seated to the left of the room is discernible. These young people have longer hair; some boys wear earrings; a few of the girls have pierced noses. The remainder of the crowd observes the loud boys in the front row. Some parents escort their children. They take seats at the rear of the gymnasium on the bleachers. (Fieldnotes, 23 April 1998)

In the gymnasium there are symbols of nation: flags, the image of a cultural hero, and an image of members of the Olympic hockey team. Outstanding members of the school body are celebrated through display of their names on rolls and trophies. Teams are identified by gender; their banners hang ready for the next regional competition with other schools. Like party-goers at the Mogul Smoker, the crowd at this performance gathers into visually discernible social groups. Since the 1950s, sideshows have been touring North America, staging their performances in nontraditional arenas such as the school gymnasium (Stebbins 1984:11).

> There are large speakers on the stage – the hypnotist adjusts controls on the sound system. He is wearing a neon blue blazer and black T-shirt with an orange spiral. The audience was becoming impatient. From the bleachers, boys began to throw pennies at those of us seated in front of them. Ponytails are tugged. Some boys in the front row shout out opportunities to buy tickets in a 50/50 draw. I went outside. Four boys on skateboards rolled towards me and stopped abruptly to ask: "How much is it to get hypnotized?" They rushed inside and then passed by me, saying: "Five bucks! And that's just to watch!"

Clearly these boys were not impressed with the role of spectator that has ensured the success of stage hypnotism as a form of mass entertainment in America. During the nineteenth century, somnambulists sprang up everywhere. The largely middle-class audiences thronged to these spectacles. It was not always so. In eighteenth-century Europe, "mesmerism was the guarded secret of a privileged aristocracy" (Fuller 1982:30). It was developed in Vienna as a scientific theory and method. According to its originator: "There is only one illness and one healing" (Franz Mesmer 1779 in Fuller 1982:1). Mesmerism challenged eighteenth- and nineteenth-century medical practices, prompting theories grounded in the relationship between therapist and patient that were to contribute to the establishment of modern psychiatry. At the centre of the theory of mesmerism was the concept of "animal magnetism," postulated as a "universal substance [fluid or energy] linking together every orderly process throughout nature" (Fuller 1982:1-3). As a form of healing, mesmerism involved manual gestures; magnets were passed across the patient's body, sometimes pausing over affected organs in order to re-establish the flow of animal magnetism. One symptom caused by the "passing" of magnets was the "somnambulic state," now recognized as hypnotic trance.

> Loud music brings everyone to his or her seats. "Mesmer! America's foremost hypnotist!" His show: "One Step Beyond!" At the end of the introduction: "Due to copyright, video, flash-photo and audio recording is strictly prohibited for the first fifteen minutes of the show. Tapes are available after the show for five dollars." Mesmer calls up twenty-four volunteers on whom he conducts a "suggestibility test." His speech is fast, evangelistic; he uses loud music and touch, and then he slaps

his hand on the tops of their heads. Those who "snap out of it" dramatically are chosen.

Mesmerism had its debut into the popular imagination in America without endorsement from the scientific community. European "Professors of Animal Magnetism" included phrenologists. These scientists embarked on lecture tours to promote mesmerism as a theory and method of healing. Lectures were accompanied by demonstrations of the "magnetic state of consciousness" that prompted feats of telepathy and clairvoyance. Showmen eventually took up the performance. Dropping the use of magnets and "passes," they concentrated on "assertions and commands" through which audience members were led into a "state of acquiescence" (Fuller 1982:17-20, 31-32). The shift from scientific arenas to the popular stage excluded animal magnetism from serious medical consideration.[2] In the American press there were charges of demonic possession, charlatanism, sexual overtones, and exploitation.

A hundred years later, a modern Mesmer began his show in Fernie with a taped statement on copyright. It suggests that the first fifteen minutes of the performance hold the secret to his power. He did not use magnets. Through touch, speech, and loud music he overwhelmed the senses of his subjects. For those on stage, whose eyes were closed, the sound escalated, music building behind his voice. He issued a rapid-fire barrage of orders, followed by the surprise of touch.

The volunteers were between approximately twelve and eighteen years of age. Many of these people were selected from the group of gregarious front-row males. Intrigued, leaning forward in our seats, we anticipated the spectacle about to unfold. Young people observed their classmates; they pointed and laughed at their onstage responses.

The first situation the hypnotist leads them through is a scenario on the bridge of the USS *Enterprise* from *Star Trek*. They are travelling at warp speed, shooting photon torpedoes, when they encounter a bad smell. Afterwards they are led into particular activities: in Hawaii, surfing the huge waves; throwing a boomerang; and riding a motorcycle. Mesmer calls an intermission, leaving them with a suggestion. "When you hear music you will fall asleep. Your friends won't matter anymore, just my voice, just truth." He snaps them out of their hypnotized state. They return to their seats where their friends test their memories. (Fieldnotes, 23 April 1998)

The hypnotized teenagers performed their feats in astoundingly uniform ways. It was obvious that they shared knowledge of the movements and postures appropriate to the characters in *Star Trek*. Although the boomerang throwing was less than consistent, the conformity of body movements continued throughout the next series of suggestions. Like repertoires of gesture and word enacted in other public performances, there is a shared set of expectations and understandings at this event: "Entertainment magic deals ... with the everyday empirical world that is understandable and recognizable to an audience seeking diversion. It is an application of science using an array of familiar objects, animals, processes, materials, and situations" (Stebbins 1984:3).

While magic may not be the best way to categorize the hypnotist's performance, there was something in the act that evoked that tension around belief. As the teenagers returned to their seats, I was made aware of how this performance depended greatly on the social connection between members of the audience and those who had become entranced. The excitement in the room balanced on the tip of dis/belief. Friends attempted to trick the somnambules into confessions of acting. The latter professed their authenticity through blank stares and serious demeanours. It was a dialogue flirting with the unexplainable that pivoted on an understanding of the legitimacy of hypnotism. It also called into question the ways in which people know each other. Predictably, as the music began again, the hypnotized slumped in their chairs, fast asleep and ready for another session on stage. One or two remained in their seats, unable to reattain their mesmerized state.

> Mesmer set up a series of situations that revolve around sexual tensions. One of the scenarios calls for an embrace between two boys that will be cued by a song. This is played to the extreme, and the audience responds with uncomfortable laughter. Settings in the second act include a movie theatre and behind the scenes at a Hollywood screen test. The hypnotized are asked to compete with each other as bodybuilders and Highland dancers. Next they are told that they are Arnold Schwarzenegger in combat, Roger Rabbit, and Superman. Finally Mesmer suggests that when they are cued they will hear a fire alarm and must evacuate the gymnasium "speaking Chinese." (Fieldnotes, 23 April 1998)

Mesmer chose emotionally charged scenarios for this age group. Homosexuality is particularly loaded, and the audience reacted accordingly. Some stood up to see if the two boys would actually participate in the socially taboo situation. Other scenarios tapped into understandings from popular culture. At the Hollywood screen test, the teenagers strutted, ran their hands through their hair, and flexed their hips. Their enactments of the movie star in combat also revealed a shared mental image. Their bodies became sturdy, almost crouching under the weight of their weapon; they shook with the firing force. Mesmer's suggestions emphasized body image, and expressions of sexuality seemed to dominate these teenagers' understandings about the movie industry. It would seem that stage mesmerism is still immersed in "sexual overtones" and in images of "animal magnetism" now popularized by Hollywood.

During the second act the hypnotist asked performers to imitate two ethnic groups. Scottish traditions play a prominent role in official performances in Fernie, and the hypnotized youth managed a recognizable Highland fling. Their frenzied evacuation of the gymnasium "speaking Chinese" also revealed a shared set of understandings. They shouted gibberish and the audience responded – heaving with laughter at the chaos created by this scenario. It reminded me of the written descriptions of "foreigners" and hysteria during the Fernie fire.

> Mesmer closes with a little speech about "being hypnotized by TV."
> He informs people that there will be "a time lapse" for those who
> participated, that they will eventually remember what they did. His last
> suggestion is that they will achieve self-confidence, sleep well, do their
> homework, do well at job interviews, and not be frightened at the
> dentist. (Fieldnotes, 23 April 1998)

According to Robert Fuller (1982:xiii): "Mesmerism's only surviving contribution to American culture [is] the cult of positive thinking." At the end of the performance, the hypnotized were gently brought back to the realities of their daily regime. They were given a blessing of sorts to do well at work, maintain their health, and strive for achievement. Mesmer's understated critique of the power of television highlighted the medium that largely ensured the success of his performance. He tapped into a world of action where individuals easily identify with movie stars, superheroes, cartoon characters, and sports figures. The settings were places that are part of dominant visual culture.

Another field of imagery in which young people are immersed is roleplaying video games or RPGs, which engage players in an arena of programmed scenarios.

Video Games

Video games are everywhere. In people's homes, subtle electronic beeps signal their presence in the bedrooms of children. They are prohibited in Fernie's schools, and one girl told me that you can't play them on airplanes or in restaurants. I saw GameBoys poking out of jacket pockets and heard the excitement in children's voices as they traded different versions. Players told me that Pocket GameBoys cost $87, Colour GameBoys are $99, and each individual game is $45. Mastering video games requires intensive tracts of time, "patience, attentiveness and a well developed memory" (Strong 1996:408). The "creation of expert knowledge about these products" is an important part of the social world for many young people (Provenzo 1991:16). Not unlike the performances cued by the hypnotist, the games provide scenarios for "action," in which players identify with an imaginary character. "In the most common scenario found in the games, an anonymous character performs an act of aggression – typically mediated through some type of technology – against an anonymous enemy" (Provenzo 1991:118).

The games employ old ideas of difference embedded in new mediums of truncated story. Each game involves a series of quests; they are episodic rather than narrative. Players advance to higher levels by accomplishing particular tasks. In order to be successful, they must acquire and use a detailed knowledge of symbols, objects, and characters. Video games are "value laden" and "rule driven" (22-23); players are led through moves and procedures dictated by software programmers. There are some recognizable characters in video games: sorcerers, princesses, fairies, warriors, and monsters. Some characters are robotic; many are genetically mutated beings. There are secrets to discover and palaces to infiltrate, treasure to acquire, and evil to overcome. In one game, evolution, conquest, and imperialism are fused with biology.

I spoke with a ten-year-old girl and a fifteen-year-old boy about *Pokémon,* a Nintendo game that is played on a GameBoy.

Okay, *Pokémon* is an RPG – a role-playing game. You're this little kid who's ten who sets off on a Pokémon journey to become a Pokémon master. You capture Pokémon on the way and collect badges on the way that get you into the Pokémon League.
What happens when you make a capture?
The screen goes black for two seconds and this music goes doodoo-doodlededoo. Say you have a Charlemander, and then on the thing it says: "Get them, Char." You just see the back of your Pokémon going into battle. It shows the attack that you do. Say it's a flame-thrower, you see a little flame coming out of its mouth. If your Pokémon has this much life in it [gesturing a tiny amount], you can throw a Poké ball. See, if it bursts open you weren't successful. If it wriggles and rolls on its side, then you were successful in the capture. Say you're close to town, you go and heal the Pokémon at the Poké centre.
What is the geography like there?
Palate Town is home, like, where you start. Veridian City everything's, like, you can just walk into people's houses and they don't say anything. You can talk to them and they say things like "My Pokémon's the best" or "Your Pokémon needs more training" and stuff. (Interview, 13 February 2001. Girl, born 1991.)

Video games create places where even short conversations are programmed. In *Pokémon,* the object is to earn "experience points" through battle while maintaining "health" as measured by "hit points."

In the year 2000 there were 201 individual Pokémon. When I asked what a Pokémon is, the fifteen-year-old boy laughed and said: "How can I put it? They're monsters. They were just found in the world." He listed eleven types: water, fire, grass, electricity, psychic, normal, dark, light, steel, poison, and mixed. Some are shape-shifters; all are wild until they are captured. "Some Pokémon come out of eggs, unless they're Kangascon. They're like kangaroos they come out of their mom." According to the Nintendo booklet, Pokémon are arranged in a complicated taxonomy based in reproductive vigour. Only two have fixed genders: male and female Nidoran "evolve" into Nidorino and Nidorina and eventually into Nido King and Nido Queen. Some "will never produce eggs"; male or female, they are infertile. "Some do not have a gender but you can still hatch their eggs with Ditto's help" (Nintendo 2000:10). Ditto is a Pokémon with no "gender," but it produces eggs with males or females. "The egg produced will always hatch at the lowest evolution of a particular Pokémon" (Nintendo 2000:95). Other Pokémon can be either male or female and are capable of mating in the more advanced Gold and Silver games. In the earlier games (Red, Blue, and Yellow) they had no gender and couldn't mate.

How do you move between levels?
By experience points, by winning battles. Defence goes up, attacks go up, intelligence goes up, speed. It's quite violent if you think about it. There are more attacks than [there are] Pokémon now. You can learn new attacks. Some have weaknesses against each other. (Interview, 13 February 2001. Boy, born 1986.)

Pokémon are "typecasted for battle" and particular forms of attack: "absorb, poison, freeze, burn, paralyze, sleep etc." (Nintendo 2000:10-12, 85). Most Pokémon can evolve: "The most basic way to evolve one is by entering it into many battles and building up its level" (14). Amongst the types of evolution cited in the guide are "Stone evolution, Link-trade evolution and Friendship evolution … If it really likes you it may evolve … use it in battle often, never let it faint, groom it!" (14).

Some can't evolve at all, like Snorlax or Articuno or Zapdos or Moltres. None of them can mate either. The new ones evolve by day or night. Sometimes you can go back and it's evolved overnight. Evolving is kind of like changing form, like the first humans evolved into us, like the dinosaurs evolved and the monkeys. Like the theory of evolution I guess. (Interview, 13 February 2001. Boy, born 1986.)

This game is laced with scientific authority. Like the commonsense knowledge of evolution expressed by this boy, technology and biological fact are a given. Human characters appearing in *Pokémon* reveal understandings about story and authority. They are the hero, the rival, Bill, Mom, Professor Oak, Kurt, and Professor Elm. The named men appear in the more advanced games. They are built-in computer specialists who attest to the celebration of technology.[3] I asked the ten-year-old girl what Mom does. "She gives you moral support and helps you save money and buys you stuff. A Poké ball costs ten g – gills." *Pokémon* has its own economic system, and throughout the game players send money to the "First Bank of Mom." In the newer Gold and Silver games, there are "bad guys" known as "Team Rocket."

They're pretty much the bad guys. There's no background story of why anything is. I know a quick background story of James, who's in Team Rocket. He used to be rich but he ran away because he didn't want to be rich. Talking Cat learned how to talk while trying to impress a female. She thought of him as a freak. [Laughing] Now a walking, talking freak. Jessie is a mystery, an enigma.
Where did you learn who these guys are?
Cartoons. It's pretty boring. Sometimes they become lame and dumb, it's the same plot over and over again. (Interview, 13 February 2001. Boy, born 1986.)

Video games are promoted through television shows aimed at young players. Their repetitive plots provide the basic premise of the game. While this boy suggests that there is "no background story" to explain the world of *Pokémon,* he is able to recite a complex classificatory scheme for its characters. It is interesting that the "bad guys" are people who have rejected wealth or outstepped the bounds of their species. There is a hard edge of essentialized categories in the world of *Pokémon.* Computer games promote the "consumption of objectified difference" (Strong 1996:419) through a new regime of commonsense ideas.

Players require knowledge of a complex taxonomy in order to progress to higher levels.[4] Individual Pokémon are distinguished by reproductive vigour and by their prowess in battle. Some are infertile, others produce eggs, one appears to be a marsupial. Gender is slippery. Most Pokémon are genderless and bisexual, capable of mating with either males or females.

Reproduction is tied to ideas of evolution. It is telling that the male and female Nidorans eventually evolve, at their highest state, into king and queen. Pokémon "evolve" through battle; their "types" are derived from fighting capabilities and weaponry. Battle is the only means through which players acquire "experience," by "capturing" wild Pokémon. Like troops, these beings must be kept healthy, and finance also plays a role. Players have to purchase Poké balls in order to fight battles.

The logic of conquest is intact. *Pokémon* evokes the cluster of ideas at the centre of imperial propaganda: militarism, social hierarchy, racial typology, and social Darwinism. There is no narrative in *Pokémon,* only a daily series of battles circumscribed by roles and rules programmed by technical specialists. The ranking of Pokémon through reproductive ability is reminiscent of a eugenic worldview and also of new reproductive technologies. Technology is the new authority supporting these old story-realms.

The performance of the hypnotist and the worlds created by video games both depend somewhat on the authority of science. As forms of entertainment, they provide a glimpse of the imagery now engaging young people. They are both examples of visual culture. One attests to the almost seamless familiarity with television and film. Through innovative technologies, video games offer up new worlds filled with strange images that require specific forms of knowledge. Perhaps most significantly, video games and performance hypnosis are about role-playing. Young audiences, or consumers, are acting out old themes of sexual transgression, gender conformity, and conquest. The media in which these themes appear are sites of rupture between generations.

I hiked often with an elderly woman. Sometimes we took the chairlift up the ski hill and she talked to trees. One day on the lift she spotted and named a flower fifty feet below us. This inspired her to recite a poem that she had memorized as a child. Then she asked me to do the same. I had bits and pieces of "Clancy of the Overflow" and most of "Bound for Botany Bay" (both examples of Australian colonial literature), but I was basically unable to perform what she considered to be a simple task. She was shaking her head by this point, lamenting the fact that people of my age were so carelessly educated, that we didn't remember because we weren't drilled. Many old-timers told me that their children constitute a lost link in the transmission of traditions and ideas from elsewhere. Languages, songs, and customs (with the exception of culinary talents) have been largely neglected, or else they are collected, stored, or displayed as artifacts of ancestral identity.

I visited the woman who recites poetry on another occasion. When she opened her book of Czech fairy tales, the smell of cloves escaped into the air. She thought it would be good to translate the stories into English;

then she changed her mind. "It's such a shame that children don't have any stories anymore. My grandchildren," she said, "are all into Nitendos [sic] and action figures. They don't know these stories. It's all different." Technology constitutes a major site of disjuncture between the youngest and the eldest generations, for they no longer share a repertoire of images and stories. I heard passionate statements about computer technology from the eldest age groups. An eighty-four-year-old man said: "That Internet is going to blow up in your faces!" A woman in her seventies told me: "Computers don't produce a damned thing! It's just about powerful people who convince everybody they need it!" Many elderly people suggested to me that young people now communicate in a "different language," unintelligible to them. Language has certainly shifted.

I asked my friends' children about labels that are used amongst their peers. "Gay" is by far the most common insult. Not unlike the stigmas of "DP" and "foreigner," being "gay" carries ideas of stupidity and social pollution. I was surprised to hear the term "white trash." When I asked what it meant, one eleven-year-old told me that these are the "skinheads," who are "tough and racist." From many children I heard the term "whigger." I was told simply that whiggers are "white kids who think they're black." During my interview with the teenagers, they identified a complex field of social groups that sheds some light on these appellations. "Race" remains salient. Age, sexuality, and social identity are the clearest markers used by young people I spoke with in Fernie. Young locals also use genealogy to assert privilege.

A woman who holds a prominent position in town told me about going to a Ghostrider game and unwittingly choosing a seat in a three-row area that was empty. "What a mistake!" she said. "They call it the zoo. It's the area where the local teenagers sit." She said that someone brought in a horn that they were blowing throughout the game. At one point they were spitting on the players on the ice. The woman reprimanded them, saying: "You don't treat human beings like that!" Someone replied: "You're not from Fernie!" She told them that she lives and works here and they said: "But you weren't born here!" (from Fieldnotes, 29 February 1998). Once again, birthright surfaces in an interaction between residents in Fernie. Here wielded by a teenager, it is a discourse intended to strip this woman of any authority she may assume as an adult. Importantly, the verbal exchange takes place in a space charged with significance for local teenagers and adults. The arena is imbued with regional pride and serves as the forum for masculine display. Within the arena, the "zoo" is a space over which teenagers have dominion. These distinctions of genealogy, locality, gender, and age are evident in the ways in which young people in Fernie express their ideas of difference. Like their predecessors, they identify places with particular categories of persons.

Narrative Maps: Hanging Out

The teenagers I interviewed narrated a social landscape within which complex fields of identities compete. Their perception of space, like that of their grandparents, is focused on social groups, although now displaced from neighbourhoods. The train tracks, main street, and courthouse are intergenerational sites in the reckoning of space. In contrast to other generations, who orientated themselves using residences and physical features, teenagers use stores and fast-food outlets as central landmarks on their maps. Other sites are age specific: schools, the skate park, and parking lots of various businesses. The teenagers' map is dotted with the sites where people "hang out" rather than where they live. Named categories of peers are associated with different places in town. Like their parents, the teens give these categories implicit class designations. Unlike their parents, whose class categories were based on occupation, education, and environmentalism, the young people draw heavily from popular culture and visual style.

A twelve-year-old girl also worked on a map with me. Space was less specific here. Her map depicted the structured activities of a child. On its edges she listed categories of people based on different age grades and arranged by sports, school, and gender.

Town

Narratives about the areas that make up town have changed substantially. Teenagers identified the Airport, the Annex, Ridgemont, West Fernie, and the ski hill. "Main" replaces "Downtown" and includes only the two blocks at the commercial and administrative core. One young woman referred to Parkland Terrace as "East Fernie." The Airport now includes what the eldest generations used to call the South End. The North End does not appear as a name on their map. When I asked them if it has a name, one person replied: "Not really, just 'down by 7-Eleven' or 'down by A&W.'"

The teenagers mentioned a few entirely new areas. The "Rainforest" describes the educational forest off the road towards Coal Creek on the edge of town. This is where they "party." It is now the site of a future golf course. "B-Patch, or 4:20," lies to the side of the highway, beside a marsh at the eastern entrance to town. At the time of the interview, this area encompassed a cluster of weather-beaten houses and barns. According to the teenagers, the term "4:20" signifies legal use of marijuana and hashish in Amsterdam and is derived from either the name of a hotel there, the time when it is legal to serve the drugs, or the time when people indulge in them. In Fernie, "B-Patch is where teenagers smoke pot." (In the three years since this interview, the B-Patch buildings have been torn down, and the marsh is now filled in. A sprawling Best Western Hotel greets drivers as they enter Fernie. Soon McDonald's will open its doors there, adjacent to Fernie's first shopping mall, Ghostrider Crossing.)

For younger children, landmarks and places are structured around their range of movement. The twelve-year-old showed me where they swim in the Elk River. An area beyond Ridgemont was marked simply "bush"; inhabited by bears, it is a place that parents warn their children away from. She also identified the Annex, the Airport, Cokato, Ridgemont, and West Fernie. To her, West Fernie includes the ski hill. It is where "kids who take the bus" live. Outlined on her map are the different playing fields for soccer and baseball. She filled the margin of the map with a list of people corresponding to age grades and sport teams. School presents the clearest ranking: kids in kindergarten to grade three are known as "Primary"; people in grades four to seven are "Intermediate." "Secondary" includes grades eight to eleven, and grade twelve people are "Seniors." When I asked her who different groups of people were, she began with "girls and boys." She told me: "Popular girls are the ones who play sports." As far as boys go, these are the "BMX-ers, skateboarders, and rollerbladers" who "hang out" in various parking lots.

"Hanging Out"

For teenagers, as for people of all ages, some places are socially relevant and some are not. West Fernie is where "mostly older people live." When I asked who lived at the Airport, I was told: "You don't hang out there. People live there, but they always come into town." It was the same with the ski hill. Teenagers' social landscape is arranged by the places where different groups "hang out" and by a remarkable list of categories.

b: And the skaters.
c: They're, like, everywhere! In the summertime they're at Isabella Dicken [school]. Yeah, the tennis courts. They're, like, in here [marking the map].
b: Skatepark ...
a: The pucks – hockey players.
c: Right here, at the arena, they all hang here. And the ...
[supermarket] parking lot, that's where the cowboys hang.
a: Yeah, the hicks.
c: They all sit in their trucks and listen to country music really, really loud ...
b: And [a mini-mall], that's where ...
a: Oh, Westside Gang.
c: Where they used to be ...
c: You see granolas over here [pointing to the Annex on the map]. And you can get some over that way too [in the North End].

[Laughing] They have been seen, have they?
c: There's some in Ridgemont too.
a: And on Main ...
c: The Northern Hotel's pretty popular too.
   Who hangs out there?
c: ... what would you call them?
a: It's the freaks, like the, uh ...
b: The punks ... They kind of, like, are individual.
c: Yeah. They're their own selves. They stand out.
   Are there kids who come from farms and ranches?
c: The inbreeds! That's what they call them. The ones from out of
town ...
   And what about the people in Parkland?
b: Parkland Terrace, well, not very many people – it's, like, kids that
are younger mostly live up there.
c: Goodie-goodies ... Coal Creek area, there's lots of kids over there.
a: Yeah, there is, but they're, like, rich ...
   What about Cokato?
c: I find a lot of preppies live out there ...
   What about the trailer park?
c: No one lives there.
b: Well, lots of people live there but, like, old ... (Interview, 24
February 1998. Young women, born ca. 1980-1982.)

According to these young women, the social landscape is punctuated with
Skaters, Pucks, Hicks, members of the Westside Gang, Punks and Freaks,
Preppies, Inbreeds, and Granolas. Their social cartography leaves out areas
where either the "old" or "rich" or younger children reside. Social groups
are defined through identity categories based on activities, outsiderness,
and expressions of individuality. There is some resonance here with the
descriptions of their parents' generation, where occupation, regionalism,
and ideology circumscribe groups. Gone are the neighbourhood affiliations experienced by their grandparents in their youth. I asked the young
women how these various groups of people get along with each other.
Their taxonomy became even more complex.

b: The Westside people kind of really don't like the granolas.
c: They, like, fight.
b: And nobody likes the pucks!
a: Except for the preps.
c: Except for the preppies. They're the Ghostrider riders.
   The preps and the pucks are together?
b: Yep! The clan! The girls.

c: The Ghostrider riders. The clan.

Tell me about this.

c: The clan are the girls that, like ...

a: Grade 11 girls that go out with all the Ghostriders.

c: They idolize them ...

What about the preps?

b: Girls and guys.

a: They do, like, this rotation. They go out with everyone, then they go out with them again.

... So what about the hicks? Do they get along with everybody?

All: No!

b: Nobody messes with them because they're, like, tough.

c: They're big, big ...

a: And they all have trucks and wear cowboy boots and stuff ... They all look alike!

b: They all have their hair the same way and – that's why we call them inbreeds.

What about you guys, where do you fit in here?

a: Okay, I'm, like, with the granolas and ...

c: Yeah, me too – I've been with the granolas and ...

a: Then we get our normal sessions.

b: ... [gesturing towards her friends] They'd just be classified as normal people ...

What are the characteristics of a granola?

a: My one teacher, she said: "They are people that try to act poor that walk around in Birkenstocks, but you know they're really rich."

Unlike older adults, these teenagers exhibit little hesitation in naming and describing social categories. Like other generations, however, they "classify" themselves "as normal people." I am intrigued by their self-identification as granolas. When I asked them about the characteristics of a granola, they spoke about welfare, snowboarding and hiking, humility, and the Volkswagen vans that they drive. Perhaps most importantly, granolas are young adults who are "really nice to talk to." The enormous social boundaries around age dissolve. These teenagers like granolas because they are included in their social sphere. True outsiderness is ascribed to the hicks and inbreeds. It is the perceived conformity of their appearance that is mentioned, as well as their aggression. Spatially, these people are not "local"; they live in outlying areas.

Gender is central in these descriptions of different groups of people. The number of appellations assigned to the girls who go out with the Ghostriders is particularly notable. During the interview, "bunnies" and "groupies" were added to the list of preppies, the clan, and Ghostrider riders. The hockey-playing males remain monolithic as Ghostriders and pucks. This is not surprising given the official recognition awarded to this team by adults, their inclusion in municipal ceremony, and the regional pride they inspire. Hockey figures greatly in the awarding of social capital in Fernie. Across generations, several families are known for their sons' participation in the National Hockey League. This position of privilege is challenged by teens through denigating the hockey players' female partners. In 1997 some graffiti appeared on the side of the ice arena. One of the inscriptions said: "Goat-riders suck." There are other spray-painted messages in town that serve as doorways to various sites of difference.

Graffiti Site: "Race" and Visualism

At an industrial ruin in Hosmer, on towering walls built by Italian masons, a huge pink W is spray-painted next to the word "Gangster" (see Figure 20). I noticed these Ws at the 7-Eleven and at the mini-mall, in back alleys, and on curbs and benches in Fernie. I first assumed that the scribbled W was the graffiti signature of one individual. I found out later, through teenagers, that the W is the mark of the Westside Gang. I asked the young women who these people are.

a: They're just a bunch of guys that wear their hats backwards.
c: And they think they're all black.
b: Yeah. They think they can beat up people and everything, and listen to rap music.
c: And they stalk. They stalked ____ and other kids. (Interview, 24 February 1998. Young women, born ca. 1980-1982.)

Members of the Westside Gang are male. They are described through signature dress style and the genre of their music. They are perceived as violent and predatory. One young woman sums up their attitude as "think[ing] they are black." She speaks from the position of someone who is racialized in this community.

Where do you think racism comes from?
a: Could be from TV.
c: Jealousy.
b: I think a lot of it comes from people, like, parents of Westside people.
c: And video games.
a: Yeah, the thing is, they rent it from other people who they see, like, music too.
c: Their music.

a: A lot of hip hop and rap and stuff. Some of the rap guys walk around calling each other all these names and swearing.

When you say parents –

a: Yeah, that's where racism is – they tell you who the bad people are, different origins or whatever ... Kids pick up on it. If her dad says: "Hey, blah blah, a guy with a different religion," that kid says: "Hey, my dad says that it's okay for me to say that."

Racism here includes discrimination on the basis of religion, class (jealousy), and ethnicity (name-calling). Transmission of ideas between generations is clearly acknowledged, and these teenagers link the racist attitudes to the sharing of music and video games, circulating products of popular culture. According to these young women, the style and vocabulary used by the Westside Gang are appropriated from African-American music artists. The "names and swearing" these boys use evoke the history of violent representations of African Americans, who are now reappropriating them. Sherry Ortner (1998:1; see also hooks 1992:27-29) might see these cross-appropriations as one product of "radical" approaches to identity. "Embracing stigma and turning it into the basis of political agency has in fact been truly disruptive over the past two decades or so" (Ortner 1998:1). Members of the Westside Gang are young Euro-Canadian males who have

Figure 20   Members of the Westside Gang spray-painted their pink graffiti on the walls of an abandoned mine site near Fernie. *Photograph by L. Robertson.*

taken on the language and style of African-American rap artists currently engaged in this radical process. In so doing, they ignore the context of "white supremacy" within which these artists are seeking empowerment (hooks 1992:26). Ruth Frankenberg (1993:15) calls the lack of attention to such invisible terrains "power evasiveness." Young people in Fernie have a name for these identity appropriators: whiggers – "white kids who think they're black." At the same time, in local idiom they are also called "white trash" because of their racist attitudes, judged through the vocabulary they employ. It is interesting that the critique is aimed at unacceptable cross-cultural labels and not, for instance, at gender violence. There is an unsettling inside-outness to all of this that reflects the disguises used by the previous generations. These young women acknowledge the power of cursing, the meanings that negative representations carry. I asked them what they thought about political correctness.

> a: Like, what do you mean?
>   *Have you heard of it?*
> c: No.
> a: I've seen the show *Politically Incorrect!*
> c: Me too!

Yet another reference to television and its power to transmit ideas.

During our conversation I asked them about their "cultural backgrounds." Youth "a" is Czech and Ukrainian and English and Irish and Polish. Youth "b" told me she is mostly English and Irish with a little Polish. Youth "c" distinguished between her maternal line and her paternal line. She is Danish, Scottish, African Canadian, and "one-eighth Indian." They were reckoning their descent through parents and grandparents on both sides. It is another reminder of the movements of people across the world and a potential explanation for the dropping away of nationality as a social category to the youngest generations. I asked them if they could tell me about the "cultures" here.

> a: It's Italian.
> b: A lot of Pakis and Indonesian.
> c: Like people from India and Pakistan.
> b: Lots of people from Australia.
> c: There's some Natives.
> a: Italians – yeah, the Aussies, lots.
> c: There's a lot of Kiwis too.
> b: Italians.
> a: There's some people from Denmark.
> c: A lot of England, Germans.

b: A whole mix of people.
a: There's not any black people.
b: There's lots of Japanese too.
c: A lot of Japanese exchange students down here.
   What about people who live here?
a: Italian, Italian, and more Italian.
b: Chinese.
c: Yeah, there's some Chinese.

Although two of these teenagers hail from Slavic backgrounds, they do not mention these cultural groups. Italians are named four times. Five Asian nationalities are offered in this list of "cultures" – one through an ethnic slur. Demographically, these people constitute a fraction of the community. Australians are clearly new arrivals on the international scene in Fernie. Only one of the teenagers lists English people and indigenous people, two groups that are largely invisible, albeit for different reasons. She also notes the often overlooked distinction between Australians and New Zealanders. To her surprise, her friend states confidently that there are "no black people."

   Do you think there's racism in this town?
   All: Oh yeah!
   c: I got nailed in English class. Last year [my English teacher] was
   speaking and she said: "If you look around, there's not too many
   black people." And her coming from South Africa. She nailed me one
   day because I was the only black person in my English class out of
   all white.
   How did she nail you?
   c: Just the way she was talking. I felt about *this* big. I said something
   to her afterwards – she apologized.

I am reminded of the scene in the Fernie High School in 1966 where a Ktunaxa woman became the living specimen in a lesson on racial categories. What these scenarios have in common is the perception of being objectified through the typology of race. That the speaker on this occasion is South African evokes the apartheid taxonomy in which "blacks" constituted the lowest-ranked majority. South Africans who speak about "blacks" summon understandings of historical relationships between people, as well as political and social violence. It is the perception of a vocabulary of power that affects this self-identified African-Canadian woman. Historical understandings shape the contexts in which certain people are licensed to speak. In this situation, both teacher and student concede to current sanctions of representation.

a: It's not just like it's racist against people of different colours, it's racist against how you dress.

c: How you dress.

a: How you talk – like, there's hicks, pucks.

c: Who you go out with too, I've noticed ...

a: One of my friends was going out with a Russian, right? And her family's Irish and they're all, like, "Yeah, bring him over – does he run around naked in the bush?" Dumb things like that.

Is he Doukhobor?

c: I notice a lot of the Russians have long faces and red cheeks too, so ...

So that's another culture here?

a and c: I just know one.

Another history of discrimination emerges in this conversation, this one aimed at Doukhobors.[5] The age-old emphases on language and appearance are noted. A kind of visualism saturates most people's perceptions of human difference. As we are speaking, I think about an elderly woman who was reeling from an editorial in the paper. In it, she said, a newcomer was telling old people that they looked "dowdy" and had to start improving their dress because it reflects upon the image of the town. Visualism was an avenue through which hippies were judged by the eldest generations. It is also part of the ire directed at granolas by members of the middle generations. While making a generalization about the physical features of Russians, these young women speak about "race" as appearance through dress! New frontiers of difference are telling. Categories have changed, but people are ascribed fixed characteristics based on group membership and described through appearance, behaviour, language, and historical relationships. The teenagers name all of it "racism."

How about multiculturalism?

c: Hmmm [laughing].

b: I've heard of it, but I don't know what it is.

a: Isn't that like culturally you act as one?

[I explained the policy and the concept to them and asked them if they thought that was true in Canada.]

a: Yeah. I think if people want to, like, they don't have to all go Canadian and have to do everything they say, like Americans or something. Everyone has their own individuality.

c: I think it's kind of neat when someone else stands up when they want to. I was reading in one of my magazines that the Italians or the Spics, the Spanish people, or the blacks, just the normal

Canadians right, the Japanese – they all, at school, they're all together
as one, but at lunch hour they all go off into their own little way.
So, like, they're not racist towards one another, but they prefer to
hang out with their own kind.

Phrased in terms of "individuality" or being "with their own kind," difference and patterns of sociality are naturalized. Regarding ideas of race,
there is much that is consistent with previous generations. What has
shifted appears to be the shared understandings about how one speaks
regarding particular relationships and the effects of such verbal acts of
racialization. Old categories of "Slavs" and "foreigners" are not mentioned.
The targets of racism revolve around their own experiences of the world
and popular culture.

Graffiti Site: Religion

One night in October 1997, I was telephoned by a friend who told me
about graffiti that had appeared on the side of the United Church in
Jaffray.[6] It said: "God is dead Long Live Hitler." I drove out to Jaffray the
next morning and spoke with an elderly man who was repairing the door
jamb on the church. I asked him about the graffiti. He said: "It meant
nothing. Just a bunch of kids. It was harmless stupidity."

In his paper on "white supremists and neo-fascists" in Canada, Stanley
Barrett (1991:85-86) states that such messages are often treated as "random racial incidents" that are the work of "poorly socialized individuals."
The approach dangerously ignores the extent to which social structures
and institutions in wider society are "conducive to racism" (86-87).[7] In
this case, however, the message itself may be telling. While anti-Semitism
is a central element of white supremacist ideology, members of these
groups "see themselves as the saviours ... of Western Christian civilization" (90).[8] There is, perhaps, another way to approach the inscription
that has more to do with provocation across generations.

In February 1998 I was speaking on the phone with another friend.
She told me about her childhood in a European household; how she and
her sister had learned to identify important topics through their parents'
silence about the Second World War. As we were speaking, her children
were buzzing around her. One of her daughters asked: "What war?" It
made me realize that the Second World War is a common point of reference for our generation, but for her children, "war" could be one of many
national and international conflicts now raging. Is this why the man at
the church felt that the graffiti was "harmless stupidity"? Did the spray-
painters recognize the potency of their transgression without understanding its significance? The tension that the spray-painted message caused

between generations is acute. It attacked perhaps the most revered European consensus – never to let something like the Holocaust happen again. It also attacked religious faith through the content of the message and through the site where it was written – a church.

Superficially, however, religion seems to have disappeared as a primary marker of difference for young people. Only one church was marked on the map drawn up by the teenagers. Halfway through our interview, someone exclaimed:

> c: You know who we forgot? The Jehovah's Witnesses!
> a: Oh yeah! JWs!
> c: Everywhere!
> b: My grandma's a Jehovah's Witness.
>   *So what about religions here?*
> a: There's lots of them.
> b: There's Mormons, JWs.
> a: The Mormons come from Jaffray.
> b: There's Catholics, lots of Baptist.
> a: All the Italians are Catholic ... I go to the Anglican.
> b: I'm not really a religious person.
> c: I've never been to church in my life. I know of nothing against people who have one, but when they bring it in my face! (Interview, 24 February 1998. Female teenagers, born ca. 1980-1982.)

The young woman whose grandmother is a member of the Jehovah's Witnesses emphasized the diversity of religious groups in Fernie. Another expressed the common knowledge that "all the Italians are Catholic." Jaffray was identified as a Mormon town. While these teenagers circled one corner of the Annex and marked it with "JW," there is the perception that they are "everywhere." Jehovah's Witnesses are active door-to-door proselytizers. On one visit at my front doorstep, a young woman told me that there are 65 members of her church in Fernie and 150 in the entire Elk Valley. From the middle generations I heard stories about assertive encounters on their doorsteps or people ducking away from windows and trying to keep perfectly still. Some old people hang warnings to them on their front verandahs. Others are cautious about answering the front door as they know that people "who know them" come around the back.

> *So there's no tension around religion then, hey?*
> b: Except for sometimes the Jehovah's Witnesses, if you go out with a JW you sometimes have to become them. Or, like, Mormons, remember when ___ and ___ were going out?
> c: That's just the parents though.

Religious difference is marked through the precarious arena of dating. They note that Mormons and Jehovah's Witnesses both have proscriptions about romantic relationships – you "have to become them." The grand-daughter of the Jehovah's Witness is quick to point out that it is their parents' generation that insists upon these strictures. While sanctions on endogamy are the domain of previous generations, concern about sexuality is very much a part of the social world of adolescents.

Graffiti Site: Sexuality
"I hate People!! God is Gay!!! Luv?" appeared in bold red and blue paint across the side wall of a business on the main street in Fernie. The centrality of this site is apt given the anxiety around sexuality that currently preoccupies young people. There is some ambiguity in the spray-painted message. Is it intended to reveal hegemonic assumptions in the same way that feminists claim God as a woman? Or is it a denouncement of God using the most common insult in local idiom? It is different from other messages I saw scratched into surfaces or painted on walls and doorways on routes to schools – messages that name individuals and pronounce them "gay." I asked a mother what categories of difference her seven-year-old daughter was aware of. "She understands sexual difference. She understands that because she came back to me asking what 'fag' was. She came back from school asking what 'whore' was too."

I heard from many mothers about bullying in schools. One woman spoke about her teenaged son and a kind of evolution of harassment. "He went through it all! 'You're a nerd!' 'You're fat!' Then when he started to lose weight it was: 'You're gay!'" (from Fieldnotes, 24 July 1998. Mother, born ca. 1955). This kind of name-calling is rampant amongst children and teenagers in Fernie.

> Right now in high school the word "gay" means stupid. That's what
> it means. "Don't be so gay" means "don't be so stupid" ... There's
> real homophobia in this community, like, huge. Mostly in the high
> school ... What happens in the school yards, what happens in the
> hallways, what happens in the locker rooms when there isn't an adult
> present is just a simplified, juvenile representation of what's actually
> occurring in the community. It's just the new fear. They get it from
> adults around them. (Interview, 4 September 1998. Mother, born 1959.)

In February 1998 an article appeared in the *Free Press* telling a story of remembered trauma narrated by a gay man who once attended the Fernie High School. He mentions how, in grade seven, a daily regime began: "name-calling, taunting and ostracizing ... and never, did [my] teachers intervene." When contacted to speak about homophobia in schools, the superintendent of the district stated: "Any special treatment of this issue may do more harm than good ... Sometimes a policy differentiates and accentuates that [difference] more" (*FFP* 17 February 1998:3). The "special treatment" he is reluctant to address refers to adequately educating students about healthy forms of sexuality and enforcing sanctions against discriminating behaviour. It is an old argument; to address difference directly is to encourage prejudiced behaviour, but protecting targeted groups with silence ensures the views of the majority go unchallenged. To queer theorists, this new frontier of public dialogue confronts heterosexuality that saturates "the taken for granted, naturally occurring and unquestioned" (Ingraham 1994:204).

> *So there was an article in the paper last week about gay people.*
> a: I haven't seen anybody gay!
> c: Well if you were to see, like, last year they had this lesbian convention at [a hotel in town].
> b: Did they say that they were?
> c: Yeah. This big lesbian convention.
> b: It doesn't really matter to me. I'm not homophobic or anything ...
> c: But they did, like, you know, they walked down the street holding hands!
> b: It's 'cause we don't see that in Fernie. (Interview, 24 February 1998. Young women, born ca. 1980-1982.)

These young women use the term "homophobic" and acknowledge the difference between being labelled gay or lesbian and openly self-identifying. Through my own acquaintances, I knew several women who came to Fernie regularly to ski. It is interesting how a long-weekend trip here has been transformed into a "lesbian convention." This perception ignores the idea of social community and reflects a popular discourse of identity politics in which gays and lesbians have been "made into a political minority by social prejudice" (Seidman 1994:171). There is a suggestion that these people may be recognized by sight. What makes them visible is their public show of affection. Finally, someone recognizes the invisibility of same-sex couples in Fernie, and a more inclusive elsewhere is evoked.

> c: I have no problem with it. I mean, I have a [relative] that's a lesbian ... I was used to it [in a large city]. They used to have something called Gay Pride Week. A whole week where they'd march down the street saying: "We're proud to be gay!" I was used to it, but out here [pause].

Her pause is noticeable. If it is possible for silence to be echoed, this was surely evident in the way that these teenagers' sentences trailed off when it came to speaking about Fernie. It is a knowledge of community values that emerges here.

Two years after this interview, on a summer night in the parking lot of a supermarket in Fernie, an openly gay woman in her forties was assaulted by a group of teenage boys. Her story appeared in the paper. They "circled around her and began yelling obscenities and hateful slurs" (*FFP* 4 July 2000:1). Using a pseudonym, she stated that her decision not to press charges was based on the ways that her openness would affect her family's reputation and threaten their careers. Her reluctance exposes another kind of social knowledge about homophobia in that community. Notably, harassment on the basis of sexual orientation is now dealt with as a "hate crime."[9]

> a: The thing is, if it was, like, guys – guys don't bother me that much if I know they're gay because I know that I won't have them coming on to me or anything like that 'cause they're gay. But if they're girls, if I knew, like, ___, right? And all of a sudden she tells me she's a lesbian. Okay. I'd still be her friend, except, if she asked me to sleep over I'd kind of be, like [gesturing distance], "I can't. I'm moving to [pause] Germany." [All laughing]
>
> *Do you think it's just what people have been exposed to? Is it fear?*
> a: It's differency – is that a word? Because they're different. And each people stand out in their own way. Like a lot of people wear lots of makeup. They just express themselves differently ... and sometimes it scares people.
> c: Yeah. But I don't know, Sparwood is known for gay people.
> a: So is Elkford.
> c: Sparwood and Elkford. They'll dress really punk, chains and stuff, and they run around holding each other's hand and kissing and, you know? But my [relative] was talking: "If you look at ten of your friends, at least one of them ... will be gay or lesbian." So far I've counted ten and, nope! Well, except for one. But she's ...
> a: She's bi.
> c: She's bi and she's really cool. I like her, she's nice.

Unlike members of previous generations, these young women offer no theories about the causes of homosexuality. One comment suggests a fear of contagion. The identification of particular towns with gay people is interesting. Again it is the public display of affection that makes these places visible. "Differency" is used to define what "scares people." There are references to styles of dress and makeup as forms of "expression" that characterize "gays." Another category appears here, seemingly free of the essentialized imagery of homosexuality. Bisexuality interrupts what Judith Butler (1990:336) calls "the regulatory fiction of heterosexual coherence." While these young women possess a certainty about gay and lesbian persons, their bisexual friend is neither gay nor straight. Challenges to reified identities are important to consider.

Ideas of difference converge at this point. Bisexuality suggests a kind of hybridity somewhere in between the either/or binaries of identity. Such conversations remind me of historical discussions around "half-breeds" and "transculturated" fur traders, as well as more current notions about overassimilated cultural others (see Crosby 1997:24). Several scholars working with ethnic, gender, and sexual difference advocate attention not to the explanations of pure identities, but to the political and historical contexts wherein identity categories become fixed. The object of scrutiny is the closure of meaning itself, propagated within particular contexts of power. Thus, in reference to sexuality, the emphasis should be placed, not on the polarized positions of "gay" and "straight," but on the social and political conditions that normalize heterosexuality (Butler 1990:39; see also Epstein 1994:197). Regarding ethnicity and "racial" categories, scholars direct attention to dominating political ideologies – Nazism, apartheid, colonialism – that carve out taxonomies of difference, creating homogeneous images that do not allow for fluid and diverse expressions of identity (see Laclau 1996; Norval 1996; Roseberry 1996). As Aletta Norval (1996:62-63) writes:

> Rather than standing in need of a theory of ethnicity as such ... we need to have the theoretical tools which can account for the mechanisms of identification involved in the constitution of imaginaries and symbolic universes of meaning ... For what is at stake here is no longer simply a question of how actors themselves interpret their own belonging to a community, but the very construction of discursive horizons of meaning.

Dominant and popular modes of thinking through binaries – gay/straight, black/white, self/other – might give way to "a map of tensions and resonances between [these] fixed ends" (Harraway 1991:194). To the teenagers I interviewed, homosexuality is one of these fixed and essentialized ends.

Transmission of Popular Myths

Several means of transmitting ideas about difference have already appeared in this chapter. Teachers told one young woman about the disguised wealth of granolas. The teenagers agree that racism is passed from parents to children and is also propagated through certain forms of mass media. Although I persisted in my questions about old stories and ideas, these young women clearly wanted to speak about other things that are relevant to them.

> c: What's another myth out here? The glowing stone at the graveyard. Superstitions.
> a: You go out there when the full moon is out, and we have to go in this certain way, in the graveyard, and we look at this one gravestone. It glows, because, you know how the moon goes onto it – it glows. One night we looked for it. We thought we saw it once.
> c: We had to be careful because it was, like, bear season when we went in there ...
> a: This town's, like, gossip town. (Interview, 24 February 1998. Young women, born ca. 1980-1982.)

The use of the term "superstition" is revealing in the context of "myth." The comment was meant to inform me of the story's truth-value. In popular usage, "myth" has a pejorative meaning; it designates "beliefs clung to against all evidence" (P. Cohen 1969:337).[10] We spent much time discussing the way in which "talk" affects the lives of these teenagers. Our conversation was not about oral traditions. It was about the social repercussions of teenage rumour and all of the anxieties that balance and tip over gendered difference.

Gossip, Rumour, and Scholarly "Myths"

> b: One thing happens and, like, everybody knows about it!
>   *What sort of things do people talk about?*
> b: Mostly people – other people.
> a: Yeah, about other people, and it always keeps going.
> b: Everybody knows everybody in this town.
> c: "Did you hear about so and so? She moved." And the whole town would know in one day.
> b: If you got pregnant or something.
> a: Or breaking up – everybody knows then.
> b: Yep. There's not much to talk about in this town. Not much happens.

To these young women, gossip turns private relationships into public knowledge and is especially aimed at pregnancy, the quintessential marker of teenage promiscuity. Gender expectations appear to have changed little. Across generations, women are the targets of gossip. People of all age groups told me that silence is a political strategy to avoid the sting of gossip and the speedy realignments of families that ensue.

Have you ever seen shunning?
After a story? [Pause] Yes, I think it can happen. Particularly with young people ... I think about stories of people not being clean, you know, clean housekeepers. All right, let's take that one ... No matter which nationality you bring up, I hear from them all. So it maybe has something to do with class. [Laughing] I heard a man the other day and he said: "You better be wearing your work clothes when you go visiting, because her house ... " I couldn't believe this man making this comment. "You better be wearing your work clothes ... because you're bound to get dirty." Imagine. And he would be my age. (Interview, 16 April 1998. Grandmother, born 1933.)

Hygiene was brought up often by members of the eldest generations. To these people it is a critical signifier of difference and a topic of gossip. I heard stories about pigs in the house and chickens in the kitchen, tables swarming with flies, and unruly, dirty children. These were always directed at women. They are speech acts fuelled by older ideas about "foreigners" and "peasants." Where the eldest generations used stories of housekeeping and hygiene to mark particular women, people in the middle generations spoke about adultery.

What are other ways [that ideas are conveyed in this community]?
Gossip is one, probably the dominant one in this community. Man, I wished I knew how it works [laughing]. I wish I knew how it moved. It's used as a form of control. In a small town, all people are impacted by gossip when they are being gossiped about. They feel incredible community pressure. It always comes back to you. It's what initiates stoppage in community. If you want someone to stop their behaviour, you talk about it.
And what gets talked about?
Adultery. I wish they would do it over abuse, but they don't ... It's hard for people to make a really strong stand ... People are very uncomfortable with women who don't fit in the gender roles that they expect. (Interview, 4 September 1998. Mother, born 1959.)

Across time, gender expectations have maintained the veracity of the curse legend. Gender is evident in the differentiating scripts of political policies, traditional sanctions around belief, ideas of pollution and witchcraft, perceptions of place, and ranges of mobility. While gossip is popularly associated with women as a "weapon of the powerless," I found that this was not the case. Rumour is a potent social act that scapegoats particular categories of people, blaming or marking them with failure in the face of disaster, or dehumanizing them in the context of war and colonialism. It is a popular medium through which to discredit powerful corporations and other bodies of authority.

Like rumour and gossip, scholarly theories constitute a kind of promiscuous knowledge brought into use at strategic moments. Perhaps the most popular of these is the scientific theory of race. Anthropologists are currently acknowledging the damage this concept has wrought, and in 1998 the American Anthropological Association published a "Statement on Race":

> Numerous arbitrary and fictitious beliefs about different peoples were institutionalized and deeply embedded in American thought ... fus[ing] behaviour and physical features together in the public mind ... Evidence from the analysis of genetics (e.g., DNA) indicates that there is greater variation within racial groups than between them. This means that most physical variation, about 94%, lies *within* so-called racial groups ... The continued sharing of genetic material has maintained all of humankind as a single species ... Physical variations in the human species have no meaning except the social ones humans put on them ... Race subsumed a growing ideology of inequality devised to rationalize European attitudes and treatment of the conquered and enslaved people ... The ideology magnified the differences among Europeans, Africans and Indians, established a rigid hierarchy of socially exclusive categories ... and provided the rationalization that the inequality was natural or God-given. Different physical traits ... became markers or symbols of their status differences. (3)

Calling upon the scientific authority of genetics, the statement denounces monogenist theories and implicitly addresses miscegenation. Explanations of "natural" or "God-given" difference are condemned as conscious ideological projects that rationalize conquest, social exclusion, and hierarchy. The meanings given to appearance are recognized as social constructs intended to mark status. Throughout the remaining body of the statement, references are made to geographical proximity, movement through enslavement, imperialism, colonialism, and immigration. The discussion of transnational processes highlights dominating ideas of difference and the effects that these have on "others." "How people have been accepted and treated within the context of a given society or culture has a direct impact on how they perform in that society."

Genetics has replaced social Darwinism, comparative anatomy, genealogy, eugenics, and scientific race theory. Assertions of social, economic, and political power are at the heart of race theory. In the words of the AAA statement:

> Racial beliefs constitute myths about diversity in the human species and about the abilities and behavior of people homogenized into racial categories ... The racial world view was invented to assign some groups to perpetual low status, while others were permitted access to privilege, power and wealth ... Racial groups are ... products of historical and contemporary social, economic, educational and political circumstances. (American Anthropological Association 1998:3)

It is interesting that anthropologists use the term "myth." Their official statement suggests that the scientific theory of race creates a narrative that supports a "racial world view" or cosmology. Race theory is traced to "countless errors" wrought by "reliance on folk beliefs about human difference." As I have shown in this book, these "folk" are scientists and scholars, colonial administrators, explorers, educators, journalists, politicians, physicians, immigration officials, and ordinary people.

> Even modern thought and science furnish elements to folklore, in that certain scientific statements and certain opinions, torn from their context, fall into the popular domain and are "arranged" within the mosaic of tradition. (Gramsci 1995:187)

The "racial world view" is orally transmitted between generations through mass media and more specialized avenues of education and public policy. Like other forms of legend and folklore, its veracity depends upon recognition of a shared set of images and ideas. The "Statement on Race" appears in a publication for a specialized audience of anthropologists, many of whom teach at universities and colleges throughout North America. It is a sign of the resurgence in essentialist ideologies. It is also an appeal to educators to perform an act of narrative resistance in the face of old and dangerous ideas propagated by anthropology in its infancy.

While people in the youngest age groups tap into technologies globalized and commodified in new forms of media, ideas about human difference remain intact across generations. Categories based on "race," age, gender, religion, nationality, sexuality, and class are still evident. To children, age is perhaps the most important distinction between people. It marks the power that adults have over their daily activities. To teenagers, sexuality is the major arena of social concern, and sexual preference is their new frontier of human difference. Adolescent anxieties around dating and pregnancy lead teenagers to speak about religion. Although teenagers I spoke with acknowledge bisexuality, their comments still work from poles of gay and straight. Social distance is marked by appearance and style largely derived from popular media. In the idiom of teenagers, it is "race." To diffuse lines of authority and assert their status as locals, young people in Fernie continue to use genealogical privilege.

Identity politics have complicated notions of representation. Ethnic slurs, now traditionalized in everyday vocabularies, are being appropriated and remodelled by those people they targeted. Young people in positions of dominant privilege have reappropriated these politicized expressions as tags of style and social identity. An awareness of the politics of representation is still grounded in particular locations, measured by distance to dominant power. Old story-worlds of social evolution and conquest appear through new technologies sold for entertainment. While scholars now recognize the violence inherent in particular concepts, these themes maintain a stubborn grip on the social imagination.

Recently I caught a glimpse of another video game called *Warcraft II, Battle.net Edition*. I was drawn into a room by a low Cockney voice repeating the words: "Ready to serve, me Lord." On the screen there were men dressed in olive green smocks. Their short brown pants were tattered at the edges. I asked the girl who was playing about the identity of these characters. "Peasants," she replied and then added: "They sound like they're drunk!" The figures enter into violent skirmishes with armoured opponents. They then trudge slowly back to the king, who is the player in this game, "continuing the struggle for domination over Azeroth." I was told that this context is one of many that may be entered through the *Warcraft* game. When the screen initially opens, the first set of choices available to the player is "Choose your race." The knowledge exists, but ...

Epilogue: Waiting

As we approached the cabin, butterflies rose from the lips of puddles, wafting into the gusty air. On this overcast day, their colours stung our eyes. Inside, deer skulls hung from door frames; on the walls hung a knife strap, a rifle, several saw blades, and thermometers. On a window ledge an ostrich egg sat alongside a unicorn, and next to that a rubbery Bugs Bunny grimaced atop an old tin. Although there were four of us in the kitchen that day, the only sound was the clock and the wind. One of the sisters broke the silence: "I just feel as though everything is waiting. Everything in here – it's just waiting. Do you feel that?"

I was offered a cup of tea. The youngest sister rose to remove the heavy plate from the wood stove. Aggressively, she stoked the remains of the last fire and then joined us at the table. The stove spewed two puffs of smoke, surprising the women who had known its moods for decades and once again bringing the fire-tender to her feet. "He has old coal stuck back there," she said, stirring the oven's guts.

Tea was ready. The middle sister said she'd take hers black; she stood and walked silently out the door, up the hillside, behind the woodshed. The eldest sister surveyed the room, taking in everything that was waiting. She sang a compliment to the complexity of objects in a cabinet at her elbow. "See the Chinese cup?" she said, pointing.

"Take it out so she can see it," directed her sister.

The teacup was emblazoned with raised colours, like string strung carefully in place to form an image – looking as though it could fall free and loosen the dragon on its surface.

"... face on the bottom – look," said the younger sister.

I raised the cup to the light. As if projected, a woman's face appeared at the base of the cup. Hair piled round in tiers.

"Chinese or Japanese?"

"She looks Japanese to me, don't you think so, Leslie?"

I didn't know. I said something about dragons.

A visitor arrived and we walked outside to greet her. She admired the beauty of the butterflies and told us that she was worried about running them down with her truck. We assured her it would be fine. One of the sisters left with the visitor, and I sat for a time on the porch with the eldest.

"Don't you wish we had a flying carpet that would take us gently up the side of the mountain?" she said.

For a while we discussed the pleasures of flying in carpeted comfort, easing the burden on ninety-year-old knees. Then we set off down the road.

The eldest sister took small steps, lifted her staff, and made clucking noises as she crossed the bridge by the chicken coop. She came to a sudden halt some distance down the road. "Ooh! Ooh, look!" Near the end of her walking stick was a butterfly – stuck. One wing was flattened in the mud, a delicate membrane branded with tire ridges. The other wing was almost translucent, like a tattoo in the clay. "We can't leave him on the road. Put him in the grass. He'll feel better there."

On my finger, the insect's legs sprawled and then kicked as they found the surface of my skin.

"He's still alive – put him on the grass."

The first attempt left the butterfly sideways, teetering perilously on a tall tower of grass. I placed him on a budding plant and we walked away.

"He had no idea that was going to happen to him today."

"No."

We walked a few more steps and the old woman stopped deliberately. "Am I dreaming this day?"

Yes, the mountains are breath taking, but they also carry rich folklore ... Numerous legends ... have a profound effect on the type of experience available in Fernie. A hike ... in Fernie is not some hike up an anonymous place. The place holds a story, a past, a feeling. (Rino 2001:121)

In a glossy, eighteen-dollar, oversized quarterly, a writer celebrates her town's move into a new economy. Luisa Rino (120) quotes a local entrepreneur: "We are going toward an experience economy. At first we had to deliver a product, then the product had to come with a service, and now people want an experience along with it." As one reads through her piece, the "experience" that Fernie offers begins to take shape. A local pub is compared to the television program *Northern Exposure;* the Ghostrider Trading Company sells "Fernie logo wear"; restaurants offer a "Rocky Mountain menu"; "a well-rooted indigenous population imbues Fernie with a unique authenticity" (121). Rino's comments bring to mind a new condominium project where "small, vinyl-clad houses [are] modelled after the 100-year-old coal miners' cottages scattered throughout Fernie" (*National Post* 21

April 2001). In Rino's piece, titled "Fernie: Cinderella of the Kootenays," folklore is an important element of this vision of authenticity. Given the latest interpretations of the curse legend by children, her invocation of the Cinderella story is appropriate. To her, the rags-to-riches narrative is analogous to Fernie's transformation from an "old mining community" into a "magnet for skiers and sports followers in every season" (118). It would seem that Fernie's metamorphosis is complete. The physical shape of the town has changed as condominiums, gated housing projects, chalets, and franchises spring up at a rapid rate.

Rino suggests that Fernie "holds a story" and "a past." Her words imply a single history and one narrative of place. Multiple and often conflicting interpretations do not translate well into promotional literature. She concludes her piece with a narrative lure. Visitors are invited to explore local knowledge: "If the city's progress is any indication, we can assume that the curse-lifting ceremony in 1964 worked. If you want to know what happened, you'll have to pay a visit to Fernie. Just ask any local ... about the Ghost Rider whose shadow haunts Mt. Hosmer every night" (124).

There is no mention of the profusion of interpretations about the curse legend, its ritual resolution, or the identity of the shadow Rider. In the context of development, these many voices are reduced into one homogenous vision generated for experience-seeking outsiders. As a form of social knowledge, the curse legend appears to be slipping from the realm of oral transmission in Fernie. The commercialized icon of the Ghostrider will, perhaps, ensure the story's preservation in a concise visual format. In the early months of 2002, the Ghostrider Trading Company issued T-shirts inscribed with the curse legend. Now a souvenir, the Rider carries on into an unbounded globalized future.

Throughout this book, the curse story has opened dialogues about intercultural conflict and social distance, the colonial appropriation of traditional knowledge, labour exploitation, and gender transgression. People in Fernie summoned the legend to explain tragedies or to provide practical advice about the rigours of travel. Some tied the story to their own family histories, to anecdotes of immigration, or to their sense of foreignness or locality. Conversations about the legend inspired people to speak about their traditional beliefs and their ideas about human difference. At base it is a narrative about social justice that deeply implicates perceptions of power. Cursing itself is an expression through which power is negotiated, contested, or claimed. It evokes the force of ideas cast into circulation, deeply affecting the ways that people imagine others and themselves.

I have explored ideas of human difference generated and transmitted through time and through narratives, as well as the ways that particular histories are invoked and others forgotten. My interpretations are grounded in specific historical contexts of colonialism, wars, immigration, nationalism, labour strife, local tragedy, treaty making, and development. Ideas circulating in these contexts reveal surprisingly similar images of human difference. Although rephrased and sometimes disguised, taxonomies of difference remain malleable, constructed upon the fundamental forms of gender, class, nationality, religion, age, "race," sexual preference, and locality. These categories are propagated through stories; they are transmitted across generations, enforced by political structures, and given credence by scholarly theories. I have attempted to keep afloat the complicated locations from which people spoke and to track the sites where personal experiences intersect with official narrative.

Some people mark difference in essentialized ways; they naturalize the boundaries between themselves and others. Some look sideways, casting an inclusive web around those who share locations grounded in belief, class, gender, "race," or locality. The eldest generations proudly wield a "working class" identity, generating a sense of solidarity that surpasses nationality. "Foreigners," in particular, look sideways based on their shared experience of poverty and marginalization from Anglo-European privilege. People of all age groups speak about religion as a marker of difference, and for some, ritual and faith define perceptions of affinity cast between themselves and others. To others, difference is invisible, people unmarked, and privilege unnoticed.

I hope I have brought attention to these spaces in noticing, these times, places, and events where difference was and is rendered natural or unquestioned. It is not the use of identity categories that signals danger, for these are inevitable social tools by which we navigate our lives. The real threat is the closure of meaning that freezes forms of difference. We must look to the processes that generate these closures.

Colonialism saturates public consciousness with stories-become-histories that are well embedded in the national imagination and in our personal repertoires of difference. What is striking about these stories is a simultaneous documentation of the absence and presence of indigenous peoples. Grand narratives of discovery camouflaged the workings of global capital during the early colonial period, romanticizing the corporate and imperial quest for land and resources. Explorers and princesses and chiefs played their fixed roles in performances staged for colonizing populations, but always, in uneasy juxtaposition, were the "terrifying narrations" of savagery and primitivism. Broadcast through explorers' journals and maps, rituals of conquest served to erase the political presence of peoples in the new world, while Europeans' scientific gaze measured, classified, and inscribed them as eminently knowable.

Theories of social evolution and race were particularly useful justifications for colonial incursion, creating taxonomies of difference launched from the British standard of "civilization," with its attendant assumptions of morality, productivity, and knowledge. Not coincidentally, anthropology was then vying for recognition as a valid scientific enterprise, and ideas generated by the discipline were accessible through the transnational flow of mass media. During my research I became acutely aware of the stubborn hold these nineteenth-century theories continue to have on public consciousness and on ways that people express perceptions of difference from indigenous societies. Participants in this research drew upon old theories of comparative anatomy, phenotype, and "racial types" to explain contemporary and historical relationships.

Absences accumulate in the collective memories of those whose presence has been systematically diluted and distorted. Legacies of colonial representation are evidenced in current indigenous assertions of self-representation and control over cultural property, lands, and political processes. Now, in what some are calling a "post-colonial" present, indigenous activists and scholars still struggle to overcome the colonial mythologies so well instilled in popular belief. Treaty making in British Columbia has reactivated ideas of the empty land, of the threat of rebellion, and of "racial" difference. Special rights discourses are especially imbued with radical difference. Although disassociated from early theories of scientific race, proponents of special rights tap into shared understandings about dangerous ideas by exposing what they claim to be the assertion of "racial" privilege. In the process, specific histories of colonialism continue to be erased even as they are acknowledged in symbolic rituals of reconciliation and historical exposition.

National narratives are imbued with the property of plasticity necessary to accommodate the flux in transnational and indigenous populations. Processes of immigration and settlement generated the raw stuff of national identity, carving collective visions of citizens and others. Those who drafted early immigration policy relied upon theories of race, eugenics, philology, social Darwinism, and Nordic superiority to select so-called desirable citizens. Theories of race were applied to European peoples, sparking the tinder of xenophobia expressed in the still potent categories of "foreigner" and Anglo-Saxon. These ideas already had solid foundations in earlier theories of European "types" that delineated rural Mediterranean and Alpine populations from urban Nordic and Aryan peoples. At the vortex of these constructions was a project of assessing what was then emerging as nation-state dominance through histories of conquest. Throughout the early years of immigration, official categories of "foreigner," "imbecile," "idiot," and "insane" appeared in contrast to "citizen." The categories were based in criteria of cultural competency that highlighted class markers. "Paupers," "peasants," "folk," and "labourers" corresponded with national, religious, and regional populations that in turn reflected labour hierarchies. Eugenic theorists used pedigree charts and genealogies to argue for sterilization and institutionalization of the "less fit." Poverty was seen to be hereditary, and with the rise in medical authority it was linked to public concern over national health. Not unlike the detoxified stories of colonial incursion, processes of immigration reified classifications of difference based on ideas of morality, intellect, and criminality.

Immigration is an experience as well as a political process, and those who have made journeys of citizenship carry within them multiple histories of collective memory. They conjure the social barb of words like "DP," "POW," and "enemy alien," official labels that transformed their daily lives during particular episodes of inter-nation conflict. War generates specific histories of group relations through state-sanctioned atrocity myths that mark indelible distances between "us" and "them," between madness and sanity, morality and licentiousness. Like the "terrifying narrations" of colonial stories, these myths create taxonomies of otherness still potent in social interactions many decades later. "Totalitarian mentalities" are enforced through structures of authority that manifest power in displays extending from corporal discipline to informal sanctions on speech and action. That the proscriptions of authoritative regimes have somehow become embodied is evident in the stories of participants who experienced war from many locations. Acts of self-censorship, silencing, and social distancing enable the intergenerational transmission of particular ideas of difference that are now "traditionalized" in our repertoires.

Storytelling animates imageries of human difference, propagating understandings about who others are. While some representations are jettisoned, others maintain a vigour that deserves attention. People spoke with me about old world ways and the challenges of exile, about labour upheaval and natural disasters, about dreams and visions, all through the many lenses of tradition, but there were topics that were not spoken about, subjects muted by understandings that surround the transmission of traditional knowledge, shifting political sanctions on public speech, and social repercussions. Certain formulae and prayers are guarded items of sacred knowledge; war and immigration carry their own secrets. The silences are as important as the words, for they mark the places where meaning is lost or judged irrelevant or too powerful to convey.

Each successive generation, it seems, overlooks the confusion of voices and pasts that melts away in the present. There is a seeming inevitability to the shrinking public memory of other eras when views of difference became hegemonic, commonsense understandings. In the apparently limitless space of globalization, older traditions of othering are cloaked in new technologies, disguised by discourses that promise the dissolution of restrictive frontiers. Ironically, new regimes of cultural politics denounce older schemes of difference while reinforcing the criteria upon which they are constituted. Social class, now transformed into "lifestyle," implies individual choice and personal responsibility; visualism and special rights have blunted the scientific edge of race theories, while still evoking essentialized differences. Sexuality remains a matter of biological debate for all but the youngest generations. In such a decontextualized present, it is worth noting an accompanying, unrelenting quest for authenticity. Nowhere is this demonstrated more clearly than through the processes of place-making in Fernie. Development for tourism revives grand narratives of exploration and discovery, inviting machinery that moulds culture and history into a marketable product. New myths are born and old ones are snipped to conform to advertising formats. Replicas of place and people lose the uneven edges of the originals. Like the Ghostrider shadow, they are fashioned into a single image, reified by a single story, mass-produced, and sold.

I must stress that the views and actions presented in this book are not exclusive to the residents of Fernie. Every location has its own rendering of the past in the present, where differently situated people negotiate their place in the world through malleable imaginative resources.

Postscript

I returned to Fernie the day after British and American forces began military action in Afghanistan. At this time the United States was on "high alert," three cases of anthrax had been reported, and Americans abroad were being advised not to "dress American," to keep their voices down, and to avoid crowds. Along the highway, signs on hotels sent best wishes to overseas troops and hopes for a speedy return. In the 7-Eleven a Red Cross donation box was set up. Printed on it were the words "Help my American neighbour" and the flags of Canada and the United States crossed over each other. An advertisement appeared in the *Free Press* with the headline "Operation Enduring Freedom" and the portraits of President George Bush and Osama bin Laden. At its centre was an image of an aircraft carrier against the background of a topographical map. The text of the ad said: "The world's events and issues continue to shape and impact our daily lives. Catch up on all the breaking news and current affairs from around the world and locally – hook up to _____ Cable" (*FFP* 2 October 2001).

These uneasy days revived memories of other conflicts. One woman recalled the words of her mother: "You still make love and gather together to eat good food, but always you have this heaviness under war." During a conversation at the hospital I was told: "The enemy is within us, they live among us." Another said: "Round them up and send them all home. That's what they have to do! When I found out that they're all here on welfare – that was it for me." I asked whom she was talking about. "The terrorists! We just let them in and then they just go on welfare. That fellow they caught in Toronto was on it for a while – they all go on it! All those [she laughed] boat people. They're being fed and housed here and they've been here a long time."

"Do you mean the jails, the encampments where refugees are being held?" I asked.

"Yes. They might as well be on welfare ... And my parents went through that! They never talked about it, but they were Germans here during the war."

One woman was worried that her son, a cadet, might be conscripted. She told me that her mother was British and her father had fought in the Second World War. I asked her about Britain's stance in the war against terror. "It's all about re-establishing the empire," she said.

Many felt that this conflict signalled the beginning of the Third World War. Pearl Harbor was mentioned here and there. An Italian woman spoke about wartime leadership. "I grew up always hearing about how wonderful Benito Mussolini was. My father just always said he was great. When I got older I asked him why he says that. 'He put food on the table and clothes on the backs of the people. He raised up the poor people.' Now, what this coalition is doing will make people hate them! People aren't interested in the ideologies of the state – they want basic homes. You're not going to get the support of the people by bombing the poor civilians."

My conversations that autumn included speculations about difference. "Who are Afghans culturally? I mean, what do they look like?" We had been talking about racial profiling and the question seemed appropriate. Another person answered it: "They're Caucasian! They have beautiful blue eyes, some of them, and red hair, and they're tall." She pulled out an edition of *National Geographic* with a stunning green-eyed woman on the cover. Our conversation about racial profiling continued, and one woman told me about the "latest theory," which proposes two "original races." She asked me what my blood type was and I told her. "Berber," she said. She could see it in my face, the cheeks and the shape of my eyes. According to her typology, those with type B blood are descendants of Genghis Khan. The other "race" consists of those hailing from Celts and Druids, whose blood type is O.

People asked me if I was frightened to live in a large city where there are skyscrapers and other sites that may be targets for terrorist attacks. There was a general consensus that most felt safe in Fernie. I told them about public attacks on the large Muslim population in Vancouver. I had been reading various South Asian papers distributed there. In one, called *The Link*, I came across an article by Dr. Kala Singh, who counselled people about the stress and paranoia caused by the 11 September 2001 attacks, and who had encountered superstitious attitudes towards illness:

Because of a lack of information, there are a lot of misgivings about mental illness. Some treat it as "jadoo, toona," evil spirit, evil eye, black magic, ghosts, "bhoot, pret" and curses. Despite claims by some people to treat these through supernatural powers, the fact is that there is no remedy for these problems except through proper medication. (*The Link* 13 October 2001: A18)

The *Fernie Free Press* also invoked belief: "The only answer at a time like this is to turn to God ... We are all members of the human race regardless of our ethnic backgrounds ... let us continue to pray for all the suffering people in the world because ultimately we are all brothers and sisters in this global village" (*FFP* 2 October 2001:5). Perhaps most profoundly, this writer states: "It has now become politically correct to talk and write about prayer and faith." Another woman told me that she was careful about what she said to people: "I state my views and people don't say anything – they say nothing back. They just look at me. I don't know if I'm crazy or what!" The events of 11 September have ushered in what some are calling the death of political correctness through a rebirth of patriotism and faith.

Perhaps not surprisingly, the curse legend was drawn into service during this current period of uncertainty. *Free Press* reporters asked an eleven-year-old in Fernie to respond to the "attacks": "It's more comical when I talk about it with my friends than with my family. My friends joke about hiding in a cave on Hosmer Mountain if there is a war, stuff like that" (*FFP* 2 October 2001:5).

Like other imaginative resources, the legend will continue to communally unfold to fill the ideational spaces left bare by our struggles. Perhaps the most difficult challenge before us is to remember and recite complexities in our expressions of social reality and to notice when these expressions are reduced to a single vision.

In October 2002, I was again in Fernie. On the main street, four businesses had left empty shells, the false front of a saloon had been erected over a local hotel, and some of the once fading advertisements were repainted. There are mugs with images of the Griz and the Three Sisters for sale, along with transparent ski boots and holographic snowboards. One store was selling magnetic bracelets as health aids. Real estate agents were running for city council in Fernie civic elections, and a group of residents were fighting to protect their water from international interests. From a shoebox, a sepia portrait of Geronimo stares out the window at shoppers on the street.

Notes

Introduction: Ideas Make Acts Possible

1 In anthropology, fieldnotes are surrounded by a certain mystique that draws attention to the boundaries between public and private property, professional and personal writing (see Sanjek 1990; Robertson 1998). They are an intensely individualistic form that rarely appears in published texts intact (for exceptions see Michael Jackson 1986, and Margery Wolf 1992).

2 In 1998 the Royal British Columbia Museum sponsored folk dancing, bocce tournaments, Italian opera, historical exhibits, and banquets in Fernie as part of the museum's provincial celebration.

3 Appadurai's concept of ethnoscape is: "The landscape of persons who constitute the shifting world in which we live: tourists, immigrants, refugees, exiles, guestworkers and other moving groups ... [who] affect the politics of (and between) nations" (1991:6). He is writing about present "global interactions"; however, I suggest that this reading is equally relevant to other historical periods.

4 Both theorists contest popular distinctions between territorially defined units of culture, or locals, and what has come to be regarded as a new phenomenon of transnational diasporas. I suggest that the international flow of populations is also a historical phenomenon.

5 Anglo Europeans are those people from English-speaking countries, including the United Kingdom, Ireland, the USA, Canada, Australia, New Zealand, etc. Non-Anglo Europeans are those people of European origin whose primary language is other than English.

6 I have no way to determine whether this reflects people's knowledge of my research interests or a local way of speaking and introducing oneself. The general knowledge that people carry about each other's stories, however, suggests that the exchange of information is vital to members of this small community.

7 Perhaps the first widespread challenge to written and verbal language use came out of the 1970s feminist movement. These scholars called for a reformation of language use towards gender inclusion (Leydesdorff, Passerini, and Thompson 1996:2). At base here is the assumption that older forms of speech and inscription perpetuate male dominance (2).

8 They distinguish between censure and censorship. The former takes the form of disapproval or reprimand aimed at the speaker *after* the transgression. Censorship is stronger and is focused on the actual idea or form of expression: it aims to prevent "disapproved expressions or ... their spread ... before it can be repeated" (Smith and Saltzman 1995:86).

9 Complex sanctions on "everyday social practice" are committed to a culture of human rights (Richer and Weir 1995:6). Scholars in this edited volume on political correctness approach it as a "neo-conservative appropriation" that acts to "dismiss human rights initiatives as forms of intolerant fanaticism and oppression" (3).

10 Culhane (1987, 1998) examines philosophical and political assumptions at the heart of legal processes and government structures that constitute barriers to Aboriginal communities in British Columbia. Her works detail histories of European social theory and political, legal, and social discourses constituting sites of colonial power. Furniss (1999) examines

"myths" circulating in a BC forest town. She reveals the "systematic way in which a dominant colonial culture operates in multiple dimensions of ordinary life" (204). Both scholars highlight ideas about history and the colonial past and the ways these are presently used to negotiate new relationships between Aboriginal and non-Aboriginal people in Canada.

11 See Chapter 1. I spoke with many members of the Ktunaxa Nation. In this work I highlight excerpts from the taped interview with one woman who grew up in Fernie. I do not wish for her voice to appear as token or representative. This Ktunaxa woman is included because she is/was a Fernie "local," well versed in the social idiosyncrasies of the town as experienced from her location.

12 Stolcke (1995:5) defines xenophobia as "hostility towards strangers and all that is foreign."

13 See Culhane (1998:24-25) for her criticism of the term "indigenous" and for her thorough discussion of the many complications that arise from these labels. Culhane's critique speaks to the way that this term obliterates the particularities of a group's history, language, and political, religious, and economic systems. I agree that such erasures are part of the colonial machinery of representation. My discussion, however, focuses on discourses that have been used to reify original inhabitants of lands across the world and across North America in a variety of colonial situations.

14 The language used in the act is worth noting: "A reference in this Act to an Indian does not include any person of the race of aborigines commonly referred to as Inuit" (Indian Act, RSC 1985, c. 1-6, s. 1:4).

15 Prior to the 1985 amendment of section 31 of the Indian Act, non-status First Nations people included women married to non-Aboriginal men, "illegitimates," and those who had been enfranchised (Brizinski 1989:176; Hedican 1995:11).

16 The mining company was incorporated in 1889. In 1893 the assets of the Crow's Nest Coal and Mineral Company were absorbed by the BC Coal, Petroleum and Mineral Company. In 1901, the Canadian Geographic Board renamed the region, changing "Crow's Nest" to Crows Nest. References to the company's name vary. Most writers use the Crowsnest Pass Coal Company and I follow their lead throughout the book. Prior to the Kaiser Steel takeover in the 1970s, the company was Crowsnest Industries.

17 There are notable exceptions, and to some extent the discipline is moving towards such investigations (see Crapanzano 1986; Dominy 1995; Stewart 1996).

Chapter 1: Conversations among Europeans

1 Although there are several published accounts of the story of the curse, I have chosen Hutcheson's on the basis of detail: his use of actual persons and places. There is also a sense of oral narration in his writing that resonates with the ways in which people in Fernie narrate the story.

2 Following the lead of many scholars, I place the concept of race in quotation marks throughout this book in order to flag its shifting definitions and applications.

3 Mackenzie defines propaganda as: "The transmission of ideas and values from one person, or group of persons, to another, with the specific intention of influencing the recipient's attitudes in such a way that the interests of its authors will be enhanced" (1984:3). He states that such efforts are deliberate in contrast to a more social process whereby ideas are reinforced through repetition (3). In this chapter I will be looking at both conscious forms of information management and forms arising from practical social and political contexts.

4 Michael Phillipps's descendants informed me of the correct spelling of his name. Most published accounts use "Phillips."

5 In what follows I work from Hudson's Bay Company dispatches compiled by Rich (1947). Journal entries from the 1857-1860 explorations of John Palliser, Thomas Blackiston, and James Hector are taken from Spry (1963).

6 Spry (1963:2) describes John Palliser as "the heir of a wealthy Irish landowner," well-educated, with a military background and political aspirations.

7 Thomas Blackiston is described by Spry (1963:163) as an "ambitious young artillery officer" who had great difficulty subordinating himself to the orders of Palliser.

8   George Dawson was born in Nova Scotia. His father was Sir William Dawson, known as "the father of McGill University" (Barkhouse 1989:foreword). He studied geology at the Royal School of Mines in London, England, until he was appointed to the British North American Boundary Commission in 1873 (40-65).

9   In Henry Morgan's journals of his travels up the Missouri River in 1862, he comments on the "gossip" surrounding powerful men. Among those whom he met was Father DeSmet, who was "a count by birth" (in White 1993:166).

10   John Pelly's 1825 dispatch is a detailed example of this endeavour (in Rich 1947:161-166). The "history" scrolls through a series of corporate takeovers and expeditions. Alexander Mackenzie's 1793 crossing of the Rockies to the coast is followed by the construction of a series of trading posts, beginning with the North West Company of Montreal, which established trade "among the Flathead and Coutonais Tribes" (162). Pelly dismisses any claims made by Lewis and Clark and notes the establishment of the Pacific Fur Company in the area of the Columbia River (162). In 1818, an agreement between Americans and the North West Company established "formal possession of the settlement" by the US government. Regarding this agreement, Pelly wrote: "I think it right to observe that the settlement and whatever had been previously occupied in that country by American subjects had been acquired by the North West Company by purchase for a valuable consideration and not by capture" (163). In 1821 the Hudson's Bay Company "acquired possession of all the trading Posts and Stock" of the North West Company (164). In 1881 the US and Great Britain drew up a convention that left the country to the west of the Rockies open to trade for ten years (163). Questions of the citizenship of Americans at the time of British possession (181) led to references to Cook and Drake, the history of North West Company trading posts and the Pacific Fur Company, and the routes of explorers.

11   The distinction between Nation and State is important here. According to Williams (1976:213), "nation" was commonly used in the "primary sense of a racial group rather than a politically organized grouping."

12   George Stocking pinpoints a shift in the use of the concept of civilization. In the early eighteenth century civilization was regarded as the "destined goal of all of humanity"; later in the century it was used to account for apparent "racial" differences (1968:36). The next century made civilization into the achievement of "certain races" (36).

13   Dawson distinguished the nature of these names by their largely "descriptive character," which "express[ed] some noted feature or product of each locality" (1892:35).

14   There is some suggestion here that the gesture of a kiss implies earlier contact with the Spanish.

15   "Images of colonized populations ... became the object of conflict" (Miles 1989:26). Since the late eighteenth century, public debates on slavery had been especially heated. They revolved around conflicting theories about human difference that were then constructed from the accounts of explorers, traders, and missionaries.

16   Hallowell traces the phenomenon to the late eighteenth century when "'Squaw Men' of the South Seas" included runaway sailors, captives, and missionaries (1963:524).

17   Hallowell used the term "Indianization" (1963:520). I suggest that the concept remains salient, although now phrased as "going native" or losing one's objectivity.

18   Van Kirk (1981:10-15) points to the differing strategies of the Hudson's Bay Company and the North West Company, which reflect national and class hierarchies within the two corporations.

19   Simpson himself entered into two such unions (1821 and 1825), both of which he cast off when he married his British cousin in 1830 (Van Kirk 1980:163). The Welsh trader David Thompson journeyed into Ktunaxa territories in 1808. His party included his "Indian" wife and children (Johnson 1969:48; Scott and Hanic 1979:41; Ktunaxa-Kinbasket Tribal Council 1992). James Sinclair, categorized by Palliser in 1841 as "a very intelligent ... half breed gentleman" from Red River, had led a group of emigrants through Ktunaxa lands some years before Palliser's expedition (Spry 1963:7). Michael Phillipps may also be placed in this category. In 1866 he married Rowen David, daughter of Chief David on the Tobacco Plains. He spoke Ktunaxa fluently (Miller 1998:29, 31).

20 Van Kirk states that this was especially the case amongst people who shared English ancestry in contrast to French (Van Kirk 1980:163). The observation suggests the two European nationalities held differing ideas of social inclusion.

21 Canada was well represented in these international exhibitions and by 1891 had a permanent display (Mackenzie 1984:102).

22 As Noel Dyck points out, "public problems" involve the interplay of moral judgment and available theories, which create the "facticity of the situation" (1986:32).

23 Leon Poliakov cites Friedrich Blumenbach (1754-1840) as the "founder of physical anthropology" (1974:173). It was Blumenbach who coined the term "Caucasian" and proposed a theory of five distinct "races," although asserting a monogenist stance (173).

24 See Poliakov (1974) for an illuminating examination of philology through the "Aryan" hypothesis and the nationalistic and racializing uses of this theory.

25 To Tylor (1871:vol 1:385), religion was a faulty attempt at true knowledge, in contrast to science, which was the pinnacle of reason and unarguable experience. James Frazer was more specific in his outline of the stages of human development from magic, through religion, and finally to science (Langham 1981:17).

26 It is interesting that studies of language were used to elucidate relationships between "races." In 1891 Alexander Chamberlain published a paper titled "The Aryan Element in Indian Dialects," in which he discussed elements of "incorporation" in the Kootenay language. His work traces effects of the "Aryan conquerors" upon language systems as a result of "the intermingling of races and intellects" (1, 6). Boas's 1918 *Kutenai Tales* signals an approach to language that sought common motifs or traits in the folklore of different indigenous groups. While this work may be viewed in the tradition of salvage anthropology, it also evokes a fluid model of interaction and movement in a theoretical context that remained invested in the idea of distinct and separate categories of people.

27 There are notable exceptions (see Holden 1976 and Wickwire 1994).

28 I have drawn heavily here from Patrick Wolfe's (1991) analysis of the Australian Aboriginal "Dreaming" and his outline of European conceptual traditions that serve to reinforce colonial relationships.

Chapter 2: Látkép ⁂ Ansicht ⁂ View ⁂ ВИД

1 The Viennese government first issued postcards in 1869. A year later, Britain began producing them (Willoughby 1992:30). In 1871 Canada became "the first non-European country" to issue postcards, and three years later they were available in Russia, Italy, and the United States (31).

2 Members of the Greek Orthodox faith, including Russians and Serbians, use the Cyrillic alphabet.

3 See Malkki (1997:61-66) for her discussion about "refugees" as a category of persons "pathologized" through their condition of deterritorialization.

4 In his capacity as superintendent of Indian affairs, Sifton asserted a similar constellation of ideas regarding compulsory school attendance: "An Indian neither had the physical, mental nor moral get-up to enable him to compete" with the white man (1894 in Ktunaxa-Kinbasket Tribal Council 1992).

5 There is no mention of the nationality of these workers. Between 1881 and 1884, 15,700 Chinese labourers arrived in Canada, contracted by the CPR (Palmer 1975:22). According to Donald Avery (1979:26), the CPR excluded Slav and Scandinavian workers. In 1896 the corporation was charged with gross mistreatment of Welsh, Scottish, and English workers on the Crow's Nest Pass Railway. The charges stemmed mostly from appalling sanitary conditions (25). The Alien Labour Act was passed in 1897, outlawing the "solicitation or importation or immigration of any alien or foreigner ... under contract or agreement" (32).

6 McLaren traces intellectual connections to Britain through medical doctors and zoologists at McGill, the University of Toronto, and the Nova Scotia Hospital for the insane (1990:23-24).

7 The *Free Press* article (18 March 1899:2) summarizes the report of the minister of the

interior and also provides a table of birth rates and death rates in different countries. The total number of immigrants reported for 1897 was 27,209.

8 In this capacity in 1919 Bryce outlined measures to prevent the growing population of the "unfit" (McLaren 1990:54). These included prohibiting this group from marrying and reproducing, while denying access to birth control to those who were "fit." Notably, he had much to say about selecting the "right" kind of immigrant and denying entry to the "degenerate" (54).

9 Canadian schoolchildren had used texts published by the Royal Colonial Institute since the 1870s and by the Royal Geographical Association since 1889 (Mackenzie 1984:175). From the turn of the century, children in schools were singing the national anthem, marching, and saluting the British flag (237).

10 The term "Aryan" came from Herodotus and was recast into circulation during the early 1800s in Europe. Through the work of philologists, it came to be associated with the discovery of the "Indo-European" or "Indo-German" language family (Poliakov 1974:193). Scholars studying Sanskrit recognized similarities between that language and Greek and Latin. They theorized that Indians were the original conquerors of Europe and had broken through the Caucasus Mountains to "civilize" the west (196). What Poliakov calls the "Aryan myth" appeared in the "histories," dictionaries, and philosophical treatises of many leading scholars in Europe. By 1845 the myth was elaborated to include a notion of white superiority based on the lighter-skinned, higher castes of India (196-209). The theory reinforced Friedrich Blumenbach's (1754-1840) category of "Caucasian," which also derived from the same region (173). While "Caucasian" was used as a category for selective immigration into North America, the British were not fond of the proposed relationship between Indians and Aryans (268).

11 Yu Bromley (1987:31) cites the ethnologist Chernishevsky and the physical anthropologist Miklouho-Maklay as two Russian scholars engaged in virulent opposition to reigning ideas of Nordic superiority in late-nineteenth-century Europe.

12 These "laws" suggest the two dominant approaches to eugenics at this time. Biometrics used statistical methods in an analysis of correlation between measurements (mostly bodily) seen to be proof of inheritance. Mendelians, on the other hand held to rules of dominance and recessiveness of particular traits. The presence or absence of such traits was deemed as proof of inheritance. Americans were seen as "vulgar Mendelians," while the British adhered mostly to the statistical approach (Mazumdar 1992:59-60).

13 In their histories of British and Canadian eugenics, Pauline Mazumdar (1992:65-66) and Angus McLaren (1990:24) both mention E.W. McBride, a Cambridge-educated zoologist who held a position at McGill University between 1897 and 1909. He was notorious in England because he largely ignored class and concentrated on "race" (Mazumdar 1992:65). In Canada he advocated sterilization of "mental defectives," who, he said, "place a heavier burden on the shoulders of the Nordic race, who form the bulk of the taxpayers" (McBride 1924 in McLaren 1990:24).

14 I was surprised at my ability to follow and participate in the discussion of clan history. Both of my grandfathers were from Scotland, and I became aware of a kind of osmosis of knowledge picked up here and there simply by virtue of being a member, through my mother's and father's patriline, of a "Scottish" family.

15 Postcard images were personalized early on in production through the use of studio portraits and snapshots (Baskin 1981:xi).

16 See Thomas and Znaniecki (1918:127) re: Russian Poland; Arlacchi (1983:25-29) re: Calabria; Miller and Sharpless (1985:192-195) re: "Slavs."

17 In 1903 the Salvation Army created a Department of Migration and Settlement and became a major organization of emigration. Its role was to aid in the transportation and "placement of the deserving poor of Great Britain" (Avery 1979:20). Emigrants included some of the approximately 100,000 children who were transported involuntarily as part of the anglicization policy of settlement (Mackenzie 1984:161). In exchange for these services, the Canadian government gave the Salvation Army a cash bonus for each agricultural worker (161).

18   The "problem of the feeble-minded" warranted a Royal Commission in Britain in 1909. Its purpose was to develop new laws for those people not then covered by the Lunacy or Idiot Acts (Great Britain 1909:2). In its report, the commission described "feeble-minded" persons as those "who may be capable of earning a living under favourable circumstances, but are incapable from mental defect existing from birth or from an early age: (a) of competing on equal terms with their normal fellows; or (b) of managing themselves and their affairs with ordinary prudence" (5).

19   Between 1902 and 1913, 8,741 people were deported; numbers declined during the First World War and then sharply rose to 11,114 from 1925 to 1930. The highest number of deportees was 24,744 during the period from 1930 to 1936 (Avery 1979:197). Between 1903 and 1909, 73.1 percent of deportations were to the United Kingdom, 4.7 percent to the United States, and 22.2 percent to the "rest of the world" (W.G. Smith 1920:76).

20   It is interesting to consider how the once official labels of "idiot" and "imbecile" have come to inhabit a detoxified place in everyday language. Regina Bendix and Barbro Klein (1993:4) note that the vocabularies of "official language" change constantly. Many terms continue to circulate in expressive culture as slurs. In the early 1900s, "idiots" were persons "so deeply defective in mind ... that they are unable to guard themselves from physical danger" (Great Britain 1909:4). "Imbeciles" were regarded as capable of self-protection but unable to earn their own living (5).

21   The symbols of the pedigree were "standardized" in 1911 by Leonard Darwin, son of Charles and president of the Eugenics Research Committee in Britain (Mazumdar 1992:77). They have an eerie resemblance to kinship diagrams developed by the discipline of anthropology around this time. I have not investigated this relationship, but do note Pauline Mazumdar's reference to William Rivers and Alfred Haddon, two very eminent anthropologists, attending lectures of the British Eugenics Society (77).

22   In a letter proposing extensive research into "changes in Immigrant Body Form," Franz Boas recommended that "male and female observers on Ellis Island ... collect data relating to the immigrants and ... make similar arrangements on emigrants leaving this country" (Boas 1908:204). Data consisted of "three head-measurements"; measurements of "stature, weight, circumference of chest, strength of muscles"; and observations on hair and eye colour (203). Boas's project also included comparison of the Ellis Island results with "observations ... in public and parochial schools ... in which the foreign population is more strongly represented" (204). As well he recommended that the "families of natives of foreign countries" who have been long-time residents in America be included. Later he saw the need for comparative research to be carried out in Galicia, southern Italy, and southern Germany. The data were to be collected at steamship stations through inspection of passengers before embarking (209).

23   By this time, corporate interests were pushing the government away from British labour and towards those people who were not vocal about working conditions. In violation of the Alien Labour Act and in secret agreement with the government, seventy thousand workers from the Austro-Hungarian Empire had been recruited by the North Atlantic Trading Company (Avery 1979:20-25). Strike actions in the Welsh mines and in the metalliferous mines of BC saw labour agencies bring in "foreign scabs," mostly Italians and Slavic people (32). One such agency was in Fernie. In response to labour unrest and immigration concerns, a series of Royal Commissions were established. In 1899, William Fernie testified before the Commission on Mining Conditions in BC. Regarding miners employed by the Crow's Nest Mining Company, he said: "Nearly all are British subjects except one or two foreigners" (British Columbia 1899:306). By 1912 the majority of miners were Slavic and Italian (Avery 1979:57).

24   Chinese miners had already been excluded from underground labour in 1900 (Yarmie 1998:201). The United Mine Workers of America solidified this recommendation in 1906 by prohibiting Asian workers from its membership (203). At issue now was the hiring of "Italian, Slav, Belgian, Bohemian, German, Finn, Pole and Russian workers" favoured by the mining companies of southeastern BC (201-202).

25   A charge for stealing coal carried the penalty of $200 or three days in jail. Vagrants were subject to a one-month prison term, and people found riding the train without a ticket

could spend twenty days in jail. One man was deported to the United States for the charge of drunkenness. Profane language carried a charge of ten dollars or ten days (FDHS Archives 1911).

26 At this time Austro-Hungarians included Czechoslovakians and Ukrainians.

27 Smith states that women and children who have not landed in Canada are not entitled to citizenship through marriage or through parentage.

28 As Wayne Norton and Ella Verkerk (1998:92) note, First World War internment files were destroyed by the Department of National Defence in 1953. They provide a concise bibliography of available references.

29 According to a 1994 article in the *Free Press*, 8,579 men, 81 women, and 156 children were interned across Canada between 1914 and 1920 (14 December 1994:8). One hundred and seven people died at the camps (8). Internees at Morrissey took legal recourse for unlawful confinement. The attempt was quashed by an Order in Council passed 28 October 1914: "aliens of enemy nationality" were henceforth "to be classified as prisoners of war" (Carter 1980:20).

30 Men could be put to work straightening roads for a wage of twenty-five cents per day; the coal company would retrieve some of what was lost through labour by renting the building and property for the internment camp (*FFP* 20 August 1915:1).

31 Institutionalization was later combined with sterilization. In 1933 the Sexual Sterilization Bill was passed in BC (McLaren 1990:103). "Even Tom Uphill, the independent member from Fernie who had in the past been critical of the medical profession, fell into line ... he apologized for his opposition" (103). After 1937, consent was no longer required for sterilization. Roman Catholic and Greek Orthodox eastern Europeans overrepresented those who were sterilized (160). "Indians and Métis, who represented only 2.5 per cent of Alberta's population, accounted for over 25 per cent of those sterilized" (160). Angus McLaren notes that the "typical" candidate for sterilization was "a young, unwed mother who had been diagnosed as mentally retarded" (160).

Chapter 3: "The Story As I Know It"

1 Coal Creek was the mine site five miles outside of Fernie. Morrissey mines were open from 1901 to 1910, ten miles south of Fernie. Michel, later Michel-Natal, was twenty-two miles north. The mines here were established in 1898 and operated until 1970 (Sloan 1998:40-41).

2 Respectively, see Brunvand 1971:186; Dundes 1971a:24; and Mullen 1971:409, citing Wayland Hand.

3 Karel Skalický (1989:297-298) suggests that this was a popular response to techniques used by states to manipulate populations during different waves of nationalism and empire.

4 Phillips Stevens (1997:33) warns against "interpreting belief systems engendered in and structured by one cultural framework, through models of 'reality' and principles of etiology developed from the perspective of another."

5 Phillips Stevens (1997:200) makes the distinction between magical (sorcery) and mystical (witchcraft) acts. The former involve "the manipulation of objects and/or the uttering of words with intent to bring about that which is symbolically communicated or enacted in the rite." Witchcraft requires "a belief in extrasomatic (psychic or mystical) power vested in uncertain individuals which operates without recourse to magic" (200). Cursing, as a supernatural act, slides between these categories depending on whose cultural interpretation is to be followed.

6 See J.G. Lockhart (1938) for an interesting compilation of curses plaguing British aristocratic families. Donna Shai (1978:43-44) discusses "house" curses affecting extended families of Kurdish Jews.

7 Discourses of authenticity amongst miners seem to revolve around actual body markings. I was told that workers "in the old days" were rightly suspicious of the qualifications of men with whom they worked and, to some degree, entrusted their lives. Mining in England was apparently carried out in tunnels with very low ceilings. Scrapes and cuts were typical in these conditions. Coal dust entered their wounds, leaving a kind of tattoo that served as a mark of experience recognized by other miners (from Fieldnotes, 16

October 1997). Contemporary residents in the Crownest Pass speak of "miner's mascara" – the unwashable line of coal, telltale of underground work.

8   Korson (1938:139-148) outlines the use of charms and the belief in omens, witches, fairies, and ghosts that provided miners with a sense of how to proceed in their dangerous occupation.

9   More recently, the performance has become an expression of good wishes for the newly-weds and is most prevalent in rural Canada (Darnton:666).

10 In 1895, William Fernie sold his interests in the Crow's Nest Pass Coal Company and returned to England where he retired in comfort.

11 St. Barbara converted to Christianity while confined in a tower built by her father to pre-vent her marriage. Her father turned her over to Roman authorities, and under torture she refused to relinquish her faith. He then took her to a mountaintop and beheaded her, at which time he was struck down by lightning (MEE 2000; see also Korson 1965:50). The Church removed St. Barbara from the calendar of saints in 1969, suppressing her cult and denying her existence (www.catholicforum.com).

12 Jeanne Favret-Saada (1977:6) outlines three interpretive options available to a parish priest confronted by witchcraft: deny religious significance, attribute the incident to divine interference, or "interpret misfortunes as the work of the devil."

13 When methane gas was ignited in the mines, the explosion was called a "bump."

14 The interpretive centre now marking the Frank Slide also mentions indigenous fore-knowledge of the geological instability of Turtle Mountain.

15 Writing about "Sicilian Peasants" in 1897, Salvatore Salomone-Marino (202-205) describes the merging of beliefs in sorcery and witchcraft with the power of saints and invocations of the church. See also a discussion on the role of parish priests in bewitchment cases in contemporary rural France (Favret-Saada 1977:14-15).

16 Writing in the same present as the postcard, Astra Cielo (1918:36) defines "mascot" as "anything from a piece of string to a human being that is supposed to influence The Fates for the benefit of the possessor."

17 Robert Darnton (1984:90-92) presents versions of the ritual killing of cats across Europe and burnings in various regions of France and Germany. Many coincided with Lent and saints' days. James Frazer (1922:610) states that cat burning continued as late as 1840 in France. He describes the "fire-festivals" across Europe, where animals were burnt as "an infallible means of preserving [livestock and persons] from disease and witchcraft" (656).

Part Two: Imagining Difference

1   In August 1997 a television documentary in the Czech Republic broadcast the message that Roma would be given automatic refugee status and welfare benefits upon arrival in Canada. Flyers appearing on the streets of Prague invited them to leave and guaranteed them $1,500 per month when they arrived here. Some regional officials were offering to pay the bulk of their airfare (*Globe and Mail* 23 August 1997:1, 6).

2   "King Frederick William of Prussia decreed in 1725 that any Gypsy over 18 ... should be hanged. In the Holy Roman Empire it was decreed in that same year that Gypsy men were to be put to death. In Silesia and Moravia, Gypsy women were to have their left ears cut off. In Bohemia ... the right ears of Gypsy women were to be severed ... In his quest for an Aryan Europe, Adolph Hitler exterminated 500,000 Gypsies ... With the col-lapse of communism, it was again almost open season on Gypsies" (*Globe and Mail* 23 August 1997:1).

Chapter 4: A Moment of Silence

1   May's works about Native Americans sold over two million copies in Germany and were published in sixty-five volumes (Kamenetsky 1984:147).

2   Particularly underrepresented in this chapter on war are Anglo-European men. Many chose not to speak about this period in their lives.

3   In Italy, rules and rites around the tricolour flag were instituted in 1890 (Dogliani 1999:16-17). In Germany, the tricolour flag emerged from student movements and was well insti-tuted after 1848. Hitler "abandoned the traditional tricolour design, possibly because of

its associations with nineteenth century liberalism, possibly as not sufficiently indicative of a break with the past" (Hobsbawm 1994:273).

4 The Knights of Columbus were started in the United States by an Irish priest named James McGiddon. Christopher Columbus is the patron of the lodge, whose members follow values of the "faithful navigator" (Interview, 8 July 1998. Italian-Canadian man, born 1936).

5 Eric Hobsbawm (1989:272-275) notes that memorials to battles began to appear in European states after 1890, and those erected to fallen soldiers sometime after 1914. The Fernie cenotaph was erected and dedicated in 1923 (Phillips 1977:81).

6 The swastika was in common use before Hitler's National Socialist Reich appropriated and significantly transformed its use. During the early 1920s, the women's ice hockey team was known as the Fernie Swastikas.

7 Members of the Salvation Army are evangelical Methodists. The group was formed in 1878 in the climate of "popular militarism of the Russo-Turkish war" (Mackenzie 1984:5).

8 Under Austro-Hungarian rule, Slovak nationalists were imprisoned. Slovakian territories, characterized as areas of "peasant culture," were ruled by the colonial administration in Budapest. In contrast to highly industrialized Czech regions, where education was accessible, in Slovakia Magyar was the "only language of political, judicial and administrative intercourse" (Leff 1988:13-20).

9 There are resonances here with the Indian Act. In 1935 the Nuremberg Laws stated that "to be classified as a full Jew one had to have three Jewish grandparents or two if one actively practiced Judaism" (Pauley 1997:160).

10 I heard similar typecasting comments about "Indians," Doukhobors and Russians, "Slavs," and Italians.

11 In 1938 identifying names were forced on people classified by the German Reich as Jewish; men were required to add "Israel," and women the name "Sarah" (Pauley 1997:161).

12 Anti-Semitism is a potent tool of scapegoating used by political regimes, especially in areas where Jewish communities are largely unassimilated. In Slovakia, against the backdrop of Roman Catholicism, anti-Semitism was aimed at Jewish professionals, who were targeted as "sapping the national wealth and peasant welfare" (Leff 1988:21).

13 In March 1994, *North Shore News* columnist Doug Collins wrote an article titled "Hollywood Propaganda" in which he critiqued the film *Schindler's List*. The review included a trivialization of the numbers of deaths during the Holocaust and an attack on "the Jewish-owned media." The Pacific region of the Canadian Jewish Congress filed a human rights complaint against Collins and the North Vancouver newspaper that sparked a nation-wide debate over censorship and political correctness. The seventy-six-year-old writer retired before the tribunal dismissed the complaint (see Brook 1997:59-115). After a second complaint in 1999, the BC Human Rights Tribunal ordered Collins and the paper to pay two thousand dollars to an individual who cited four other columns written by Collins with anti-Semitic content. Doug Collins died in 2001, while this ruling was under appeal (Fulford 2001:no page).

14 "Freemasons have been blamed for both the French and Russian revolutions, for the assassination of Archduke Ferdinand ... or the German inflation of the 1920s, and for the Spanish Civil War" (Daniel Cohen 1972:92-106). In Europe during the Second World War, speculation circulated about Hitler's membership in a secret society.

15 The Pest House was used in the 1930s to quarantine people who had infectious diseases. I heard about people moving into the sanatorium for smallpox, meningitis, measles, chicken pox, and mumps.

16 When Michel and Natal were dismantled and people relocated to Sparwood, the mine companies hoped to discourage a long-standing trend of managers living in Fernie. Their efforts were not entirely successful; many employees live now in Ridgemont.

Chapter 5: Getting Rid of the Story

1 A CBC radio crew was on site to record that day's activities. I was unable to obtain copies or transcripts of the program they aired. Archivists could not locate the piece.

2 South Africa originally established a "reserve system" in 1913. The reserves were later known as "homelands" (Crapanzano 1986:xviii). In 1950 all South Africans were assigned

racial classifications under the ideology of "apartheid," meaning "separateness" in Afrikaans (xix). In the early 1960s, apartheid policies were severely criticized by the United Nations and world press. Protests and boycotts across the world led to South Africa's withdrawal from the Commonwealth in 1961.

3   Further international scrutiny via the Human Rights Commission of the United Nations changed the status clauses in the Indian Act, which excluded membership of Native women married to non-Native men, and their children (Suagee 1994:196).

4   Eric Hobsbawm (1994:127) cites the "nationalist resentment against Peace Treaties 1918-20" as one of the factors that precipitated the rise of fascist regimes. Veterans of the First World War were an important component of mobilization in all European nations.

5   Prohibitions on religious and ceremonial expression in the form of Sun Dances and potlatches were instituted in amendments to the Indian Act in 1884. They were deleted from the act in 1951.

6   There are two avenues by which indigenous leaders approach the Canadian state. One is to argue the status of Aboriginal people through claims of "traditional ways of life" and particular rights to lands (C. Scott 1993:312). Central to their efforts is the assertion that culture is changing, albeit "distinctive" (C. Scott 1993:312; see also Cruikshank 1997:17). The other tactic used by First Nations' leaders argues for "special constitutional and administrative status [based on First Nations'] long experience as the involuntary clients of a paternalistic and stifling form of federal administration" (Dyck 1986:32).

7   The Great Northern Railway (1904-1926), the Canadian Pacific Railway (1898-1964), and the Morrissey, Fernie, and Michel Railroad (1898-1958) provided regular passenger transport through the South Country into the United States, farther west into the BC interior, east to Michel, and more locally to Coal Creek, where the mines were operated (Mangan 1977a:41). There was nostalgia about the "Galloping Goose," a slow train that travelled the CPR tracks between Elko and Fernie, moving at a speed slow enough for passengers to hop off where they wanted to go fishing or hunting. "In 1938 the tracks were lifted from Elko clear through to the border" (41).

8   The ten-thousand-year-old remains of Kennewick Man were found on the Columbia River in Oregon in 1996.

9   Miscegenation is defined as "interbreeding of races, esp. of Whites with non-Whites" (OED 1982:646). It is derived from *miscere* mix + *genus* race (646). The givenness of "race" and designation of white and non-white is interesting to consider.

Chapter 6: Development, Discovery, and Disguise

1   Previous cards are inscribed with "The Ghostrider, Fernie, BC." These provide a thumbnail sketch of the curse story (see Introduction) and mention its lifting by the "Kootenay Indian Band in 1964." The shadow is presented as "the Ghost of Captain Fernie," who "must flee the angry Indian Chief and his daughter."

2   In 1998 a seasonal ski pass sold for $599. I heard many parents of young families comment on their children's exclusion from the social world of skiing because they are unable to afford gear and the lift tickets.

3   In Greek mythology, Zeus was regarded to be the "divinity of the sky, the rain and the thunder" (Frazer 1922:159). Ancient Italians and Greeks performed rituals and prayed to him for rain (159).

4   Ski-run names, in some cases, depict the internationalism of skiing: Kangaroo, Wallaby, and Boomerang reflect what some residents have called the latest "wave of Australian immigrants." Other runs are named after wildflowers and animals; a few follow from the old names of ridges and mountains; some are the first names of particular individuals.

5   Scholars present various interpretations. He is the stepson of the sky god, Thor, who reigns through thunder and lightning (Branston 1980:121). Guerber (1912:139) cites Sif as his father, "one of the dreaded frost giants." According to Branston (1980:122), Sif was one of Thor's wives, "the golden-haired fertility goddess, the emblem of the ripe cornfield."

6   The *Eddas* constitute the earliest written works on Norse mythology; one is a collection of poems by unknown writers, and the other is the *Prose Edda*, authored in 1241 by Icelander Snorri Sturluson (Branston 1980:26).

7   Guerber's work (1912:xi) is illustrative of another era in which Nordic superiority was becoming established: "It may safely be asserted that the Edda is as rich in the essentials of national romance and race-imagination, rugged though it be, as the more graceful and idyllic mythology of the South."

8   Kimberley is an interesting example of another town that consciously transformed itself into a destination ski resort after the 1990 closure of the Cominco zinc mines. Agnes Koch (1996) provides an interesting analysis of the process of "Bavarianization" undertaken by this community in the late '70s to lure tourists.

9   One woman explained to me how "habitat" was used in public debates to disguise class discrimination in one suburb. A proposal for a "low-income housing project" was floated for public discussion. Residents in the district banded together and scripted a petition against the proposal, arguing that the housing would destroy the greenbelt and threaten wildlife habitat.

10   The men were Australians who asserted "squatters rights." They were not charged. The story offered implicit kudos for their ingenuity.

11   "Local" should be viewed as an "ideal type," loaded with assumptions about the flow of meaning through face-to-face interactions within territorially defined spaces (Hannertz 1990:238-239).

12   Hal Rothman (1998:19-20) describes "travellers" as an identity category, a "marker of belonging" for those who "collect the difference embodied in travel experience."

13   Ulf Hannertz (1990:239) identifies "cosmopolitans" with a "coexistence of cultures within the individual experience." These people are characterized by their mobility, which allows them to participate in transnational "networks of meaning" (239).

14   In 1969 the Criminal Law Amendment Act (1968-69, SC 1968-69, Chap. 38, s.7) decriminalized sexual practices between individuals of the same sex in Canada.

15   I contacted a number of people in Fernie who were recommended to me as "openly gay" members of the community. It became clear very quickly that several of these people were not aware of this designation, nor were they interested in speaking about their ideas of difference as it pertains to sexuality. One couple met with me, at their insistence, in a busy cafe, where we were unable to speak openly. I telephoned a regional resource centre for contact numbers of gay and lesbian groups in the area. I was told that the number was "hidden somewhere," then that it was "out of date" and could they get back to me. The woman asked me if it would be "safe" to leave a message on my telephone and wished me a sincere "good luck."

16   When I asked one man what the name meant, he exclaimed defensively: "I came here to ski. I didn't come for the girls." The term refers to the noticeably higher number of men than women in town.

17   Over New Year's 1998, an out-of-province man was violently beaten by locals.

Chapter 7: One Step Beyond

1   No author is cited on this sheet. I received another copy of this ballad signed by Mae Turner, "with apologies to those who know the legend better than I." I do not know what route this work took to enter the school system in Fernie or who this writer is. Her nod to local knowledge is important to note.

2   On a return visit to Fernie in the summer of 2000, I was surprised to hear the testimonies of people now using magnets as a form of healing. They wore them in the soles of their shoes, on eyeglass frames, and stitched into their clothing; some had them attached to wheelchairs and sofas; others lined their mattresses with magnets. Healing or alleviation of every ailment was aided by the use of these restorative metals. I heard no talk of animal magnetism, but the theory of balancing flows seemed consistent.

3   Bill appears to be a hacker who "has made it possible to store Pokémon electronically." Professor Oak provides "consultant services," Kurt is a "Pokéball craftsman," and Professor Elm is "the rising star in Pokémon research" (Nintendo 2000:6-7).

4   I was told that it is common to use "cheats" from the Internet in order to reduce the time it takes to learn information. With "cheats," people who are renting RPGs over the weekend are able to play immediately at higher levels.

5   I heard many old-timers ascribe to Doukhobors essentialized features of the terrorist, in combination with judgments of morality based on forms of protest used by an offshoot sect called the Sons of Freedom. During the time I was in Fernie, an advertisement appeared each week in the *East Kootenay Weekly*. It was a call for people to join a group action suit seeking compensation from the government for Doukhobor children's forced attendance at residential schools.

6   Jaffray is a lumber town approximately twenty minutes' drive west of Fernie. It was established around the turn of the century. Now it is described by many in Fernie as a "Mormon" community.

7   During the 1920s the American Ku Klux Klan was perceived by its members as an "ordinary, unremarkable social club" (Blee 1993:601). As Kathleen Blee (601) notes, its ideology was infused throughout everyday life, the institutions and events of common communities. Under the headline "KKK in Fernie," the following appeared in 1927. "An effort is being made to form a branch of the Ku Klux Klan in Fernie. A large number of invitations to join have been sent out, but the citizens generally in this community have little use for an organization of this type" (*FFP* 13 July 1927).

8   Stanley Barrett (1991:90) lists other elements as anti-communism, anti-liberalism, and racism. "Anti-liberalism attacks a whole range of issues associated with social change and presumed moral decay ... homosexuality, drugs, pornography, modern art and modern music" (90). Supremacists rally under the assumption that "whites" risk "race suicide" through "non-Aryan" immigration and miscegenation (91).

9   In 1996 sexual orientation was added to the Canadian Human Rights Act as a "prohibited ground of discrimination" (www.ilga.org). British Columbia included "protection from discrimination on grounds of sexual orientation" in its anti-discrimination legislation in 1992 (ibid.).

10   Like legend, myth has been greatly debated. In contrast to legend, characters and events in mythology are set outside historical time, and the content refers to origins and transformations linked symbolically to a particular cosmology (P. Cohen 1969:337).

References

Abrahams, Roger
  1976   The Complex Relations of Simple Forms. In *Folklore Genre*s, edited by Dan Ben-Amos, 193-214. Austin: University of Texas Press.
  1992   The Past in the Presence: An Overview of Folkloristics in the Late Twentieth Century. In *Folklore Processed: In Honour of Lauri Honko,* edited by R. Kvideland, 32-51. Helsinki: Studia Fennica.

Absalom, Roger
  1999   Peasant Memory and the Italian Resistance 1943-1945. In *Italian Fascism: History, Memory and Representation,* edited by R. Bosworth and P. Dogliani, 31-44. New York: St. Martin's Press.

Abu-Lughod, Lila
  1991   Writing against Culture. In *Recapturing Anthropology,* edited by R. Fox, 137-162. Santa Fe, NM: School of American Research Press.

Ackelsberg, Martha
  1992   Mujeres Libres: The Preservation of Memory under the Politics of Repression in Spain. In *Memory and Totalitarianism,* edited by L. Passerini, 125-143. Oxford: Oxford University Press.

Allport, G.W.
  1979   *The Nature of Prejudice.* Cambridge, MA: Addison Wesley.

American Anthropological Association
  1998   AAA Statement on Race. *American Anthropology Newsletter,* September.

Appadurai, Arjun
  1991   Global Ethnoscapes: Notes and Queries for a Transnational Anthropology. In *Recapturing Anthropology,* edited by R. Fox, 191-210. Santa Fe, NM: School of American Research Press.

Arlacchi, Pino
  1983   *Mafia, Peasants and Great Estates: Society in Traditional Calabria.* Translated by Jonathan Steinberg. New York: Cambridge University Press.

Armstrong, Jeanette (editor)
  1993   *Looking at the Words of Our People: First Nations Analysis of Literature.* Penticton, BC: Theytus Books.

Avery, Donald
1979   *"Dangerous Foreigners": European Immigrant Workers and Labour Radicalism in Canada 1896-1932.* Toronto: McClelland and Stewart.

Baker, Paul
1955   *The Forgotten Kutenai.* Boise, ID: Mountain States Press.

Bakhtin, Mikhail Mikhailovich
1981   *The Dialogic Imagination.* Edited by M. Holquist. Austin: University of Texas Press.

Balibar, Etienne
1991   Is There a Neo-Racism? In *Race, Nation, Class: Ambiguous Identities,* edited by E. Balibar and I. Wallerstein, 17-27. New York: Verso.

Balibar, Etienne, and Immanuel Wallerstein (editors)
1991   *Race, Nation, Class: Ambiguous Identities.* New York: Verso.

Banton, Michael
1987   The Classification of Races in Europe and North America 1700-1850. *International Social Science Journal* 39(1):45-60.

Barkhouse, Joyce
1989   *George Dawson: The Little Giant.* Toronto: Natural Heritage.

Barrett, Stanley
1991   White Supremists and Neo-Fascists: Laboratories for the Analysis of Racism in Wider Society. In *Racism in Canada,* edited by O. McKague, 85-99. Saskatoon, SK: Fifth House.

Barth, Frederick
1969   *Ethnic Groups and Boundaries: The Social Organization of Cultural Difference.* Boston: Little, Brown.
1995   *Balinese Worlds.* Chicago: University of Chicago Press.

Barton, Josef
1975   *Peasants and Strangers: Italians, Rumanians and Slovaks in an American City, 1890-1950.* Cambridge, MA: Harvard University Press.

Barzun, Jacques
1937   *Race: A Study in Superstition.* New York: Harper and Row.

Baskin, John
1981   Foreword. In *Prairie Fires and Paper Moons: The American Photographic Postcard 1900-1920,* edited by H. Morgan and A. Brown, vii-xiii. Boston: David Godine.

Basso, Keith H.
1979   *Portraits of "The Whiteman": Linguistic Play and Cultural Symbols among the Western Apache.* Cambridge: Cambridge University Press.
1996   *Wisdom Sits in Places: Landscape and Language among the Western Apaches.* Albuquerque: University of New Mexico Press.

Bauman, Richard
1986   *Story, Performance, and Event: Contextual Studies of Oral Narrative.* New York: Cambridge University Press.

Bauman, Richard (editor)
1992   *Folklore, Cultural Performances and Popular Entertainments.* Oxford: Oxford University Press.

Ben-Amos, Dan (editor)
1976   *Folklore Genres*. Austin: University of Texas Press.

Bendix, Regina, and Barbro Klein
1993   Foreigners and Foreignness in Europe: Expressive Culture in Transnational Encounters. *Journal of Folklore Research* 30(1):1-14.

Bendyshe, T.
1863   The History of Anthropology. In *Memoirs Read before the Anthropological Society of London*. Vol. 1, 335-459. London: Trubner and Co.

Bennett, Gillian
1988   Legend: Performance and Truth. In *Monsters with Iron Teeth*. Perspectives on Contemporary Legend Series, edited by G. Bennett and P. Smith, 3:13-36. Sheffield: University of Sheffield Press.

Bennett, Gillian, and Paul Smith (editors)
1988   *Monsters with Iron Teeth*. Perspectives on Contemporary Legend Series, vol 3. Sheffield: University of Sheffield Press.

Berkhofer, Robert F.
1979   *The White Man's Indian: Images of the American Indian from Columbus to the Present*. New York: Vintage Books.

Bieder, Robert
1986   *Science Encounters the Indian, 1820-1880: The Early Years of American Ethnology*. Norman: University of Oklahoma Press.

Blee, Kathleen
1993   Evidence, Empathy, and Ethics: Lessons from Oral Histories of the Klan. *Journal of American History* September:596-606.

Blinkhorn, Martin
1984   *Mussolini and Fascist Italy*. New York: Methuen.

Boas, Franz
1908   Changes in Immigrant Body Form. Reprinted in *A Franz Boas Reader: The Shaping of American Anthropology, 1883-1911*, edited by G. Stocking, 202-214, Selection 29. Chicago: University of Chicago Press.
1918   *Kutenai Tales*. Smithsonian Institution Bureau of American Ethnology Bulletin 59.
1928   *Anthropology and Modern Life*. New York: W.W. Norton.

Bogdan, Robert
1988   *Freak Show: Presenting Human Oddities for Amusement and Profit*. Chicago: University of Chicago Press.

Böhning, W.R.
1972   *The Migration of Workers in the United Kingdom and the European Community*. London: Oxford University Press.

Boon, J.A.
1982   *Other Tribes, Other Scribes: Symbolic Anthropology in the Comparative Study of Cultures, Histories, Religions, and Texts*. New York: Cambridge University Press.

Borneman, John
  1992   State, Territory, and Identity Formation in the Postwar Berlins, 1945-1989. *Cultural Anthropology* 7:45-62.

Bosworth, R.J.B., and Patrizia Dogliani (editors)
  1999   *Italian Fascism: History, Memory and Representation.* New York: St. Martin's Press.

Bourget, Marie-Noelle, Lucette Valensi, and Nathan Wachtel (editors)
  1990   *Between Memory and History.* London: Harwood.

Bowen, Lynne
  1998   Friendly Societies in Nanaimo: The British Tradition of Self-Help in a Canadian Coal-Mining Community. *BC Studies* 118:67-92.

Brace, C.L.
  1964   On the Race Concept. *Current Anthropology* 5(4):313-320.

Branston, Brian
  1980   *Gods of the North.* New York: Thames and Hudson.

Braroe, N.W.
  1975   *Indian and White: Self-Image and Interaction in a Canadian Plains Community.* Stanford: Stanford University Press.

Brison, Karen
  1992   *Just Talk: Gossip, Meetings, and Power in a Papua New Guinea Village.* Berkeley: University of California Press.

British Columbia
  1899   Report of the Royal Commission on Mining Conditions in British Columbia: Evidence. R.C. Clute, commissioner. Toronto: Micromedia Ltd.

British Columbia Ministry of Education
  1998   School Curriculum. Vancouver: BC Ministry of Education.

British Columbia Treaty Commission
  1996   *British Columbia Treaty Commission Annual Report 1995-1996.* Vancouver: BC Treaty Commission.

Brizinski, Peggy
  1989   *Knots in a String: An Introduction to Native Studies in Canada.* Saskatoon: University of Saskatchewan Press.

Bromley, Yu
  1987   Anthropology, Ethnology and Ethnic and Racial Prejudice. *International Social Science Journal* 39(1):31-43.

Brook, Paula
  1997   Freedom's Just Another Word ... for Saying 6 Million Didn't Die. *Saturday Night* November.

Brues, Alice
  1964   Statement on Statements on Racism. *Current Anthropology* 5(2):107-108.

Bruner, Edward
1986   Ethnography as Narrative. In *The Anthropology of Experience,* edited by V. Turner and E. Bruner, 139-155. Chicago: University of Illinois Press.

Bruner, Edward (editor)
1984   *Text, Play and Story: The Construction and Reconstruction of Self and Society.* 1983 Proceedings of the American Ethnological Society. Prospect Heights, IL: Waveland Press.

Bruner, Edward, and Phyllis Gorfain
1984   Dialogic Narration and the Paradoxes of Masada. In *Text, Play and Story: The Construction and Reconstruction of Self and Society,* edited by E. Bruner, 56-79. Prospect Heights, IL: Waveland Press.

Brunvand, Jan
1971   Modern Legends of Mormondom, or Supernaturalism Is Alive and Well in Salt Lake City. In *American Folk Legend: A Symposium,* edited by W. Hand, 185-202. Berkeley: University of California Press.

Brunvand, Jan (editor)
1996   *American Folklore: An Encyclopedia.* New York: Garland.

Butler, Judith
1990   Gender Trouble, Feminist Theory, and Psychoanalytic Discourse. In *Feminism/ Postmodernism,* edited by L. Nicholson, 324-340. New York: Routledge.

Canada. Department of Indian Affairs and Northern Development
1985   *Indian Act RSC 1985.* Ottawa: Government of Canada.
1995   *Aboriginal Self-Government: Executive Summary.* Ottawa: DIAND.
1998   *Statement of Reconciliation.* 7 January 1998. Ottawa: Government of Canada.

Canada. Department of Labour
1905   *Report of Commissioner and Evidence: Immigration of Italian Labourers and the Alleged Fraudulent Practices of Employment Agencies.* Sessional Paper No. 36b. Ottawa: Department of Labour.

Canada. Royal Commission on Bilingualism and Biculturalism
1970   Historical Background. Reprinted in *Immigration and the Rise of Multiculturalism,* edited by H. Palmer, 17-31. Vancouver: Copp Clarke, 1975.

Cardinal, Harold
1969/   *The Unjust Society.* Edmonton: M.G. Hurtig. Repr. Vancouver: Douglas and
1999   McIntyre.

Carter, David
1980   *Behind Canadian Barbed Wire: Alien, Refugee and Prisoner of War Camps in Canada 1914-1916.* Calgary: Tumbleweed Press.

Chamberlain, Alexander
1891   The Aryan Element in Indian Dialects I. *Canadian Indian* February.

Cielo, Astra
1918   *Signs, Omens and Superstitions.* London: Skeffington.

Clifford, James
1988   *The Predicament of Culture: Twentieth-Century Ethnography, Literature, and Art.* Cambridge, MA: Harvard University Press.

1997   *Routes: Travel and Translation in the Late Twentieth Century.* Cambridge, MA: Harvard University Press.

Clifford, James, and George Marcus (editors)
1986   *Writing Culture: The Poetics and Politics of Ethnography.* Berkeley: University of California Press.

Clifton, James
1990   *The Invented Indian: Cultural Fictions and Government Policies.* New Brunswick, NJ: Transaction Publishers.

Cohen, David
1989   The Undefining of Oral Tradition. *Ethnohistory* 36(1):9-18.
1994   *The Combing of History.* Chicago: University of Chicago Press.

Cohen, Percy
1969   Theories of Myth. *Malinowski Memorial Lecture at London School of Economics.* 8 May 1969. London: London School of Economics.

Cohen, Ronald
1978   Ethnicity: Problem and Focus in Anthropology. *Annual Review of Anthropology* 7:379-403.

Corbey, Raymond
1995   Ethnographic Showcases, 1870-1930. In *The Decolonization of Imagination,* edited by J. Pieterse and B. Parekh, 57-80. London: Zed Books.

Crapanzano, Vincent
1986   *Waiting: The Whites of South Africa.* New York: Random House.

Crosby, Marcia
1991   Construction of the Imaginary Indian. In *Vancouver Anthology: The Institutional Politics of Art,* edited by Stan Douglas, 267-291. Vancouver: Talonbooks.
1997   Lines, Lineage and Lies, or Borders, Boundaries and Bullshit. In *Nations in Urban Landscapes: Faye HeavySheild [sic], Shelley Nino and Eric Robertson.* Texts by Marcia Crosby and Paul Chaat Smith. Guest curated by Marcia Crosby, 23-30. Vancouver: Contemporary Art Gallery.

Crowsnest Pass Historical Society
1979   *Crowsnest and Its People.* Coleman, AB: Crowsnest Pass Historical Society.
1990   *Photo Companion: Crowsnest and Its People.* Coleman, AB: Crowsnest Pass Historical Society.

Cruikshank, Julie
1994   Oral Tradition and Oral History: Reviewing Some Issues. *Canadian Historical Review* 75(3):403-418.
1997   Negotiating with Narrative: Establishing Cultural Identity at the Yukon International Storytelling Festival. *American Anthropologist* 99(1):56-69.
1998   *The Social Life of Stories: Narrative and Knowledge in the Yukon Territory.* Lincoln/Vancouver: University of Nebraska Press/UBC Press.

Culhane, Dara
1987   *An Error in Judgement: The Politics of Medical Care in an Indian/White Community.* Vancouver: Talonbooks.
1998   *The Pleasure of the Crown: Anthropology, Law and First Nations.* Burnaby: Talonbooks.

Dafoe, Chris
1999   The Other Side of the Mountains. *Globe and Mail* 9 January:A15.

Damm, Kateri
1993   Says Who: Colonialism, Identity and Defining Indigenous Literature. In *Looking at the Words of Our People: First Nations Analysis of Literature*, edited by J. Armstrong, 9-25. Penticton: Theytus Books.

Danet, Brenda, and Bryna Bogoch
1992   "Whoever Alters This, May God Turn His Face From Him on the Day of Judgment": Curses in Anglo-Saxon Legal Documents. *Journal of American Folklore* 105(416):132-165.

Darnton, Robert
1984   *The Great Cat Massacre and Other Episodes in French Cultural History*. New York: Basic Books.

Das, Veena
1998   Specificities: Official Narratives, Rumour and the Social Production of Hate. *Social Identities* 4(1):109-131.

Davidson, H.R. Ellis
1993   *The Lost Beliefs of Northern Europe*. New York: Routledge.

Davis, Owen
1999   *Witchcraft, Magic and Culture 1736-1951*. New York: Manchester University Press.

Dawson, Brian
1995   *Crowsnest: An Illustrated History and Guide to the Crowsnest Pass*. Vancouver: Altitude.

Dawson, George
1879   Sketches of the Past and Present Condition of the Indians of Canada. *Canadian Naturalist* 9(3).
1883   *Evidence of Dr. Dawson before the Immigration and Colonization Committee of the House of Commons*. Ottawa: Maclean, Roger.
1892   *Elementary Geography of the British Colonies*. New York: Macmillan.

Deloria, Vine
1969   *Custer Died for Your Sins: An Indian Manifesto*. Norman: University of Oklahoma Press.

DeSmet, Pierre-Jean
1905   *Life, Letters and Travels of Father Pierre-Jean De Smet, S.J.*, edited by H. Chittendon and A. Richardson. Vols. 3 and 4. New York: Kraus Reprint.

Diamond, Stanley
1964   Reply to Statement on Statements on Racism. *Current Anthropology* 5(2):108.

Dimen-Schein, Muriel
1977   *The Anthropological Imagination*. Toronto: McGraw-Hill.

Dogliani, Patrizia
1999   Constructing Memory and Anti-Memory: The Monumental Representation of Fascism and Its Denial in Republican History. In *Italian Fascism: History, Memory and Representation*, edited by R. Bosworth and P. Dogliani, 11-30. New York: St. Martin's Press.

Dominguez, Virginia
   1992   Invoking Culture: The Messy Side of "Cultural Politics." *South Atlantic Quarterly* 91(1):19-42.

Dominy, Michele
   1995   White Settler Assertions of Native Status. *American Ethnologist* 22(2):358-374.

Douglas, Mary
   1973   *Natural Symbols: Explorations in Cosmology.* London: Barrie and Jenkins.

Douglas, Stan (editor)
   1991   *Vancouver Anthology: The Institutional Politics of Art.* Vancouver: Talonbooks.

Duff, Wilson
   1969   *The Indian History of British Columbia.* Vol. 1, *The Impact of the White Man.* Anthropology In British Columbia Memoir No. 5. Victoria: Royal British Columbia Museum.

Dundes, Alan
   1971a On the Psychology of Legend. In *American Folk Legend: A Symposium,* edited by W. Hand, 21-36. Berkeley: University of California Press.
   1971b A Study of Ethnic Slurs: The Jew and the Polack in the United States. *Journal of American Folklore* 84(332):186-203.

Dundes, Alan (editor)
   1981   *The Evil Eye: A Folklore Casebook.* New York: Garland.

Dyck, Noel
   1986   Negotiating the Indian "Problem." *Culture* 6(1):31-41.

Dyck, Noel, and James Waldram (editors)
   1993   *Anthropology, Public Policy and Native Peoples in Canada.* Montreal: McGill-Queen's University Press.

Elder, Charles, and Roger Cobb
   1983   *The Political Uses of Symbols.* New York: Longman.

Epstein, Steven
   1994   A Queer Encounter: Sociology and the Study of Sexuality. *Sociological Theory* 12(2):188-202.

Evans-Pritchard, E.E.
   1937   *Witchcraft, Oracles and Magic among the Azande.* Oxford: Clarendon Press.

Fabian, Johannes
   1990   Presence and Representation: The Other and Anthropological Writing. *Critical Inquiry* 16(4):753-773.

Fanon, Franz
   1966   *The Wretched of the Earth.* New York: Grove Press.

Favret-Saada, Jeanne
   1977   *Deadly Words: Witchcraft in the Bocage.* New York: Cambridge University Press.

Featherstone, Mike (editor)
   1990   *Global Culture: Nationalism, Globalization and Modernity.* Newbury Park, CA: Sage Publications.

Fernie and District Historical Society (editors)
1977   *Backtracking*. Fernie: Fernie and District Historical Society.

Fernie Free Press
1898- [From microfiche – Fernie Public Library]
2001
1994   *Historical Booklet to Commemorate the 90th Anniversary of Fernie*. Fernie: *Fernie Free Press*.
1998   *100 Years, 100 Stories: 100th Anniversary*. Fernie: *Fernie Free Press*.

Fidler, Peter
1793   *Journal of Journey Overland from Buckingham House to the Rocky Mountains in 1792 and 1793*. Winnipeg: Manitoba Provincial Archives.

Fiume, Giovanna
1996   Cursing, Poisoning and Feminine Morality: The Case of the "Vinegar Hag" in Late Eighteenth-Century Palermo. *Social Anthropology* 4(1):117-132.

Fox, Richard (editor)
1991   *Recapturing Anthropology*. Santa Fe, NM: School of American Research Press.

Francis, Daniel
1992   *The Imaginary Indian: The Image of the Indian in Canadian Culture*. Vancouver: Arsenal Pulp Press.

Frankenberg, Ruth
1993   *White Women, Race Matters: The Social Construction of Whiteness*. Minneapolis: University of Minnesota Press.

Frazer, James
1922   *The Golden Bough: A Study in Magic and Religion*. Ware, Hertfordshire: Wordsworth.

Fulford, Robert
2001   Robert Fulford's column about Doug Collins and Allan Fotheringham. *National Post* 3 November. <www.robertfulford.com>.

Fuller, Robert
1982   *Mesmerism and the American Cure of Souls*. Philadelphia: University of Pennsylvania Press.

Furniss, Elizabeth
1998   Pioneers, Progress, and the Myth of the Frontier: The Landscape of Public History in Rural British Columbia. *BC Studies* 115/116:7-41.
1999   *The Burden of History: Colonialism and the Frontier Myth in a Rural Canadian Community*. Vancouver: UBC Press.

Gaudet, Marcia
1988   The Curse of St. John the Baptist. In *Monsters with Iron Teeth*. Perspectives on Contemporary Legend Series, edited by G. Bennett and P. Smith, 3:201-210. Sheffield: University of Sheffield Press.

Geary, Christraud, and Virginia-Lee Webb
1998   *Delivering Views: Distant Cultures in Early Postcards*. Washington: Smithsonian Institution Press.

Georges, Robert
  1971   The General Concept of Legend: Some Assumptions to Be Re-examined and Reassessed. In *American Folk Legend: A Symposium,* edited by W. Hand, 1-20. Berkeley: University of California Press.

Ginsburg, Faye
  1989   Dissonance and Harmony: The Symbolic Function of Abortion in Activists' Life Stories. In *Interpreting Women's Lives: Feminist Theory and Personal Narratives,* edited by Personal Narratives Group, 59-84. Indianapolis: Indiana University Press.
  1994   Culture/Media: A Mild Polemic. *Anthropology Today* 10(2):5-15.

Gluckman, Max
  1963   Gossip and Scandal. *Current Anthropology* 4(3):307-315.
  1968   Psychological, Sociological and Anthropological Explanations of Witchcraft and Gossip: A Clarification. *Man* 3:20-34.

Goodwin, Marjorie
  1982   Instigating: Storytelling as Social Process. *American Ethnologist* 9(4):799-819.

Görög-Karady, Veronica
  1992   Ethnic Stereotypes and Folklore: The Jew in Hungarian Oral Literature. In *Folklore Processed: In Honour of Lauri Honko,* edited by R. Kvideland, 114-126. Helsinki: Studia Fennica.

Gramsci, Antonio
  1995   *Prison Notebooks.* Vol. 1, *1929-1933.* Edited by J. Buttigieg. Translated by J. Buttigieg and A. Callari. New York: Columbia University Press.

Great Britain
  1909   *The Problem of the Feeble-Minded: An Abstract of the Report of the Royal Commission on the Care and Control of the Feeble-Minded.* London: P.S. King and Son.

Guerber, H.A.
  1912   *Myths of the Norsemen from the Eddas and Sagas.* London: George Harrap and Co.

Guerra, Elda
  1999   Memory and Representations of Fascism: Female Autobiographical Narratives. In *Italian Fascism: History, Memory and Representation,* edited by R. Bosworth and P. Dogliani, 195-215. New York: St. Martin's Press.

Gupta, Akhil, and James Ferguson (editors)
  1997   *Culture, Power, Place: Explorations in Critical Anthropology.* Durham: Duke University Press.

Hallowell, Irving
  1963   American Indians, White and Black: The Phenomenon of Transculturation. *Current Anthropology* 4(5):519-531.

Hand, Wayland (editor)
  1971   *American Folk Legend: A Symposium.* Berkeley: University of California Press.

Hannertz, Ulf
  1990   Cosmopolitans and Locals in World Culture. In *Global Culture: Nationalism, Globalization and Modernity,* edited by Mike Featherstone, 237-257. Newbury Park, CA: Sage Publications.

Harraway, Donna
1991   *Simians, Cyborgs, and Women: The Reinvention of Women*. New York: Routledge.

Harrowitz, Nancy
1994   *Antisemitism, Misogyny, and the Logic of Cultural Difference: Cesare Lombroso and Matilde Serao*. Lincoln: University of Nebraska Press.

Hedican, Edward
1995   *Applied Anthropology in Canada: Understanding Aboriginal Issues*. Toronto: University of Toronto Press.

Hill, Jonathan (editor)
1988   *Rethinking History and Myth: Indigenous South American Perspectives on the Past*. Urbana, IL: University of Illinois Press.

Hobsbawm, Eric
1989   Mass-Producing Traditions: Europe 1870-1914. In *The Invention of Tradition*, edited by E. Hobsbawm and T. Ranger, 263-307. New York: Cambridge University Press.
1994   *Age of Extremes: The Short Twentieth Century 1914-1991*. London: Abacus.

Hobsbawm, Eric, and Terrence Ranger (editors)
1989   *The Invention of Tradition*. New York: Cambridge University Press.

Hodgen, M.T.
1964   *Early Anthropology in the Sixteenth and Seventeenth Centuries*. Philadelphia: University of Pennsylvania Press.

Holden, Madronna
1976   Making All the Crooked Ways Straight: The Satirical Portrait of Whites in Coast Salish Folklore. *Journal of American Folklore* 89:271-293.

Holquist, Michael (editor)
1981   Introduction. *The Dialogic Imagination*. Austin: University of Texas Press.

Holy Family Church
1988   *Seventy-Five Diamond Years*. Fernie: Holy Family Parish.

hooks, bell
1990   *Yearning: Race, Gender, and Cultural Politics*. Toronto: Between the Lines.
1992   *Black Looks: Race and Representation*. Toronto: Between the Lines.

Hutcheson, Sydney
1973   *The Curse and Other Stories from the Wella Board*. Fernie: Fernie and District Historical Society.

Huxley, Julian
1964   Reply to On the Race Concept. *Current Anthropology* 5(4):316-317.

Hymes, Dell (editor)
1974   *Reinventing Anthropology*. New York: Pantheon Books.

Ignatieff, Michael
2000   *The Rights Revolution: CBC Massey Lectures Series*. Toronto: Anansi Press.

Indian and Northern Affairs
  1978   Act for Better Protection of the Lands and Property of the Indians in Lower
         Canada (1850). Reprinted in *The Historical Development of the Indian Act.* Ottawa:
         Treaties and Historical Research Centre.

Ingraham, Chrys
  1994   The Heterosexual Imaginary: Feminist Sociology and Theories of Gender. *Soci-
         ological Theory* 12(2):203-219.

Jackson, Michael (editor)
  1996   *Things As They Are: New Directions in Phenomenological Anthropology.* Indi-
         anapolis: Indiana University Press.

Jay, Timothy
  1996   Cursing. In *American Folklore: An Encyclopedia,* edited by J. Brunvand, 185-186.
         New York: Garland.

Jobes, Gertrude
  1962   *Dictionary of Mythology, Folklore and Symbols.* New York: Scarecrow Press.

Johnson, Olga Weyermeyer
  1969   *Flathead and Kootenay: The Rivers, the Tribe and the Region's Traders.* Glendale,
         CA: Arthur H. Clarke.

Jones, Louis
  1981   The Evil Eye among European-Americans. In *The Evil Eye: A Folklore Casebook,*
         edited by A. Dundes, 150-167. New York: Garland.

Kallen, Evelyn
  1982   *Ethnicity and Human Rights in Canada.* Toronto: Gage.

Kamenetsky, Christa
  1984   *Children's Literature in Hitler's Germany: The Cultural Policy of National Socialism.*
         Athens: Ohio University Press.

Kecskemeti, P. (editor)
  1952   *Essays on the Sociology of Knowledge.* London: Routledge.

Kerr, James
  1980   The Great Landslide at Frank, NWT (1903). In *Crowsnest and Its People,* edited
         by Crowsnest Pass Historical Society, 57-64. Calgary: Crowsnest Pass Historical
         Society.

Khubova, Daria, Andrei Ivankiev, and Tonia Sharova
  1992   After Glasnost: Oral History in the Soviet Union. In *Memory and Totalitarian-
         ism,* edited by L. Passerini, 89-101. Oxford: Oxford University Press.

Kirkham, Della
  1998   The Reform Party of Canada: A Discourse on Race, Ethnicity and Equality. In
         Racism and Social Inequality in Canada, edited by V. Satzewich, 243-267. Toronto:
         Thompson Educational Publishing.

Klein, Kerwin
  1992   Frontier Tales: The Narrative Construction of Cultural Borders in Twentieth-
         Century California. *Comparative Studies of Society and History* 34(4):464-490.

Koch, Agnes
1996　*Kimberley in Transition: A Case Study of Sociocultural Change in a Mining Community.* Cranbrook: College of the Rockies.

Kolfage, Don
1967　Indian Woman's Curse Believed Responsible for Fernie Fire. *Nelson Daily News* May 26:11.

Kootenai Cultural Committee
1997　*Ktunaxa Legends.* Pablo, MT: Salish Kootenai College Press.

Korson, George
1938　*Minstrels of the Mine Patch: Songs and Stories of the Anthracite Industry.* Philadelphia: University of Pennsylvania Press.
1965　*Coal Dust on the Fiddle: Songs and Stories of the Bituminous Industry.* Hatboro, PA: Folklore Associates.

Ktunaxa-Kinbasket Tribal Council
1992　*Ktunaxa Land Claims Presentation.* Video with an introduction by Chief Sophie Pierre. Narrated by Lexine Phillipps. St. Mary's: Ktunaxa-Kinbasket Tribal Administration.

Kuklick, Henrika
1991　*The Savage Within: The Social History of British Anthropology, 1885-1945.* Cambridge: Cambridge University Press.

Kuper, Leo
1981　*Genocide: Its Political Use in the Twentieth Century.* New Haven: Yale University Press.

Kvideland, Reimund (editor)
1992　*Folklore Processed: In Honour of Lauri Honko.* Helsinki: Studia Fennica.

Laclau, Ernesto
1996　Universalism, Particularism, and the Question of Identity. In *The Politics of Difference: Ethnic Premises in a World of Power,* edited by E. Wilmsen and P. McAllister, 45-58. Chicago: University of Chicago Press.

Langford, Tom
1998　"Workers of the World Unite": Celebrating May Day. In *The Forgotten Side of the Border: British Columbia's Elk Valley and Crowsnest Pass,* edited by W. Norton and N. Miller, 48-57. Kamloops, BC: Plateau Press.

Langham, Ian
1981　*The Building of British Social Anthropology: W.H.R. Rivers and His Cambridge Disciples in the Development of Kinship Studies, 1898-1931.* London: D. Reidel.

Leach, Edmund
1954　*Political Systems of Highland Burma: A Study of Kachin Social Structure.* Cambridge: Harvard University Press.

Leff, Carol Skalnik
1988　*National Conflict in Czechoslovakia: The Making and Re-making of a State, 1918-1987.* Princeton: Princeton University Press.

Lehmann, Arthur
   1997   Eyes of the Ngangas: Ethnomedicine and Power in a Central African Repub-
          lic. In *Magic, Witchcraft and Religion: An Anthropological Study of the Supernat-
          ural,* edited by A. Lehmann and J. Myers, 138-146. Toronto: Mayfield.

Lehmann, Arthur, and James Myers (editors)
   1997   *Magic, Witchcraft and Religion: An Anthropological Study of the Supernatural.* 4th
          ed. Toronto: Mayfield.

Lessa, William, and Evon Vogt
   1979   Introduction: Magic, Witchcraft and Divination. In *Reader in Comparative
          Religion: An Anthropological Approach,* edited by W. Lessa and E. Vogt, 332-334.
          4th ed. San Francisco: Harper and Row.

Leydesdorff, Selma, Luisa Passerini, and Paul Thompson
   1996   Introduction. In *Gender and Memory,* edited by S. Leydesdorff, L. Passerini, and
          P. Thompson, 1-16. Oxford: Oxford University Press.

Li, Peter
   1988   *Ethnic Inequality in a Class Society.* Toronto: Wall and Thompson.

Linke, Uli
   1990   Folklore, Anthropology, and the Government of Social Life. *Comparative Study
          of Society and History* 32:117-148.
   1997   Gendered Difference, Violent Imagination: Blood, Race, Nation. *American
          Anthropologist* 99(3):559-573.

Lips, Julius
   1937   *The Savage Hits Back.* New Haven, CT: Yale University Press.

Lithman, Yngve
   1984   *The Community Apart: A Case Study of a Canadian Indian Reserve Community.*
          Winnipeg: University of Manitoba Press.

Lockhart, J.G.
   1938   *Curses, Lucks and Talismans.* London: Geoffrey Bles.

Lombardi-Satriani, Luigi
   1974   Folklore as Culture of Contestation. *Indiana University Folklore Institute Journal*
          11:99-121.

MacGregor, Gwen
   1997   *Fold It Up and Put It Away: Fernie's Curse.* Multimedia Installation. Lethbridge:
          Southern Alberta Art Gallery.

Mackenzie, John
   1984   *Propaganda and Empire: The Manipulation of British Public Opinion 1880-1960.*
          Manchester: Manchester University Press.

Mahon, Maureen
   2000   Black Like This: Race, Generation, and Rock in the Post-Civil Rights Era. *Amer-
          ican Ethnologist* 27(2):283-311.

Malinowski, Bronislaw
   1965   *Coral Gardens and Their Magic.* Vol. 2. Bloomington: Indiana University Press.

Malkki, Liisa
1997   National Geographic: The Rooting of Peoples and the Territorialization of National Identity among Scholars and Refugees. In *Culture, Power, Place: Explorations in Critical Anthropology*, edited by A. Gupta and J. Ferguson, 52-74. Durham: Duke University Press.

Mangan, Loretta
1977a   Devastation and Restoration. In *Backtracking*, edited by Fernie and District Historical Society, 25-51. Fernie: Fernie and District Historical Society.
1977b   Neighbouring Towns. In *Backtracking*, edited by Fernie and District Historical Society, 53-67. Fernie: Fernie and District Historical Society.

Mannheim, Karl
1952   The Problem of Generations. In *Essays on the Sociology of Knowledge*, edited by P. Kecskemeti, 276-320. London: Routledge.

Mazumdar, Pauline
1992   *Eugenics, Human Genetics and Human Failings: The Eugenics Society, Its Sources and Its Critics in Britain*. New York: Routledge.

McKague, Ormond (editor)
1991   *Racism in Canada*. Saskatoon: Fifth House.

McLaren, Angus
1990   *Our Own Master Race: Eugenics in Canada, 1885-1945*. Toronto: Oxford University Press.

McMaster, Gerald, and Lee-Ann Martin (editors)
1992   *Indigena: Contemporary Native Perspectives*. Hull: Canadian Museum of Civilization.

MEE
2000   Barbara Saint. In *Microsoft Encarta Encyclopaedia*. Microsoft Corporation.

Memmi, Albert
1968   *Colonizer and the Colonized*. New York: Orion Press.

Migliore, Sam
1997   *Mal'uocchiu: Ambiguity, Evil Eye, and the Language of Distress*. Toronto: University of Toronto Press.

Miles, Robert
1989   *Racism*. New York: Routledge.

Miller, Donald, and Richard Sharpless
1985   *The Kingdom of Coal: Work, Enterprise, and Ethnic Communities in the Mine Fields*. Philadelphia: University of Pennsylvania Press.

Miller, Naomi
1998   Michael Phillips: Prominent Kootenay Citizen. In *The Forgotten Side of the Border: British Columbia's Elk Valley and Crowsnest Pass*, edited by W. Norton and N. Miller, 29-39. Kamloops, BC: Plateau Press.

Mirzoeff, Nicholas (editor)
1998   *Visual Culture Reader*. New York: Routledge.

Montagu, A.
1972   *Statement on Race*. London: Oxford University Press.

Morgan, Hal, and Andreas Brown
1981   *Prairie Fires and Paper Moons: The American Photographic Postcard: 1900-1920*. Boston: David Godine.

Mullen, Patrick
1971   The Relationship of Legend and Folk Belief. *Journal of American Folklore* 84(334):406-413.

Muratorio, Blanca
1998   Indigenous Women's Identities and the Politics of Cultural Reproduction in the Ecuadorian Amazon. *American Anthropologist* 100(2):409-420.

Nicholson, Linda (editor)
1990   *Feminism/Postmodernism*. New York: Routledge.

Nintendo
2000   *Pokémon Official Nintendo Player's Guide: Gold/Silver Edition*. Redwood, CA: Nintendo of America.

Norris, Rosalie (editor and translator)
1981   *Customs and Habits of the Sicilian Peasants*. Original by Salvatore Salmone-Marino 1897. Toronto: Associated University Press.

Norton, Wayne, and Ella Verkerk
1998   Communities Divided: The Internment Camps of World War One. In *The Forgotten Side of the Border: British Columbia's Elk Valley and Crowsnest Pass,* edited by W. Norton and N. Miller, 66-92. Kamloops, BC: Plateau Press.

Norton, Wayne, and Tom Langford (editors)
2002   *A World Apart: The Crowsnest Communities of Alberta and British Columbia*. Kamloops, BC: Plateau Press.

Norton, Wayne, and Naomi Miller (editors)
1998   *The Forgotten Side of the Border: British Columbia's Elk Valley and Crowsnest Pass*. Kamloops, BC: Plateau Press.

Norval, Aletta
1996   Thinking Identities: Against a Theory of Ethnicity. In *Politics of Difference: Ethnic Premises in a World of Power,* edited by E. Wilmsen and P. McAllister, 59-70. Chicago: University of Chicago Press.

Okely, Judith
1996   *Own or Other Culture*. New York: Routledge.

Opie, Iona, and Moira Tatem
1990   *A Dictionary of Superstitions*. New York: Oxford University Press.

Ortner, Sherry
1998   Identities: The Hidden Life of Class. *Journal of Anthropological Research* 54(1):1-17.

Ouston, Rick
1998 B.C. Indian Chiefs Lay Claim to Entire Province, Resources. *Vancouver Sun* 2 February:1-2.

OED
1982 *The Concise Dictionary of Current English.* Oxford: Clarendon Press.

Paine, Robert
1968 What Is Gossip About? An Alternative Hypothesis. *Man* 2:278-285.

Paine, Robert (editor)
1985 *Advocacy and Anthropology: First Encounters.* St. John's: Memorial University Press.

Palmer, Howard
1975 Attitudes towards Immigration and Immigration Policy. In *Immigration and the Rise of Multiculturalism,* edited by H. Palmer, 16-21. Vancouver: Copp Clarke.
1982 *Patterns of Prejudice: A History of Nativism in Alberta.* Toronto: McClelland and Stewart.

Palmer, Howard (editor)
1975 *Immigration and the Rise of Multiculturalism.* Vancouver: Copp Clarke.

Palsson, Gisli (editor)
1993 *Beyond Boundaries: Understanding, Translation and Anthropological Discourse.* Oxford: Berg Publishers.

Passerini, Luisa (editor)
1992 *Memory and Totalitarianism.* Oxford: Oxford University Press.

Pauley, Bruce
1997 *Hitler, Stalin, and Mussolini: Totalitarianism in the Twentieth Century.* Wheeling, IL: Harlan Davidson.

Pearce, Roy Harvey
1953 *Savagism and Civilization: A Study of the Indian and the American Mind.* Berkeley: University of California Press.

Perry, Adele
1995 "Oh I'm Just Sick of the Faces of Men": Gender Imbalance, Race, Sexuality and Sociability in Nineteenth-Century BC. *BC Studies* 105-106:27-44.

Personal Narratives Group (editor)
1989 *Interpreting Women's Lives: Feminist Theory and Personal Narratives.* Indianapolis: Indiana University Press.

Phillips, Lloyd
1977 The Social Advancements. In *Backtracking,* edited by Fernie and District Historical Society, 69-97. Fernie: Fernie and District Historical Society.

Pieterse, Jan
1996 Varieties of Ethnic Politics and Ethnicity Discourse. In *The Politics of Difference: Ethnic Premises in a World of Power,* edited by E. Wilmsen and P. McAllister, 25-44. Chicago: University of Chicago Press.

Pieterse, Jan, and Leon Poliakov
1974   *The Aryan Myth: A History of Racist and Nationalist Ideas in Europe.* Translated by Edmund Howard. New York: Basic Books.

Porter, John
1965   *The Vertical Mosaic.* Toronto: University of Toronto Press.

Povinelli, Elizabeth
1994   Sexual Savages/Sexual Sovereignty: Australian Colonial Texts and the Post-Colonial Politics of Nationalism. *Diacritics* 24(2-3):122-150.
1995   "Do Rocks Listen?" The Cultural Politics of Apprehending Australian Aboriginal Labour. *American Anthropologist* 97(3):505-518.

Pratt, Mary-Louise
1986   Fieldwork in Common Places. In *Writing Culture: The Poetics and Politics of Ethnography,* edited by J. Clifford and E. Marcus, 27-50. Berkeley, CA: University of California Press.
1998   From the Victoria Nyanza to the Sheraton San Salvador. In *Visual Culture Reader,* edited by N. Mirzoeff, 263-272. New York: Routledge.

Provenzo, Eugene
1991   *Video Kids: Making Sense of Nintendo.* Cambridge, MA: Harvard University Press.

Rappaport, Roy
1992   Ritual. In *Folklore, Cultural Performances and Popular Entertainments,* edited by R. Bauman, 249-260. Oxford: Oxford University Press.

Ratch, Noel
1998   An Impossible Curse: The Ghostrider on Hosmer Mountain. In *The Forgotten Side of the Border: British Columbia's Elk Valley and Crowsnest Pass,* edited by W. Norton and N. Miller, 3-14. Kamloops, BC: Plateau Press.

Ray, Verne F.
1939   *Cultural Relations in the Plateau of Northwestern America.* Publication of the Frederick Webb Hodge Anniversary Publication Fund 3. Los Angeles: Southwest Museum.

Rich, E.E. (editor)
1947   *Part of Dispatch from George Simpson Esq. Governor of Rupert's Land to the Governor and Committee of the Hudson's Bay Company London.* Toronto: Champlain Society.

Richer, Stephen, and Lorna Weir (editors)
1995   Introduction. In *Beyond Political Correctness: Toward the Inclusive University,* edited by S. Richer and L. Weir, 3-22. Toronto: University of Toronto Press.

Rino, Luisa
2001   Fernie: Cinderella of the Kootenays. *Nuvo* 4(1):118-124.

Robertson, Leslie A.
1994   Poetics of Coexistence: Bloods, Saints and Scribes. MA thesis, Department of Anthropology, University of Calgary.

Roosens, Eugeen
1989   *Creating Ethnicity: The Process of Ethnogenesis.* Vol. 5, *Frontiers of Anthropology.* Newbury Park: Sage Publications.

Rosaldo, Renato
   1989   *Culture and Truth: The Remaking of Social Analysis.* Boston: Beacon Press.

Roseberry, William
   1996   Hegemony, Power, and Languages of Contention. In *The Politics of Difference: Ethnic Premises in a World of Power,* edited by E. Wilmsen and P. McAllister, 71-84. Chicago: University of Chicago Press.

Roseman, Marina
   1998   Singers of the Landscape: Song, History and Property Rights in the Malaysian Rainforest. *American Anthropologist* 100(1):106-121.

Rothman, Hal
   1998   *Devil's Bargains: Tourism in the Twentieth Century American West.* Lawrence: University Press of Kansas.

Roy, Beth
   1994   *Some Trouble with Cows: Making Sense of Social Conflict.* Berkeley: University of California Press.

Ryan, Stephen
   1996   "The Voice of Sanity Getting Hoarse?" Destructive Processes in Violent Ethnic Conflict. In *The Politics of Difference: Ethnic Premises in a World of Power,* edited by E. Wilmsen and P. McAllister, 144-161. Chicago: University of Chicago Press.

Said, Edward
   1978   *Orientalism.* New York: Vintage.

Salmone-Marino, Salvatore
   1897   *Costumi e Usanze Dei Contadini di Sicilia.* Translated by Rosalie Norris. Toronto: Associated University Press.

Satzewich, Vic (editor)
   1998   *Racism and Social Inequality in Canada.* Toronto: Thompson Educational Publishing.

Schaeffer, Claude
   1934-   Claude Schaeffer Papers. Glenbow-Alberta Institute Archives Division. Calgary,
   1969   AL. Accession #2464.
              Kootenay Fur Trade Period. M1100/37.
              Miners and Settlers. M1100/42.
              Economic Activities. M1100/8.
              Chiefs and Warriors. M1100/19.
              Fur Buyers. M1100/32.
              Reservation Days. M1100/43.
              Kootenay Chiefs. M1100/57.
   1965   The Kootenai Female Berdache: Courier, Guide, Prophetess and Warrior. *Ethnohistory* 12(3):193-236.

Scott, Andrew
   1997   *The Promise of Paradise: Utopian Communities in B.C.* Vancouver: Whitecap Books.

Scott, Colin
   1993   Customs, Tradition, and the Politics of Culture: Aboriginal Self-Government in Canada. In *Anthropology, Public Policy and Native Peoples in Canada,* edited

by N. Dyck and J. Waldram, 311-333. Montreal: McGill-Queen's University Press.

Scott, David, and Edna Hanic
1979   *East Kootenay Chronicle: The Story of Settlement, Lawlessness, Mining Disasters and Fires Stretching across British Columbia from the Alberta Border to Creston on Kootenay Lake.* Langley: Mr. Paperback.

Seidman, Steven
1994   Symposium: Queer Theory/Sociology: A Dialogue. *Sociological Theory* 12 (2):166-177.

Shai, Donna
1978   Public Cursing and Social Control in a Traditional Jewish Community. *Journal of Western Folklore* 37:39-46.

Siikala, Anna-Leena
1992   Understanding Narratives of the "Other." In *Folklore Processed: In Honour of Lauri Honko,* edited by R. Kvideland, 200-213. Helsinki: Studia Fennica.

Skalický, Karel
1989   The Vicissitudes of the Catholic Church in Czechoslovakia, 1918 to 1988. In *Czechoslovakia: Crossroads and Crises, 1918-1988,* edited by N. Stone and E. Strouhal, 297-324. New York: St. Martin's Press.

Sloan, Bill
1998   Prosperity and Recession before the 1930s. In *The Forgotten Side of the Border: British Columbia's Elk Valley and Crowsnest Pass,* edited by W. Norton and N. Miller, 40-47. Kamloops, BC: Plateau Press.

Slotkin, Edgar
1988   Legend Genre as a Function of Audience. In *Monsters with Iron Teeth.* Perspectives on Contemporary Legend Series, edited by G. Bennett and P. Smith, 3:89-111. Sheffield: University of Sheffield.

Slotkin, Richard
1973   *Regeneration through Violence: The Mythology of the American Frontier, 1600-1860.* Middletown: Wesleyan University Press.
1992   *Gunfighter Nation: The Myth of the Frontier in Twentieth Century America.* New York: Atheneum.

Sluga, Glenda
1999   Italian National Memory, National Identity and Fascism. In *Italian Fascism: History, Memory and Representation,* edited by R. Bosworth and P. Dogliani, 178-194. New York: St. Martin's Press.

Smith, Dorothy
1995   "Politically Correct": An Ideological Code. In *Beyond Political Correctness: Toward the Inclusive University,* edited by S. Richer and L. Weir, 23-50. Toronto: University of Toronto Press.

Smith, Moira
1996   Shivaree. In *American Folklore: An Encyclopedia,* edited by J. Brunvand, 665-666. New York: Garland.

Smith, Moira, and Rachelle Saltzman
1995   Introduction to Tastelessness. *Journal of Folklore Research* 32(2):85-99.

Smith, W.G.
1920   *A Study in Canadian Immigration.* Toronto: Ryerson Press.

Spry, Irene
1963   *The Palliser Expedition: An Account of John Palliser's British North American Expedition 1857-1860.* Toronto: Macmillan.

Stebbins, Robert
1984   *The Magician: Career, Culture, and Social Psychology in a Variety Art.* Toronto: Clarke Irwin.

Stein, Howard
1981   Envy and the Evil Eye among Slovak-Americans: An Essay in the Psychological Ontogeny of Belief and Ritual. In *The Evil Eye: A Folklore Casebook,* edited by A. Dundes, 223-256. New York: Garland.

Stephen, Michele
2000   Witchcraft, Grief, and the Ambivalence of Emotions. *American Ethnologist* 26(3):711-737.

Stevens, Phillips
1997   Some Implications of Urban Witchcraft Beliefs. In *Magic, Witchcraft and Religion: An Anthropological Study of the Supernatural,* edited by A. Lehmann and J. Myers, 199-207. Toronto: Mayfield.

Stewart, Kathleen
1996   *A Space on the Side of the Road: Cultural Poetics in an "Other" America.* Princeton: Princeton University Press.

Stocking, George
1968   *Race, Culture, and Evolution: Essays in the History of Anthropology.* New York: Free Press.
1987   *Victorian Anthropology.* New York: Free Press.

Stocking, George (editor)
1974   *A Franz Boas Reader: The Shaping of American Anthropology, 1883-1911.* Chicago: University of Chicago Press.

Stolcke, Verona
1995   Talking Culture: New Boundaries, New Rhetorics of Exclusion in Europe. *Current Anthropology* 36(1):1-24.

Stone, Norman, and Eduard Strouhal (editors)
1989   *Czechoslovakia: Crossroads and Crises, 1918-1988.* New York: St. Martin's Press.

Strong, Janice
1998   Cursed! The Ghost in the Mountain: The Legend of Fernie's Ghost Rider. *East Kootenay Weekly:*11.

Strong, Pauline Turner
1986   Fathoming the Primitive: Australian Aborigines in Four Explorers' Journals, 1697-1845. *Ethnohistory* 33(2):175-194.

1992   Captivity in White and Red. In *Crossing Cultures: Essays in the Displacement of Western Civilization,* edited by D. Segal, 33-104. Tucson: University of Arizona Press.
1996   Animated Indians: Critique and Contradiction in Commodified Children's Culture. *Cultural Anthropology* 11(3):405-424.
1999   *Captive Selves, Captivating Others: The Politics and Poetics of Colonial American Captivity Narratives.* Boulder: Westview Press.

Strong, Pauline Turner, and Barrik Van Winkle
1996   "Indian Blood": Reflections on the Reckoning and Refiguring of Native North American Identity. *Cultural Anthropology* 11(4):547-576.

Stymeist, D.H.
1975   *Ethnics and Indians: Social Relations in a Northwestern Ontario Town.* Toronto: Peter Martin Associates.

Suagee, Dean
1994   Human Rights and Cultural Heritage: Development in the UN Working Group on Indigenous Populations. In *Intellectual Property Rights for Indigenous Peoples,* edited by T. Greaves, 191-208. Oklahoma City, OK: Society for Applied Anthropology.

Tambiah, Stanley
1968   The Magical Power of Words. *Man* 3:175-288.

Taussig, Michael
1984   Culture of Terror, Space of Death: Roger Casement's Putumayo Report and the Explanation of Torture. *Comparative Study of Society and History* 26(3):467-497.
1987   *Shamanism, Colonialism, and the Wild Man: A Study in Terror and Healing.* Chicago: University of Chicago Press.

Teneese, Kathryn
1997   A Treaty in the Making. *Kootenay Advertiser* 24 November:6.

Thomas, Nicholas
1994   *Colonialism's Culture: Anthropology, Travel and Government.* Princeton: Princeton University Press.

Thomas, William, and Florian Znaniecki
1996   *The Polish Peasant in Europe and America: A Classic Work in Immigration History* [1918], edited by Eli Zaretsky. Urbana, IL: University of Illinois Press.

Thompson, Richard
1989   *Theories of Ethnicity: A Critical Appraisal.* New York: Greenwood Press.

Todd, Loretta
1992   What More Do They Want? In *Indigena: Contemporary Native Perspectives,* edited by G. McMaster and L. Martin, 71-81. Hull: Canadian Museum of Civilization.

Turnbull, Elsie
1983   Fernie: City under a Curse. In *Tragedies of the Crowsnest Pass,* 74-85. Surrey, BC: Heritage House.

Turner, Ian
1977a   "... In the Beginning." In *Backtracking,* edited by Fernie and District Historical Society, 5-14. Fernie: Fernie and District Historical Society.

1977b The Second Go-Round. In *Backtracking,* edited by Fernie and District Historical Society, 15-24. Fernie: Fernie and District Historical Society.

Turner, Patricia
1992 Ambivalent Patrons: The Role of Rumor and Contemporary Legends in African-American Consumer Decisions. *Journal of American Folklore* 105(418):424-441.

Turner, Terence
1993 Anthropology and Multiculturalism: What Is Anthropology That Multiculturalists Should Be Mindful Of? *Cultural Anthropology* 8(4):411-429.

Turner, Victor, and Edward Bruner (editors)
1986 *The Anthropology of Experience.* Urbana, IL: University of Illinois Press.

Turney-High, H.H.
1941 *Ethnography of the Kootenai.* American Anthropological Association Memoir no. 56. New York, NY: American Anthropological Association.

Tylor, Edward
1871 *Primitive Culture.* 2 Vols. London: Murray.
1964 *Researches into the Early History of Mankind and the Development of Civilization.* Chicago: University of Chicago Press.

Van Kirk, Sylvia
1980 *Many Tender Ties: Women in Fur Trade Society, 1670-1870.* Winnipeg: Saults and Pollard.

Venne, Sharon
1981 *Indian Acts and Amendments 1868-1975: An Indexed Collection.* Saskatoon: University of Saskatchewan Native Law Centre.

Vogt, E.Z., and E.M. Albert (editors)
1966 *People of Rimrock: A Study of Values in Five Cultures.* Cambridge, MA: Harvard University Press.

Wachtel, Nathan
1990 Introduction. In *Between Memory and History,* edited by Marie-Noelle Bourget, Lucette Valenci, and Nathan Wachtel, 1-18. London: Harwood.

Walker, Deward (editor)
1970 *Systems of North American Witchcraft and Sorcery.* Moscow: University of Idaho.

Ward, Donald
1996 Superstition. In *American Folklore: An Encyclopedia,* edited by J. Brunvand, 692-696. New York: Garland.

Watson, Rubie
1994 Introduction. In *Memory, History and Opposition under State Socialism,* edited by R. Watson, 1-20. Sante Fe, NM: School of American Research.

Weeks, Jeffrey
1991 *Against Nature: Essays on History, Sexuality and Identity.* London: Rivers Oram Press.

Westerman, William
1996 The Politics of Folklore. In *American Folklore: An Encyclopedia,* edited by J. Brunvand, 571-574. New York: Garland.

White, Leslie (editor)
1993   *Lewis Henry Morgan: The Indian Journals 1859-1862.* Mineola: Dover Publications.

Wickwire, Wendy
1994   To See Ourselves as the Other's Other: Nlaka'pamux Contact Narratives. *Canadian Historical Review* 75(1):1-20.

Wiercinski, Andrzej
1964   Reply to On the Race Concept. *Current Anthropology* 5(4):318-319.

Wikan, Unni
1992   Beyond the Words: The Power of Resonance. *American Ethnologists* 19(3): 460-481.

Williams, Gwyn
1979   *Madoc: The Making of a Myth.* London: Eyre Methuen.

Williams, Patrick, and Laura Chrisman (editors)
1994   *Colonial Discourse and Post-Colonial Theory.* New York: Columbia University Press.

Williams, Raymond
1976   *Keywords: A Vocabulary of Culture and Society.* London: Fontana Press.

Willoughby, Martin
1992   *A History of Postcards: A Pictorial Record from the Turn of the Century to the Present Day.* London: Studio Editions.

Wilmsen, Edwin
1996   Introduction. In *The Politics of Difference: Ethnic Premises in a World of Power,* edited by E. Wilmsen and P. McAllister, 1-23. Chicago: University of Chicago Press.

Wilmsen, Edwin, and Patrick McAllister (editors)
1996   *The Politics of Difference: Ethnic Premises in a World of Power.* Chicago: University of Chicago Press.

Wolf, Eric
1966   *Peasants.* Englewood Cliffs: Prentice-Hall.
1982   *Europe and the People without History.* Berkeley: University of California Press.
1994   Perilous Ideas: Race, Culture, People. *Current Anthropology* 35(1):1-12.
1999   *Envisioning Power: Ideologies of Dominance and Crisis.* Berkeley: University of California Press.

Wolfe, Patrick
1991   On Being Woken Up: The Dreamtime in Anthropology and in Australian Settler Culture. *Society for Comparative Study of Society and History* 33(2):197-224.

Yarmie, Andrew
1998   Community and Conflict: The Impact of the 1902 Explosion at Coal Creek. In *The Forgotten Side of the Border: British Columbia's Elk Valley and Crowsnest Pass,* edited by W. Norton and N. Miller, 195-205. Kamloops, BC: Plateau Press.

Zaretsky, Eli (editor)
1996   Foreword. In *The Polish Peasant in Europe and America* [1918], W. Thomas and F. Znaniecki, 1-53. Urbana, IL: University of Illinois Press.

Index

Printed and bound in Canada by Friesens

Set in Stone by Brenda and Neil West, BN Typographics West Ltd.

Copy editor: Audrey McClellan

Proofreader: Deborah Kerr

Cartographer: Eric Leinberger